EXAM CRAM™

CCNP Advanced Cisco Router Configuration

The Cram Sheet

This Cram Sheet contains the distilled, key facts about CCNP Advanced Cisco Router Configuration. Review this information last thing before you enter the test room, paying special attention to those areas where you feel you need the most review. You can transfer any of these facts onto a blank sheet of paper before beginning the exam.

SCALABLE INTERNETWORKS

1. Router Roles:
   - Core—At the top of your internetwork hierarchy.
   - Distribution—In the mid-sections of your hierarchy providing connectivity from the core backbone to the individual sites.
   - Access—At the bottom of the hierarchy providing end user access to internetwork resources.

2. Compression is best-utilized on low speed serial links.

TRAFFIC MANAGEMENT

3. IP standard access-lists:
   - Filter only on source IP address.
   - Use list numbers between 1 and 99.

4. IP extended access-lists:
   - Filter on source IP address, destination IP address, protocol and port number.
   - Use list numbers between 100 and 199.

5. A wild card mask is the inverse value of a subnet mask. To find an appropriate wildcard mask for a specific subnet, change the binary value of each bit in the subnet mask. For example, a subnet mask of 255.255.255.240 would use a wildcard mask of 0.0.0.15.

6. IPX standard access-lists:
   - Filter in source and destination IPX address.
   - Use list numbers between 800 and 899.

7. IPX SAP access-lists:
   - Filter based on SAP type.
   - Use list numbers between 1000 and 1099.

8. Standard access-lists should be placed as close as possible to the destination of the filtered traffic.

9. Extended access-lists should be placed as close as possible to the source of the filtered traffic.

10. Any traffic not specifically permitted by an access-list is denied. The last line of all access-lists is an implicit deny.

11. A static route specifying an outbound interface of null 0 is a good alternative to access-lists.

12. The command **line vty 0 4** will change you to the virtual terminal configuration prompt.

13. IP helper addresses should be placed on the inbound interface that will be receiving the broadcast to be forwarded.

14. The command **ipx routing** will enable the forwarding of IPX traffic on your router.

15. Required information for tunnel configuration:
    - Tunnel Source—The outbound interface through which to depart this router.
    - Tunnel Destination—The next logical hop IP address where the tunnel terminates.
    - Tunnel Mode—The definition of the mode used to encapsulate the traffic to be carried (*tunnel mode gre-ip* is the command to set it to Generic Route Encapsulation).

- Use ip route 0.0.0.0 0.0.0.0 <out int I next hop address> to set static default route.

47. Stopping Routing updates:
    - Use the **passive interface <int>** command to force a routing protocol to stop sending updates.
    - Use distribute lists with access-lists to filter routes.

CONNECTING TO AN ISP

48. Use BGP to connect to ISP when you need multiple exit points or when specified by ISP.

49. EBGP is a BGP connection to an external AS while IBGP is a BGP connection within the local AS.

50. Use a default route to point your AS to the ISP rather than redistributing.

NLSP

51. Novell's Link State replacement for the distance vector IPX RIP protocol.

52. Define ipx internal network number, area designation, and enable on each interface.

INTRODUCTION TO WANS

53. Possible encapsulations are HDLC, Frame Relay, ATM, SDLC, PPP, and SMDS.

54. Default encapsulation on Cisco serial interface is HDLC. All others must be configured.

ISDN INTERNETWORKING

55. Use PPP or HDLC encapsulation.

56. Can be native ISDN (TE1) or non-native ISDN (TE2). TE2 must connect to TA.

57. Required DDR information:
    - Set ISDN switch type at global config (**isdn switch-type <type>**).
    - Static route to destination network beyond ISDN link.
    - Define interesting traffic with dialer-list (can point to access-list if necessary).
    - Apply dialer list to interface as dialer-group.
    - Create a dialer-map to destination.

58. Optional PAP (clear text) or CHAP (encrypted) authentication with PPP.

59. PPP Multilink will bind two channels together as one link. *Dialer load-threshold <load>* tells router when to initialize second channel.

60. **Dialer idle-timeout <seconds>** tells router when to bring link back down when interesting traffic stops.

BRIDGING

61. Transparent bridging is unknown to end hosts.

62. Encapsulated bridging is the encapsulation of a bridged frame inside of a serial frame.

63. Source Route Bridging is a Token Ring implementation for routing frames from ring to bridge to ring.
    - Create Virtual Ring if more than two active SRB ports.
    - RIF tells route that traffic should take.
    - If RIF is present, first bit of source MAC address is set to 1 (so the hex value will be in range 8 – f).
    - RIF consists of Routing Control field and Route Descriptor Fields.

64. Source Route Transparent bridging is used when moving between Token Ring hosts that are transparent bridged and those that are Source route bridged. RIF is added and removed as needed.

65. Source Route Translational bridging is the translation of Ethernet frames to Token Ring frames and back.

66. Integrated Routing and Bridging allows passage of bridging traffic out of routed interfaces as well as the passage of routed traffic out of bridged interfaces via a logical Bridged Virtual Interface (BVI).

T1/E1 AND PRI OPTIONS

67. Configure integrated CSU/DSU (controller) with framing, line coding and clock source (all telco provided information).

68. Framing choices in North America are SF or ESF for T1 and Multiframe for E1.

69. Line Coding choices in North America are AMI and B8ZS for T1 and AMI and HDB3 for E1.

70. PRI uses same line coding and framing as T1. You must define switch type.

**Certification
Insider** Press

- Election of DR/BDR will only occur on broadcast media (such as Ethernet and Token Ring).
31. Routing Updates:
  - Routing updates sent to DR and BDR if present via 224.0.0.6.
  - DR forwards routing updates to other OSPF routers via 224.0.0.5.
  - If no DR/BDR, simply forward update to neighbor(s).
  - Routing updates are called LSAs are disseminated in flooding fashion.
32. Required Information for OSPF neighbors:
  - Neighbor ID
  - Area ID
  - Router Priority
  - DR IP Address
  - BDR IP Address
  - Authentication Type
  - Authentication Password
  - Stub Area Flag
33. OSPF Router Designations:
  - Internal Router—Any router with all interfaces in one area.
  - Area Border Router—Any router with interfaces in multiple areas.
  - Backbone Router—Any router with an interface in area 0.
  - Autonomous System Boundary Router—Any router with a connection to an external autonomous system.
34. Stub Areas:
  - Stub area—Contains only one exit point (via the ABR to area 0), all intra-area routes, summary routes to other areas and a default route.
  - Totally Stubby Area—Contains only one exit point (via the ABR to area 0), all intra-area routes and a default route. It contains no external routes.
  - All routers in stub or totally stubby area must agree that the area is a stub.
  - Use the *area* **<number> stub no-summary** command on the ABR to create totally stubby area.
  - Use the area <number> stub on internal routers to tell them they're part of a stub area.
  - Do not stub area 0.
35. Virtual links must be configured on areas that cannot connect directly to area 0.

36. Show commands:
  - **show ip protocols**—Show active routing protocols
  - **show ip ospf neighbors**—Show neighbor database

EIGRP

37. Routes for IP, IPX, and AppleTalk.
38. Metric is composite of bandwidth, delay, load, reliability and MTU.
39. Best route is called successor or current successor. Selected based on lowest feasible distance.
40. Second best route is called feasible successor. Advertised distance of this route must be lower than feasible distance of best route to be considered a feasible successor.
41. Automatic redistribution between EIGRP and IGRP if AS numbers are same.
42. Use the *ip summary-address eigrp* <**as number**> <**network address**> <**prefix**> on the outbound interface to configure summarization.
43. Use the **ipx sap-incremental** command to force incremental RIP/SAP updates on a particular interface.
44. Show commands:
  - **show ip eigrp neighbors**—Displays the EIGRP ip neighbor table.
  - **show ip eigrp topology**—Displays the EIGRP ip topology table.
  - **show ip route**—Displays the ip routing table.

OPTIMIZING ROUTING UPDATES

45. Static routes:
  - ip route <dest.network> <dest. netmask> <next hop addr I out int> <distance>
  - Specifying outbound interface sets administrative distance to 0 and automatically redistributes.
  - Specifying next hop address sets administrative distance to 1 and requires manual redistribution.
  - Manipulating administrative distance to a high number so that the dynamic route will show and use the static route as a backup is called a floating static route.
46. Default Route:
  - Use the **ip default network <network address>** command to set on each router.

- Encapsulated protocol attributes (such as IPX network number, AppleTalk, Cable-range, and Zone).

QUEUING

16. Queuing is best used on slower (T1 and below) Serial links that are subject to bursty traffic.

17. Weighted Fair Queuing:
    - Low volume traffic gets priority on outbound interface.
    - On by default on Serial interfaces 2Mbps and below.

18. Priority Queuing:
    - Four queues—High, Medium, Normal and Low
    - Assign various traffic types to queue using priority-list command (for example, **Priority-list 1 protocol ipx medium** will place all outbound IPX traffic into the medium queue).
    - **show queuing priority** will display the current priority queuing configuration.

19. Custom Queuing:
    - All queues processed in round-robin fashion.
    - There are 17 queues, 0 through 16. 0 is for system traffic and is not configurable. 1 through 16 are configurable queues.
    - **show queuing custom** displays custom queuing configuration.

ROUTING PROTOCOL OVERVIEW

20. Routing Protocol Metrics:
    - OSPF—Cost (based on bandwidth)
    - EIGRP—Bandwidth, delay, load, reliability, and MTU

21. Administrative Distance—The believability of a route learned by a particular routing protocol:
    - OSPF—110
    - EIGRP—90
    - Static Route—0 or 1 (depends on configuration. see next item)
    - Use the **distance** command to manipulate administrative distance from the config-router prompt.

ADVANCED IP ADDRESSING

22. IP Addressing:
    - Routing decision based on longest match of routing table entry to destination address.
    - Class A—1 to 126
    - Class B—128 to 191
    - Class C—192 to 223
    - To find number of subnets created or number of hosts per subnet use 2^x-2 formula.
    - Subnet address derived through *logical AND* process.

23. Private Internetwork Space:
    - Class A—10.0.0.0 to 10.255.255.255
    - Class B—172.16.0.0 to 172.31.255.255
    - Class C—192.168.0.0 to 192.168.255.255

24. VLSM
    - Routing protocol must be capable of passing the prefix in routing-updates to support VLSM.
    - RIP and IGRP do not support VLSM.
    - OSPF does support VLSM.
    - EIGRP support for VLSM must be enabled (*no auto-summary* under the EIGRP configuration).
    - Further subdivide the address space.
    - Mask for Serial links is 255.255.255.252 to provide for only two hosts.

25. Route summarization:
    - Find a common bit boundary in the sequence of network addresses.
    - Count the number of bits the addresses have in common to create the prefix.
    - Use the command *area* <**number**> *range* <**network address**> <**prefix**> for OSPF route summarization. This command is entered under the OSPF configuration.
    - Use the command *ip summary-address eigrp* <**as number**> <**network address**> <**prefix**> for EIGRP route summarization. This command is entered on the outbound interface that will be advertising the summary route. Enter the command **no auto-summary** under the EIGRP to support summarization.

26. Network Address Translation (NAT) is used to convert private internal IP addresses to public external IP addresses, which should exist in your registered space.

OSPF

27. OSPF is a link state routing protocol.

28. Developed to overcome RIP limits:
    - Fast convergence
    - No hop count limit
    - Support for VLSM
    - Metric is cost based on bandwidth
    - Efficient routing updates via multicast

29. Uses Hello protocol to establish neighbor relationship.

30. DR election:
    - Highest priority is DR
    - Second highest priority is BDR
    - Router ID used to break tie on priority.
    - Router ID is highest IP address or IP address of Loopback 0 interface.

CCNP Advanced Cisco Router Configuration

Brian Morgan
Mike Shroyer

CCNP Advanced Cisco Router Configuration Exam Cram

© 1999 The Coriolis Group. All Rights Reserved.

Limits Of Liability And Disclaimer Of Warranty

The author and publisher of this book have used their best efforts in preparing the book and the programs contained in it. These efforts include the development, research, and testing of the theories and programs to determine their effectiveness. The author and publisher make no warranty of any kind, expressed or implied, with regard to these programs or the documentation contained in this book.

The author and publisher shall not be liable in the event of incidental or consequential damages in connection with, or arising out of, the furnishing, performance, or use of the programs, associated instructions, and/or claims of productivity gains.

Trademarks

Trademarked names appear throughout this book. Rather than list the names and entities that own the trademarks or insert a trademark symbol with each mention of the trademarked name, the publisher states that it is using the names for editorial purposes only and to the benefit of the trademark owner, with no intention of infringing upon that trademark.

The Coriolis Group, LLC
14455 N. Hayden Road, Suite 220
Scottsdale, Arizona 85260

480/483-0192
FAX 480/483-0193
http://www.coriolis.com

Library of Congress Cataloging-in-Publication Data
Morgan, Brian (Brian Edward)
    CCNP advanced Cisco configuration exam cram / by Brian Morgan and Mike Shroyer
        p.   cm.
    Includes index.
    ISBN 1-57610-439-7
    1. Electronic data processing personnel--
Certification.   2. Internetworking (Telecommunication)
--Examinations Study guides.   3. Computer networks--Examinations Study
guides.   I. Shroyer, Mike.   II. Title.
QA76.3.M65   1999
004.6--dc21   99-29059
                                                        CIP

Printed in the United States of America
10 9 8 7 6 5 4 3 2 1

Publisher
Keith Weiskamp

Acquisitions Editor
Shari Jo Hehr

Marketing Specialist
Cynthia Caldwell

Project Editor
Dan Young

Technical Reviewer
Glen Shok

Production Coordinator
Kim Eoff

Cover Design
Jesse Dunn

Layout Design
April Nielsen

14455 North Hayden Road, Suite 220 • Scottsdale, Arizona 85260

Coriolis: The Training And Certification Destination ™

Thank you for purchasing one of our innovative certification study guides, just one of the many members of the Coriolis family of certification products.

Certification Insider Press™ has long believed that achieving your IT certification is more of a road trip than anything else. This is why most of our readers consider us their *Training And Certification Destination*. By providing a one-stop shop for the most innovative and unique training materials, our readers know we are the first place to look when it comes to achieving their certification. As one reader put it, "I plan on using your books for all of the exams I take."

To help you reach your goals, we've listened to others like you, and we've designed our entire product line around you and the way you like to study, learn, and master challenging subjects. Our approach is *The Smartest Way To Get Certified*™.

In addition to our highly popular *Exam Cram* and *Exam Prep* guides, we have a number of new products. We recently launched Exam Cram Live!, two-day seminars based on *Exam Cram* material. We've also developed a new series of books and study aides—*Practice Tests Exam Crams* and *Exam Cram Flash Cards*—designed to make your studying fun as well as productive.

Our commitment to being the *Training And Certification Destination* does not stop there. We just introduced *Exam Cram Insider*, a biweekly newsletter containing the latest in certification news, study tips, and announcements from Certification Insider Press. (To subscribe, send an email to **eci@coriolis.com** and type "subscribe insider" in the body of the email.) We also recently announced the launch of the Certified Crammer Society and the Coriolis Help Center—two new additions to the Certification Insider Press family.

We'd like to hear from you. Help us continue to provide the very best certification study materials possible. Write us or email us at **cipq@coriolis.com** and let us know how our books have helped you study, or tell us about new features that you'd like us to add. If you send us a story about how we've helped you, and we use it in one of our books, we'll send you an official Coriolis shirt for your efforts.

Good luck with your certification exam and your career. Thank you for allowing us to help you achieve your goals.

Keith Weiskamp

Keith Weiskamp
Publisher, Certification Insider Press

This book is dedicated to my wife Beth and my daughters Emma and Amanda for their patience in putting up with me during its production. Also included in this dedication is Michelle Smith. Her willingness to give a kid a chance so long ago made this possible.

—Brian Morgan

This book is dedicated to my wife Dianne whose love and support makes all things possible.

—Mike Shroyer

About The Authors

Brian Morgan is a Certified Cisco Systems Instructor (CCSI) for GeoTrain Corporation, Cisco's first and largest Certified Training Partner. He has been teaching Cisco courses for over two years and has been involved in the networking world for 10 years. The Cisco courses he teaches include the Introduction to Cisco Router Configuration (ICRC), Advanced Cisco Router Configuration (ACRC), Cisco Campus ATM (CATM) and Cisco Voice Over Frame Relay, IP and ATM (CVOICE) courses.

Prior to teaching for GeoTrain, Brian spent a number of years with IBM in the Network Services division where he attained MCNE and MCSE certifications. He was involved in a number of larger LAN/WAN installations for many of IBM's largest clients including Bell Helicopter, Federal Reserve and Hallmark.

Today, Brian is GeoTrain's representative to the ATM Forum, a standards body reporting to the ITU for ATM Standards and Specifications. He is actively involved in the expansion of ATM as a technology.

Brian is the proud father of fraternal twin girls, Emma and Amanda (age 4) who keep him quite busy when he's at home.

Mike Shroyer is President of J.M. Shroyer Associates, Inc. (JMSAI) a 20-year old, Denver-based data communications consulting company. He has over 35 years experience at all levels in the computer field. Mike is a Cisco Certified Internet Expert (CCIE #2280) and Certified Computer Professional (CCP). As a Certified Cisco Systems Instructor (CCSI). Mike has worked as a contract instructor for GeoTrain, Inc. and its predecessor, Protocol Interface, Inc. for over five years. The Cisco courses he teaches or has taught include the Introduction to Cisco Router Configuration (ICRC), Advanced Cisco Router Configuration (ACRC), Cisco Campus ATM (CATM), Cisco Internetwork Design (CID) and Introduction to Cisco Works Configuration (ICWC).

Mike has lectured and consulted extensively in the United States, Europe and Asia on Internetworking, SNA, network security and audit of data networks, Unix, C language programming, and other technical topics. In addition to his consulting practice Mike has taught for the University of Denver in its Masters in Computer Science program and for Metropolitan State College.

Mike is married to Dianne and lives in Denver, Colorado.

Acknowledgments

I'd like to thank Mike Shroyer for putting in some long hours in writing as a co-author. Special thanks to GeoTrain Corporation (especially Guy, Marty and Dolores) for their on-going support of me and my professional development. Thanks to Bill Wagner for providing a sounding board for my frustrations and ideas. He is and has been a good friend to my family and me. A great deal of work went into this book from its writing, to its final production. I want to say thanks to the Coriolis team of editors and production personnel.

This book was a definite test of patience and abilities. I want to thank Glen Shok for his role as a technical editor and his willingness to ask me what the heck I was thinking on a few topics. He's definitely done more than his share for this book. Thanks to Bonnie Trenga for making Mike and I sound like we can actually write with some degree of competence. Her copy editing skills proved to be a major asset. Thanks to Glen Shok for the technical review. I look forward to doing this again soon. I hope to have as good a team next time.

—*Brian Morgan*

First and foremost, I want to thank Brian Morgan for inviting me to work on this project. He's spent many hours helping to write this book and his efforts are appreciated. I also want to thank the many people who have helped along the way by carrying on intense discussions, answering difficult questions, and contributing great ideas for this book.

Also I wish to thank our Coriolis editors especially Bonnie Trenga, Dan Young, and our technical editor Glen Shok. An effort like this is a group effort and much credit goes to them.

I also want to thank the rest of the team at The Coriolis Group, including Keith Weiskamp for publishing our book, Kim Eoff for production coordination, Cynthia Caldwell for marketing, Jesse Dunn for the cover design, and April Nielsen for the layout design. I really appreciate all of the effort you've put into this book.

—*Mike Shroyer*

Contents At A Glance

Table Of Contents

Introduction

Welcome to the *CCNP Advanced Cisco Router Configuration Exam Cram*! This book aims to help you get ready to take—and pass— the Cisco career certification test numbered 640-403, "Advanced Cisco Router Configuration (ACRC)". This Introduction explains Cisco's certification programs in general and talks about how the *Exam Cram* series prepare for Cisco's career certification exams.

Exam Cram books help you understand and appreciate the subjects and materials you need to pass Cisco career certification exams. *Exam Crams* are aimed strictly at test preparation and review. They do not teach you everything you need to know about a topic (such as the ins and outs of managing a Cisco router implementation). Instead, we (the authors) present and dissect the questions and problems we've found that you're likely to encounter on a test. We've worked from Cisco's own training materials, preparation guides, and tests, and from a battery of third-party test preparation tools. Our aim is to bring together as much information as possible about Cisco certification exams.

Nevertheless, to completely prepare yourself for any Cisco test, we recommend that you begin your studies with some instructor-led classroom training. You should also pick up and read one of the many study guides available from Cisco or third-party vendors, including The Coriolis Group's *Exam Prep* series. We also strongly recommend that you install, configure, and fool around with the Internetwork Operating System (IOS) software or environment that you'll be tested on, because nothing beats hands-on experience and familiarity when it comes to understanding the questions you're likely to encounter on a certification test. Book learning is essential, but hands-on experience is the best teacher of all!

The Cisco Career Certification Program

The Cisco Career Certification Program is relatively new on the internetworking scene. The best place to keep tabs on it is the Cisco Training Web site, at **www.cisco.com/training/**. Before Cisco developed this program, Cisco Certified Internetworking Expert (CCIE) certification was the only available Cisco certification. Although CCIE certification is still the most coveted and prestigious certification that Cisco offers (possibly the most prestigious in the internetworking industry), lower-level certifications are now available as stepping stones on the road to the CCIE. The Cisco career certification program includes four certifications in addition to the CCIE, each with its own new acronym. If you're a fan of alphabet soup after your name, you'll like this program:

➤ **Cisco Certified Network Associate (CCNA)** The CCNA is the first career certification. It consists of a single exam that covers information from the basic-level classes such as Introduction to Cisco Router Configuration (ICRC) and Cisco LAN Switch Configuration (CLSC). Cisco also offers a class aimed at the CCNA certification known as Cisco Routing and LAN Switching (CRLS). You must obtain CCNA certification before you can get any other Cisco certification.

➤ **Cisco Certified Design Associate (CCDA)** The CCDA is a basic certification aimed at designers of high-level internetworks. The CCDA consists of a single exam that covers information from both the Designing Cisco Networks (DCN) and the Cisco Internetwork Design (CID) course. You must get CCDA certification before you can move up to the CCDP certification (discussed shortly).

➤ **Cisco Certified Network Professional (CCNP)** The CCNP is a more advanced certification. It is not an easy certification to obtain. To earn CCNP status, you must be a CCNA in good standing, and you must pass two additional tests. The first is the Foundation Routing/Switching exam (number 640-409), which consists of information from the ACRC course (covered in this book), CLSC, and Configuring, Maintaining and Troubleshooting Dial-up (CMTD). If you're not up for a long test—this one takes from two to three hours—you can take each of the exams for these classes individually. The second test that you must pass to complete CCNP certification is the Cisco Internetwork Troubleshooting (CIT) exam.

Once you have completed the CCNP certification, you can further your career (not to mention beef up your resume) by branching out and passing one of the CCNP specialization exams. These include:

➤ Security (Managing Cisco Network Security—MCNS)

➤ LAN ATM (Campus Asynchronous Transfer Mode—CATM)

➤ Voice Access (Cisco Voice over Frame Relay, ATM and IP—CVOICE)

Table 1   Cisco CCNA, CCNP, And CCIE Requirements*

CCNA

Only 1 Exam Required	
Exam 640-407	CCNA (Cisco Certified Network Associate)

CCNP

All 5 of these are required	
Exam 640-407	CCNA (Cisco Certified Network Associate)
Exam 640-403	ACRC 11.3 (Advanced Cisco Router Configuration)
Exam 640-404	CLSC (Cisco LAN Switch Configuration)
Exam 640-405	CMTD (Configuring, Monitoring, and Troubleshooting Dial-up Services)
Exam 640-406	CIT (Cisco Internetwork Troubleshooting)

CCIE

1 Written Exam and 1 Lab Exam Required	
Exam 350-001	CCIE Routing and Switching Qualification
Lab Exam	CCIE Routing and Switching Laboratory

* This is not a complete listing. We have included only those tests needed for the Routing and Switching track.

➤ SNA Solutions (SNA for Multiprotocol Administrators—SNAM— and Data Link Switching plus—DLSW)

➤ Network Management (Managing Cisco Routed Internetworks— MCRI—and Managing Cisco Switched Internetworks—MCSI)

➤ **Cisco Certified Design Professional (CCDP)** The CCDP is another advanced certification. It's aimed at high-level internetwork designers who must understand the intricate facets of putting together a well-laid-out network. The first step in the certification process is to obtain the CCNA and CCDA certifications (yes, both). As with the CCNP, you must pass the Foundation Routing/Switching exam (number 640-409) or pass the ACRC, CLSC, and CMTD exams individually. Once you meet those objectives, you must pass the CID exam to complete the certification.

➤ **Cisco Certified Internetworking Expert (CCIE)** The CCIE is possibly the most influential certification in the internetworking industry today. It is famous (or infamous) for its difficulty and for how easily it holds its seekers at bay. The certification requires only one written exam, which qualifies you to schedule time at a Cisco campus to demonstrate your knowledge in a two-day practical laboratory setting. You must pass the lab with a score of at least 80 percent to become a CCIE. Recent statistics have put the passing rates at roughly 2 percent for first attempts and 35 through 50 percent overall. Once you achieve CCIE certification, you must recertify every two years by passing a written exam administered by Cisco.

➤ **Certified Cisco Systems Instructor (CCSI)** To obtain status as a CCSI, you must be employed (either permanently or by contract) by a Cisco Training Partner in good standing, such as GeoTrain Corp. That training partner must sponsor you through Cisco's Instructor Certification Program, and you must pass the two-day program that Cisco administers at a Cisco campus. You can expand on CCSI certification on a class-by-class basis. Instructors must demonstrate competency with each class they are to teach thereafter by completing the written exam that goes with each class. Cisco also requires that instructors maintain a high customer satisfaction rating, or they will face decertification.

Taking A Certification Exam

Alas, testing is not free. Each computer-based exam costs between $100 and $200. If you do not pass, you must pay the testing fee each time you retake the test. In the United States and Canada, tests are administered by Sylvan Prometric. Sylvan Prometric can be reached at (800) 755-3926 or (800) 204-EXAM, any time from 7:00 A.M. to 6:00 P.M., Central Time, Monday through Friday. You can also try (612) 896-7000 or (612) 820-5707.

To schedule an exam, call at least one day in advance. To cancel or reschedule an exam, you must call at least 24 hours before the scheduled test time (or you may be charged regardless). When calling Sylvan Prometric, have the following information ready for the telesales staffer who handles your call:

➤ Your name, organization, and mailing address.

➤ Your Cisco Test ID. (For most U.S. citizens, this is your Social Security number. Citizens of other nations can use their taxpayer IDs or make other arrangements with the order taker.)

➤ The name and number of the exam you wish to take. For this book, the exam name is "Advanced Cisco Router Configuration (ACRC)," and the exam number is 640-403.

➤ A method of payment. The most convenient approach is to supply a valid credit card number with sufficient available credit. Otherwise, Sylvan Prometric must receive check, money order, or purchase order payments before you can schedule a test. (If you're not paying by credit card, ask your order taker for more details.)

When you show up to take a test, try to arrive at least 15 minutes before the scheduled time slot. You must bring and supply two forms of identification, one of which must be a photo ID.

All exams are completely closed book. In fact, you will not be permitted to take anything with you into the testing area. However, you are furnished with a blank sheet of paper and a pen. We suggest that you immediately write down on that sheet of paper all the information you've memorized for the test. While the amount of time you have to actually take the exam is limited, it does not start until you tell it to. So you can spend as much time as necessary writing notes on the provided paper. If you think you will need more paper than what is provided, ask the test center administrator before entering the exam room. You must return all pages prior to exiting the testing center.

In Exam Cram books, the information that we suggest you write down appears on a tear-out sheet inside the front cover of each book. You will have some time to compose yourself, to record this information, and even to take a sample orientation exam before you must begin the real thing. We suggest you take the orientation test before taking your first exam, but because they're all more or less identical in layout, behavior, and controls, you probably won't need to do this more than once.

When you complete a Cisco certification exam, the software will tell you whether you've passed or failed. All tests are scored on a basis of 100 percent, and results are broken into several topic areas. Even if you fail, we suggest you ask for—and keep—the detailed report that the test administrator should print for you. You can use this report to help you prepare for another go-round, if needed. Once you see your score, you have the option of printing additional copies of the score report. It is a good idea to have it print twice.

If you need to retake an exam, you'll have to call Sylvan Prometric, schedule a new test date, and pay another testing fee. Cisco has recently implemented a new policy regarding failed tests. The first time you fail a test, you can retake the test the next day. However, if you fail a second time, you must wait 14 days before retaking that test. The 14-day waiting period is in effect for all tests after the first failure.

Tracking Cisco Certification Status

As soon as you pass any Cisco exam (congratulations!), you must complete a certification agreement. You can do so online at the Certification Tracking Web site (**www.galton.com/~cisco/**), or you can mail a hard copy of the agreement to Cisco's certification authority. You will not be certified until you complete a certification agreement and Cisco receives it in one form or the other.

The Certification Tracking Web site also allows you to view your certification information. Cisco will contact you via email and explain it and its use. Once you are registered into one of the career certification tracks, you will be given a login on this site, which is administered by Galton, a third-party company that has no in-depth affiliation with Cisco or its products. Galton's information comes directly from Sylvan Prometric, the exam-administration company for much of the computing industry.

Once you pass the necessary exam(s) for a particular certification and complete the certification agreement, you'll be certified. Official certification normally takes anywhere from four to six weeks, so don't expect to get your credentials overnight. When the package arrives, it will include a Welcome Kit that contains a number of elements, including:

➤ A Cisco certificate stating that you have completed the certification requirements, suitable for framing, along with a laminated Cisco Career Certification identification card with your certification number on it.

➤ A promotional item, which varies based on the certification. For example, for CCNA, you will receive a CCNA shirt, whereas a CCDA gets you a leather (or reasonable facsimile thereof) organizer folder.

Many people believe that the benefits of the Cisco career certifications go well beyond the perks that Cisco provides to newly anointed members of this elite group. We're starting to see more job listings that request or require applicants to have a CCNA, CCDA, CCNP, CCDP, and so on, and many individuals who complete the program can qualify for increases in pay or responsibility. In fact, Cisco has started to implement requirements for its Value Added Resellers: To attain and keep silver, gold, or higher status, they must maintain a certain number of CCNA, CCDA, CCNP, CCDP, and CCIE employees on staff. There's a very high demand and low supply of Cisco talent in the industry overall. As an official recognition of hard work and broad knowledge, a Cisco career certification credential is a badge of honor in many IT organizations.

How To Prepare For An Exam

Preparing for any Cisco test (including ACRC) requires that you obtain and study materials designed to provide comprehensive information about Cisco router operation and the specific exam for which you are preparing. The following list of materials will help you study and prepare:

➤ **Instructor-led training** There's no substitute for expert instruction and hands-on practice under professional supervision. Cisco Training Partners, such as GeoTrain Corporation, offer instructor-led training courses for all of the Cisco career certification requirements. These companies aim to help prepare network administrators to run Cisco routed and switched internetworks and pass the Cisco tests. Although such training runs upwards of $350 per day in class, most of the individuals lucky enough to partake find them to be quite worthwhile.

➤ **Cisco Connection Online** This is the name of Cisco's Web site (**www.cisco.com**), the most current and up-to-date source of Cisco information.

➤ **The CC Prep Web site** This is the most well-known Cisco certification Web site in the world. You can find it at **www.ccprep.com** (formerly known as **www.CCIEprep.com**). Here, you can find exam prep materials, practice tests, self-assessment exams, and numerous certification questions and scenarios. In addition, professional staff is available to answer questions that you can post on the answer board.

➤ **Cisco Training Kits** These are available only if you attend a Cisco class, at a certified training facility, or if a Cisco Training Partner in good standing gives you one.

➤ **Study guides** Publishers like Certification Insider Press and Sybex offer informative Cisco study guides of one kind or another. The Certification Insider Press series includes:

   ➤ **The Exam Cram series** These books give you information about the material you need to know to pass the tests.

   ➤ **The Exam Prep series** These books provide a greater level of detail than the Exam Cram series.

   Together, the two series make a perfect pair.

➤ **Other publications** You'll find direct references to other publications and resources in this text: There's no shortage of materials available about Cisco routers and their configuration. To help you sift through some of the publications out there, we end each chapter with a "Need To Know More?" section that provides pointers to more complete and exhaustive resources covering the chapter's information. This should give you an idea of where we think you should look for further discussion.

By far, this set of required and recommended materials represents an unparalleled collection of sources and resources for Cisco router configuration guidelines. We anticipate that you'll find that this book belongs in this company. In the next section, we explain how this book works, and we give you some good reasons why this book counts as a member of the required and recommended materials list.

About This Book

Each topical Exam Cram chapter follows a regular structure, along with graphical cues about important or useful information. Here's the structure of a typical chapter:

➤ **Opening hotlists** Each chapter begins with a list of the terms, tools, and techniques that you must learn and understand before you can be fully conversant with that chapter's subject matter. We follow the hotlists with one or two introductory paragraphs to set the stage for the rest of the chapter.

➤ **Topical coverage** After the opening hotlists, each chapter covers a series of at least four topics related to the chapter's subject. Throughout this section, we highlight topics or concepts likely to appear on a test using a special Exam Alert layout, like this:

This is what an Exam Alert looks like. Normally, an Exam Alert stresses concepts, terms, software, or activities that are likely to relate to one or more certification test questions. For that reason, we think any information found offset in an Exam Alert format is worthy of unusual attentiveness on your part. Indeed, most of the information that appears on the Cram Sheet appears as Exam Alerts within the text.

Pay close attention to material flagged as an Exam Alert; although all the information in this book pertains to what you need to know to pass the exam, we flag certain items that are really important. You'll find what appears in the meat of each chapter to be worth knowing, too, when preparing for the test. Because this book's material is very condensed, we recommend that you use this book along with other resources to achieve the maximum benefit.

In addition to the Exam Alerts, we have provided tips that will help build a better foundation for ACRC knowledge. Although the information may not be on the exam, it is certainly related and will help you become a better test taker.

This is how tips are formatted. Keep your eyes open for these, and you'll become an CCNP guru in no time!

➤ **Practice Questions** Although we talk about test questions and topics throughout each chapter, this section presents a series of mock test questions and explanations of both correct and incorrect answers. We also try to point out especially tricky questions by using a special icon, like this:

Ordinarily, this icon flags the presence of a particularly devious inquiry, if not an outright trick question. Trick questions are calculated to be answered incorrectly if not read more than once, and carefully, at that. Although they're not ubiquitous, such questions make regular appearances on the Cisco exams. That's why we say exam questions are as much about reading comprehension as they are about knowing your material inside out and backwards.

➤ **Details and resources** Every chapter ends with a section titled "Need To Know More?" It provides direct pointers to Cisco and third-party resources offering more details on the chapter's subject. In addition, this section tries to rank or at least rate the quality and thoroughness of the topic's coverage by each resource. If you find a resource in this collection that you like, use it, but don't feel compelled to use all the resources. On the other hand, we recommend only resources we use regularly, so none of our recommendations will be a waste of your time or money (but purchasing them all at once probably represents an expense that many network administrators and would-be CCNPs might find hard to justify).

The bulk of the book follows this chapter structure slavishly, but there are a few other elements that we'd like to point out. Chapter 16 is a sample test that provides a good review of the material presented throughout the book to ensure you're ready for the exam. Chapter 17 is the answer key. Additionally, you'll find a Glossary that explains terms and an index that you can use to track down terms as they appear in the text.

Finally, the tear-out Cram Sheet attached next to the inside front cover of this Exam Cram book represents a condensed and compiled collection of facts, figures, and tips that we think you should memorize before taking the test. Because you can dump this information out of your head onto a piece of paper before answering any exam questions, you can master this information by brute force— you need to remember it only long enough to write it down when you walk into the test room. You might even want to look at it in the car (not while driving) or in the lobby of the testing center just before you walk in to take the test.

How To Use This Book

If you're prepping for a first-time test, we've structured the topics in this book to build on one another. Therefore, some topics in later chapters make more sense after you've read earlier chapters. That's why we suggest you read this book from front to back for your initial test preparation. If you need to brush up on a topic or you have to bone up for a second try, use the index or table of contents to go straight to the topics and questions that you need to study. Beyond the tests, we think you'll find this book useful as a tightly focused reference to some of the most important aspects of ACRC.

Given all the book's elements and its specialized focus, we've tried to create a tool that will help you prepare for—and pass—Cisco Career Certification Exam 640-403, "Advanced Cisco Router Configuration (ACRC)." Please share your feedback on the book with us, especially if you have ideas about how we can improve it for future test-takers. We'll consider everything you say carefully, and we'll respond to all suggestions.

Please send your questions or comments to us at **craminfo@coriolis.com**. Please remember to include the title of the book in your message; otherwise, we'll be forced to guess which book you're writing about. Also, be sure to check out the Web pages at **www.certificationinsider.com**, where you'll find information updates, commentary, and clarifications on documents for each book that you can either read online or download for use later on.

Thanks, and enjoy the book!

Self-Assessment

The reason we included a Self-Assessment in this Exam Cram is to help you evaluate your readiness to tackle CCNP certification. It should also help you understand what you need to master the topic of this book—namely, Exam 640-403, "Advanced Cisco Router Configuration (ACRC)." But before you tackle this Self-Assessment, let's talk about concerns you may face when pursuing a CCNP, and what an ideal CCNP candidate might look like.

CCNPs In The Real World

In the next section, we describe an ideal CCNP candidate, knowing full well that only a few real candidates will meet this ideal. In fact, our description of that ideal candidate might seem downright scary. But take heart: Although the requirements to obtain a CCNP may seem pretty formidable, they are by no means impossible to meet. However, you should be keenly aware that it does take time and requires some expense and substantial effort to get through the process.

The first thing to understand is that the CCNP is an attainable goal. You can get all the real-world motivation you need from knowing that many others have gone before, so you will be able to follow in their footsteps. If you're willing to tackle the process seriously and do what it takes to obtain the necessary experience and knowledge, you can take—and pass—all the certification tests involved in obtaining an CCNP. In fact, we've designed these Exam Crams, and the companion Exam Preps, to make it as easy on you as possible to prepare for these exams. But prepare you must!

The same, of course, is true for other Cisco career certifications, including:

➤ CCNA, which is the first step on the road to the CCNP certification. It is a single exam that covers information from Cisco's Introduction to Cisco Router Configuration (ICRC) class and the Cisco LAN Switch Configuration (CLSC) class. Cisco also has developed a class that is geared to CCNA certification, known as Cisco Routing and LAN Switching (CRLS).

➤ CCDA, which is the first step on the road to the CCDP certification. It also is a single exam that covers the basics of design theory. To prepare for it, you should attend the Designing Cisco Networks (DCN) class and/or the Cisco Internetwork Design (CID) class.

➤ CCDP, which is an advanced certification regarding internetwork design. It consists of multiple exams. There are two ways to go about attaining the CCDP. You could pass the individual exams for ACRC, CLSC, CMTD, and CIT. However, if you're not one for taking a lot of exams, you can take the Foundation Routing/Switching exam and the CIT exam. Either combination will complete the requirements.

➤ CCIE, which is commonly referred to as the "black belt" of internetworking. It is considered the single most difficult certification to attain in the internetworking industry. First you must take a qualification exam. Once you pass the exam, the real fun begins. You will need to schedule a two-day practical lab exam to be held at a Cisco campus, where you will undergo a "trial by fire" of sorts. Your ability to configure, document, and troubleshoot Cisco equipment will be tested to its limits. Do not underestimate this lab exam.

The Ideal CCNP Candidate

Just to give you some idea of what an ideal CCNP candidate is like, here are some relevant statistics about the background and experience such an individual might have. Don't worry if you don't meet these qualifications, or don't come that close—this is a far from ideal world, and where you fall short is simply where you'll have more work to do.

➤ Academic or professional training in network theory, concepts, and operations. This includes everything from networking media and transmission techniques through network operating systems, services, and applications.

➤ Three-plus years of professional networking experience, including experience with Ethernet, token ring, modems, and other networking media. This must include installation, configuration, upgrade, and troubleshooting experience.

➤ Two-plus years in a networked environment that includes hands-on experience with Cisco routers and related equipment. A solid understanding of each system's architecture, installation, configuration, maintenance, and troubleshooting is also essential.

➤ A thorough understanding of key networking protocols, addressing, and name resolution, including TCP/IP, IPX/SPX, and AppleTalk.

➤ Familiarity with key TCP/IP-based services, including ARP, BOOTP, DNS, FTP, SNMP, SMTP, Telnet, TFTP, and other relevant services for your internetwork deployment.

Fundamentally, this boils down to a bachelor's degree in computer science, plus three years of work experience in a technical position involving network design, installation, configuration, and maintenance. We believe that well under half of all certification candidates meet these requirements, and that, in fact, most meet less than half of these requirements—at least, when they begin the certification process. But because thousands of people have survived this ordeal, you can survive it too—especially if you heed what our Self-Assessment can tell you about what you already know and what you need to learn.

Put Yourself To The Test

The following series of questions and observations is designed to help you figure out how much work you must do to pursue Cisco career certification and what kinds of resources you should consult on your quest. Be absolutely honest in your answers, or you'll end up wasting money on exams you're not yet ready to take. There are no right or wrong answers, only steps along the path to certification. Only you can decide where you really belong in the broad spectrum of aspiring candidates.

Two things should be clear from the outset, however:

➤ Even a modest background in computer science will be helpful.

➤ Extensive hands-on experience with Cisco products and technologies is an essential ingredient to certification success.

1. Have you ever taken any computer-related classes? [Yes or No]

   If Yes, proceed to question 2; if No, proceed to question 4.

2. Have you taken any classes included in Cisco's curriculum? [Yes or No]

If Yes, you will probably be able to handle Cisco's architecture and system component discussions. If you're rusty, brush up on basic router operating system concepts, such as, RAM, NVRAM, and flash memory. You'll also want to brush up on the basics of internetworking, especially IP subnetting, access lists, and WAN technologies.

If No, consider some extensive reading in this area. We strongly recommend instructor-led training offered by a Cisco Training Partner.

However, you might want to check out a good general advanced routing technology book, such as *Cisco CCIE Fundamentals: Network Design and Cast Studies* by Andrea Cheek, H. Kim Lew, and Kathleen Wallace (Cisco Press, Indianapolis, IN, 1998 ISBN 1-57870-066-3). If this title doesn't appeal to you, check out reviews for other, similar titles at your favorite online bookstore.

3. Have you taken any networking concepts or technologies classes? [Yes or No]

If Yes, you will probably be able to handle Cisco's internetworking terminology, concepts, and technologies. If you're rusty, brush up on basic internetworking concepts and terminology, especially networking media, transmission types, the OSI Reference model, and networking technologies such as Ethernet, Token Ring, FDDI, and WAN links.

If No, you might want to read one or two books in this topic area. Check out the "Need To Know More?" section at the end of each chapter for a selection of resources that will give you additional background on the topics covered in this book.

4. Have you done any reading on routing protocols and/or routed protocols (IP, IPX, AppleTalk, and so on)? [Yes or No]

If Yes, review the requirements stated in the first paragraphs after Questions 2 and 3. If you meet those requirements, move on to the next question.

If No, consult the recommended reading for both topics. A strong background will help you prepare for the Cisco exams better than just about anything else.

The most important key to success on all of the Cisco tests is hands-on experience with Cisco routers and related equipment. If we leave you with only one realization after taking this Self-Assessment, it should be that there's no substitute for time spent installing, configuring, and using the various Cisco products upon which you'll be tested repeatedly and in depth. It cannot be stressed enough that quality instructor-led training will benefit you greatly and give you additional hands-on configuration experience with the technologies upon which you are to be tested.

5. Have you installed, configured, and worked with Cisco routers? [Yes or No]

If Yes, make sure you understand basic concepts as covered in the class Introduction to Cisco Router Configuration (ICRC), before progressing into the materials covered here, because this book expands on the basic topics taught there.

You can download objectives and other information about Cisco exams from the company's Training and Certification page on the Web at **www.cisco.com/training**.

If No, you will need to find a way to get a good amount of instruction on the intricacies of configuring Cisco equipment. You need a broad background to get through any of Cisco's career certification. You will also need to have hands-on experience with the equipment and technologies on which you'll be tested.

 If you have the funds, or your employer will pay your way, consider taking a class at a Cisco Training Partner (preferably one with "distinguished" status for the highest quality possible). In addition to classroom exposure to the topic of your choice, you get a good view of the technologies being widely deployed and will be able to take part in hands-on lab scenarios with those technologies.

Before you even think about taking any Cisco exam, make sure you've spent enough time with the related software to understand how it may be installed and configured, how to maintain such an installation, and how to troubleshoot that software when things go wrong. This will help you in the exam, and in real life!

Whether you attend a formal class on a specific topic to get ready for an exam or use written materials to study on your own, some preparation for the Cisco career certification exams is essential. At $100 to $200 (depending on the exam) a try, pass or fail, you want to do everything you can to pass on your first try. That's where studying comes in.

6. Have you taken a practice exam on your chosen test subject? [Yes or No]

   If Yes, and you scored 70 percent or better, you're probably ready to tackle the real thing. If your score isn't above that crucial threshold, keep at it until you break that barrier.

   If No, obtain all the free and low-budget practice tests you can find (see the list above) and get to work. Keep at it until you can break the passing threshold comfortably.

We have included a practice exam in this book, so you can test yourself on the information and techniques you've learned. If you don't hit a score of at least 70 percent after this test, you'll want to investigate the other practice test resources we mention in this section.

For any given subject, consider taking a class if you've tackled self-study materials, taken the test, and failed anyway. The opportunity to interact with an instructor and fellow students can make all the difference in the world, if you can afford that privilege. For information about Cisco classes, visit the Training and Certification page at **www.cisco.com/training** or **www.geotrain.com** (use the "Locate a Course" link).

If you can't afford to take a class, visit the Training and Certification page anyway, because it also includes pointers to additional resources and self-study tools. And even if you can't afford to spend much at all, you should still invest in some low-cost practice exams from commercial vendors, because they can help you assess your readiness to pass a test better than any other tool. The following Web sites offer some practice exams online:

➤ CCPrep.com at **www.ccprep.com** (requires membership)

➤ Network Study Guides at **www.networkstudyguides.com** (pay as you go)

When it comes to assessing your test readiness, there is no better way than to take a good-quality practice exam and pass with a score of 70 percent or better. When we're preparing ourselves, we shoot for 80-plus percent, just to leave room for the "weirdness factor" that sometimes shows up on Cisco exams.

Assessing Readiness For Exam 640-403

In addition to the general exam-readiness information in the previous section, there are several things you can do to prepare for the ACRC exam. You will find a great source of questions and related information at the CCprep Web site at **www.ccprep.com**. This is a good place to ask questions and get good answers, or simply to watch the questions that others ask (along with the answers, of course).

You should also cruise the Web looking for "braindumps" (recollections of test topics and experiences recorded by others) to help you anticipate topics you're likely to encounter on the test.

When using any braindump, it's OK to pay attention to information about questions. But you can't always be sure that a braindump's author will also be able to provide correct answers. Thus, use the questions to guide your studies, but don't rely on the answers in a braindump to lead you to the truth. Double-check everything you find in any braindump.

For ACRC preparation in particular, we'd also like to recommend that you check out one or more of these resources as you prepare to take Exam 640-403:

➤ Douglas Comer. *Internetworking with TCP/IP, Volume 1: Principles, Protocols, and Architecture*, Prentice Hall, Englewood Cliffs, NJ, 1995. ISBN 0-13-216987-8.

➤ W. Richard Stevens. *TCP/IP Illustrated, Volume 1: The Protocols*, Addison-Wesley, Reading, MA, 1994. ISBN 0-201-63346-9.

➤ Huitema, Christian. *Routing in the Internet*, Prentice Hall, Englewood Cliffs, NJ, 1995. ISBN 0-13-132192-7.

➤ Perlman, Radia: *Interconnections: Bridges and Routers*, Addison-Wesley, Reading, PA, 1992. ISBN 0-201-56332-0.

Stop by your favorite bookstore or online bookseller to check out one or more of these resources. We believe the first two are the best general all-around references on TCP/IP and advanced routing available, and the second two complement the contents of this Exam Cram for test preparation very nicely.

One last note: Hopefully, it makes sense to stress the importance of hands-on experience in the context of the ACRC exam. As you review the material for that exam, you'll realize that hands-on experience with the Cisco IOS with various technologies and configurations is invaluable.

Onward, Through The Fog!

Once you've assessed your readiness, undertaken the right background studies, obtained the hands-on experience that will help you understand the products and technologies at work, and reviewed the many sources of information to help you prepare for a test, you'll be ready to take a round of practice tests. When your scores come back positive enough to get you through the exam, you're ready to go after the real thing. If you follow our assessment regime, you'll not only know what you need to study, but when you're ready to make a test date at Sylvan Prometric. Good luck!

Cisco
Certification
Exams

Terms you'll need to understand:

√ Radio button

√ Checkbox

√ Exhibit

√ Multiple-choice question formats

√ Careful reading

√ Process of elimination

Techniques you'll need to master:

√ Preparing to take a certification exam

√ Practicing (to make perfect)

√ Making the best use of the testing software

√ Budgeting your time

√ Saving the hardest questions until last

√ Guessing (as a last resort)

√ Breathing deeply (to calm frustration)

Exam taking is not something that most people anticipate eagerly, no matter how well prepared they may be. In most cases, familiarity helps ameliorate test anxiety. In plain English, this means you probably will not be as nervous when you take your fourth or fifth Cisco certification exam as you will be when you take your first one.

Whether it is your first exam or your tenth, understanding the details of exam taking (how much time to spend on questions, the environment you will be in, and so on) and the exam software will help you concentrate on the material rather than on the setting. Likewise, mastering a few basic exam-taking skills should help you recognize—and perhaps even outfox—some of the tricks and gotchas you are bound to find in some of the exam questions.

This chapter, besides explaining the exam environment and software, describes some proven exam-taking strategies that you should be able to use to your advantage.

Assessing Exam-Readiness

Before you take any more Cisco exams, we strongly recommend that you read through and take the Self-Assessment included with this book (it appears just before this chapter, in fact). This will help you compare your knowledge base to the requirements for obtaining an CCNP, and it will also help you identify parts of your background or experience that may be in need of improvement, enhancement, or further learning. If you get the right set of basics under your belt, obtaining Cisco certification will be that much easier.

Once you've gone through the Self-Assessment, you can remedy those topical areas where your background or experience may not measure up to an ideal certification candidate. But you can also tackle subject matter for individual tests at the same time, so you can continue making progress while you're catching up in some areas.

Once you've worked through an *Exam Cram*, have read the supplementary materials, and have taken the practice test, you'll have a pretty clear idea of when you should be ready to take the real exam. We strongly recommend that you keep practicing until your scores top the 70 percent mark; 75 percent would be a good goal to give yourself some margin for error in a real exam situation (where stress will play more of a role than when you practice). Once you hit that point, you should be ready to go. But if you get through the practice exam in this without attaining that score, you should keep taking practice tests and studying the materials until you get there. You'll find more information about other practice test vendors in the Self-Assessment, along with even more pointers on how to study and prepare. But now, on to the exam!

The Exam Situation

When you arrive at the testing center where you scheduled your exam, you will need to sign in with an exam coordinator. He or she will ask you to show two forms of identification, one of which must be a photo ID. After you have signed in and your time slot arrives, you will be asked to deposit any books, bags, or other items you brought with you. Then, you will be escorted into a closed room. Typically, the room will be furnished with anywhere from one to half a dozen computers, and each workstation will be separated from the others by dividers designed to keep you from seeing what is happening on someone else's computer.

You will be furnished with a pen or pencil and a blank sheet of paper, or, in some cases, an erasable plastic sheet and an erasable felt-tip pen. You are allowed to write down any information you want on both sides of this sheet. Before the exam, you should memorize as much of the material that appears on The Cram Sheet (inside the front cover of this book) as you can so you can write that information on the blank sheet as soon as you are seated in front of the computer. You can refer to your rendition of The Cram Sheet anytime you like during the test, but you will have to surrender the sheet when you leave the room.

Most test rooms feature a wall with a large picture window. This permits the exam coordinator standing behind it to monitor the room, to prevent exam takers from talking to one another, and to observe anything out of the ordinary that might go on. The exam coordinator will have preloaded the appropriate Cisco certification exam—for this book, that's Exam 640-403—and you will be permitted to start as soon as you are seated in front of the computer.

All Cisco certification exams allow a certain maximum amount of time in which to complete your work (this time is indicated on the exam by an onscreen counter/clock, so you can check the time remaining whenever you like). Exam 640-403 consists of 72 randomly selected questions. You may take up to 90 minutes to complete the exam. You must get a score of at least 70 percent to pass.

All Cisco certification exams are computer generated and use a multiple-choice format. Although this may sound quite simple, the questions are constructed not only to check your mastery of basic facts and figures about Cisco router configuration, but they also require you to evaluate one or more sets of circumstances or requirements. Often, you will be asked to give more than one answer to a question. Taking the exam is quite an adventure, and it involves real thinking. This book shows you what to expect and how to deal with the potential problems, puzzles, and predicaments.

Exam Layout And Design

Some exam questions require you to select a single answer, whereas others ask you to select multiple correct answers or fill in the blank with a *non-abbreviated* code command. The following multiple-choice question requires you to select a single correct answer. Following the question is a brief summary of each potential answer and why it is either right or wrong.

Question 1

What is the key piece of information on which routing decisions are based?

○ a. Source network-layer address

○ b. Destination network-layer address

○ c. Source MAC address

○ d. Destination MAC address

Answer b is correct. The destination network-layer, or Layer 3, address, is the protocol-specific address to which this piece of data is to be delivered. The source network-layer address is the originating host and plays no role in getting the information to the destination. Therefore, answer a is incorrect. The source and destination Media Access Control (MAC) addresses are necessary for getting the data to the router, or the next hop address. However, they are not used in pathing decisions. Therefore, answers c and d are incorrect.

This sample question format corresponds closely to the Cisco certification exam format—the only difference on the exam is that questions are not followed by answer keys. To select an answer, position the cursor over the radio button next to the answer. Then, click on the mouse button to select the answer.

Let's examine a question that requires choosing multiple answers. This type of question provides checkboxes rather than radio buttons for marking all appropriate selections.

Question 2

Which of the following are possible encapsulations for an ISDN-capable interface? [Choose the four best answers]

❑ a. Frame Relay

❑ b. LAPB

❑ c. PPP

❑ d. HDLC

❑ e. ATM

Answers a, b, c, and d are correct. Integrated Services Digital Network (ISDN) is also capable of supporting X.25 encapsulation. Answer e is incorrect because Basic Rate Interfaces (BRIs) are not capable of providing Asynchronous Transfer Mode (ATM) services. Specialized ATM interfaces are required for utilization of ATM technology.

For this type of question, more than one answer is required. Cisco does not give partial credit for partially correct answers when the test is scored. For Question 2, you have to check the boxes next to items a, b, c, and d to obtain credit for a correct answer. Notice that picking the right answers also means knowing why the other answers are wrong!

Let's take a look at a fill in the blank question. Remember, you may not abbreviate the commands in any way.

Question 3

Enter the command to display information regarding custom queuing operations. [Fill in the blank]

_____

"Show queueing custom" is the answer. You will have to know the exact command. Unfortunately for most of us, you cannot abbreviate the commands in the blank as if you were actually at the command line interface. You must know the exact syntax and command variables of the question to get credit for this one. Also notice that the word "queueing" is misspelled. That is the way it is coded into the router's operating system.

Although these three basic types of questions can appear in many forms, they constitute the foundation on which all the Cisco certification exam questions rest. More complex questions include so-called exhibits, which are usually network scenarios, screen shots of output from the router or even pictures from the course materials. For some of these questions, you will be asked to make a selection by clicking on a checkbox or radio button on the screenshot itself. For others, you will be expected to use the information displayed therein to guide your answer to the question. Familiarity with the underlying utility is your key to choosing the correct answer(s).

Other questions involving exhibits use charts or network diagrams to help document a workplace scenario that you will be asked to troubleshoot or configure. Careful attention to such exhibits is the key to success. Be prepared to toggle frequently between the exhibit and the question as you work.

Using Cisco's Exam Software Effectively

A well-known principle when taking exams is to first read over the entire exam from start to finish while answering only those questions you feel absolutely sure of. On subsequent passes, you can dive into more complex questions more deeply, knowing how many such questions you have left.

Fortunately, Cisco exam software makes this approach easy to implement. At the top-left corner of each question is a checkbox that permits you to mark that question for a later visit. (Note: Marking questions makes review easier, but you can return to any question if you are willing to click on the Forward or Back button repeatedly.) As you read each question, if you answer only those you are sure of and mark for review those that you are not sure of, you can keep working through a decreasing list of questions as you answer the trickier ones in order.

There is at least one potential benefit to reading the exam over completely before answering the trickier questions: Sometimes, information supplied in later questions will shed more light on earlier questions. Other times, information you read in later questions might jog your memory about router configuration facts, figures, or behavior that also will help with earlier questions. Either way, you will come out ahead if you defer answering those questions about which you are not absolutely sure.

Keep working on the questions until you are certain of all your answers or until you know you will run out of time. If questions remain unanswered, you will want to zip through them and guess. Not answering a question guarantees you will not receive credit for it, and a guess has at least a chance of being correct.

 At the very end of your exam period, you are better off guessing than leaving questions unanswered.

Exam-Taking Basics

The most important advice about taking any exam is this: Read each question carefully. Some questions are deliberately ambiguous, some use double negatives, and others use terminology in incredibly precise ways. The authors have taken numerous exams—both practice and live—and in nearly every one have missed at least one question because they did not read it closely or carefully enough.

Here are some suggestions on how to deal with the tendency to jump to an answer too quickly:

➤ Make sure you read every word in the question. If you find yourself jumping ahead impatiently, go back and start over.

➤ As you read, try to restate the question in your own terms. If you can do this, you should be able to pick the correct answer(s) much more easily.

➤ When returning to a question after your initial read-through, read every word again—otherwise, your mind can fall quickly into a rut. Sometimes, revisiting a question after turning your attention elsewhere lets you see something you missed, but the strong tendency is to see what you have seen before. Try to avoid that tendency at all costs.

➤ If you return to a question more than twice, try to articulate to yourself what you do not understand about the question, why the answers do not appear to make sense, or what appears to be missing. If you chew on the subject for awhile, your subconscious might provide the details that are lacking or you might notice a "trick" that will point to the right answer.

➤ Breathe. Deep rhythmic breathing is a stress reliever. Breathe in for a count of four, hold it for two, and then exhale for a count of four. You will be surprised how this can clear your mind of the frustration that clouds it and allow you to regain focus.

Above all, try to deal with each question by thinking through what you know about Cisco routers and their configuration—the characteristics, behaviors, facts, and figures involved. By reviewing what you know (and what you have written down on your information sheet), you will often recall or understand things sufficiently to determine the answer to the question.

Question-Handling Strategies

Based on exams the authors have taken, some interesting trends have become apparent. For those questions that take only a single answer, usually two or three of the answers will be obviously incorrect, and two of the answers will be plausible—of course, only one can be correct. Unless the answer leaps out at you (if it does, reread the question to look for a trick; sometimes those are the ones you are most likely to get wrong), begin the process of answering by eliminating those answers that are most obviously wrong.

Things to look for in obviously wrong answers include spurious menu choices or utility names, nonexistent software options, and terminology you have never seen. If you have done your homework for an exam, no valid information should be completely new to you. In that case, unfamiliar or bizarre terminology probably indicates a totally bogus answer.

Numerous questions assume that the default behavior of a particular utility is in effect. If you know the defaults and understand what they mean, this knowledge will help you cut through many Gordian knots.

As you work your way through the exam, another counter that Cisco thankfully provides will come in handy—the number of questions completed and questions outstanding. Budget your time by making sure that you have completed one-quarter of the questions one-quarter of the way through the exam period (or the first 18 questions in the first 22 minutes) and three-quarters of them three-quarters of the way through (54 questions in the first 66 minutes). If you are not finished when 85 minutes have elapsed, use the last 5 minutes to guess your way through the remaining questions. Remember, guessing is potentially more valuable than not answering, because blank answers are always wrong, but a guess may turn out to be right. If you do not have a clue about any of the remaining questions, pick answers at random, or choose all a's, b's, and so on. The important thing is to submit an exam for scoring that has an answer for every question.

Mastering The Inner Game

In the final analysis, knowledge breeds confidence, and confidence breeds success. If you study the materials in this book carefully and review all the exam prep questions at the end of each chapter, you should become aware of those areas where additional learning and study are required.

Next, follow up by reading some or all of the materials recommended in the "Need To Know More?" section at the end of each chapter. The idea is to become familiar enough with the concepts and situations you find in the sample questions that you can reason your way through similar situations on a real exam. If you know the material, you have every right to be confident that you can pass the exam.

After you have worked your way through the book, take the practice exam in Chapter 16. This will provide a reality check and help you identify areas you need to study further. Make sure you follow up and review materials related to the questions you miss on the practice exam before scheduling a real exam. Only when you have covered all the ground and feel comfortable with the whole scope of the practice exam should you take a real one.

 If you take the practice exam and do not score at least 75 percent correct, you will want to practice further.

Armed with the information in this book and with the determination to augment your knowledge, you should be able to pass the certification exam. However, you need to work at it, or you will spend the exam fee more than once before you finally pass. If you prepare seriously, you should do well. Good luck!

Additional Resources

A good source of information about Cisco certification exams comes from Cisco itself. Because its products and technologies—and the exams that go with them—change frequently, the best place to go for exam-related information is online.

If you haven't already visited the Cisco Certified Professional site, do so right now. The Cisco Connection Online home page resides at **www.cisco.com/ warp/public/10/wwtraining/certprog/index.html**, as shown in Figure 1.1.

> *Note:* *This page might not be there by the time you read this, or it might have been replaced by something new and different, because things change regularly on the Cisco site. Should this happen, please read the sidebar later in this chapter titled "Coping With Change On The Web."*

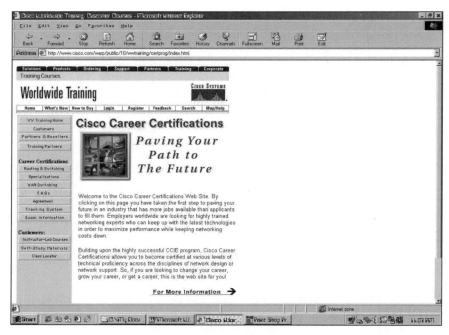

Figure 1.1 The Cisco Career Certifications home page.

The menu options in the left column of the home page point to the most important sources of information in the Cisco Career Certification pages. Here's what to check out:

➤ **Routing Switching** Use this entry to explore the Cisco Certified Internetworking Expert (CCIE) certification track for routing and switching.

➤ **Specializations** Use this entry to explore different Cisco Certified Networking Professional (CCNP) specialization options.

➤ **WAN Switching** Use this entry to explore the CCIE certification track for WAN switching.

➤ **F.A.Q.s** Use this entry to access the most commonly asked questions regarding any Cisco Career Certification.

➤ **Agreement** Use this entry to complete the certification agreement. Prior to certification, all candidates must do so or Cisco will not recognize them as certified professionals.

➤ **Tracking System** Use this entry to keep up with your progress on the certification tracking system. Once you have registered with Sylvan Prometric, and taken any Cisco exam, you will automatically be added to it.

➤ **Exam Information** Use this entry to go to a class locator. It should be noted that no book is an adequate replacement for instructor-led, Cisco-authorized training. This entry will assist you in your efforts to find a class that meets your scheduling needs.

These are just the high points of what's available in the Cisco Career Certification pages. As you browse through them—and we strongly recommend that you do—you will probably find other informational tidbits that are every bit as interesting and compelling.

Coping With Change On The Web

Sooner or later, all the information we have shared with you about the Cisco Career Certification pages and the other Web-based resources mentioned throughout the rest of this book will go stale or be replaced by newer information. In some cases, the URLs you find here might lead you to their replacements; in other cases, the URLs will go nowhere, leaving you with the dreaded "404 File not found" error message. When that happens, do not give up.

There's always a way to find what you want on the Web if you are willing to invest some time and energy. Most large or complex Web sites—and Cisco's qualifies on both counts—offer a search engine. Looking back at Figure 1.1, you can see that a Search field appears along the top edge of the page. As long as you can get to Cisco's site (it should stay at **www.cisco.com** for a long while yet), you can use this tool to help you find what you need.

The more focused you can make a search request, the more likely the results will include information you can use. For example, you can search for the string "training and certification" to produce a lot of data about the subject in general, but if you are looking for the preparation guide for Exam 640-403, "Advanced Cisco Router Configuration" or ACRC, you are more likely to get there quickly if you use a search string similar to the following:

```
"Exam 640-403" AND "preparation guide"
```

Finally, feel free to use general search tools—such as **www.search.com**, **www.altavista.com**, and **www.excite.com**—to search for related information. The bottom line is this: If you can't find something where the book says it lives, start looking around. If worst comes to worst, you can always email us.

Internetwork Overview

Terms you'll need to understand:

√ Scalable internetworks

√ Hierarchical infrastructure

√ Core router

√ Distribution router

√ Access router

√ Hierarchical routing

√ Traffic prioritization

√ Route redundancy

√ Network accessibility

Techniques you'll need to master:

√ Designing scalable networks

√ Creating a hierarchical structure

√ Provisioning appropriate hardware

√ Implementing route redundancy

√ Creating an accessible, secure network

This chapter serves simply as an overview of the technologies that are covered in the remainder of the book. We will address a number of topics that relate to the basic design of your internetwork. In doing so, we will address some of the issues that arise in the design of any network. The topics described in this chapter are discussed from a very high level viewpoint. The goals of any network can fall into any or all of the guidelines discussed.

Scalable Networks

Any network design has goals, including deploying internetworking devices appropriately to create a logical structure for the internetwork. Cisco has developed routers and other devices that fulfill many of these goals. Figure 2.1, which serves as an example for our discussions throughout the chapter, shows a basic Internetwork deployment.

Scalability

In order to be scalable, your network must meet the predefined objectives of its existence. For your network to work for you, you must first design it properly.

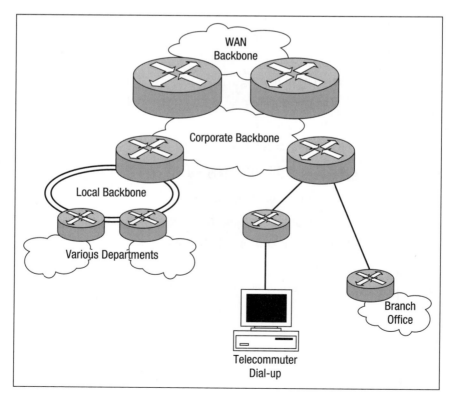

Figure 2.1 An example of a scalable network.

Before we can discuss design, we must define some roles that routers can play in your internetwork. Consider Figure 2.1. It is easy to see the role that each type of router plays in the network. The largest, most powerful devices exist at the highest level of the hierarchy. These routers carry the highest load of your internetwork traffic from site to site. They are typically attached to the highest-level backbone, otherwise known as the *core* of the network. Appropriately, these devices are known as *core routers*.

The next level down in the hierarchy is comprised of somewhat powerful routers as well. These routers pass traffic to the core from the lower levels and back again. This functionality has deemed these devices *distribution routers*.

At the lowest level of the hierarchy, the mission-specific routers are deployed. These are the routers that provide users with access to the internetwork infrastructure. They can provide users based in home offices with access to the network via dial-up services. These routers can also provide access from a satellite office to a larger centralized office network. These devices have been deemed the *access routers*.

Each type of router has its appropriate place in the network. Obviously, an outage would have some effect at any level in the hierarchy. If a core router failed, significantly more users would be affected than if you lost an access router.

 You need to understand the different roles of the various routers in your internetwork. It is important for you to understand the position of core, distribution, and access routers.

One of the key elements in designing an internetwork is defining what you want to get out of the network once it is complete. To be successful, a network should be:

➤ Reliable and available

➤ Responsive

➤ Efficient

➤ Adaptable

➤ Accessible

➤ Secure

Reliability And Availability

We mention these two topics together because they go hand in hand. If the network is not reliable, its availability could be compromised. Obviously, if it is not available, it is not reliable.

What factors come to mind when you think about network reliability? The first answer is usually redundancy. If one piece of the network goes down, we would rather the end users not notice it. Providing redundancy requires additional hardware, multiple data pathways, software, or any number of other factors.

When we are planning any redundancy in the network, we should be careful not to create what is commonly known as a *single point of failure*—one device on which the operation of the entire network (or large portions thereof) depends. Should this single device fail in any way, a catastrophic outage would occur. You should carefully plan single points of failure out of existence.

Hardware Redundancy

Notice in Figure 2.1 that there is not simply one very large router functioning as the core router. Why not? What issues (a better word is nightmares) come to mind when you imagine a single router providing your core services? The core router is many times the most heavily loaded router and the one you can least afford to lose. How do you avoid losing it?

One of your options is to ensure that the larger routers operate in the network by providing redundant hardware in the same chassis where possible. Many of the high-end routers, such as the 7500 series routers, can use dual power supplies. Other hardware options provide some level of additional protection from various failures that can occur within the device itself.

Another choice may be to implement multiple devices to do the job of the one. The purpose here is not to replace the single device, just to augment it. For instance, in Figure 2.1, you can see two core routers. Is it conceivable that one router could provide the core function? Yes, that is possible, depending on the nature of the network and the amount of traffic going across it. Implementing additional core routers—although not absolutely necessary to get the traffic across the network adequately—can provide peace of mind for the administrator. As far as the routers are concerned, the benefit of having two devices is lower traffic load because much of the traffic has been distributed between them.

Route Redundancy

If the hardware is functioning properly, but routing information is lost, the result is basically the same as the hardware failure, no data flow. Actually, the loss of routing information is many times more difficult to troubleshoot than are hardware issues. With hardware issues, there are sometimes physical manifestations, good or bad: red or amber Light Emitting Diodes (LEDs), Simple Network Management Protocol (SNMP) events, pops, sparks, smoke, or—in extreme cases—fires. Physical manifestations are quite straightforward, usually, whereas with routing inconsistencies, it's not so easy to find the causes.

A way to provide route redundancy is to run multiple dynamic routing protocols simultaneously. Obviously, doing so to some degree impacts the amount of system resources used; however, route redundancy is often a benefit in such scenarios. Should one protocol experience problems, lost routes, and so on, the other routing protocol may still have reachability to specific networks. Of course, that is the case only if the cause of the issue is not physical.

In the case of physical outages, it may be prudent to install multiple redundant pathways between points of extreme importance. Internet Protocol (IP) routing protocols automatically seek out equal-metric pathways to a particular destination and load balance traffic across those pathways. Should one pathway fail, the other pathway is present to pick up the slack.

It's also a good idea to use a dynamic routing protocol that can intelligently adapt to routing changes. You may want to implement a protocol that allows you to create a hierarchical routing structure. Advanced routing protocols can minimize the impact of a topology change by localizing the impact and decreasing convergence time. By logically dividing the internetwork into separate areas, you can localize the routing change to that area. Convergence simply occurs within that area.

One implementation of redundancy in pathways is known as *dial backup*. Dial backup places into service a secondary pathway that is used only when the primary pathway is overloaded or down. Dial backup is discussed in detail in Chapter 13.

 You should know the basic information regarding hardware and route redundancy. You need to understand that convergence issues, routing loops, and lost reachability can occur and that specific technologies (including dial backup) are available to deal with each.

Responsiveness

Responsiveness refers to how fast the network responds to topology changes, delivers requested resources, or provides any other function that it should. If the network can't perform these tasks promptly, it lacks responsiveness.

In some cases, the transport of multiple protocols can become an issue. The timing issues involved with protocols, such as IBM's System Network Architecture (SNA) protocol, can create the need for traffic prioritization. SNA does not tolerate delay well. Should congestion occur in the network—or any other condition that causes additional delay—SNA could cease to function properly, which becomes a problem very quickly. Traffic prioritization allows the high-priority traffic to be processed before the lower-priority traffic types, thereby ensuring less delay through the network. Traffic prioritization is discussed in detail in Chapter 4.

Efficiency

Efficiency is heavily enmeshed with responsiveness. If the network lacks responsiveness, efficiency is reduced. Efficiency can refer to bandwidth utilization, hardware deployment, or any number of other issues.

One way to make your network efficient is to implement access lists to filter traffic. Doing so keeps traffic from areas of the network where it is not wanted or needed. Access lists are meant to provide basic security, not to replace firewall implementations. If you have a Fiber Distributed Data Interface (FDDI) backbone where no NetWare servers exist, you can use access lists to filter out unnecessary SAP broadcast traffic. Access lists are covered in detail in Chapter 3.

You can improve efficiency in many different ways. Using compression on slower-speed links allows you to increase the efficiency of your WAN links. However, you should take care not to overload the router. If the router's CPU utilization is already high, compression increases it, which could cause a failure. On higher-speed links, compression may actually slow down the transfer of data. There comes a point where it is faster to send the data than it would be to compress, send, and decompress it.

You can take advantage of snapshot routing to increase efficiency in dial-on-demand routing (DDR) situations where routing updates are not desirable on Integrated Services Digital Network (ISDN) links. Snapshot routing was designed to freeze the routing tables on each side of the link when distance-vector protocols are in use. Snapshot routing stops the normal periodic updates of Routing Information Protocol (RIP) or Interior Gateway Routing Protocol (IGRP) and freezes the routing table for a number of hours (known as a *quiet period*). Once the quiet period expires, the routers exchange updates for a few minutes, and then they resume the quiet state. DDR and snapshot routing are covered in more detail in Chapter 13.

You can make routing tables more efficient in several ways. Route summarization, for instance, reduces the overall size of the routing table. A smaller routing table means faster routing table lookups as well as lower memory and CPU utilization overall. Route summarization greatly increases the efficiency of the network's operations.

Adaptability

The network must be able to handle multiple protocols. In a multiprotocol environment, the network must be able to react to network topology changes quickly as well as to deal with the possibility of non-routable protocols. Non-routable protocols are those that do not contain a network-layer address. Thece protocols must be bridged or switched. Bridging protocols should not be taken lightly. Once layer 2 support has been enabled on the router, the router becomes a simple bridge. Unlike routers, bridges forward broadcasts by default.

Should you decide not to bridge the non-routable protocols, you can deal with them in another way, by encapsulating non-routable protocols inside IP packets. Protocol encapsulation adds a significant amount of overhead. It is common to encapsulate NetBIOS and/or SNA or other layer 2 non-routable protocols inside of IP so that those protocols may be transported across an internetwork.

Accessibility

The network should be accessible when needed. Whether your users are local or remote, you need to make some accommodations for them. If some of your users are remote or mobile users, you must consider some special issues.

How will they connect to the network? Will routers be placed at their homes for home-office access? What technology will be used to allow connectivity to these users? If ISDN is to be used, you may need to implement DDR. If you are going to use some sort of Serial technology (such as High-Level Data Link Control—HDLC), you must make special provisions in the network to receive these remote users' data.

Will users be provided with mobile electronics such as a laptop for access to the network? How many dial-up accounts will be necessary? What kind of dial-capable hardware will be put in place to accommodate these users? If many dial-up users will be using your network, you will need specific hardware to accomplish this somewhat large task.

Security

All of these network issues that we have discussed are extremely important. However, an intruder out to exploit your network can undo all of the security in a short time. It is unfortunate that some individuals make it their life's work to maliciously exploit network infrastructure. Without some security measures in place, the network is in danger.

Security can come in the form of a firewall placed between your network and the public data network. Firewall products are widely available and come in many implementations. There are many Unix or Windows NT-based software-based firewall solutions; some hardware-based firewall solutions, such as Cisco's PIX Firewall product, are also available. Firewalls are beyond the scope of the ACRC course and exam as well as this book.

Practice Questions

Question 1

> What are the routers at the top of the internetwork hierarchy known as?
>
> ○ a. Core routers
>
> ○ b. Distribution routers
>
> ○ c. Accesc routers
>
> ○ d. None of the above

Answer a is correct. Core routers make up the very backbone of your internetwork and are generally the highest-horsepower routers in the internetwork. These routers are the cornerstones of your infrastructure. Answer b is incorrect because distribution routers provide a pathway between the lower-level routers and the core routers at the top. Answer c is incorrect because access routers actually provide the end-user network facilities. Answer d is incorrect because a correct answer is given.

Question 2

> Which items are goals of the internetwork? [Choose the two best answers]
>
> ❏ a. Accessibility
>
> ❏ b. Dial-on-demand routing
>
> ❏ c. Firewall
>
> ❏ d. Efficiency

Answers a and d are correct. Accessibility and efficiency are a couple of small pieces in the overall big picture of internetwork design. Answer b is incorrect because DDR is not one of the goals; rather, it is an implementation of an internetwork goal: It is one method of making the network efficient. Answer c is incorrect because it is one method of making the network secure. Security is the goal, not just a firewall implementation.

Question 3

> Redundancy in the network is not a useful tool and should not be implemented.
>
> ○ a. True
>
> ○ b. False

Answer b is correct, False. Redundancy has become one of the most, if not *the* most, important aspects of network planning.

Question 4

> Which types of protocols determine the degree of adaptability needed for internetwork design and implementation? [Choose the two best answers]
>
> ❑ a. Routing protocols
>
> ❑ b. Routable protocols
>
> ❑ c. Non-routable protocols
>
> ❑ d. None of the above

Answers b and c are correct. Routable and non-routable protocols that exist in your network require the network be adaptable to handle both types. You must be able to deal with the various traffic types on your network. Answer a is incorrect because routing protocols provide path determination and reachability for routed protocols only. They do not necessarily have anything to do with the network's adaptability where multiple protocol types are concerned. Answer d is incorrect because a correct answer is given. The trick in this question lies in the fact that you may not read all of the answers adequately. If you find the basic word forms that you're looking for you'll usually pick that answer. Hopefully you read the answers and saw that answer a, "routing" protocols is incorrect and that answer b "routable" protocols is correct.

Question 5

Where is compression best utilized?

○ a. Low-speed Serial links

○ b. High-speed Serial links

○ c. Ethernet interfaces

○ d. Token Ring interfaces

Answer a is correct. Low-speed Serial links are much easier to push into a congestion condition. Compression on these links provides additional overhead for the router but reduces the size of the data transmitted over the link. Answer b is incorrect because high-speed Serial links can transmit traffic in less time than it takes to compress, send, and decompress the data. Answers c and d are incorrect because Ethernet and Token Ring interfaces are high-bandwidth interfaces that do not require the use of compression algorithms.

Need To Know More?

 Cheek, Andrea, Kim H. Lew, and Kathleen Wallace. *Cisco CCIE Fundamentals: Network Design and Cast Studies.* Cisco Press, Indianapolis, IN 1998. ISBN 1-57870-066-3. Part I of this book deals with internetwork design concepts.

 Huitema, Christian. *Routing in the Internet.* Prentice Hall, Englewood Cliffs, NJ, April, 1995. ISBN 0-13-132192-7. This book is a great resource for finding regarding IP internetwork design and routing operations.

 Visit Cisco's Web site at **www.cisco.com** and perform a search on any of the concepts discussed here (such as Scalable Internetworks, Core, Distribution, or Access).

Traffic Management

Terms you'll need to understand:

√ Standard access-lists

√ Extended access-lists

√ Wildcard masks

√ Access class

√ Null interfaces

√ Helper addresses

√ Service Advertising Protocol (SAP) filters

√ Get Nearest Server (GNS) filters

√ Tunnels

Techniques you'll need to master:

√ Coding wildcard masks

√ Configuring standard and extended IP access-lists

√ Understanding access-list positioning

√ Limiting virtual terminal access

√ Using a static route to the null interface as an alternative to access-lists

√ Understanding helper address configuration

√ Using standard and extended IPX traffic, SAP filters, and GNS filters

√ Using tunnels to connect network islands

In this chapter, we'll look at some of the Cisco IOS features used to make IP more efficient and secure. We'll start by reviewing standard IP access-lists, commonly called filters, and move on to the more complicated extended versions. Along the way, we'll talk about issues such as the placement of access-lists for correct operation and maximum efficiency in the network. Additionally, we'll examine an alternative to access-lists called the null interface. We'll illustrate how to use access-lists to increase router security with access classes as well as examine the concept of the IP helper address.

Access-lists can be used with all protocols, including IPX, which has special needs such as SAP and GNS filtering. We will also discuss the concept of a protocol encapsulation method known as a tunnel, which can to connect discontiguous network layer protocol implementations.

This chapter is basically about access-lists and the many ways to use them. At times they may be confusing, but they are an important part of the Cisco IOS and will be found on the ACRC exam.

Defining Access-Lists

Other than hierarchical design issues (which we discuss in Chapters 6 through 8), the most common problem with efficiency in networks is that LAN protocols make heavy use of broadcasts to transfer information. In a small network with a few LAN segments, broadcasts work well and cause few problems. Unfortunately, as networks scale upward in size, broadcast traffic grows to the point where it may compromise successful network operation. This is where access-lists come in.

Access-lists are filters that administrators use to separate traffic of all protocols. IP access-lists come in two varieties: standard and extended. Access-lists provide a facility to sort traffic and are used with many IOS features including the following:

➤ **Traffic filtering** Allow filtering or forwarding traffic into or out of an interface based on administrative policy

➤ **Security** Allow or prevent Telnet access to or from router virtual terminals

➤ **Dial-on-demand routing (DDR)** Select interesting traffic to force dialing (covered in Chapter 13)

➤ **Priority and custom queuing groups** Assign traffic to queues with more precision than simply specifying an interface or a protocol allow (covered in Chapter 4)

➤ **Route filtering** Restrict the contents of routing updates (we discuss IPX route filtering in this chapter; see Chapter 9 for a discussion of IP route filtering)

➤ **Service filtering** Restrict Novell SAPs, and AppleTalk Zone update filtering

Basic Operation

When an administrator wants to select traffic for one of the purposes listed above, he or she creates one or more rules to test against traffic packets. If the address being checked matches, the packet is selected and either permitted or denied (denied also means *dropped* or *filtered*) immediately. If a packet being tested does not match any of the rules in the access-list, it is dropped at the end of the list. If the packet is filtered either explicitly (due to one of the rules) or implicitly (by not matching any rule), an Internet Control Message Protocol (ICMP) "Administratively Prohibited" message is sent. Standard access-lists use only the packet's source address for comparison. In other words, IP standard access-lists can make filtering decisions base solely on the source address of the packet. Extended access-lists provide for selection based on source address, destination address, protocol, and port numbers. Extended access-lists require more processing but provide finer tuning of the selection process.

Access-list functionality is available for a large variety of protocols and is identified by the router based on the list number and the range into which it falls. Table 3.1 provides some of the ranges supported by the router.

Other access-lists exist. See the Cisco Documentation CD or Web site for further information.

Table 3.1 List number ranges for access-lists.	
Range	**Description**
1 through 99	Standard IP
100 through 199	Extended IP
200 through 299	Ethernet type code (transparent and source-route bridging)
300 through 399	DECnet
400 through 499	Xerox Network Services (XNS)
500 through 599	Extended XNS
600 through 699	AppleTalk

(continued)

Table 3.1 List number ranges for access-lists (continued).	
Range	Description
700 through 799	Vendor code (transparent and source-route bridging)
800 through 899	Standard Internetwork Packet eXchange (IPX)
900 through 999	Extended IPX
1000 through 1099	IPX Service Advertising Protocol (SAP)
1100 through 1199	Extended transparent bridging
1200 through 1299	NetWare Link Services Protocol (NLSP) route summary route

Managing IP Traffic

Sorting of IP traffic with access-lists for any of the uses listed earlier comes in two flavors. Standard IP access-lists use only the packet's source address for comparison. Extended access-lists provide for more precise packet selection based on source and destination addresses, protocol and port numbers.

Standard IP Access-Lists

All access-lists are coded globally and then associated with an interface for traffic filtering. Once the interface for the access-list has been determined, you must decide the direction for the access-list. You can filter traffic inbound to the router or outbound from the router. If you filter inbound, the filtering decision is made prior to the routing table lookup. If you filter outbound, the routing decision has been made and the packet switched to the proper outbound interface before it is tested against the access-list. The lists default to the outbound direction on the interface for compatibility with older IOS versions. However, the in or out direction is part of the interface assignment statement. You may use this same list for DDR, priority and custom queuing, and traffic filtering.

Access-List Processing Logic

The rules of the basic IP access-lists are processed in accordance to the sequence illustrated in Figure 3.1.

As you can see in the figure, at each of the one or more rules the source IP address is matched or not. A match causes immediate processing of the permit or deny statement depending on how the statement is coded. If the logic is "permit," whatever action the access-list is associated with (for example, filtering/forwarding, DDR, sorting traffic for queuing) is performed. In this case the example shows a simple traffic filter, so the packet is forwarded out of the

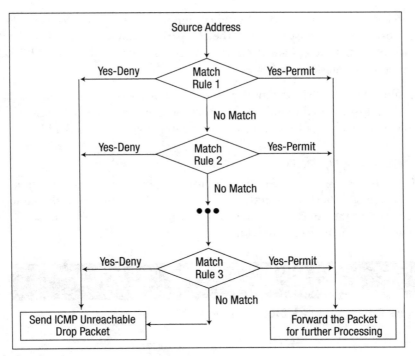

Figure 3.1   Standard access-list processing.

interface to which this filter is attached. If the action is "deny," the packet is dropped and an ICMP "Administratively Prohibited" (RFC-1812) message is returned to the source address.

Some security administrators don't like to let someone who may be attacking the network have any detail on denied access. To avoid this situation, use an access-list to deny the return "Administratively Prohibited" messages at the security domain boundary.

Wildcard Masks

It is necessary, when configuring access-lists, to specify the traffic you are trying to filter by address. You can be very specific regarding an address or very general. To specify the generality or specificity of a filter, access-lists use a wildcard mask. The wildcard mask is a way to specify which bits must match and which bits don't matter, octet by octet, in the comparison of the packet's address to the rule. The masking process is similar to the AND used for subnet processing, which was discussed in the Introduction to Cisco Router Configuration (ICRC) course. The difference is that the wildcard mask uses bits that are 1s to indicate bit positions that should be ignored in the comparison and 0s for bit positions that must match in the comparison. Sometimes, bits in the wildcard mask that are 1s are referred as don't care bits. Tables 3.2 and 3.3 compare the two masking processes.

The result is that 1 bits in the mask are used to indicate don't care bits, and 0 bits in the mask are used to indicate bits that must match. Table 3.4 shows an example of a match that keeps only the 8-bit subnet on the Class B address.

Coding Description

The Cisco IOS allows one access-list per protocol, per interface, per direction. If two IP access-lists that currently exist should both be applied to the same interface and in the same direction, you must combine them into a single list and assign it to the interface instead.

Table 3.2   Logical AND mask processing used for subnet derivation.

Address Bit	Mask Bit	Result
1	1	1
1	0	0
0	1	0
0	0	0

Table 3.3   Wildcard mask processing for access-lists.

Address Bit	Mask Bit	Result	Indication
1	1	0	Ignore (don't care)
0	1	0	Ignore (don't care)
1	0	1	Must match
0	0	0	Must match

Table 3.4   Wildcard mask example.

Component	Dotted Decimal	Binary
Source address	172.16.5.1	10101100.00010000.00000101.00000001
Wildcard mask	0.0.255.255	00000000.00000000.11111111.11111111
Result	172.16.0.0	10101100.00010000.00000000.00000000

Please refer to the command format in Listing 3.1 below. The access-list number does two things. First, it tells the IOS what kind of access-list is being coded (numbers between 1 and 99 indicate a standard IP access-list). Second, it ties the statements of the access-list together.

Notice also in Listing 3.1 below that the access-list does not have line numbers. The commands are executed from top to bottom. Therefore, for the access-list to work correctly, it is critical that you enter the statements in the correct order. Address selections must go from more specific to more general. Essentially, individual addresses must come before subnets, subnets before networks, and networks before **permit any** or **deny any** statements. The "any" implies a match for every address. Remember that each packet is selected by the first line of the access-list it matches. So, if the same packet matches as an individual address and as part of a subnet, the individual address must come first. If the subnet match occurs first, the packet never reaches the individual address statement.

Use the following tips to help assure that you correctly place and operate an access-list:

➤ First, it is usually much more reasonable to create the list on a desktop computer with a text editor of your choice, then use Trivial File Transfer Protocol (TFTP) to deliver it to the router. If you do this, remember to put the no access-list statement at the beginning of your file (which will remove all lines of access-list). Otherwise, the new statements are added to the end of the existing list rather than replacing it.

➤ If a network management tool such as Netsys (see the Cisco Web site or the Documentation CD for details) is available, allow it to look at your list before you install it into a production network, especially in a remote router.

Note: If you place a list in a router that accidentally blocks more traffic than desired, the list may even block Telnet access for the administrator trying to fix the problem, thereby cutting off remote access to the router.

➤ Allow a colleague or group of colleagues to review the access-list and the location within the network where you will place the list.

➤ When you load the access-list into the remote router, you should load it into active RAM (the running-config). Do not save it initially in case there are problems with it and you get cut off from the router due to the effects of the access-lists. At that point, power cycling the router by a person that is local to the router can remove the list's effect.

Command Syntax And Examples

The basic format of the global access-list command is shown in Listing 3.1.

Listing 3.1 Global access-list command.

```
[no] access-list number {permit | deny } source-ip-address
    wildcard-mask [log]
```

Listings 3.2 through 3.6 show some standard IP access-lists. They also illustrate the sequence-of-commands issue. The first line would make all other lines ineffective because all traffic is permitted immediately and never reaches the lines below it.

Listing 3.2 Permitting all IP source addresses because all of the wildcard bits are 1s.

```
access-list 20 permit 0.0.0.0 255.255.255.255
```

Listing 3.3 Permitting all packets from the network number 172.16.0.0—all subnet and host bits are ignored.

```
access-list 20 permit 172.16.0.0 0.0.255.255
```

Listing 3.4 Permitting traffic from subnet 172.16.1.0 (assuming a 24-bit prefix or subnet mask).

```
access-list 20 permit 172.16.1.0 0.0.0.255
```

Listing 3.5 Permitting traffic from the host 172.16.1.1 only.

```
access-list 20 permit 172.16.1.1 0.0.0.0
```

Listing 3.6 Permitting traffic from subnets 172.16.0.0 through 172.31.0.0 (assuming a subnet prefix of 24 bits).

```
access-list 20 permit 172.16.0.0 0.15.255.255
```

Listings 3.7 and 3.8 show some common access-list mistakes.

Listing 3.7 An erroneous access-list line example.

```
access-list 21 permit 172.16.0.0
```

This code does not function because the default mask is 0.0.0.0. No source address would ever have the address 172.16.0.0 as a host address. This address is actually the network number without subnet or host.

Listing 3.8   Another erroneous access-list line example.

```
access-list 21 deny 0.0.0.0 255.255.255.255
```

This code is referred to as a **deny any** and is not required. If a packet's address does not match an earlier statement, an implicit **deny any** occurs at the end of every access-list automatically.

In IOS version 10.3, several new changes were added to make the access-lists more legible and their coding less error prone. The first are code words to replace common patterns. The second is a named access-list. Listings 3.9 and 3.10 show common errors in access-list coding.

Listing 3.9   These two statements are identical in operation.

```
access-list 22 permit 0.0.0.0 255.255.255.255
access-list 22 permit any
```

Listing 3.10   These two statements are also identical.

```
access-list 23 permit 172.16.1.1 0.0.0.0
access-list 23 permit host 172.16.1.1
```

Named access-lists were first introduced in IOS 11.2. Named access-lists are an attempt to overcome one of the major configuration issues with access-lists, the inability to selectively remove lines from a list. For example, refer back to listing 3.10. If this represented only one line of a 30 line access-lists, the command no access-list 23 permit host 172.16.1.1 would completely remove all lines for access-list 23. Named access-lists allow the selective removal of access-lists lines (but it's still easier to work with text files and TFTP servers or cut an paste from a terminal emulator). Listing 3.11 shows a named access-list.

Listing 3.11   Named access-list example.

```
ip access-list standard mike
permit host 10.1.1.1
deny 10.2.0.0 0.0.255.255
permit any
!
interface serial 1
ip access-group mike in
```

The access-list, coded globally (for the whole router), is associated with a specific interface and direction with the command shown in Listing 3.11.

Let's review some issues to remember when configuring access-lists:

➤ Processing is line by line from top to bottom. Tests must be manually sorted from more specific addresses to the more general. Also, to boost efficiency, place more frequently accessed items before less frequently accessed ones.

➤ New lines are added only at the end of the current list (IOS 11.2 allows individual line changes with named access-lists only).

➤ Undefined lists (the existence of an access-group statement on an interface but no corresponding global access-list definition in the router configuration) imply a **permit any**. Watch out: Prior to IOS 10.3, the default was **deny any**. All the interface knew was that there was supposed to be an access-list and the only line it could assume was the implicit deny.

➤ The last line of an access-list is an implicit **deny any** (usually what you want).

Extended IP Access-Lists

Extended IP access-lists are similar in operation to standard IP access-lists, but they provide for more extensive filtering and allow you to be more flexible when placing them within the router hierarchy. Extended IP access-lists allow filtering on source address, destination address, protocol, port, and other conditions. The processing flow of an extended IP access-list is shown in Figure 3.2.

As you can see from the figure, the processing logic of the Extended access-list is similar to, but more extensive than, the Standard access-list. In order for the explicit permit or deny action to apply, all conditions must match. The test sequence is as follows: source address then destination address (both of which must have wildcard masks associated with them), then protocol field, and finally, port number or protocol options.

The extended IP access-list uses the range 100 through 199. The general format for an extended access-list is illustrated in Listing 3.12.

Listing 3.12 Extended **access-list** command parameters.

```
[no] access-list number {permit | deny} { protocol | protocol
      keyword }
        { source-ip-address source-wildcard-mask | any }
        { destination-ip-address destination-wildcard-mask | any}
        [ protocol-specific options ] [ log ]
```

In the access-list command, you must specify the protocol to be matched. This parameter can support a number of different protocol options. The protocol

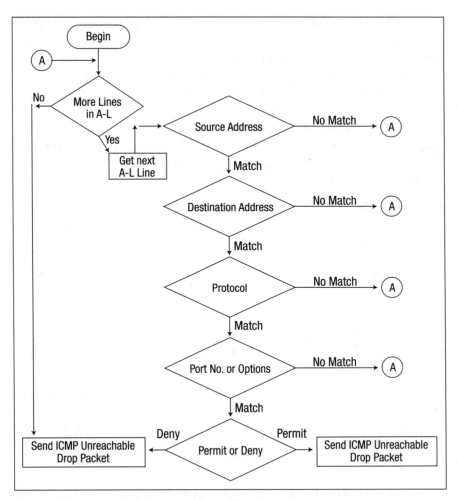

Figure 3.2   Extended IP access-list processing.

keywords are **eigrp, icmp, igmp, igrp, ip, nos, ospf, tcp**, or **udp**. These can be used to filter specific traffic types beyond the simple IP realm.

You must configure source and destination addresses that must be matched. Each must contain a wildcard mask or a keyword representing the wildcard mask (such as, any, host, and so on). The terms "address" (source or destination) and "keyword" mean the same as for the standard access-lists.

The optional keyword **log** causes each packet that matches this statement to generate a log entry, which is recorded by the router. This can generate significant processing and uses bandwidth if it is logging to a remote syslog server, or router memory. One strategy would be to use this feature to monitor the traffic periodically. Another approach might be to use a **show** command that displays the number of times a statement has been matched. By using the **show** command or using Simple Network Management Protocol (SNMP) to retrieve the information over a known period of time, you can track the information without constant logging, thereby saving valuable processor resources.

TCP Specific Access-Lists

You can use extended access-lists to filter the transport layer protocol TCP. TCP is a connection-oriented protocol. The format for TCP protocol specific format is shown in Listing 3.13.

Listing 3.13   TCP access-lists syntax.

```
[no] access-list <number> {permit | deny} tcp { source-ip-address
        source-wildcard-mask| any } [ operator source-port | source-
        port ]
        { destination-ip-address  destination-wildcard-mask | any}
        [ operator destination-port | destination-port ] [ estab
        lished ]
```

The operator option is used to specify application port numbers or a group of port numbers. The values for **operator** include **gt** (greater than or equal), **eq** (equal), or **lt** (less than or equal).

The port number itself, as mentioned, can be application specific. Port numbers range from 0 through 65535. In most cases, the port number can use a name rather than number for clarity. Here is a partial list of the names in the IOS along with the port number:

➤ **bgp**   Border Gateway Protocol (179)

➤ **bootpc**   Boot Protocol Client (68)

➤ **bootps**   Boot Protocol Server (67)

➤ **discard**   Dump Port (9)

➤ **domain**   Domain Name Server (53)

➤ **finger**   Finger Port (79)

➤ **ftp-control**   FTP Control Port (21)

➤ **ftp-data**   FTP Data Port (20)

➤ **gopher**   Gopher Port (70)

➤ **hostname**   NIC Hostname Port (101)

- **klogin**   Kerberos login port (543)

- **kshell**   Kerberos shell port (544)

- **nntp**   Network News Transfer Protocol (119)

- **pop3**   Post Office Protocol version 3 (110)

- **smtp**   Simple Mail Transfer Protocol (25)

- **snmp**   Simple Network Management Protocol (161)

- **sunrpc**   Sun Remote Procedure Call (111)

- **syslog**   Syslog port (514)

- **tacacs-ds**   TACACS Database Service (65)

- **telnet**   Telnet – Network Virtual Terminal port (23)

- **tftp**   Trivial File Transfer Protocol (69)

- **uucp**   Unix-to-Unix Copy path (117)

- **whois**   Whois port (43)

- **www**   World Wide Web port (80)

- and a few hundred more

Another very handy keyword that you can use is **established,** which means, if it came from within my network and had to leave my network (possibly out to the Internet), let it back into my network. It was designed to allow outbound traffic to come back through the security of a firewall or access-lists. Any TCP header that contains the ACK (Acknowledge) and/or RST (Reset) bit matches. Figure 3.3 shows the effect of the established keyword.

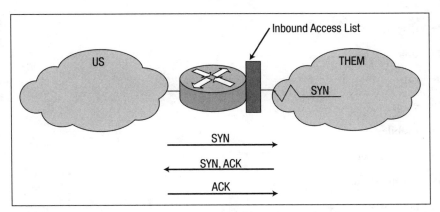

Figure 3.3   Operation of the **established** keyword for TCP conversations.

The ACK bit is not set (equal to one) on the SYN message in the first packet that initiates the three-way handshake. The ACK bit is set in every other packet in the TCP connection. Placing an inbound access-list, using the **established** keyword, (on the interface shown,) allows sessions to be started from within our part of the network. Conversations cannot originate from outside the network. This assumes that our own people may start TCP conversations freely. This is useful, but remember that an access-list is not a firewall. For more information, check the Cisco Web site (**www.cisco.com**), Documentation CD, or the Computer Emergency Response Team (CERT) bulletins.

UDP Extended Access-List Syntax

You can use access-lists to filter protocol specific options of UDP. UDP is a connectionless protocol, which has much less overhead than its connection oriented brother, TCP. The syntax of the UDP version of the extended access-list command is illustrated in Listing 3.14.

Listing 3.14   UDP extended **access-list** command syntax.

```
[no] access-list <number> {permit | deny} udp { source-ip-address
        source-wildcard-mask| any }
        [ operator source-port | source-port ]
        { destination-ip-address destination-wildcard-mask | any}
        [ operator destination-port | destination-port ]
```

Notice that no **established** keyword exists in Listing 3.16 since UDP is connectionless. The concept of connection orientation is TCP based. The words to replace port numbers are similar to those used in the TCP format. Here are some of them:

➤ bootpc

➤ bootps

➤ discard

➤ dns

➤ dnsix

➤ echo

➤ mobile-ip

➤ nameserver

➤ netbios-dgm

➤ netbios-ns

➤ ntp

➤ rip

➤ snmp

➤ snmptrap

➤ sunrpc

➤ syslog

➤ tacasds-ds

➤ talk

➤ tftp

➤ time

➤ whois

ICMP Extended Access-List Syntax

TCP and UDP are not the only protocol specific options available for filtering traffic. You can use access-lists to filter ICMP traffic. ICMP is an extremely powerful and useful protocol. Its versatility is also its downfall. It can be used by a hacker to search out possible exploits in your network. To avoid that, you can filter any of the ICMP protocol options. Listing 3.15 shows the Internets Control Message Protocol (ICMP) format prototype.

Listing 3.15   ICMP extended access-list command syntax.

```
[no] access-list <number> {permit | deny} icmp { source-ip-address
      source-wildcard-mask | any } { destination-ip-address
      destination-wildcard-mask | any} [ icmp-type [ icmp-code]
      | icmp-message ]
```

For ICMP, the protocol-specific options are message types that range from 0 through 255. Message codes, used to further subdivide message types, have the same range. Here are some protocol-specific keywords that you can use instead of the numeric message types and message codes for ICMP:

➤ administratively-prohibited

➤ alternate-address

➤ conversion-error

➤ dod-host-prohibited

➤ dod-net-prohibited

➤ echo

- ➤ echo-reply
- ➤ general-parameter-problem
- ➤ host-isolated
- ➤ host-tos-redirect
- ➤ host-tos-unreachable
- ➤ host-unknown
- ➤ host-unreachable
- ➤ information reply
- ➤ mask-reply
- ➤ mask-request
- ➤ mobile-redirect
- ➤ net-redirect
- ➤ net-tos-redirect
- ➤ net-tos-unreachable
- ➤ net-unreachable
- ➤ network-unknown
- ➤ no-room-for-option
- ➤ option-missing
- ➤ packet-too-big
- ➤ parameter-problem
- ➤ port-unreachable
- ➤ reassembly-timeout
- ➤ redirect
- ➤ router-advertisement
- ➤ router-solicitation
- ➤ time-exceeded
- ➤ traceroute
- ➤ ttl-exceeded
- ➤ unreachable

Placing Access-Lists

It's very important to effectively decide where you should place access-lists. When you are using the access-list as a traffic filter, you can attach it to an interface in the inbound or outbound direction. The amount of processing the router must do and which routers in the hierarchy do the processing may greatly affect the network's performance.

Remember that much access-list processing is done in the process routing path. On newer versions of the IOS and on larger routers, the traffic, after the first packet is routed and has survived the access-list, may take one of the fast switch paths. In other words, the first packet from a specific source to a specific destination is routed using a routing table lookup. The result of the routing decision is placed into a switching cache in the router. Subsequent packets from that source to that destination are switched based on the switching cache entry, not the routing table. The difference in placement determines whether the traffic is to be filtered before or after the routing table lookup. All packets must be examined with an inbound access-list that results in a significant processor load if the packets are not dropped. This is justifiable for lists placed primarily for security. Penetration-attempt traffic (if it can be identified) would be dropped without the overhead of a routing table lookup.

It is also important to determine how many interfaces would be involved on the router. If, for example, six outbound lists could be replaced by an inbound list, the result is probably better. By default, all access-lists are outbound unless otherwise specified. Figure 3.4 illustrates the difference between inbound and outbound processing within a single router for all access-lists (standard and extended for all protocols).

Standard IP access-lists use only source addresses and require fewer CPU cycles than extended access-lists. However, you must place standard IP access-lists as close to the destination as possible. Otherwise, traffic is blocked unnecessarily and perhaps incorrectly. Positioning the access-list within the router hierarchy is shown in Figure 3.5.

Position 4 would be the location for placing a basic access-list to block access from Device A to Device B. If you placed a standard access-list at other positions, Device A would be blocked from all positions beyond the access-list in the hierarchy.

Extended access-lists are much more flexible than standard access-lists, but they add to the CPU load. You should try to place the filter as close to the source as possible. This approach keeps the undesired traffic and the ICMP messages from traversing the network backbone. In addition, administrators can choose which routers will take the CPU hit associated with the access-list

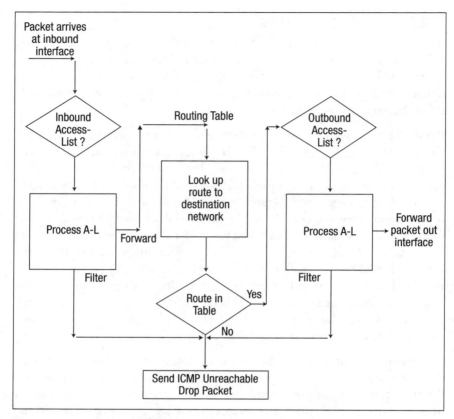

Figure 3.4 Inbound versus outbound access-list processing.

processing. They can put the access-lists into access routers or distribution routers. The tradeoff is between managing a large number of possibly identical lists in the access routers (where each router has plenty of processing power) and managing a single list (or at least fewer lists) in the distribution routers. In the latter case, the distribution routers would do more processing but it would be much easier to manage the access-lists.

Notice in Figure 3.5 that you could place extended access-lists at positions 1 or 2 based on the comments made previously about processing power and list management issues. You should not place access-lists of either type at location 3, in the core. To maximize efficiency, you should do the filtering before the traffic enters the backbone. Figure 3.5 and this discussion also show how important it is to have a hierarchical network design. If the network were fully meshed at the lower levels, you would have to place extended access-lists in several locations to prevent access from Device A to Device B when routing tables changed. Not only would this require more work for the administrator

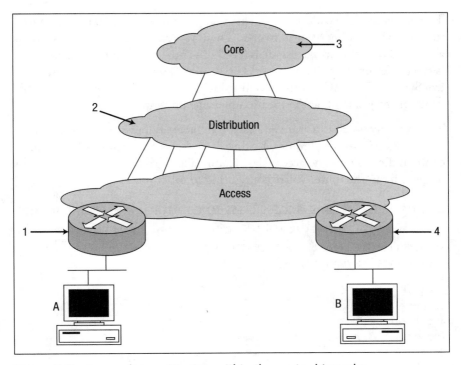

Figure 3.5   Access-list positioning within the router hierarchy.

and the router, but it would also add to the complexity and increase the probability of error.

Permitting Or Denying Telnet Access Using Access Classes

You can use standard IP access-lists to prevent Telnet connections to (inbound) or from (outbound) a Cisco router. You could configure inbound traffic filters to prevent Telnet access from any source to each router interface, but doing so is cumbersome. Another drawback is that access-lists won't block traffic that originates from within the router itself. That is, Telnet traffic passing through the router can be filtered with extended IP access-lists but you cannot block outbound Telnet traffic (originating from "this" router) with a traffic filter. You would much rather keep Telnet sessions from specified sources (to this router) from starting or restrict Telnet sessions originating in this router to specified destinations. The way to do it is by using an access class, an IOS feature that is specifically designed for controlling Telnet access into and out of a router. It's not so much for traffic control as it is to supplement security.

The procedure is to code an access-list that permits or denies traffic from particular devices, subnets, or networks. Then, you create an access class that is associated with the virtual terminals (vtys). Essentially, before any security check is run (for example, password checks or Terminal Access Control Access Control System, (TACACS), traffic coming into a vty is checked. Only if the traffic is permitted is a login authentication message presented.

The same access class feature allows you to block Telnet access to other locations from within "this" router. Listing 3.16 shows an example of just such a configuration. The same access class feature allows you to block Telnet access originating in the router you're configuring to other routers.

Listing 3.16   Using access class to control Telnet traffic to and from the router.

```
access-list 30 permit 172.16.5.0 0.0.0.255
access-list 31 deny any
!
line vty 0 4
access-class 30 in
access-class 31 out
login
password cisco
```

The access-list number 30, when applied inbound, allows only 172.16.5.X source addresses to Telnet into this router. The access-list number 31, when applied outbound, denies all outbound Telnet from this router.

 You must configure all vty (0 through 4 by default) lines identically in order for the access class security to work properly. Use the line vty 0 4 command to apply the configuration to all vty lines simultaneously.

An Alternative To Access-Lists

In any situation when you need to prevent all traffic from reaching a remote portion of the network, you can use a very efficient alternative to an access-list. You can statically route to a null interface all packets bound for a specific destination network. Essentially a bit bucket, the null interface simply is a logical software destination interface that drops the packet. An advantage is that routing to the null interface is a normal routing process, so you can use fast switching to dispose of unwanted traffic. The null interface works for protocols other than IP as well.

A sample configuration that an ISP can use to block private addresses from accidentally reaching the Internet is shown in Listing 3.17.

Listing 3.17   Using null interfaces.

```
ip route 172.16.0.0 255.240.0.0 null 0
ip route 10.0.0.0 255.0.0.0 null 0
ip route 192.168.0.0 255.255.0.0
```

The statements in Listing 3.17 are equivalent to those in Listing 3.18 but with much less overhead.

Listing 3.18   Access-list equivalent to null interface command.

```
access-list 101 deny ip any 172.16.0.0 0.15.255.255
access-list 101 deny ip any 10.0.0.0 0.255.255.255
access-list 101 deny ip any 192.168.0.0 0.0.255.255
```

No ICMP messages are returned when the null interface is used. An advantage is reduced traffic. The disadvantage is that no indication is given of the drop. For example, if someone in network management were doing connectivity tests with pings, the pings would simply disappear.

Helper Addresses

Routers will segment a broadcast domain. In other words, routers do not, by default, forward broadcast traffic. There are times when you might want to forward broadcasts selectively. Sometimes it is not so important to filter all broadcasts. Instead, it is desirable to provide a way for certain broadcasts to be passed through a router. If hosts don't know a destination, they attempt to use a local broadcast (255.255.255.255) to obtain a service such as DHCP (Dynamic Host Configuration Protocol), DNS (Domain Name Service), or TFTP. Routers block local broadcasts, which is usually considered to be good. However, placing servers on every LAN segment so that local broadcasts would reach them may be cumbersome.

IP helper addresses are a feature that allows traffic sent to local broadcast addresses to be re-addressed to a unicast (single destination) address. Once this is done, the packet may be routed just like any other.

It is not usually desirable to forward all broadcasts. When you use the IP helper-address on an interface command, only traffic from certain UDP ports (on that particular inbound interface) is forwarded by default. Table 3.5 shows a list of UDP ports.

If you need to forward other ports, include an IP forward-protocol UDP statement for that port. To forward only DNS (for example), you should enter a "no IP forward-protocol" (where represents the protocols you do not wish to forward) statement for each protocol to be blocked. The general format of the IP forward-protocol statement is shown in Listing 3.19.

Table 3.5   UDP ports forwarded by default when the IP helper address is used.

Port Number	Description
37	Time
49	TACACS
53	DNS
67	BootP client
68	BootP server (DHCP)
69	TFTP
137	NetBIOS name service
138	NetBIOS packet service

Listing 3.19   Syntax of the ip forward-protocol statement.

```
[no] ip forward-protocol { udp [port] | nd | sdns }
```

The **nd** keyword refers to an old Sun protocol for diskless workstations: network disk. The **sdns** keyword refers to Network Security Protocol.

Examples Of IP Helper Address Usage

When you want to use helper address functionality, you must consider three scenarios: single server at a remote location, multiple servers that share a remote subnet, and multiple servers on multiple remote subnets. Use Figure 3.6 along with the listing to view helper address functionality.

Listings 3.20, 3.21, and 3.22 show how to code the Denver router, shown in Figure 3.6.

Listing 3.20   Adding UDP port 5000 to those being forwarded.

```
!
ip forward-protocol udp 5000
```

Listing 3.21   Not forwarding NetBIOS name requests.

```
no ip forward-protocol udp 137
!
interface Ethernet 0
ip address …
```

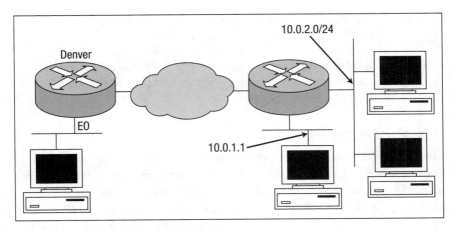

Figure 3.6 Helper address operation.

Listing 3.22 Pointing the broadcasts to a single remote server on a single LAN segment.

```
ip helper-address 10.0.1.1
```

If other servers are available on other segments, put an address in for them also. In this case, there are redundant servers on the same subnet, so use a directed broadcast, as shown in Listing 3.23.

Listing 3.23 Using IP helper address to forward to a directed broadcast address.

```
ip helper-address 10.0.2.255
```

Managing IPX Traffic

In general, the issues and techniques for Novell IPX traffic management are exactly the same as those for IP. IPX also supports both standard and extended access-lists. Protocols such as DHCP, DNS, TFTP, and Telnet don't exist in the Novell world. However, extra filter types are needed to support Novell's Service Advertising Protocol (SAP) and Get Nearest Server (GNS) traffic.

There are also helper addresses and null interface usage for Novell. These subjects are mentioned in ACRC but very little time is spent describing them. You can find examples on the Cisco CD or Web site but it is unlikely that Cisco will spend its limited number of test questions on their configuration.

Cisco's courses focus on configuration of the router to support other (non-IP) protocols. However, Cisco is not creator or the

> full source of information for learning about the other proto-
> col. The detail in the ACRC course and in this section is at a
> level necessary to support IPX protocol options. Test questions
> will focus on the material here. For full detail on protocol-
> specific values and issues, you need to consult the keeper of
> the IPX protocol, Novell.

IPX Protocol Review

The IPX address consists of a network and node number. The network is 32 bits and is written in hexadecimal. You can specify the 48-bit node number when the IPX protocol is enabled on the router using the **ipx routing <node address>** command. Otherwise, the node number is copied from the layer 2 burned in MAC address for the interface. Serial interfaces do not have MAC addresses, so the router uses the MAC address of the lowest numbered LAN interface that contains a MAC address as the node number on the serial inter-face. All serial interfaces will pull the same node address. Their address will be unique because you will assign unique network numbers to each interface. Multiple IPX network numbers may co-exist on the same physical wire. This is commonly done to support different layer 2 frame formats (encapsulations).

IPX-RIP is the default routing protocol and is on by default when IPX routing is enabled in the router. IPX-RIP is a traditional distance vector routing protocol. Its metric is ticks, with hop count used as a tiebreaker. The maximum network diameter is still 15 hops. IPX-RIP and SAP do support split horizon. That is, route information is not advertised back out of an interface from which it was learned. Novell calls split horizon the BIA—Best Information Algorithm.

Other routing protocols may replace IPX-RIP in the backbone. Cisco IOS supports both Novell's Link Services Protocol (NLSP, which is discussed in Chapter 11) and Cisco's Enhanced IGRP (EIGRP, which we cover in Chap-ter 8).

In addition to routing updates, Novell uses SAP information broadcast every 60 seconds by every server. The routers do not pass the SAP broadcasts. In-stead, the router acts as a server and caches the SAP information in the same way as any other Novell server. The router then re-broadcasts the SAP infor-mation every 60 seconds (the time period is adjustable). If the router is running EIGRP or NLSP, the routing updates are incremental (changes only, and only when needed). In any case, the router has access-lists for filtering SAP updates in or out and reducing the size of the update.

Novell clients locate services/servers by using the GNS request. A GNS re-quest is broadcast on the local LAN segment to all servers. The router may serve as a destination for GNS requests if no active Novell server is on the LAN segment and the router's responses to a client may be filtered to limit the range of answers to the client. You can also configure the router to send replies to the clients for a particular type of server in round-robin sequence. For example, load sharing to a group of print servers.

Novell uses keepalive messages (also known as watchdogs) for both IPX and Sequenced Packet Exchange (SPX) client sessions. These can waste time and resources by keeping dial connections active even when no other traffic is flowing. The IOS has features to spoof these keepalives. The connection is allowed to time out and disconnect, with the router spoofing the server (by responding on behalf of the client without the dialed connection being up) keeping the client-server connection active. When a user generates a packet going to the server, the dial connection is brought up again and the data flows as normal. Keepalive/watchdogs are not spoofed if the connection is active. Spoofing is covered in Chapter 13.

Standard And Extended IPX Access-Lists

Standard IPX access-lists have much in common with their IP cousins. They may be used as traffic filters or any of the access-list uses mentioned earlier (such as DDR). An example of the general format for the standard IPX access-list is shown in Listing 3.24.

Listing 3.24   Standard IPX access-list syntax.

```
[no] access-list <number> { permit | deny } [source-network
  .source-node  source-node-mask ] [destination-network

    .destination-node  destination-node-mask ]
```

And the command for attaching it to an interface is shown in Listing 3.25.

Listing 3.25   Attach the access-list to an interface.

```
interface ethernet 0
ipx access-group number [ in | out ]
```

If your access-list line specifies only the source or destination network without the node number and node mask, all servers sharing that LAN segment are selected. The extended IPX access-list shown in Listing 3.26 is more complex but is attached to an interface in the same way.

Listing 3.26   IPX extended access-list syntax.

```
[no] access-list <list-number> { permit | deny } protocol
        source-network [ .source-node ] [ source-node-mask ]]
        [ source-socket ] destination network
        [ .destination-node [ destination-node-mask ]]
        [ destination-socket ] [ log ]
```

Extended IPX list numbers range from 900 through 999 and describe the access-list type to the router. Table 3.6 shows the values that the protocol field may contain.

Table 3.7 shows the socket numbers.

Table 3.6 Novell protocol numbers.	
Port number	**Description**
-1	Any protocol in the 900-series access-list.
0	Any protocol that refers to the socket to determine the packet type.
1	RIP
2	Cisco-specific echo packet (ping)
3	Error packet
4	IPX
5	SPX
17	NCP
20	IPX NetBIOS

Table 3.7 Socket numbers.	
Number	**Description**
0	All sockets
451	NCP process
452	SAP process
453	RIP process
455	Novell NetBIOS process
456	Novell diagnostic process
457	Novell serialization socket
4000-7FFF	Dynamic sockets
8000-8FFF	Sockets assigned by Novell
85BE	IPX EIGRP
9001	NLSP
9004	IPXWAN/IPXWAN2
9086	IPX official echo (ping)

IPX Route Filters

Unnecessary routing of update traffic on your network can eat scarce resources. This unwanted traffic can be filtered using route filters. In addition to traffic filtering, IPX traffic filters may be used to keep the size of routing updates down as well as hide routes. An example is shown in Figure 3.7.

Listing 3.27 shows the code for the Denver router shown in Figure 3.7.

Listing 3.27   Creating the access-list.

```
access-list 801 permit 2000
!
interface Serial 0
ipx network 3000
ipx output-network-filter 801
```

The access-list will allow the route to network 2000 to be advertised to the Dallas router. This is the best location for the access-list because it will prevent

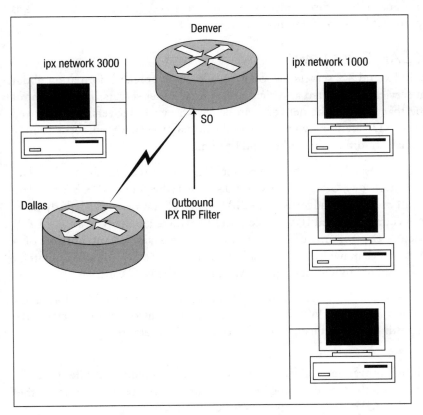

Figure 3.7   IPX RIP filters.

use of the limited bandwidth of the serial line to carry the update information when it would be dropped on the Dallas side.

Listing 3.28 shows the code for the Dallas router shown in Figure 3.7

Listing 3.28   Creating an access-list for the inbound side.

```
access-list 802 permit 2000
!
interface Serial 0
ipx network 3000
ipx input-network-filter 802
```

This inbound interface placement prevents networks other than 2000 from being included in Dallas' routing table. Unfortunately, the entire routing table would come across network 1000 before being dropped. This scenario could be used to provide security if your organization controls only the Dallas router.

Figure 3.7 and the associated coding illustrates that access-lists may be used to filter routes in both directions. The use of two access-lists on the same link is to show that it can be done, not that it should be.

IPX SAP Overview

Novell 3.x and 4.x servers use SAP broadcasts to spread information about what services are located at which servers to all other servers. The amount of traffic that flows in the network can be very heavy. Later versions of Novell that run NDS are improving the Novell world; however, we will focus on how SAPs have traditionally worked and been managed.

SAP broadcasts don't go through routers. The router receives the SAP update and builds its own SAP table. Every 60 seconds (the default IPX SAP update interval), the router advertises the SAP table. If the network is fairly large (over a couple hundred IPX devices) and flat (there are many hosts per LAN segment), the amount of SAP traffic can use a significant portion of a workstation's bandwidth. A workstation doesn't listen to SAP broadcasts; rather, they are filtered in workstation software, not by the NIC card.

Another issue is lower-bandwidth WAN links. Unnecessary SAP information that flows across the WAN link reduces the amount of relatively expensive bandwidth for actual business traffic. You can do several things to reduce the load:

➤ Filter unnecessary SAPs over the WAN links. If required, code static SAPs on the far side of the link. The router on the far end advertises the static SAP just as if the updates were running.

➤ Between two Cisco routers over a WAN link, increase the interval between SAP broadcasts.

➤ Move to an advanced protocol such as EIGRP or NLSP over the WAN or backbone links. Even with this improvement, filtering of unnecessary information is a good idea.

➤ Migrate to newer Novell software.

SAP filters (1000 through 1099) are coded as shown in Listing 3.29.

Listing 3.29   SAP filter access-list command syntax.

```
[no] access-list <list-number> {permit | deny } network
[ .node [ network ] [ network-mask [ .node-mask ]]
      [service-type [ server-name ] }
```

Table 3.8 shows some of the many SAP types.

Once the access-list is created, the next step is to assign the filter to the interface. Then, assign an input and/or output SAP filter, as shown in Listing 3.30.

Listing 3.30   Selecting the interface to which to apply the access-list.

```
interface Serial 0
ipx input-sap-filter <list-number>
ipx output-sap-filter <list-number>
```

Another possibility is the router-sap-filter, which defines the other routers from which this router accepts updates. Listing 3.31 shows the command syntax for the **ipx router-sap-filter** command.

Listing 3.31   ipx router-sap-filter command.

```
ipx router-sap-filter <list-number>
```

Table 3.8 SAP types.	
Type	**Description**
4	File Services
7	Print Services
47	Advertising Print Server
3	Print Server Queue
2E	TCP/IP Service
178	NetWare 4 NDS Server

SAP filters may be used both inbound and outbound on the same router interface. Figure 3.8 illustrates that inbound filters limit the amount of memory that the router requires to hold the table and the amount of work necessary to create the outbound update. You can use an outbound list on the router to further restrict the size of the outbound update. Doing so is especially important for lower-speed links and for segments with clients only (clients don't listen to broadcast SAPs).

If you have a WAN link through a satellite or some other high-cost facility, it may be useful to filter all of the outbound SAPs, replacing some of the missing SAPs with statically coded ones in the far-end routers. The static entries would then be advertised normally from the routers as if they had been learned dynamically. Take, for example, a company with offices in both the United States and Europe that is paying dearly for a T1 satellite link. If at one or both ends the clients need access to only a handful of servers, administrators can maintain reachability information without wasting the bandwidth and processing by coding static SAP entries. The artificial SAPs are then advertised by the remote router as if the SAPs had been received in the normal way. Listing 3.32 shows a sample configuration.

Listing 3.32 Coding the global static SAP information.

```
ipx sap 4 NYFILS 1a0.0000.0000.0001 451 1
ipx sap 4 DENFILS 1f0b.0000.0000.0001 451 2
```

This approach is not a good one if you have large number of SAPs to code or the number of servers is rapidly changing. A better choice would be a combination of SAP filters and advanced routing protocols such as NLSP (covered in Chapter 17) or EIGRP (discussed in Chapter 8) to hold the update traffic to a minimum.

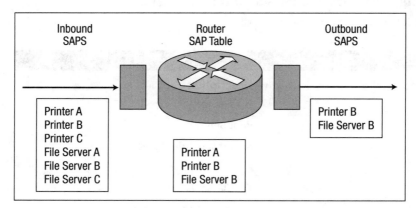

Figure 3.8 Inbound and outbound SAP processing.

In Figure 3.9, you can see that Router B is forwarding only a subset of the SAPs regarding networks 20A and 20B across the WAN link. This could be to prevent the remote site from knowing about the servers from networks 20A and 20B, but it is more likely used to hold down the amount of SAP traffic.

Listings 3.33, 3.34, 3.35, and 3.36 show a SAP filter example.

Listing 3.33 Blocking file services from all servers on network 20A.

```
access-list 1000 deny 20A 4
```

Listing 3.34 Blocking all print services from all networks.

```
access-list 1000 deny -1 7
```

Listing 3.35 Permitting all other services from all networks.

```
access-list 1000 permit -1
```

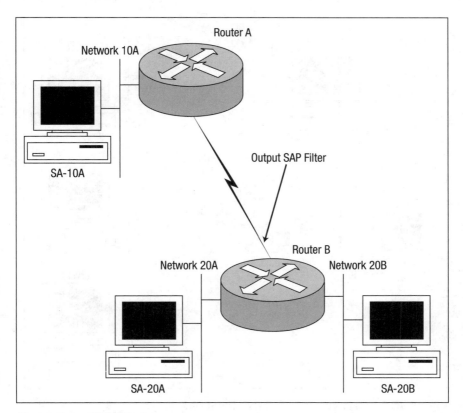

Figure 3.9 SAP filtering.

Listing 3.36 Associating the SAP filter with the outbound interface.

```
interface Serial 0
ipx-output-sap filter 1000
```

IPX GNS Overview

Cisco routers can perform other server functions. For example, if no functional Novell servers are on a segment, the router can respond to GNS requests. As it does so, it can restrict which clients receive information about certain servers by using GNS filters. Finally, the router can load balance the requests for particular servers. Figure 3.10 illustrates the GNS operation and its use with SAP filters.

Listing 3.37 shows the application of a SAP filter to an interface.

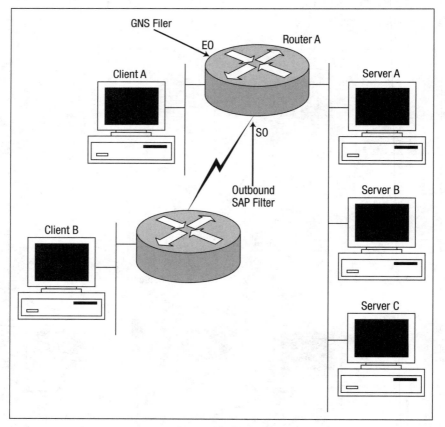

Figure 3.10 GNS versus SAP filter operation.

Listing 3.37 Application of a SAP filter to an interface.

```
access-list 1001...
!
interface Ethernet 0
ipx output-gns-filter 1001
```

In Listing 3.37, use a regular SAP filter on Serial 0 of Router A rather than a GNS filter for Client B's access. Doing so saves the bandwidth on the WAN link as well as limits Client B to a specific server or servers.

The router waits a default time of zero milliseconds before providing an answer to the GNS request. You can adjust the delay time by using the command **ipx gns-response delay xx**, where **xx** is the desired length of the delay. However the router does not provide the GNS function on segments where there is an active Novell server. How does the router know there is no active server? Simple: no SAP broadcasts.

The router may use the command **ipx gns-round-robin** as a means of sharing the load between servers. Otherwise the router responds with the server of the desired type with the lowest routing metric (closest to the router). If several servers with the same metric are not using round robin, the server whose information was received most recently is given to the client. Round robin may be great for distributing the load on print servers, but it may also include a very remote printer. An example might be an unfiltered SAP regarding a printer in London showing up in router's SAP table in Rapid City. Round robin would give the London printer its share of traffic. In current versions of the IOS, round robin is off by default.

Tunnels

As IP networks evolve, islands of legacy protocols (IPX, AppleTalk, DECnet, and so on) are left at the edges of the network. In some cases, you can migrate those protocols to IP. In others, you can use a method that allows the users to continue using the environments they wish while keeping the core of the network running only IP. The term is *tunneling*, and you accomplish it by causing the source protocol's packets to be wrapped in an IP coating.

Tunneling offers many advantages, including:

➤ An IP-only core means simpler configuration, less training required for core personnel, fewer routing updates in the core, and smaller routing tables in the core.

➤ The hop count between islands of tunneled protocols is reduced to one.

➤ You have less conversion to worry about.

➤ Client departments can continue to run protocol suites with which they are familiar.

Figure 3.11 illustrates the value of tunneling. The tunnel allows the discontiguous islands of whatever protocol to appear to be a much smaller network. A smaller number of routers and circuits will make the island protocol more manageable.

Figure 3.12 shows an example tunneling configuration.

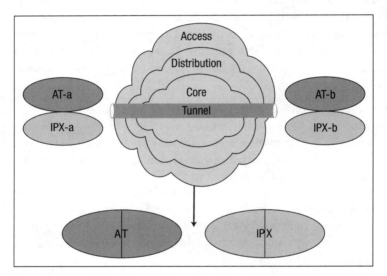

Figure 3.11 The value of tunneling.

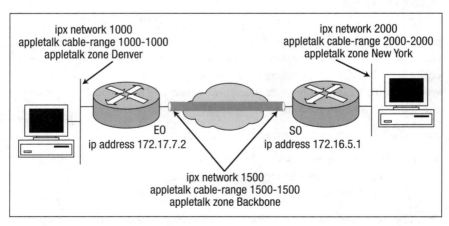

Figure 3.12 Tunneling.

Listings 3.38 and 3.39 show the code for configuring the tunnel shown in Figure 3.12.

Listing 3.38   The code for the router on the left side of
Figure 3.12.

```
interface Ethernet 1
ipx network 1000
appletalk cable-range 1000-1000
appletalk zone Denver
!
interface Ethernet 0
ip address 172.17.7.2 255.255.255.0
!
interface Tunnel 0
ipx network 1500
appletalk cable-range 1500-1500
appletalk zone Backbone
tunnel source E0
tunnel destination 172.16.5.1
tunnel mode gre ip
```

Listing 3.39   The code for the router on the right side of
Figure 3.12.

```
interface Ethernet 0
ipx network 2000
appletalk cable-range 2000-2000
appletalk zone New York
!
interface Serial 0
ip address 172.16.5.1 255.255.255.0
!
interface Tunnel 0
ipx network 1500
appletalk cable-range 1500-1500
appletalk zone Backbone
tunnel source S0
tunnel destination 172.17.7.2
tunnel mode gre ip
```

The *tunnel source* is the IP address of any active interface on this router. It is easier to use an interface name and number on this end (for example, loopback 0, serial 0). The other end of the tunnel (for example, tunnel destination) is any IP address on an active interface on the remote router. One option we have not illustrated is the *tunnel encapsulation mode*. The default is Generic Routing Encapsulation in IP (**tunnel mode gre ip**) and is the one normally used. Cisco also supports AppleTalk tunneling protocols such as AURP and Cayman, which you can use to connect with other AppleTalk routers. See the Cisco Web site (www.cisco.com) for other tunneling modes.

 Remember to filter unnecessary traffic before it goes into the tunnel. Routers along the path see only IP, and all traffic types being tunneled go to the same IP address.

 You must specify the tunnel source, destination and mode. You will then apply tunneled protocol attributes to the tunnel interface (for example, IPX network number, AppleTalk cable range, and so on). Do not put an IP address on the tunnel interface.

Useful Commands

To see the results of your work, the following commands will be most useful:

➤ **show ip route** Shows the content of the forwarding database including the next hop, metric, routing source (such as RIP, OSPF, EIGRP, IGRP).

➤ **show access-lists** Displays the access-lists that are active and the number of times each line in the list has been used.

➤ **show [ip | ipx | •••] interfaces type port** Displays the protocol specific values such as whether an access-list is associated with a particular interface, what number it is and whether it functions on the inbound or outbound path.

➤ **debug access-list** Displays hits to a line in the access-list as they occur.

 Be sure to be familiar with access-lists, SAP filters, and tunneling. The ACRC examination will probably have several questions on them.

Practice Questions

Question 1

> The following access-list has been inserted in a router and correctly tied to an interface, but it isn't working. Why?
>
> ```
> access-list 1 deny 172.16.5.0 0.0.0.255
> access-list 1 permit 172.16.5.1 0.0.0.0
> access-list 1 permit any
> ```
>
> ○ a. It works as coded.
>
> ○ b. The line that permits host 172.16.5.1 is in the wrong sequence.
>
> ○ c. The second line should have been configured as … **host 172.16.5.1**.
>
> ○ d. The **deny** statement's position blocks all traffic.

Answer b is correct. The second line should have been first. Always go from the most specific to the most general. Answer a is incorrect because the access-list does not work; either line two should not be in the list, or it must come first. Although you may use the configuration in answer c, its lack of use is not why the access-list failed. Answer d is incorrect because the **deny** blocks only one subnet. The **permit any** in line three allows all traffic that does not originate from the 172.16.5.0 subnet.

Question 2

> The following access-list has been inserted in a router and correctly tied to an interface, but it isn't working. Why?
>
> ```
> access-list 1 deny host 172.16.5.1
> access-list 1 permit 255.255.255.255 0.0.0.0
> ```
>
> ○ a. It works as coded.
>
> ○ b. It works because of the **permit any** used as the last line of the list.
>
> ○ c. It doesn't work because the **permit any** has been coded as a permit local broadcast.
>
> ○ d. It doesn't work because the first line requires a wildcard mask.

Answer c is correct. Line two should have been **0.0.0.0 255.255.255.255** or **any**. Answer a is incorrect because the list essentially denies all traffic. Answer b is incorrect because line two is not a **permit any**. Answer d is incorrect for two reasons. First, by using the "host" keyword before the IP address the result is the same as coding the wildcard mask "0.0.0.0". Second, the default wildcard mask is 0.0.0.0.

Question 3

The following access-list has been inserted in a router and correctly tied to an interface, but it isn't working. Why?

```
access-list 1 permit host 172.16.5.1
access-list 1 deny 172.16.5.0
access-list 1 permit any
access-list 1 deny 0.0.0.0 255.255.255.255
```

○ a. It works as coded.

○ b. It doesn't work. The line that denies the 172.16.5.0 subnet doesn't work because the default wildcard mask is 0.0.0.0, and no packet would contain a source address with a zero for the host number.

○ c. The **deny any** statement must come before the **permit any**.

○ d. The **deny** statement's position blocks all traffic.

Answer b is correct, for the reason given in the answer. Answer a is incorrect because the list does not block the 172.16.5.0 subnet. Answer c is incorrect because you should not code a **permit any** and a **deny any** in the same access-list. Whichever statement comes first ends the access-list as far as traffic is concerned. Answer d is incorrect because the deny any follows the **permit any** and is never reached when the code is executed.

Question 4

The following access-list has been inserted in a router and correctly tied to an interface, but it isn't working. Why?

```
access-list 1 deny 172.16.6.1 255.255.255.255
access-list 1 deny host 172.30.18.4
access-list 1 permit any
```

○ a. It works as coded.

○ b. It doesn't work. Line two should have been coded as **172.30.18.4 0.0.0.0**.

○ c. It doesn't work. Line one is essentially a **permit any**.

○ d. It doesn't work. Line one is essentially a **deny any**.

Answer d is correct. The mask shown causes all bits in the source address to be considered don't care bits. A **show access-lists** command on the router would show the statement as **access-list 1 deny any**. Answer a is incorrect because it is essentially a deny any. Answer b is incorrect because line two is correctly coded but would never have been executed because all traffic source addresses will match the deny any in line one. Answer c is backward line one is a deny any not a permit any. The coding causes line 1 to be a **deny any**, which renders every other line in the access-list ineffective.

Question 5

Access-lists can have significant overhead processing. Is there a way to reduce it? [Choose the three best answers]

❑ a. Use a static route to a loopback interface.

❑ b. Use standard rather than extended access-lists.

❑ c. Use a static route to the null interface.

❑ d. Place the access-list on the outbound side of the router if possible.

Answers b, c, and d are correct. Answer b is correct because standard access-lists use only the source address and result in less processing. Answer c is correct because the null interface is a bit bucket that is designed to allow traffic to be fast switched into oblivion. Answer d is correct because inbound access-lists process every packet before it is routed. It's probably a good idea for you to use an input (rather than an output) traffic filter if the primary reason for the list is security. However, doing so results in unnecessary processing for packets that would not have been filtered. Answer a is incorrect because the loopback interface is a place to keep addresses that must always be up. You cannot shut down the loopback interface.

Question 6

You don't want some people to be able to use the virtual terminal (Telnet) interface to your router. How might you prevent them from doing so? [Choose the two best answers]

- ☐ a. Apply inbound standard IP access-lists on every interface for every interface on the router.

- ☐ b. Apply inbound extended access-lists on every interface for every interface in my router that blocks inbound Telnet.

- ☐ c. Apply IP access-lists that block access except from desired hosts, subnets, or networks and applied as an inbound access class to all vtys.

- ☐ d. Leave the vtys configured as the IOS is delivered by Cisco.

Answers c and d are correct. Answer c is the best because it allows the administrator to be selective. Unless my address is on from our network management subnet, I won't even be presented with a login prompt. Answer d works well if no one is to be allowed Telnet access to the router because Cisco's default is to place a login process on the vty with no password. Essentially when Telnet is attempted, the source receives a message like **password required but none set….** Answer a is incorrect for several reasons. First, it causes the administrator too much work and too much overhead on the router. Second, all access to the router (such as TFTP, SNMP, and ICMP) would be blocked. Answer b is incorrect for the same reasons as answer a. However, answer b would be a better choice than answer a because TFTP and the other protocols could reach the router.

Question 7

We have too many SAPs floating around in our system. The WAN links are flooded, and our international links are too expensive to upgrade. Also, we need to add memory to some of our routers. What is a good solution?

○ a. Convert Novell from IPX to IP.

○ b. Use SAP filters on each end with static SAPs to maintain connectivity.

○ c. Block IPX RIP updates from one side and use static SAPs on the other.

○ d. Use an advanced routing protocol such as EIGRP or NLSP to send only changes to the SAP table.

Answer b is correct. Using SAP filters on each end with static SAPs results in a reduced size for the SAP tables, which in turn saves memory, processing power, and bandwidth. Answer a is a little bit of a trick. Using IP implies you're using Novell 4.x and probably NDS, which may help the problem. But the problem is the number of SAPs, not the layer 3 protocol. Answer c is incorrect because blocking IPX RIP updates fbom one side and using static SAPs on the other makes servers on the blocked networks invisible to the clients on the far end and the static SAPs do not provide a solution. The far-end server does not provide SAP information about a server on this end for which the far-end server does not have a route. Answer d is incorrect but only partly so. The problem with answer d is that no memory is saved. EIGRP and NLSP go a long way to relieving the overhead on the WAN links but do not reduce the size of the SAP tables.

Question 8

We have DECnet in our system and it won't go away. You're trying to optimize the backbone and hold down training costs for our technicians by using only IP in the backbone. What can you do?

○ a. Set up fully meshed GRE IP tunnels between the disparate groups of DEC users.

○ b. Hire new technicians directly out of college and train them in DECnet. Don't use high-end 12000 GSR routers; they're too expensive anyway.

○ c. Tunneling won't work with DECnet. Use the solution in b above.

○ d. Build a separate DEC-only network. That way, we can have an optimized solution for both groups of users.

Answer a is correct because it is the best solution. Answer b is incorrect because training new folks would be a waste of time. Answer c is incorrect because tunneling does work with DECnet. Answer d is incorrect because building a separate DEC-only network isn't necessary.

Need To Know More?

 Chappell, Laura A. and Dan E. Hakes: *The Complete Guide to NetWare LAN Analysis*, Sybex Inc. Alameda, CA, 1996. ISBN 0-78211-903-4. Part 3 discusses the NetWare protocols in depth.

 Doyle, Jeff. *CCIE Professional Development: Routing TCP/IP Volume 1*, Macmillan Technical Publishing, Indianapolis, IN, 1998. ISBN 1-57870-041-8. Appendix B has a tutorial on access-lists.

 For information on access-lists and the other topics in this section, check out the Cisco site at **www.cisco.com**.

Queuing

Terms you'll need to understand:

√ Priority queuing

√ Custom queuing

√ Weighted fair-queuing (WFQ)

√ Round-robin

√ Congestion

Techniques you'll need to master:

√ Understanding when to use queuing

√ Understanding which type of queuing is appropriate

√ Determining traffic selections for each queue

√ Setting default queues

√ Assigning a queue to an interface

This chapter introduces the concept of queuing and discusses the type of queuing appropriate for different network conditions. Managing queuing is an important part of providing network responsiveness, a goal of scalable networking. In terms of the number of topics in the Cisco Internetwork Operating System (IOS), queuing is fairly small but very important.

Buffering And Queuing

In environments where all traffic flows nicely and gets to its intended destination consistently, queuing is not needed. When the amount of traffic exceeds the data carrying capacity of the link, you will need queuing. Congestion, and thus buffering or queuing, occurs when traffic arrives on the outbound interface faster than it can be forwarded. Consider a situation involving a router with four Ethernet interfaces. If traffic flows from three of them toward the fourth, there isn't enough bandwidth to handle the packets immediately. The packets are stored in memory until they are forwarded, or until too many packets arrive at once and some are dropped.

> *Note:* *You'll often hear the terms buffering and queuing—both keep traffic in memory until it can be processed. In this chapter, we use the term queuing to specify treatment—giving priority to certain packets at the expense of others. Too many packets arriving too quickly, exceeding the number of queue entries or the number of buffers means excess traffic will be dropped.*

Normally, packets are dispatched or forwarded in a first-in-first-out (FIFO) order. In this chapter, we discuss the sequence of dispatching in orders other than FIFO. On high-speed interfaces such as the Ethernet interfaces, the CPU load necessary to resequence, the dispatch order or queue, would be too high to be of value. For example, if 40 maximum-length Ethernet packets were in a queue, the router would take a small fraction of a second to transmit them all (40 packets multiplied by 1,500 bytes multiplied by 8 bits equals 480,000 bits, or only 5 percent of the interface's speed). Using CPU cycles to re-order the packets would not make any real difference to the applications. On a 100Mbps Ethernet the processor time would actually add to the transit time packet. Now, consider the same amount of traffic on a 56K WAN link if the record number 40 is in fact a Telnet keystroke. The delay is around nine seconds, far too long for an interactive session. In this last case, using CPU cycles to send the interactive traffic ahead of any other type would be justified.

Queuing is normally restricted to interfaces slower than 2Mbps that are subject to bursty traffic conditions because the resulting processor load would likely provide more delay than simply forwarding the data.

Queuing is not your only option when you want reduce the packet transit time. You can do so in a number of ways, essentially by reducing the volume of traffic. Chapter 3 discusses reducing traffic with access lists. Adjusting the routing table to make it smaller may help (see Chapter 9). If the traffic volume is consistently too high, the only solution is to purchase more bandwidth. When the problem is bursts of traffic of short duration, queuing may be the best viable solution.

Queuing Scenarios

There are four queuing scenarios in the router. First is *no queuing*. High-speed links (faster than 2Mb per second) allow FIFO to handle the situation. Much of the problem with FIFO is that small packets get the same number of chances to be transmitted as large ones. Unfortunately, this means that the low-volume session sends a Telnet keystroke, whereas the FTP session sends a much larger volume in its packet. Delays and widely varying response times for the interactive traffic may result.

The second queuing scenario is *priority queuing*. Some types of traffic—for example, IBM's System Network Architecture (SNA) and DEC's Local Area Transport (LAT)—require networks with low round-trip (such as a higher speed). If you allow such traffic to wait at the bottom of a queue, its sessions are lost. To avoid losing sessions, administrators can use priority queuing to dedicate the circuit's entire bandwidth to this type of traffic as necessary. These packets receive priority. Such traffic is said to pre-empt bandwidth from other protocols. In this way, administrators can minimize the time delay enough to keep these time-constrained protocols from dropping sessions.

The third queuing scenario that provides some guarantees of bandwidth to users is *custom queuing*. Perhaps a particular department has paid for 50 percent of a new facility, so that department demands 50 percent of the bandwidth. Custom queuing allows administrators to allocate bandwidth.

Finally, to avoid the delays and varying response times inherent with FIFO, administrators can enhance the circuit's performance with *weighted fair-queuing* (WFQ). *WFQ* provides all available bandwidth to low-volume, interactive traffic, which then allows batch transfers to share whatever bandwidth remains. With WFQ, the interactive traffic gets a fairer share of the circuit.

Your task is determining when queuing is the proper solution and what type of queuing is appropriate.

Figure 4.1 shows a flowchart that will help you determine the appropriate queuing mechanism.

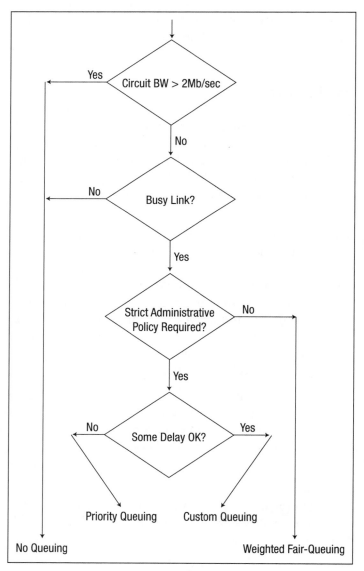

Figure 4.1 Selecting the appropriate queuing strategy.

Of course, none of the priority, custom, or weighted fair queuing strategies is necessary if you have zero congestion in your traffic flow. Regardless of the method chosen, the packets in a single conversation always flow in sequence relative to that conversation.

Now that you have a general idea about the kinds of queuing, let's discuss each in more detail.

FIFO Queuing

FIFO is not really queuing—it is more along the lines of buffering. Packets are routed to the interface and stored in router memory until it is their turn to be transmitted. The transmit order is based on the arrival order of the first bit of the packet. Essentially, the packet's outbound interface buffer is selected as soon as the packet's outbound interface is selected. This is the best approach on high-speed circuits.

 The importance of the transmit sequence being dependent on the arrival sequence is that large-volume sources transmit lots of data quickly if queuing is used somewhere along the path. Large packets tend to be transmitted together, which creates a "clumping" of the larger packets, referred to as packet trains. As a result, low-volume, interactive traffic may be squeezed out of the flow, thus getting less than its reasonable share of the bandwidth. For example, an FTP transfer is running wide open. Several large packets (large relative to the size of a Telnet packet) arrive and fill a FIFO queue. There is a large gap between the transmission times of a Telnet packet at the top of the queue and one at the bottom. To the Telnet user, there are big delays and uneven response times. Effectively, the solution is to cause the packets to be sent based on the arrival time of the last bit. This favors smaller packets, which are exactly what you will see with Telnet or voice traffic. A technique referred to as WFQ.

Priority Queuing

Priority queuing provides the network administrator with a way to reduce network delay for high-priority traffic as well as to select traffic for discard in times of serious network stress. Priority queuing has been used for years in many vendors' equipment. If you have used queuing in an IBM or DEC system, chances are it is priority queuing. Priority queuing has been in the Cisco IOS since 10.0.

The Cisco router provides four queues: high, medium, normal, and low. Within each queue, the order of process is FIFO. Simply put, all high-priority traffic is given 100 percent of the bandwidth on an interface until it there is no more high-priority traffic. Then, all medium-priority, traffic followed by normal-priority traffic, then low-priority traffic are treated the same. If new, higher-priority traffic arrives during medium, normal, or low interface, processing of the lower-priority traffic is pre-empted; the higher-priority traffic uses all bandwidth until there is no more higher-priority traffic. The result is that high-priority traffic suffers the shortest delay.

The lowest-priority traffic sits in queues in memory until it gains access to bandwidth (when no higher-priority traffic is queued on the interface). Then, it is transmitted. If too much high-priority traffic is present, the queue overflows. Once an overflow occurs, all new packets for that queue are dropped until normal queue processing space becomes available for the low-priority traffic. Each queue has a fixed length, which users can select. The defaults are as follows:

➤ **High** 20 records

➤ **Medium** 40 records

➤ **Normal** 60 records

➤ **Low** 80 records

Lower queues are larger than all the others because they are not given bandwidth until all higher-priority records have been forwarded. Thus, the lower-priority queues should always be larger than the higher-priority ones. A queue length of 0 implies that the queue may grow without limit. Once the maximum length is reached, additional records are dropped immediately as soon as they are routed to the outbound interface. Notice that increasing the size of the queue (if there is simply too much traffic) may cause congestion in the router's buffers, resulting in other problems. If a packet is dropped, a "Network unreachable" message is transmitted to the original source.

> *Note:*   *If the router's queue processing routine discovers that a record has reached its maximum age, "time-to-live (TTL) reaches zero", the record is dropped rather than transmitted and a "Network-unreachable" message is returned.*

Configuring Priority Queuing

Use the following steps to configure priority queuing:

1. Create a priority list that allocates traffic to a queue by traffic type (high, medium, normal, or low)—see the **priority-list** command used in

Listing 4.1. The logic used to assign the traffic to the proper queue, as shown in Figure 4.2, is common to both priority and custom queuing.

Once the traffic has been assigned to a queue, actual traffic dispatching begins, as shown in Figure 4.3.

2. Next, associate the priority list to the desired interface with the **priority-group** command.

3. Finally, adjust the lengths of the individual queues (only if necessary).

It is important to remember that priority queuing works best on slower interfaces that are under T1 (1.5Mbps) and E1 (2.1Mbps) speeds.

Command Syntax

The command syntax and parameter definitions for allocating traffic to an individual queue are shown in Listing 4.1.

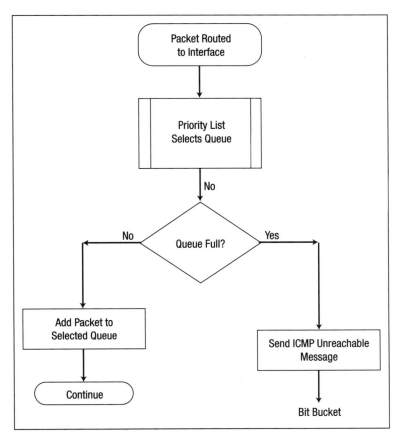

Figure 4.2 Allocating traffic to a queue.

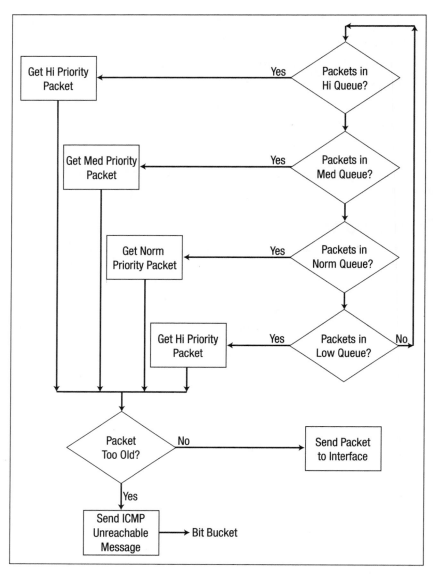

Figure 4.3 Priority queue traffic dispatch.

Listing 4.1 Allocating traffic to an individual queue.

```
priority-list <list-number> { protocol protocol-name | interface
interface-type interface-number}
{ high | medium | normal | low } <queue-keyword> <keyword-value>
```

The parameters of the priority-list command are defined as follows:

➤ **list-number** User-selected number between 1 and 16

➤ **protocol-name** Protocol field from IP header keywords are: **aarp, arp, apollo, appletalk, bridge** (transparent), **clns, clns_es, compressedtcp, cmns, decnet, decnet_node, decnet_router-11, decnet_router-12, ip, ipx, pad, rsrb, stun, vines, xns,** and **x25**

This is not a complete list of keywords and definitions. Refer to the Cisco Documentation CD or the Cisco Web site.

➤ **interface-type interface-number** Router interface, such as Serial 0

➤ **high | medium | normal | low** Priority queue level

➤ **<queue-keyword> <keyword-value>** Possible queue-keywords are **fragments** (fragments), **gt** (greater than), **lt** (less than), **list** (access-list), **tcp** (TCP), and **udp** (UDP)

A packet is compared with the conditions in the statement. If the packet matches, the packet being tested will be assigned to the queue specified. If the queue-keyword is specified in the priority-list command the keyword-values depend on the queue-keyword as follows:

➤ **fragments** The packet is a fragment of an IP datagram.

➤ **gt** *<number>* The condition will be true if the length of the packet, including layer 2 encapsulation, is larger than *number*.

➤ **lt** *<number>* This condition will be true if the length of the packet, including layer 2 encapsulation, is smaller than *number*.

➤ **list** *<number>* The condition test is an IP or IPX access list and *number* tells which one.

➤ **tcp** *<number>* The test compares the TCP port number of the packet with *number* and assigns the packet to the queue specified when they match.

➤ **udp** *<number>* The test compares the UDP port number of the packet with *number* and assigns the packet to the queue specified when they match.

These conditions are used in the same way with both priority and custom queuing.

The command in Listing 4.2 sets the default queue for packets that don't match any other rule in the priority list. The **no** form returns the default to normal.

Listing 4.2 Setting the default queue for non-matching packets.

```
[no] priority-list <list-number> default
        { high | medium | normal | low }
```

The command in Listing 4.3 sets the maximum length in buffers for each queue. A value of 0 for any of the four queues means that the queue may be of unlimited size.

Listing 4.3 Setting the maximum number of buffers for each queue.

```
[no] priority-list <list-number> queue-limit <high-limit>
        <medium-limit> <normal-limit> <low-limit>
```

The **priority-group** command associates the priority list with an interface, as shown in Listing 4.4. The **no** form removes the association.

Listing 4.4 Associating the priority list with an interface.

```
Interface Serial 0
[no] priority-group <list-number>
```

The overall configuration of priority-queuing is not extremely difficult, but it can cause problems if implemented incorrectly. Figure 4.5 shows a sample configuration of priority queuing.

Listing 4.5 Priority-list configuration example.

```
priority-list 3 ip high list 99
priority-list 3 protocol ip high udp 49
priority-list 3 interface fddi 0 medium
priority-list 3 protocol ipx normal
priority-list 3 default low
priority-list 3 queue-limit 20 40 60 80

interface serial 1
priority-group  3
```

The sequence of the priority-list lines shows use of a standard IP access list to assign traffic to the high-priority queue. Line 2 of Listing 4.5 shows assignment of traffic destined for UDP port 49 to the high-priority queue. Line 3 shows that all traffic arriving on FDDI interface 0 will be assigned to the medium priority queue. Line 4 shows assignment of all IPX traffic to the normal queue. Line 5 shows all traffic not already assigned to a queue will be dumped in the low-priority queue. The last line shows the number of buffers in the queue being modified.

Custom Queuing

If your goal is to allocate bandwidth (but possibly with delays), your choice is custom queuing. This technique allows you to provide percentage of bandwidth guarantees. The difference between this approach and priority queuing is that the queues are processed in round-robin sequence. Round-robin refers to the fact that no queue pre-empts processing for another. Each queue is given equal opportunity and is processed in order. This is different from priority queuing because priority queuing always processes the high-priority queue first. Therefore, it is possible that high-priority traffic (which doesn't really exist with custom queuing) would not be serviced quickly enough. That is, bandwidth is allocated, but not immediately. The custom queuing command first appeared in IOS 10.0. Now let's see how it works.

Custom queuing employs 17 queues. Queue 0, the system queue, is used by the system. Queue 0 has a higher priority than the remaining queues and may not be accessed by the administrator. The administrator can configure the other queues, 1 through 16, which are served on a round-robin basis.

Just as with priority queuing, a global list is created to assign the traffic to the appropriate queue. Queues not specified when the traffic is sorted are not used. The processing for each queue is shown in Figure 4.4.

The command syntax used to assign traffic to a particular queue is shown in Listing 4.6.

Listing 4.6   Assigning traffic to a particular queue.

```
queue-list <list-number> protocol <protocol-name>
          <queue-number> <queue-keyword> <keyword-value>
```

As stated above in the priority queuing section above, the **no** version in Listing 4.7 is used to remove a previously implemented assignment.

Listing 4.7 Assign all traffic from a protocol to a queue.

```
[no] queue-list <list-number> protocol <protocol-name> <queue-
number>
```

The parameter descriptions for the **queue-list** command are as follows:

➤ **list-number** Number of the queue list. An integer between 1 and 16.

➤ **protocol-name** Required keyword that specifies the protocol type: **aarp, arp, apollo, appletalk, bridge** (transparent), **clns, clns_es, clns_is, compressedtcp, cmns, decnet, decnet_node, decnet_router11, decnet_router12, dlsw, ip, ipx, pad, rsrb, stun, vines, xns,** and **x25.**

➤ **queue-number** Number of the queue. An integer between 1 and 16.

➤ **queue-keyword** Possible queue-keywords are **gt, lt, list, tcp,** and **udp.**

➤ **keyword-value** Possible keyword-values the same as those listed for priority queuing above.

After you assign the traffic to a queue, you assign a threshold value to each queue to determine the how the bandwidth is shared under load. The *byte-count-number* sets the lower bound on the number of bytes that are transferred each time this queue is given access. The default is 1,500 and allows at least 1 record. If the selected queue has fewer bytes than the limit number of bytes in all records in the queue, the pointer advances to the next queue. If this queue is the only one with any records in it, this queue will repeatedly be allowed another turn (to forward traffic) and will use all of the available bandwidth until records show up in other configured queues.

When traffic is being forwarded in all queues, the queues will share bandwidth based on the percentage of the total bandwidth represented by their *threshold* value. If only two queues are active (contain traffic to be sent) and if they have equal thresholds, each queue will get approximately 50 percent of the circuit's bandwidth. Under load (all queues forwarding data), the queues will share proportionately based on bandwidth.

The flowchart in Figure 4.4 shows the processing logic. When the queue processing routine enters a queue, the current transmission count of octets transmitted is set to 0. If there are records in the queue and the limit of octets to be transmitted has not been exceeded, a record from the top of the queue is transmitted and the length of the record is added to the transmit count. The process is then repeated. If no records remain in the transmit queue or the transmit count has been exceeded, the process moves to the next queue and is repeated.

To adjust the number of buffers (length of a queue) for a particular queue follow the example shown in Listing 4.8.

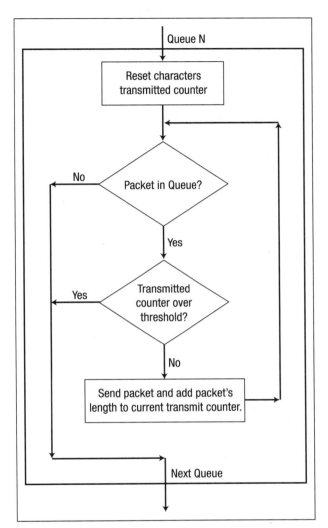

Figure 4.4 Custom queuing—per-queue processing.

Listing 4.8   Setting the length of the queue.

```
[no] queue-list <list-number> queue <queue-number>
     byte-count <byte-count-number>
```

The default length of each queue is 20 records; you can modify the default using the command as shown in Listing 4.9.

Listing 4.9   Setting the **queue-list** threshold.

```
[no] queue-list <list-number> queue <queue-number>
     limit <limit-number>
```

The parameter descriptions for the **queue-list** command are as follows:

➤ **list-number** Number of the queue list. An integer between 1 and 16.

➤ **queue-number** Number of the queue. An integer between 1 and 16.

➤ **limit-number** Maximum number of buffers for this queue. The default is 20. The range is from 0 through 32,767 entries. If the number of buffers is set to 0, that queue can be of unlimited size.

The configuration of custom queuing requires some planning in advance. As with any queuing strategy, incorrect implementation will actually hurt your router's performance in the end. An example of a custom queue list is shown in Listing 4.10.

Listing 4.10   Custom queue configuration example.

```
queue-list 25 protocol ipx 3
queue-list 25 protocol appletalk 3
queue list 25 interface e0 1
queue-list 25 list 3
queue-list 25 protocol ip 1 tcp 23
queue-list 25 protocol ip 2
queue-list 25 default 4
queue-list 25 queue 1 byte-count 4500
queue-list 25 queue 3 limit 30
!
access-list 3 permit 176.16.5.0 0.0.0.255
!
interface serial 0
custom-queue-list 25
```

In Listing 4.10, IPX, AppleTalk and any IP traffic matching access-list 3 will be placed in queue number 3. Any traffic that entered the router via interface Ethernet 0 and all Telnet traffic (TCP port 23) will be placed into queue 1. Queue 1's capacity has been modified to 4,500 bytes. Queue 3's capacity has been limited to 30 messages at any give time. By manipulating the queue capacity, you can allocate higher amounts of bandwidth to specific traffic types. The relative bandwidth, assuming traffic in all queues, will be about 50 percent (4,500 bytes/9,000 total bytes assigned for all queues) for queue 1 with each of the other queues receiving approximately 15 percent (1,500 bytes/9,000 total bytes assigned for all queues). The faster the speed of the circuit, the more even the split of the bandwidth. If traffic is available for only one queue, it uses all of the bandwidth.

Custom queuing works best with links faster than 56K. Priority queuing is designed for low-speed links (56K and 64K). Custom queuing is for queues between 1.5Mb and 2.0Mb. With the faster queues, the flows come closer to their percentage guarantees.

Please note that faster links (Ethernets, Token Rings, Optical Carrier-3 OC-3, and so on) operate at speeds too fast to take advantage of the queuing. Queuing is handled in the process routing (rather than the fast switching) path. The CPU time used to assign traffic to the queues would probably be greater than the benefit for high-speed circuit.

Weighted Fair-Queuing

As we have mentioned, FIFO queuing is often not ideal. If we could provide a way to let the Telnet and other interactive traffic have priority over the FTP and other batch transfers, things would be better. The FTP packets would get through with relatively little delay, and the Telnet users would see better and more even response times.

In IOS 11.0, Cisco introduced a queuing scheme that provides a more sensible approach than FIFO to handling the low-volume, interactive transactions. The data gets sorted into queues automatically (by the IOS) when compared with the strict regimens of the other queuing strategies.

How WFQ Works

The traffic is sorted by high- and low-volume conversations. The traffic in a session is kept within one conversation, and the records are handled FIFO within a conversation. The lower-volume interactive traffic is given a priority and flows first. All bandwidth is given to the interactive traffic, and the large-volume conversations share equally whatever bandwidth is left over. WFQ is the default on interfaces less than 2Mbps and is on by default.

Configuring WFQ

As a note, **fair-queue** (the command for WFQ) is not an option for the following:

➤ Synchronous Data Link Control (SDLC), Link-access protocol balance (LAPB), and X.25 links

➤ Links that use Silicon Switching (SSE) or autonomous switching

➤ Tunnels

The parameters used to automatically determine weighting include the following:

➤ **IP** Source and destination address, protocol type, port numbers, and Type of Service (TOS)

➤ **IPX** Source and destination network, host, and socket as well as the Level 2 protocol

➤ **AppleTalk** Source and destination network number, node, and socket

For specifications for transparent and source-route bridging, DECnet, XNS, CLNS, Frame Relay, and Vines, visit the Cisco Web site at **www.cisco.com**.

Weighting gives preference to low-volume conversations such as Telnet. As a result, the low-volume conversations are priority queued relative to the high-volume conversations. The low-volume sessions receive all of the bandwidth for a portion of the transmission cycle. The high-volume conversations then take turns sharing the remaining bandwidth equally (each sends one record at a time). The goal is to keep the interactive sessions moving.

The only adjustment that the administrator makes is to adjust the queue limit. In order to keep some conversations from overwhelming the circuit, you can configure the maximum number of records that any high-volume conversation allows into the queue. The default is 64, but the range is from 1 through 4,096. If a conversation reaches the queue-limit, no further records are *enqueued* (added to the queue) for that conversation until the percentage of the entries in the queue for that conversation drops. Essentially all new packets for the over queue-limit conversation are dropped and lost. Conversations using TCP will have their records retransmitted automatically. In addition, TCP reduces its transmit window size, reducing congestion while it does the retransmission. Note that if there isn't much traffic, the large flows go through the routers quickly and never reach a point where they are monopolizing the buffers. Hence there are no drops, which occur when congestion grows and threatens to demand more service than fairness would dictate.

Listing 4.11 shows the command syntax for activating weighted fair-queuing on an interface. The **no** version removes it. **congestive-discard-threshold**, which is optional, indicates the number of messages allowed in each queue.

Listing 4.11 Activating weighted fair-queuing on an interface.

```
[no] fair-queue [congestive-discard-threshold]
```

Listing 4.12 shows a statement that changes **congestive-discard-threshold** from the default of 64 on interface Serial 0. The command shows up in the listing only if the threshold has been changed.

Listing 4.12 Weighted fair-queuing configuration example.

```
Interface Serial 0
fair-queue 128
```

Verify Queuing Operation

The primary command to display queue operation is shown in Listing 4.13.

Listing 4.13   show command for queuing configurations.

```
show queueing [custom | fair | priority]
```

 | Notice the spelling of the word "queueing". It is wrong but that is the way the IOS expects to see it.

The results of the **show queueing** command provides a way to see the configuration of the command without being in router privileged (enable) mode.

Practice Questions

Question 1

Will the following portion of a priority list work as intended?

```
priority-list 1 default low
priority-list 1 protocol ip high tcp 23
priority-list 1 protocol ipx medium
```

○ a. False, because IPX should be in the normal priority queue.

○ b. False, the default statement at the beginning prevents processing of the other priority-list statements.

○ c. True.

○ d. False, because the default queue should always be the normal queue.

Answer b is correct. It is false because the default statement at the beginning prevents processing of the other priority-list. The items in the priority list are processed from top to bottom. The default statement catches all traffic, which renders lines two and three ineffective. The default statement will work the same way when used with the custom queue list. Answer a is incorrect because no correct queue is required for IPX. Answer c is incorrect because of the default queue's position. Answer d is incorrect because although the default queue is the normal queue, any queue can serve as the default.

Question 2

The Novell SAP table consists of 700 entries. If the default custom queue lengths are used, will the SAP processing be affected?

○ a. Yes

○ b. No, because the number of SAPs exceeds the buffers available.

○ c. No, because SAPs cannot use queuing.

○ d. Too little information is available to make a judgement.

Answer b is correct. The SAPs arrive all at one time. Seven SAPs are contained in each buffer, so we'll end up with 100 packets. We only have room for 20 in the queues. If the circuit is very fast and not busy, buffered packets might not exceed the 20 (default custom queue buffers). If the circuit is busy or too slow, the arrival rate of data will exceed the packets' transmission rate, causing the overflow to be dropped. The result is that some of the SAP information is not advertised. Eventually some of the services will drop from adjacent servers' tables, and the services will be unavailable. Answer a is incorrect for the same reason b is correct (not enough buffers). Answer c is incorrect because SAPs do use queuing. Answer d is incorrect because even though more than 20 packets might get through the odds are at least some would be dropped causing the unavailability symptom mentioned above.

Question 3

We have IBM SNA traffic coming from a 100Mbps switched Ethernet interface. Do we need to use queuing? If so, which type?

- a. Yes. Use custom queuing to provide guaranteed bandwidth for the SNA traffic.
- b. Yes. Use priority queuing to reduce the transit time in the router for the SNA traffic.
- c. No. Queuing is not necessary in this case.
- d. Yes, let Weighted fair-queuing do the job.

Answer b is correct. SNA (and DEC LAT) has a short timeout and causes sessions to be dropped if the timeout is not met. Custom queuing provides bandwidth guarantees but may allow too much delay before the bandwidth is available. By assigning the SNA or other similar traffic to the high-priority queue as SNA traffic arrives in the queue, you can give it immediate bandwidth, thereby minimizing the delay. Answer a is incorrect because although the custom queue provides some guarantee of bandwidth, the custom queues are processed in round-robin sequence and delays are possible. Answer c is incorrect because traffic piles up on the outbound interface, probably given the high speed of the input interface. If queuing does occur, the SNA needs to go first due to the possibility of low timeout values. If the timeout is exceeded, the SNA session drops. Answer d is incorrect because WFQ might help but we need the more strict priority queuing to minimize problems with the SNA traffic.

Question 4

You have a mixture of interactive Telnet traffic and large file transfers to a low-speed serial interface. The Telnet sessions seem to suffer from not enough bandwidth. The response times are slow and erratic. Queuing may be the answer. What type of queuing should you use?

○ a.   None—just let the interface run FIFO

○ b.   Priority queuing

○ c.   Custom queuing

○ d.   Weighted fair-queuing

Answer d is correct. The scenario in the question is the kind of situation that WFQ was designed to optimize. The lower-volume traffic is given priority over the high-volume traffic. In addition, you don't need to configure any queue lists. WFQ is enabled by default on serial interfaces slower than 2Mbps. Priority and custom queuing might also improve things; however, unless you have some specific administrative requirements, let the IOS do the work. Answer a is incorrect because some form of queuing probably improves the problem. Answer b might solve the problem but would require you to configure **priority-lists**. WFQ is enabled by default on slow serial interfaces and is easier—always let defaults work for you. Answer c is incorrect because although custom queuing provides some bandwidth guarantees, there is no preference for the queue dispatching as the queues are serviced round-robin. WFQ results in better performance.

Question 5

You have a mixture of interactive Telnet traffic and large file transfers to a low-speed serial interface configured for X.25. The Telnet sessions seem to suffer from not enough bandwidth. The response times are slow and erratic. Queuing may be the answer. What type of queuing should you use?

○ a.   None. You cannot use queuing on an X.25 interface.

○ b.   Priority queuing

○ c.   Custom queuing

○ d.   Weighted fair-queuing

Answer a is correct because you cannot use queuing on X.25 circuits. Answers b, c, and d are incorrect because they are types of queuing and queuing cannot be configured on X.25 circuits.

Need To Know More?

 Doyle, Jeff. *CCIE Professional Development: Routing TCP/IP Volume 1*, Macmillan Technical Publishing, Indianapolis, IN, 1998. ISBN 1-57870-041-8.

 Huitema, Christian. *Routing in the Internet*, Prentice Hall PTR, Englewood Cliffs, NJ, 1995. ISBN 0-13132-192-7. Chapter 13, "Resource Reservation," has a good discussion of queuing and weighted fair queuing

 For information on queuing, visit the Cisco Web site at **www.cisco.com**.

Routing Protocol Overview

5

Terms you'll need to understand:

√ Layer 3 forwarding (routing)

√ Distance vector routing protocol

√ Link state routing protocol

√ Hybrid routing protocol

√ Static routing

√ Metric

√ Administrative distance

Techniques you'll need to master:

√ Configuring distance vector protocols

√ Configuring link state protocols

√ Configuring static routes

√ Manipulating administrative distance

This chapter presents an overview of routing as a process. To make intelligent forwarding decisions, the router must list all of the possible destination networks, metrics to reach those networks, as well as to decide through which interface to depart from to reach a specific destination network. This is known as a routing table. We will look at how routers build routing tables by sharing information. We will focus on the methods that routers use to share this routing information as well as how a packet makes its way through the router. We will also look at all the details that must be in place for a router to make a proper decision.

Routing As A Process

Routing is routing is routing is routing. In other words, the router does not care what protocol happens to be moving across it. It treats all protocols basically the same. The routing process occurs at layer 3 (the network layer) of the Open Standards Interconnect (OSI) model. Figure 5.1 illustrates the OSI model and the names of the specific entity that exists at each layer. This is a networking book, so the OSI model has to show up somewhere, right? You are probably already familiar with it, so we will spend only a small amount of time explaining it.

The network layer's primary job is to determine the routing path. Data must go through the Physical layer, layer 1, and the Data Link layer, layer 2, to get to the network layer.

At the Physical layer, the transmission is simply binary ones and zeros. At the Data Link layer, the bit stream is interpreted by the network interface card and constructed into a frame. Once the frame is constructed, a Cyclic Redundancy Check (CRC) is performed. At that point, the device finds the destination

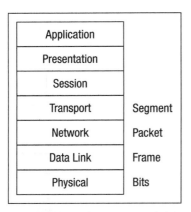

Figure 5.1 The OSI Model.

Media Access Control (MAC) address, which is part of the frame header. If the device determines that the destination MAC address belongs to it, then it begins processing the frame. To continue processing the frame, the frame must be passed to a higher layer, in this case the network layer. The data link framing is stripped away. The piece that's left is passed up to the network layer.

Once at the network layer, the device can look at the protocol-specific entity. At the network layer, this entity is known as a *packet* if the transmission is connection oriented or a *datagram* if it is connectionless. The packet consists of, among other things, a *destination protocol address* and *source protocol address*.

The router examines the destination protocol address and compares it to the entries in the routing table. The router is looking for the entry in the routing table that matches the most contiguous bits. For example, an Internet Protocol (IP) address is a 32-bit address. If an IP packet arrives with a destination IP address of 1.1.1.8, the router looks in the routing table for the longest (nearest) match. Table 5.1 is an example of the routing table.

Our packet with the address of 1.1.1.8 should be dispatched via interface Ethernet 0. In Table 5.1, all of the entries partially matched our packet. In other words, all of the routing table entries matched at least 16-bits of the destination address (2 octets). However, only the route via interface Ethernet 0 provided a longer match—24-bits was the same. It is the longest match, so it is deemed the dispatch interface. The packet is framed according to the encapsulation of the outbound interface (in this case, it is placed into an Ethernet frame) and dispatched.

Other routed protocols function in a similar fashion to the scenario described above. We discuss the longest match principle in more detail in Chapter 6. In the end, the routing process revolves around the network portion of the protocol address. If there is an entry in the routing table on which a forwarding decision can be based, the packets are forwarded accordingly. Should the router not find a match in the routing table, a "destination unreachable" message is returned to the source address.

Table 5.1 A sample routing table.

Destination Network	Outbound Interface
1.1.1.0	Ethernet 0
1.1.2.0	Ethernet 1
1.1.3.0	Ethernet 2
1.1.4.0	Ethernet 3

The router must have a method of learning these routes, maintaining them, and keeping track of which routes are no longer valid. This is the function of the routing protocol. Routing protocols have evolved over recent years. Initial attempts at the creation of intelligent routing protocols have been greatly improved upon. Today there are a number of different protocols based on differing methodologies for route calculation.

Routing Protocols

Now that we have an idea of how the router makes decisions, it is time to figure out how the router got the information about each destination network in the first place. Routers learn routes through two methods: statically and dynamically. Static routing is fairly straightforward and simple, whereas dynamic routes can be derived in a number of ways. This section covers the various ways the router can learn the necessary information.

Based on the method of calculating the best route for a given protocol, it stands to reason that one protocol may be more believable than another when it comes to our perception of what the best route should be. For example, would you trust a route based solely on hop count (with no regard for bandwidth, or lack thereof) over a route that does take aggregate bandwidth into account? RIP and IGRP/EIGRP consider these factors when comparing routes. If a route from Network A to Network B showed two hops away over 14.4 dialup lines, or six hops away via another pathway consisting of Fast Ethernet and Asynchronous Transfer Mode (ATM), which would you prefer? Which route would RIP consider to be better? Which route would IGRP/EIGRP consider to be better? It is a matter of perception in how the protocol calculates the overall route. We will cover metrics in more detail later in this chapter.

Static Routing

Static routes are entries made in the routing table manually. A router administrator can use static routes to override any dynamic route(s) by configuring the destination network and specifying next hop or outbound interface information.

Static routes have a number of uses. Administrators can use them simply to override what a dynamic routing protocol may have placed into the table, or to provide redundancy for dynamic routes. Static routes are commonly used in dial-on-demand routing (DDR) environments to keep dynamic routing updates from causing a dialer interface from staying active and wasting financial resources.

Use caution with static routes. Static routes, by default, have the distinction of being the most trusted routes the router can have in a routing table. A static route is believed over any other route that the router derives dynamically as long as the default administrative distance has not been altered. Although static routes are trusted routes, they do have their downfalls. The largest drawback is that they do not adapt to *topology changes*, any changes in the network that affect the routing table entry. Administrators define static routes, so such routes are somewhat error prone. A single route can cause a significant routing loop or other unpredictable results.

Administrators should take care when implementing static routes in any form. The static route configuration should be entered at the global configuration prompt; it consists of the following command structure:

```
ip route <dest. network><dest. mask> <next hop | out interface>
```

The command includes information about the destination network and subnet mask associated with that destination network, as well as either the next hop address or the outbound interface through which to leave the router. Optionally, an administrative distance value can be specified after the next hop or outbound interface. If left unaltered, the administrative distance of a static route for which a next hop address is specified will be 1. If an outbound interface is specified, the administrative distance will be 0 and treated as a directly connected network.

Dynamic Routing

Dynamic routing protocols are those that have some mechanism of learning, maintaining, and monitoring route and routing table status. If the route to a specific network is lost, the protocol should be able to make intelligent decisions that allow it to route around the outage, then adapt again once the route to that network has returned. Obviously, redundancy will require significant planning in the initial stages of the network design. Redundancy is one of the more common issues that administrators face in today's internetworks.

Dynamic routing protocols have evolved significantly since the creation of routable protocols. There are two well-known types of dynamic routing protocols and one type that is not quite as well known. The well-known types are *distance vector* and *link state*. The newer—and lesser known—type of dynamic routing protocol is the *hybrid* routing protocol (also called *advanced distance vector* in some industry circles). The hybrid protocols— Interior Gateway Routing Protocol (IGRP) and Enhanced Interior Gateway Routing Protocol (EIGRP)—were created by and are proprietary to Cisco. IGRP is not covered on the ACRC exam, so we will not cover it here. For more information on EIGRP, see Chapter 8.

Route Calculation

Routes are measured by *metrics*. The metric for different routing protocols varies according to the algorithm used to derive the route. Each routing protocol uses a different metric calculation to derive what it thinks is the best possible route to a specific destination. For example, Routing Information Protocol (RIP) uses a hop-count how many routers it must cross between source and destination hosts; Open Shortest Path First (OSPF) uses cost based on bandwidth; and Interior Gateway Routing Protocol (IGRP) and Enhanced Interior Gateway Routing Protocol (EIGRP) use a composite metric comprised of bandwidth, delay, reliability, load, and maximum transmittable unit (MTU). Each protocol's calculation algorithm differs based on how, and why, it was created.

Distance Vector Protocols

Distance vector protocols were the first in the family of dynamic routing protocols. They function on the premise of metric addition. Router A is four hops from Network 1. Router B is a neighbor of Router A. Router B knows of Network 1 only through Router A. The metric that is reflected in Router B's routing table is Router A's advertised metric plus 1 (because Router B is one hop from Router A). Therefore, Router B's metric to Network 1 is five hops. This algorithm is known as the Bellman-Ford algorithm.

Consider a ticket line in front of a theater. You are third in the line. What if you could not see the ticket window due to an obstruction such as a wall? Now, you know that you are third in the line only because the person ahead of you told you he was second in line. How does he know he is second in line? He knows only because the person ahead of him claims to be first. What is the ultimate destination? The destination is the ticket window. You can only know for certain that there is a person ahead of you and a person behind you. That is the principle behind distance vector technology. A router knows only its position in the network because its neighbors told it their positions in the network. The function of this type of protocol is commonly referred to as *routing by rumor*.

Distance vector protocols generally use periodic updates. A *periodic update* is one that is on a timed interval. Once the interval timer reaches zero, a routing update is broadcast out of every active interface whether there have been changes or not. Because distance vector protocols use these periodic timers, they tend to be slow to react to topological changes in the internetwork. To that end, convergence tends to be somewhat slow. In some cases, several of these protocols have implemented triggered updates to compensate for a loss of signal on the wire.

Convergence is the process of distributing routing information throughout the network, giving all routers in the internetwork a common perspective of the topology. In other words, convergence is the process of disseminating, to every router, reachability information about every network in the internetwork. This process takes time. The amount of time required depends on each protocol's attributes and abilities.

When a router first powers up, it performs a power-on-self test and figures out who it is. It then reads a configuration from nonvolatile RAM in order to find out how it should function on the network. Part of this information involves addressing on various interfaces. Based on those addresses, the router knows to which networks it is directly connected. Until it receives a routing update from a neighbor that is running a common routing protocol, it only knows the networks to which it is directly connected.

Once the distance vector routing protocol has initiated, it broadcasts all of the information it knows (at this point, directly connected networks only) out of every active interface. It does not receive routing information until the neighbor routers' periodic timer expires. Once that occurs, the neighbor router(s) broadcasts. Once this router receives the update(s), it alters its routing table accordingly. For the purposes of this discussion, we will use RIP as an example. RIP uses a hop count as the metric for determining the best pathway to a specific destination. The premise for any given destination is: "the fewer the routers it has to cross, the better the route should be to get there." Figure 5.2 shows this process from the view of the distance vector protocol RIP.

Table 5.2 shows the initial routing table of each route. The routing table at this point consists of only the directly connected networks of each router and their interface (interface) designations.

Table 5.2   Initial Routing Tables.

R1	Out Interface	Metric	R2	Out Interface	Metric	R3	Out Interface	Metric
10.1.0.0	E0	0	10.2.0.0	S1	0	10.4.0.0	E0	0
10.2.0.0	S0	0	10.3.0.0	S0	0	10.3.0.0	S1	0

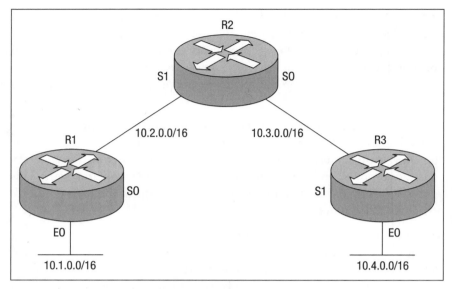

Figure 5.2 RIP operation.

As you can see, the information is limited at this point. Reachability consists only of what is directly connected to the router. Once routing updates begin to flow, the routing tables begin to converge. Table 5.3 shows each router's routing table after the first update has been received and processed. Notice that the directly connected information has not changed, but the new entries are added.

As you can see, the initial information was broadcast out of every interface. The process consisted of the expiration of the update timer, the broadcast of the update, and the processing of the update. You can also see that full convergence has not yet been reached. Also notice the metrics for each route. R1 has a new route to network 10.3.0.0 that it learned from R2 out of interface Serial 0. R2 advertised that it was zero hops from network 10.3.0.0. R1 must go through R2 to get to 10.3.0.0, so it added one hop to the metric advertised by

Table 5.3 Routing tables after one update.

R1	Out Interface	Metric	R2	Out Interface	Metric	R3	Out Interface	Metric
10.1.0.0	e0	0	10.2.0.0	s1	0	10.4.0.0	e0	0
10.2.0.0	s0	0	10.3.0.0	s0	0	10.3.0.0	s0	0
10.3.0.0	s0	1	10.1.0.0	s1	1	10.2.0.0	s0	1
			10.4.0.0	s0	1			

R2 to arrive at its metric for this particular route. The process must repeat itself in order to reach convergence. Table 5.4 shows the routing table after the next update has been received and processed. Convergence has been accomplished because all routers know about all networks.

Again, the metrics reflect the fact that to get to a particular destination, each packet must traverse one additional hop.

It is apparent that the view of the internetwork from any router's perspective is the view of its neighbors. Distance vector protocols tend to be slow to converge, as we have illustrated. Distance vector protocols also tend to use less memory and CPU power than their link state counterparts. Although distance vector protocols are less intelligent, they are less intensive than link state protocols on system resources.

Based on what we have discussed to this point, it is easy to see what happens if a topological change occurs. Should network 10.1.0.0 disappear for some reason, the update would not be immediately apparent to R2 or R3. Updates are sent out only when the periodic timer reaches zero. It would take some time before R3 knew that network 10.1.0.0 had disappeared.

The routing updates themselves are broadcasts. When broadcasts go out, all nodes on the network are affected. It makes no difference to distance vector protocols that an update may not be necessary (because nothing has changed in the network). Therefore, another consideration is unnecessary bandwidth utilization. It is a tradeoff. Do you want to use more system resources in the router, or do you want to use more bandwidth on the links between the routers?

Link State Protocols

Link state protocols were developed specifically to overcome the limitations of distance vector protocols. Whereas distance vector protocols simply broadcast updates out of each active interface when the update timer expires, link state

Table 5.4 Converged routing table.

R1	Out Interface	Metric	R2	Out Interface	Metric	R3	Out Interface	Metric
10.1.0.0	e0	0	10.2.0.0	s1	0	10.4.0.0	e0	0
10.2.0.0	s0	0	10.3.0.0	s0	0	10.3.0.0	s0	0
10.3.0.0	s0	1	10.1.0.0	s1	1	10.2.0.0	s0	1
10.4.0.0	s0	2	10.4.0.0	s0	1	10.1.0.0	s0	2

protocols send an update only when there is an update to send, and even then, only the precise change goes out. Link state protocols actually enter into a conversational state with their directly connected neighbors. This ongoing conversation consists of routing updates as well as *paranoid updates*, which occur usually every 30 minutes if there are no other routing changes. It is simply one router asking its neighbors if they are still there.

Link state protocols actually keep a map of the entire internetwork in memory. This map is a combination of a topological database and a Shortest Path First (SPF) tree derived from it. As you might expect, the map uses significant resources in the router.

Returning to our previous analogy, the movie-ticket line. Remove any obstructions in the way of your view of the destination (the ticket window). You can see that you are third in the line because you see the entire line start to finish. You can see your position in the line as well as that of everyone else. You actually know the position of everyone in the line. You know who is 10th in line, and you know who is 35th in line. You know every aspect of the line. You can even see whether or not there is a shorter line that you could be in to speed your progress to the ticket window. Why do you know all of this information? If you are a link state protocol, you know it because each individual in line told you everything it knew about its position in the line and how it would get to the ticket window.

The specific algorithm that link state protocols follow is known as the Djykstra algorithm. This algorithm consists of the following steps:

➤ Constructing a topological database

➤ Running the SPF algorithm

➤ Constructing an SPF tree diagram of the network

➤ Constructing a routing table based on the tree

This process consumes quite a bit of resources. Each time a routing update arrives, the process starts over. If an interface in the internetwork is *bouncing or flapping* (such as changing back and forth from an up-state to a down-state), a large number of updates could cause an undue load on the resources of a large number of routers.

Refer back to Figure 5.2, the distance vector example in which we saw where the routing tables evolved their way into convergence. A link state protocol, on the other hand, knows almost instantly about all the networks in the example. Within a few seconds, the routing tables of all routers resemble those shown earlier in Table 5.4.

When a new router comes up on the network, it begins to issue hello messages out of all active interfaces and awaits an answer. Once an answer is received, a conversation begins. This conversation basically consists of the new router introducing itself and the existing router(s) dumping everything it knows onto the link to the new router. Almost instantly, the new router knows the entire network and has shared what it knows with the network.

> The router will form an *"adjacency"* with neighboring routers. This is basically an information exchange and the initiation of an ongoing conversation. In the case of OSPF, the information that is exchanged here consists of the router id, hello/dead interval, neighbor routers, area id, router priority, designated router address, backup designated router address, authentication password (if any), and stub area flag. OSPF is covered in detail in Chapter 7.

Routing updates are known as *link state advertisements (LSAs)*. LSAs are sent only when there is a change to report, and they contain only the change that is being reported. LSAs propagate in a *flooding* fashion. That is, everyone on the network sees them and passes them on.

When an LSA comes in, the router examines it for a timestamp and sequence numbering to ensure that this update has not been duplicated or outdated. If the update is one that should be processed, the router makes an entry in its link state database and forwards the LSA out of every active interface (except the one through which it entered the router). It then continues to process the update according to the Djykstra algorithm.

Which Is Best?

Obviously, there are tradeoffs involved in using link state versus distance vector protocols. Link state protocols are much more intensive on system resources. It seems that unnecessary information is kept at times. They require higher-horsepower CPUs and additional RAM resources. However, they shine when it comes to convergence and intelligent route calculation. Convergence is completed within the internetwork almost instantly rather than the minutes—or sometimes hours—that it takes with distance vector protocols.

Link state protocols tend to support advanced addressing functions that distance vector protocols do not support. These include route summarization and Variable Length Subnet Masks (VLSMs), which we will discuss in Chapter 6. As you can see, the benefits of link state protocols do seem to outweigh their disadvantages. However, that is a matter of perception. The size and function of your network will weigh heavily in the decision as well.

Believability

As we have mentioned, routing protocols have differing methods of computing the "best" route. These computations are based upon a metric. The *metric* is simply a unit of measure to allow the router to compare pathways to a specific destination network.

The question "How do we tell the router what the best route should be?" arises. The answer to that question is simple if you are running only a single routing protocol. In that case, the best route is whatever the routing protocol thinks it should be. However, it is possible to run multiple routing protocols simultaneously in any given router.

The router uses a believability measurement known as *administrative distance*. Administrative distance is simply a number between 0 and 255 that gives the router an idea of which protocols to believe if two or more routing protocols come up with routing information for the same network(s). Table 5.5 lists Cisco's default administrative distances for each protocol.

 Manipulation of administrative distance is not always necessary. However, the administrative distances will allow you to understand why routes from specific protocols show up in the routing table rather than the routes of other active routing protocols.

Table 5.5   Administrative Distance Defaults.

Protocol	Administrative Distance
Connected interface	0
Static route	1
EIGRP summary route	5
External Border Gateway Protocol (EBGP)	20
Internal Enhanced IGRP	90
IGRP	100
OSPF	110
RIP	120
Exterior Gateway Protocol (EGP)	140
External Enhanced IGRP	170
Internal Border Gateway Protocol (IBGP)	200
Unknown	255

The lower the administrative distance, the more believable the route. If you have RIP and EIGRP running at the same time, you will see only EIGRP routes in your routing table. Even though both protocols are functioning as if they were running alone, only the most believable routes appear in the routing table. Should EIGRP not have a route to a particular destination and RIP can provide that route, the RIP route will show up in the routing table. However, that type of scenario is quite rare, but not impossible.

You can configure administrative distance for a particular protocol. To change the administrative distance from the default setting, you must use the **distance** command. For example, should you want to set the administrative distance for RIP to 80 (so that RIP routes override EIGRP routes), enter the following commands:

```
Router#>Configure terminal
Router(Config)#>Router rip
Router(Config)#>Network 10.0.0.0
Router(Config-router)#>Distance 80
```

> *Note:* *The steps to configure the administrative distance of other protocols are identical to those of this command example. Under the appropriate routing protocol configuration, you can use the* **distance** *command as show above.*

We should note that directly connected networks are the most believable, followed by static routes. You can configure an administrative distance value in two ways. The first involves adding a command parameter at the end of the static route command entry, as shown here:

```
ip route <dest. network><dest. mask><next hop | out int><distance>
```

 Static routes play an integral part in many technologies such as dial on demand routing. Ensure that you understand the proper command parameters and variables necessary to configure static routes on a router.

After you enter the static route command, but before pressing Enter, you need to enter the last parameter available: **distance.** You can enter a number between 0 and 255 to specify the administrative distance for this particular route. Should you not enter a distance, it defaults to 0 if you specified an outbound interface or 1 if you specified a next hop address in the command.

The second way is through manipulation of administrative distance for a specific dynamic route. Under the routing protocol configuration, you can specify distance for all routes derived by that protocol, or a single route. To configure distance for specific routes, you need to create an access list to define the networks for which the administrative distance is to be changed. Listing 5.1 shows a configuration example that defines the administrative distance for network 10.2.0.0 as 130 rather than the RIP default of 120.

Listing 5.1   Specific manipulation of administrative distance

```
!define the access-list at global configuration mode
access-list 1 permit 10.2.0.0 0.0.255.255

!configure the distance under the protocol configuration
router rip
network 10.0.0.0
distance 130 0.0.0.0 255.255.255.255 1
```

Practice Questions

Question 1

> What is the key piece of information on which routing decisions are based?
>
> ○ a. Source network-layer address
>
> ○ b. Destination network-layer address
>
> ○ c. Source MAC address
>
> ○ d. Destination MAC address

Answer b is correct. The destination network-layer address, or layer 3, is the protocol-specific address to which this piece of data is to be delivered. The source network-layer address is the originating host and plays no role in getting the information to the destination. Therefore, answer a is incorrect. The source and destination MAC addresses are necessary for getting the data to the router, or the next hop address. However, they are not used in pathing decisions. Therefore, answers c and d are incorrect.

Question 2

> In the following figure, what are the missing layers of the OSI model and the names of the entities that exist at those layers? [Choose the two best answers]
>
> ❏ a. Physical, Data Link, Network, and Transport
>
> ❏ b. Source Address and Destination Address
>
> ❏ c. Segment, packet, frame, and bits
>
> ❏ d. Application, Presentation, and Session

| Application |
| Presentation |
| Session |
| |
| |
| |
| |

Fill in the OSI Model.

Refer back to Figure 5.1, and you'll see that the correct answers are a and c. Answer b is incorrect because source and destination addresses are specific parts of the entities that exist at the Data Link and Network layers. Answer d is incorrect because those layers are listed in the figure and do not need to be added in.

Question 3

> What is the measurement information used in calculating routes from source to destination for any single protocol known as?
>
> ○ a. Longest match
>
> ○ b. Distance vector
>
> ○ c. Link state
>
> ○ d. Metric

Answer d is correct. The metric is a unit of measure used to derive the best route to a particular destination. Answers b and c are incorrect because they are specific types of routing protocols, not measurements of routes. Answer a is incorrect because the longest match principle is applied after the routing table is completed. The longest match is the route that most closely resembles the destination protocol address.

Question 4

> Distance vector protocols are faster to converge than link state protocols.
>
> ○ a. True
>
> ○ b   False

Answer b is correct, False Distance vector protocols tend to be slower to converge because they are governed by periodic updates that go out only when the timer reaches zero.

Question 5

> What is the algorithm run by link state protocols known as?
>
> ○ a. Longest match
>
> ○ b. Djykstra
>
> ○ c. Convergence
>
> ○ d. None of the above

Answer b is correct. The Djykstra algorithm defines the operation of link state protocols and how they respond to routing changes. Answer a is incorrect because it is the method of route selection. It is a function that runs based on the information the routing protocol collects. Answer c is incorrect because it is the process of all routers exchanging information to the point where they share a common perspective on the internetwork. Answer d is incorrect because a correct answer is given.

Question 6

> The believability of a route derived from one routing protocol over routes derived by another is determined by the administrative distance.
>
> ○ a. True
>
> ○ b. False

Answer a is correct, True. You can manipulate administrative distance protocol by protocol, or you can leave it to the default value for a particular protocol.

Question 7

> When running RIP and EIGRP, why would you see RIP routes in the IP routing table? [Choose the two best answers]
>
> ❏ a. RIP has a better administrative distance by default than EIGRP.
>
> ❏ b. Distance has been configured manually.
>
> ❏ c. EIGRP has a higher administrative distance by default than RIP.
>
> ❏ d. EIGRP does not have a route to that destination.

Answers b and d are correct. By default EIGRP has an administrative distance of 90 which makes it more believable than RIP at 120. If distance has been manually configured to where RIP has a distance lower than 90, or if EIGRP has been set to a distance higher than 120, the RIP route will show up. For some reason, should the situation occur where RIP has a route to a specific destination that EIGRP does not have, the RIP route will show up. Therefore, answers a and c are incorrect.

Need to Know More?

 Huitema, Christian: *Routing in the Internet*; Prentice Hall, Jersey City, NJ, 1995. ISBN 0-13132-192-7. This book is packed full of great information on Routing in the Internet.

 Perlman, Radia: *Interconnections: Routers and Bridges;* Addison-Wesley; 1992. ISBN 0-201-56332-0. This book is a great resource for quality information on Routers and Bridges.

 For more information on routing protocols, visit **www.cisco.com** and perform a search on keywords, "routing protocol".

IP Addressing Using Variable Length Subnet Masks

6

. . . .

Terms you'll need to understand:

✓ IP address

✓ Private IP address

✓ Public IP address

✓ Subnet mask

✓ Prefix

✓ Classful routing

✓ Classless routing

✓ Variable Length Subnet Mask (VLSM)

✓ Longest match

✓ Route summarization

✓ Network Address Translation (NAT)

Techniques you'll need to master:

✓ Planning and deploying IP addresses

✓ Calculating subnet masks

✓ Using private IP addressing space

✓ Calculating Variable Length Subnet Masks

✓ Deploying VLSM address space properly

✓ Configuring route summarization

This chapter will cover address deployment and memory utilization. In the past, network administrators deployed the Internet Protocol (IP) addresses without thinking about addresses becoming depleted, which is happening today. The volume of addresses on the Internet has been increasing exponentially in very small amounts of time. We will also discuss some memory utilization methods of deploying scarce IP address space more efficiently as well as how to reduce the size of the routing table.

IP Addressing Basics

If you could pick any single issue in networking and call it the most misunderstood, what would you pick? Many votes would land squarely in the realm of IP address deployment. As has been the case throughout this book, we assume that you are at least somewhat familiar with the subject matter. This book does not aim to teach subnet procedure, but you must understand it before we can delve into the rest of this chapter's subject matter. Here's a short review.

TCP/IP Address Structure

An IP address consists of a 32-bit string of ones and zeros. In order to make it simpler to work with, this 32-bit string has been divided into four equal pieces. Each of these pieces, known as an *octet*, consists of eight bits. These octets are converted from binary to decimal to create what we know as an address in dotted decimal notation. In other words, an IP address is simply four decimal numerals separated by periods.

As with any network-layer protocol, an IP address consists of two parts: the network portion and the host portion. The network portion designates a common domain or logical division. For example, an area code is a location-specific identifier that many physical devices in a geographic area share.

The host portion is an identifier that when coupled with the network portion creates a globally unique identifier for a specific end host. For example, your phone number is a unique identifier for your specific phone. Is it possible for someone in another area code to have an identical phone number? Absolutely, it is possible (and common). What makes the phone number unique to you? The coupling of that phone number with the area code makes it yours alone.

When you assign an IP address to a host, you are giving it a globally unique identifier. The question that arises is "Well, how is the device supposed to know where the network portion ends and the host portion begins?" An additional piece of information, known as a *mask*, must be present in order to tell the device where the division between network and host exists.

The mask is simply a 32-bit string very similar to an IP address. The mask is a contiguous string of ones followed by a contiguous string of zeros. The point where the ones stop and zeros start in the mask is the division between the network and host portions of the address with which this mask is associated.

IP Addressing With Class

IP addresses are viewed in terms of class. The *class* of an address makes certain assumptions about the natural network and host portions of any given address based on the decimal or binary value of the first octet. These different classes have been divided based on the value of the high-order bits (the bits furthest to the left in a binary value). If the first bit value (the leftmost bit) is a zero, the address is a Class A address. If the first two bits are one and zero, in that order, then the address is Class B. If the first three bits of the address are one, one, and zero, in that order, the address is Class C. The value of each octet is computed by converting each 8-bit string from binary to decimal. Table 6.1 illustrates the *natural* (*classful*) division of IP addressing.

As you can see, some numeric values have been omitted. Specifically, these are 0, 127, and any value from 224 to 255. The distinction of designating network addresses goes to 0, and 127 was set aside to allow the use of a diagnostic loopback address. The address 127.0.0.1 is known as an *internal loopback address*. In other words, administrators can use this address to test the configuration of an individual host's IP configuration. Pinging (the process of testing reachability to an end host) this address would result in a response from the local device (basically, you are pinging yourself). The range of 224 through 239 is known as Class D. Class D addresses have been set aside for various multicast related functions. For instance, the address 224.0.0.5 is an Open Shortest Path First (OSPF) multicast address used in disseminating routing information in an OSPF network. Class E includes the range 240 through 247 and is used only for research purposes. The remaining address space is allocated for future use. The value 255 is seen as a broadcast entity.

A common issue that arises is in simply knowing where to get the address space you need to deploy your subnetwork addressing scheme efficiently. You can obtain registered IP address space from your Internet Service Provider

Table 6.1 IP Address Classes.	
Class	**First Octet Range**
A	1 through 126
B	128 through 191
C	192 through 223

(ISP) and deploy that address space into your internetwork. Or, if your company is not planning to connect to the public Internet, you can use an address space that the internetworking industry has set aside specifically for private internetworks. Address space from each class has been set aside for private use. Anyone can use these addresses. Table 6.2 specifies this private Internetwork address space, which was originally defined in RFC 1597, but revised in RFC 1918.

 It is important that you to understand the private internetwork space and know the address ranges that have been set aside and how to use NAT to access the public Internet. NAT is discussed later in this chapter.

Subnet Mask Manipulation

By manipulating the value of the mask, you can manipulate the number of hosts per network. In their natural state, each class of address has a specific number of hosts per network. Table 6.3 illustrates examples of the natural network and host divisions for IP addresses in each class.

These addresses in their natural form cover the spectrum from a ridiculously high number of hosts (a single logical network with 16,777,214 hosts) down to what may be too few hosts. To put this in perspective, imagine a single network—not an internetwork, just a single network, as shown in Figure 6.1.

Figure 6.1 shows a single network that has been assigned to a Class B address. Sixteen bits are available for hosts on that single network, for a total host

Table 6.2   Private Internetwork space.

Class	Range
A	10.0.0.0 through 10.255.255.255
B	172.16.0.0 through 172.31.255.255
C	192.168.0.0 through 192.168.255.255

Table 6.3   Natural Network and host divisions.

Class	Network Address	Mask	Number Of Networks	Hosts
A	10.0.0.0	255.0.0.0	1	16,777,214
B	172.16.0.0	255.255.0.0	1	65,534
C	192.168.1.0	255.255.255.0	1	254

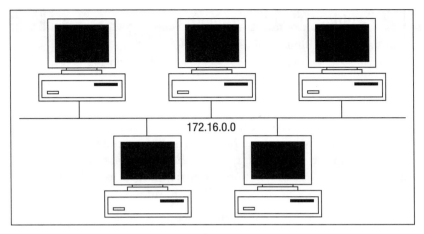

Figure 6.1 An imaginary network.

capacity of 65,534 hosts. That number is many times what a single Ethernet segment is capable of supporting. A single network obviously does not allow for scalability or growth.

Efficiency Is The Key

A current issue involving address deployment is address depletion. It is our responsibility, as responsible members of the internetworking community, to efficiently deploy the address space we have. Should you run out of address space, you may be required to justify your use of that space in order to be granted additional space. If you obtain space correctly from the beginning, you will find it much easier to obtain additional space.

To deploy address space, the first step is to plan the internetwork hierarchy and figure out how many separate subnetworks you will have and how many hosts each subnetwork will require. With that information, you can create a suitable subnet mask for your subnetwork. Referring back to Figure 6.1, should we wish to deploy additional subnetworks, we would need to segment the single network address into multiple subnetwork addresses. You accomplish this task by manipulating the subnet mask. In doing so, we have changed the natural mask for our Class B network to give us additional networks. Whereas the mask was 255.255.0.0, it is now 255.255.255.0. In effect, we have informed the router that we would like for it to look deeper into the address to make network pathing decisions.

As mentioned earlier, a mask is a contiguous string of 1's followed by a contiguous string of 0's, in binary form of course. When converted to binary, our natural mask appears as noted in Table 6.4.

Table 6.4   A mask in binary format.

Decimal Value	Binary Value
255.255.0.0	11111111.11111111.00000000.00000000

Router Logic

When distinguishing between logical networks with the same address, the router has to have a way to tell where the network portion of the address ends. It does so by using ones in the subnet mask. When the subnet mask is put together with the actual IP address in question, a function known as a *logical AND* is performed on the two 32-bit strings. Table 6.5 illustrates this process.

When the bit positions are lined up, the function is to simply to follow the rules of engagement for logical AND:

➤   1 and 1 result in a 1

➤   1 and 0 result in a 0

➤   0 and 1 result in a 0

➤   0 and 0 result in a 0

Look at the first bit position on the far left. Both values have a 1 for the first bit, so the resulting product of the logical AND is a 1. The next bit position has a 0 on the top line and a 1 on the bottom. The resulting value is 0. Apply the principle to all bit positions and you will arrive at a third 32-bit string. This string, when converted back to decimal, will yield the subnet address. Simply convert each 8-bit value into decimal to arrive at your address.

What if we were to give the router something more to look at? Assume that we would like to tell the router that it should look at the normal number of ones for a Class B address. However, we would like it to look at some additional bits, in this case 8 additional bits. Table 6.6 illustrates this premise.

Up to this point, we couldn't change the value of our assigned address, 172.16.0.0, because we had only a single network and the first two octets were set aside for network designation. We have now made it clear that the third

Table 6.5   Logical AND.

Decimal	Binary Value Equivalent
172.16.0.0	10101100.00010000.00000000.00000000
255.255.0.0	11111111.11111111.00000000.00000000
Subnet address:	10101100.00010000.00000000.00000000

Table 6.6   Logical AND with subnetting.

Decimal	Binary Equivalent
172.16.0.0	10101100.00010000.00000000.00000000
255.255.255.0	11111111.11111111.11111111.00000000
subnet address:	10101100.00010000.00000000.00000000

octet should also be used for network designation. Whereas before we had a single network, we now have many more. To be exact, 254 networks are now available for our use. However, rather than 65,534 hosts, we now have only 254 hosts per network. At this point, our network can evolve from what it was in Figure 6.1 to what it is now in Figure 6.2.

We are still using the assigned address space. We are simply making better use of the available space by manipulating the subnet mask. It is easy to see where you may be somewhat confused about various address values. The IP address itself is a useless piece of information if there is no subnet mask. Without the

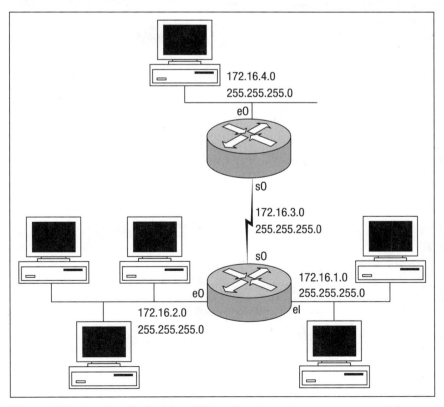

Figure 6.2   A subnetted network topology.

mask, it is impossible to tell where the division between network and host lies. Without that information, we can assume only the natural division.

You should determine where the boundary between network and hosts needs to exist during pre-deployment planning. You must know how many subnets you will need as well as how many hosts each of those subnets will need to support. Table 6.7 illustrates the subnet mask, the number of networks, and number of hosts per network that you will create when you manipulate the bit boundary between ones and zeros in the mask. The example in the table is following our example address of 172.16.0.0, first shown in Figure 6.1. The Number Of Bits field in the table is the number of bits beyond those specified by the natural mask. The formula for calculating the number of hosts and/or subnets is $2^n - 2$. In other words, if we want the router to pay attention to 5-bits beyond what it normally would for this class of address, the number of hosts would be $2^5 - 2$, for a total of 30 subnets. If we have taken 5 bits from an octet, 3 are left for the host. If we apply the same formula: $2^3 - 2 = 6$ hosts.

Table 6.7 Subnet Planning sample.			
Number Of Bits	Mask	Number Of Subnets	Number Of Hosts
0	255.255.0.0	1	65,534
1	255.255.128.0	0	32,766
2	255.255.192.0	2	16,382
3	255.255.224.0	6	8,190
4	255.255.240.0	14	4,094
5	255.255.248.0	30	2,046
6	255.255.252.0	62	1,022
7	255.255.254.0	126	510
8	255.255.255.0	254	254
9	255.255.255.128	510	126
10	255.255.255.192	1,024	62
11	255.255.255.224	2,048	30
12	255.255.255.240	4,096	14
13	255.255.255.248	8,190	6
14	255.255.255.252	16,382	2
15	255.255.255.254	32,766	0
16	255.255.255.255	N/A	N/A

What's In A Name?

The natural mask, subnet mask, or any other type of mask that you can associate with an IP address has another name: a *prefix*. The prefix is simply another way of specifying the mask. For example, we have been using the address 172.16.0.0 with a mask of 255.255.255.0. The prefix is an abbreviation. You can find out what the abbreviated prefix is by simply counting the number of ones in the mask. In our case, 24 ones are followed by 8 zeros. As stated earlier, the router cares only about the ones, not the zeros. So, the abbreviated address is 172.16.0.0/24. This address is said to have a 24-bit prefix. Eventually, most people get to where they prefer to use the abbreviation to note address and mask together.

So, why have another name for the same entity? A subnet mask is a piece of information that tells us how address space has been segmented into smaller pieces. According to what we have discussed to this point, the rules state that we cannot change our assigned address. That remains true. However, what if we were assigned a block of addresses that consisted of multiple Class B addresses? So far, our examples have shown only the assignment of a single address. The rules we have discussed up to this point are known as *classful* rules.

Classless Routing

The time has come to rise to the next level of IP address deployment and discuss what happens when the classful rules do not apply. At this point, we move partially into the realm of address assignment. We will also discuss another method of increasing the efficiency of address deployment.

Classless routing is known as *Classless Interdomain Routing (CIDR)*. CIDR is a method of assigning address space based on need. Assume that your company needs 2,000 host addresses. A Class C address is not adequate for your needs, so you automatically assume "I need a Class B address." However, if you were assigned a Class B address, it would waste a very large number of addresses. You need 2,000, whereas a Class B provides for over 65,000 addresses. In effect, that wastes over 63,000 addresses. So, what is the solution? A single Class C is not enough, and a Class B is too much. What if you were issued eight Class C addresses? That would give you a total of 254 times 8 addresses, or 2,032. That's closer to your needs without wasting space. To that end, you could be assigned the address 222.201.40.0/21. The first reaction is that this is not a legal representation of a Class C address. It should have a 24-bit prefix by default. But, this is why we call it *classless*. The rules of class do not apply. Table 6.8 breaks this address into binary to illustrate what you have been given in the above address.

Table 6.8 Classless Address example.	
Address	**Third Octet Binary Value**
222.201.40.0	00101000
222.201.41.0	00101001
222.201.42.0	00101010
222.201.43.0	00101011
222.201.44.0	00101100
222.201.45.0	00101101
222.201.46.0	00101110
222.201.47.0	00101111

Notice that all eight addresses have the first 2 octets (16-bits) in common. After that, the third octet changes. However when we view them in binary, we can see that they all have the first 5-bits of the third octet in common. We can see that with 16-bits from the 2 octets and the 5-bits of the third octet all in common, the address we were given (222.201.40.0/21) is actually a single address that represents a block of addresses. Specifically, it represents eight Class C addresses.

A common question that arises is "How do I know when my block ends?" When the first 5-bits of the third octet are no longer identical to the rest of your address, your block ends. Look at the binary form of 48, the next address in the line. It is 00110000. It no longer matches our 5-bit pattern 00101. In that case, it is not a part of our block of address space.

> **Note:**   *You will be given the address block in the form noted above, 222.201.40.0/21. You now know that this single address represents eight Class C addresses. Once the space is assigned, it is your job to efficiently deploy these eight Class C addresses in your internetwork, just as if each one had been assigned separately. You will need to plan, subnet, and deploy each of the eight addresses.*

Variable Length Subnet Masks (VLSMs)

VLSMs, defined in RFC 1009, have been around the internetworking industry for a number of years. It is far from a new technology. It is a methodology for reducing the amount of wasted IP address space on small networks, specifically point-to-point serial links.

The first point that we need to stress is that not all routing protocols support the use of VLSM. In order for VLSM to be supported, the routing protocol must be able to pass the prefix in routing updates. Protocols such as Routing Information Protocol (RIP) and Interior Gateway Routing Protocol (IGRP) do not include the prefix (such as subnet mask—remember?) in their routing updates. Therefore, they cannot advertise varied-length masks. Figure 6.3 shows two routers connected via a point-to-point serial link.

As you can see, we have deployed our address space according to the mask we came up with earlier. However, on a point-to-point serial link, only two of those addresses are used. We lose a net of 252 addresses, which is wasted space. Wasting space is not efficient deployment of scarce resources. VLSM is the answer to the problem.

As we mentioned earlier, the routing protocol must include the prefix in routing updates in order to support VLSM. If your routing protocol does not support passing the prefix, you cannot use VLSM. OSPF and Enhanced Interior Gateway Routing Protocol (EIGRP) are examples of protocols that can include prefix information in routing updates.

VLSM Methodology

To use VLSM, you must already have an internetwork design and address space allocation plan in place. Once you have decided on the subnet mask to use, in our case 255.255.255.0, you should pick a single subnet and remove it from any plans of deployment. We are going to further subdivide this address. With the wide range of address space we have available in our example, singling one out should not be a problem. We will use 172.16.30.0 255.255.255.0 as the lucky subnet.

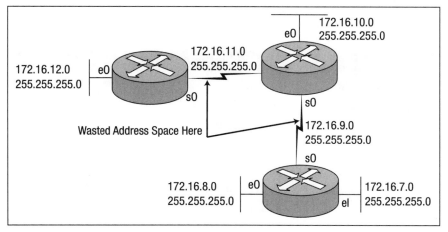

Figure 6.3 A VLSM candidate network example.

At this point, 172.16.30.0 255.255.255.0 is a single network that happens to be a piece of a larger hierarchy. We will treat this address as if it were the natural form of the address, even though we know it is not.

The procedure is simply to re-apply the same rules of engagement that we used when choosing a subnet mask for our overall internetwork. Ask the same questions. How many hosts do I need on each network? In this case, a point-to-point link, we need only two. How many additional bits do I need the router to look at in order to render two hosts? The current mask (255.255.255.0) should be able to give two hosts if we change it to the value 255.255.255.252, 30 consecutive ones followed by two zeros.

How many new subnets did I get from further subdividing the one? We gave it six additional bits, so apply the formula: $2^6 - 2 = 62$ subnets. Table 6.9 shows the subnets we just created.

> *Note:*   *You cannot use the address that was set aside for VLSM anywhere else in the network unless it is a deployment of one of the subnets derived from applying the new mask. In this example, you may not use the network 172.16.30.0 255.255.255.0 anywhere else in the internetwork. Doing so causes unpredictable results.*

We now have 62 new networks for use on serial links; we are no longer wasting space by deploying too many addresses for a single network. Figure 6.4 shows our new address deployment with VLSM in place.

VLSM was designed to work according to the rules we've set forth here, using address space removed from deployment for the specific use on serial links. However, the question "Can't I simply alter the mask anywhere I want?" arises. Yes, technically you can, but we don't recommend it. If you are running multiple routing protocols (one that supports VLSM, one that does not), VLSM

Table 6.9 VLSM Subnets.	
VLSM Calculation	**Subnets**
Original Address:	172.16.30.0 255.255.255.0
New Address:	172.16.30.0 255.255.255.252
New Subnets:	172.16.30.0 to 172.16.30.3
	172.16.30.4 to 172.16.30.5
	172.16.30.6 to 172.16.30.7
	172.16.30.252 to 172.16.30.255

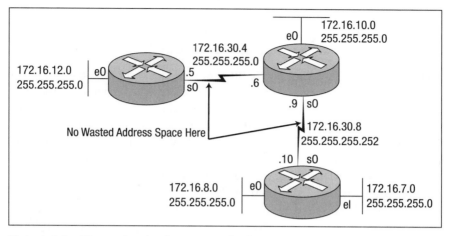

Figure 6.4   The network after VLSM deployment.

can cause reachability issues. Assume you are running RIP and OSPF in a single internetwork and you are using VLSM for serial links as discussed above.

The issue is that the VLSM-capable protocol is passing specific network and mask information in the updates. Since the non-VLSM-capable protocol does not understand the mask information in the updates, it ignores this information. Now the RIP router might be able to see the same network through two interfaces, which could be in opposite directions. The routing protocol cannot distinguish between the two networks. That limitation causes an attempt to forward data to either of the two VLSM networks to be ineffective.

 It is important to know when and when not to use VLSM and the appropriate use for VLSM networks on serial links, or other low volume subnets.

Longest Match

Routers function on the principle of *longest match*. This means that the router, in making path determination decisions, is simply looking at the 32-bit string in the destination IP address field of the packet to attempt to find a routing table match. It may not always have an exact match, so it will base the routing decision on the entry in the routing table that provides the closest to an exact match. This is known as the longest match in the routing table. Knowing this nifty piece of information gives us some very versatile functionality in the router.

Intelligent forwarding abilities focus in on a single key element, the prefix, which we discussed earlier in this chapter. At that point, it was simply an abbreviation of the subnet mask. However, if we could manipulate the prefix in a way that allows us to give reachability to the same number of networks using fewer entries in a routing table, that would be a useful tool.

Consider this analogy. Your phone number is unique. Only you have it. What makes it unique? We already discussed this earlier in this chapter, right? The combination of the area code, prefix, and exchange creates a globally unique identifier. Think of placing a long distance call. We are going to call the (fictitious) phone number (817) 555-4444 in Fort Worth, Texas. The call is being placed from Palo Alto, California. Do the telephone switches in Palo Alto have to know exact information about every phone number in the nation? Do they have an entry for (817) 555-4444? No. Think about what the switches need to know to make a decision. They need know only 817. That is enough information to tell them that the destination is somewhere other than local. The switches can decide where to route the call based on the area code; they route the call to a central office (CO) in Fort Worth, Texas.

Once they have routed the call to Fort Worth, the switches see that 817 just is not enough information, so they have entries that are more specific. The 817 switch (assuming it is not the final-destination switch) need know only (817) 555 to decide where to forward the call. Once the call arrives at the destination switch, it needs port-specific information, (817) 555-4444, to know where to send a ring to make the phone alert you to an incoming call.

Routing data works on the same basic principle. All you need to keep in a routing table is enough information to allow you to make an accurate decision. You need a longest match. However, the longest match does not necessarily have to be long.

In order to avoid maintaining unnecessary information in the routing table, routes to similar destinations can be summarized at various points. This process is known as *route summarization*. Summary routes keep the routing table smaller than it would be otherwise, increasing the speed of the routing table lookup process. Summarization also decreases overall memory utilization because there is a smaller amount of information overall in the router. Do not let the router keep information it does not need to keep. If you can give it an area code, why give it the full phone number?

Route Summarization

You can manipulate routers to cause an overall reduction in the size of the routing table. It takes some careful planning, but it is well worth it for the benefits. We have already discussed many of the benefits: lower processor and memory utilization and so on. Figure 6.5 represents a network that is a candidate for route summarization.

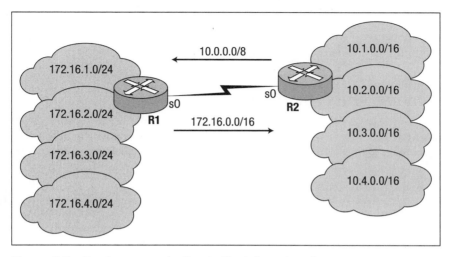

Figure 6.5 Route summarization in the internetwork.

In this example, R1 is attached directly or indirectly to many 172.16.X.0 networks. R1 can represent 254 networks. However, R1 need pass only a single route entry to its neighbor, R2. That single route is the pathway to 172.16.0.0 255.255.0.0. In fact, in this example, no other networks begin with 172.X.X.X. So, we can send into R2 a single summary that specifies 172.0.0.0 255.0.0.0. You may be saying to yourself, "Hey, that is not a legal address, it is a Class B." Actually, it is perfectly legal. Remember that all the router needs is a match in the routing table long enough to make the routing decision. If none of the other entries in the table is 172, then it will be the longest match. Table 6.10 illustrates an example of the entries in R1's routing table as well as R2's routing table with the summary routes that have been advertised to both.

In the same manner, R2 can advertise a single route to network 10.0.0.0 255.0.0.0, no matter how many 10.X.X.X networks happen to be out there.

Table 6.10 Routing tables with summarization.	
R1 Routing Table	**R2 Routing Table**
172.16.1.0/24	10.1.0.0/16
172.16.2.0/24	10.2.0.0/16
172.16.3.0/24	10.3.0.0/16
172.16.4.0/24	10.4.0.0/16
10.0.0.0/8	**172.16.0.0/16**

Note: *For summarization to work, you must exercise caution when deploying IP addresses. If even a single 172.X.X.X network is attached to R2, the summary address will lead to a routing inconsistency.*

Summarization Methodology

Route summarization focuses on reducing the routing tables of all routers in the network. It is generally performed at the edge routers at the border between two address domains, as we saw in Table 6.10. Otherwise all routers would have to keep all of the networks in Figure 6.2. Summarization is based on finding a bit boundary where multiple addresses share a common bit pattern. Table 6.11 shows an example of how to find a bit boundary.

You can summarize these routing table entries into a single statement. To create a summary address, simply find a point in one or more of the addresses where there are bits in common. Notice that all of the binary representations of the third octet begin with 10101. They all have the first 5-bits in common. Actually, when you look at the entire address, you can see that all of the addresses have 21-bits in common. The differences lie in the last 3-bits of the third octet. Using the last 3-bits as the only variable bits in the address, we can create a single address to represent all eight networks with a single routing table entry: 172.16.168.0 255.255.248.0.

As with VLSM, the routing protocol must be capable of passing the prefix along with routing updates in order to support route summarization. It is important that you understand summary addresses and where to place them.

Table 6.11	Summarizing addresses.	
Routing Table	**Third Octet Binary Value**	**Summary Address**
172.16.168.0	168 = 10101000	
172.16.169.0	169 = 10101001	
172.16.170.0	170 = 10101010	
172.16.171.0	171 = 10101011	172.16.168.0/21
172.16.172.0	172 = 10101100	
172.16.173.0	173 = 10101101	
172.16.174.0	174 = 10101110	
172.16.175.0	175 = 10101111	

Network Address Translation

As we noted earlier in the chapter, you can acquire registered address space for your internetwork, or you can simply use the space defined by RFC 1918 for private internetwork use. Should you decide to use the private space, does that mean you cannot connect to the public Internet? No. You can still connect to the public Internet using a somewhat new technology known as *Network Address Translation (NAT)*.

With NAT, you simply deploy the private space within your internetwork as we have described throughout this chapter. The added step is that you need a device that is NAT capable. As of version 11.2, Cisco's enterprise Internetwork Operating System (IOS) software meets this requirement. Other devices that can implement NAT are Cisco's PIX Firewall and many proxy server software programs. How you do it makes no difference.

NAT functions by detecting traffic destined for the Internet and simply mapping that private, unregistered address to a valid registered address on the way out. The NAT device keeps a translation table to facilitate the bi-directional passing of traffic.

When you configure NAT, you also create a pool of registered addresses. You can statically map addresses from their private values to their registered counterparts. Or, you can create a dynamic registered IP address pool in which addresses are assigned on the fly.

When you are deciding how many registered addresses to obtain for NAT purposes, you need to consider a number of factors, including:

➤ Identifying the hosts that do not need external access. You don't want to obtain too many or too few addresses.

➤ Filtering private addresses from being advertised into the Internet.

➤ Changing IP addresses from private to public, which requires time. You will experience additional transmission delay due to processor time to perform the translation.

Practice Questions

Question 1

> How many bits does an IP address consist of?
>
> ○ a. 64
>
> ○ b. 1
>
> ○ c. 32
>
> ○ d. 96

Answer c is correct. IP addresses consist of 32 bits. Answers a, b, and d are incorrect because they are not valid values for IP address lengths.

Question 2

> What are the two parts of all layer 3 protocol addresses? [Choose the two best answers]
>
> ❑ a. Network
>
> ❑ b. Host
>
> ❑ c. Range
>
> ❑ d. Boundary

Answers a and b are correct. Any layer 3 protocol address consists of network and node (or host) portions. In this lies their routability. Answer c is incorrect because it is not a valid piece of information for a network-layer address. Answer d is incorrect for a similar reason. Although we do discuss bit boundaries, or the boundary between network and host, the boundary is not a part of the address itself.

Question 3

How is the class of an address determined?

○ a. Value of the first octet

○ b. Value of the second octet

○ c. Value of the third octet

○ d. Value of the fourth octet

Answer a is correct. The value of the first octet in binary, specifically the first few bits will dictate class. Refer back to the chapter for specific address ranges. The values of the other octets have no bearing on the class of the address. Therefore, answers b, c and d are incorrect.

Question 4

What is the Class A range?

○ a. 1 through 126

○ b. 128 through 191

○ c. 192 through 223

○ d. 224 through 239

Answer a is correct. Technically, Class A is defined by value of the most significant bit. If it is a zero, the address will be Class A. The mathematical range is 0 through 127. However, we are not allowed to use 0 for address space, and 127 is reserved for diagnostic loopback addressing. Therefore, the range is 1 through 126. Since none of the other ranges begin with the proper bit pattern, answers b, c and d are incorrect.

Question 5

What is the Class B range?

○ a. 224 through 239

○ b. 1 through 126

○ c. 192 through 223

○ d. 128 through 191

Answer d is correct. If the two highest-order bits are set to 1 and 0, respectively, the address will be Class B. Since none of the other ranges begin with the proper bit pattern, answers a, b and c are incorrect.

Question 6

What is the Class C range?

○ a. 1 through 126

○ b. 192 through 223

○ c. 128 through 191

○ d. 224 through 239

Answer b is correct. If the three highest-order bits are 1, 1, and 0, respectively, the address will be Class C. Since none of the other ranges begin with the proper bit pattern, answers a, c and d are incorrect.

Question 7

What piece of information allows a router or other device to distinguish between network and host portions of an IP address?

○ a. Longest match

○ b. Subnet mask

○ c. VLSM

○ d. Class

Answer b is correct. The mask defines a string of ones followed by a string of zeros. The point at which the ones stop and the zeros start is the distinction between network and host. Answer a is incorrect since longest match is the principle routers use to make forwarding decisions, not for subnetting. Answer c is incorrect since VLSM is a method of address deployment once the mask has been determined and further subdivided. Answer d is incorrect since class is determined by the value of the high order bits of the address, not the mask.

Question 8

> What is the function that is performed on the IP address and mask to derive the actual subnet address?
>
> ○ a. Longest Match
>
> ○ b. Prefix
>
> ○ c. Logical AND
>
> ○ d. VLSM

Answer c is correct. The AND process is done by converting both the address and mask to binary the comparing each bit position vertically. If both bits are 1, the result is a 1. If either bit is a 0, regardless of the value of the other bit, the result is a 0. Answer a is incorrect since longest match is the principle routers use to make forwarding decisions, not for subnetting. Answer b is incorrect since prefix is another name for the mask itself, not the function of deriving a network address. Answer d is incorrect since VLSM is a method of address deployment once the mask has been determined and further subdivided.

Question 9

> If you have an IP address with a 26-bit prefix, what is the mask?
>
> ○ a. 255.255.255.0
>
> ○ b. 255.255.224.0
>
> ○ c. 255.248.0.0
>
> ○ d. 255.255.255.192

Answer d is correct. The rest of the answers do not have enough ones in them to make up a 26-bit prefix. The prefix is simply a string of contiguous ones. If we have a /26 prefix, that means our mask should be 11111111.11111111.11111111.11000000, which converts to 255.255.255.192. Therefore, answers a, b, and c are incorrect since they do not contain the appropriate number of contiguous 1s.

Question 10

What is the process of mapping private internal addresses to registered public addresses is known as?

○ a. Network Address Translation

○ b. Subnet Masking

○ c. Address Summarizations

○ d. Classless Interdomain Routing

Answer a is correct. Network Address Translation (NAT) is used specifically for purposes of allowing access to the public Internet without having to readdress the existing network. Subnet Masking is the process of dividing up the address space you have internally. Therefore, answer b is incorrect. Address Summarization, otherwise known as route summarization, is the process of reducing the routing table reduction through aggregating addresses based on a common bit boundary. Therefore, answer c is incorrect. Classless Interdomain Routing gives us the ability to conserve address space by giving you as close as possible to the number of addresses you need, rather than wasting addresses needlessly. Therefore, answer d is incorrect.

Need To Know More?

 Huitema, Christian. *Routing in the Internet*, Prentice Hall, Jersey City, NJ, 1995. ISBN 0-13132-192-7. It focuses on basic internetwork architecture and addressing. It is a well-written book for a basic-level to an advanced-level audience.

 For more information on VLSM, CIDR, and summarization, visit **www.cisco.com** and perform searches for these keywords.

 Visit **www.cis.ohio-state.edu/htbin/rfc/rfc-index.html** and you'll be able to download any RFC, whether complete or in progress. Related topics to this chapter are RFC 1812 defines subnet masking, RFC 1009 defines VLSM, RFC 1918 defines private address space, RFC 1631 defines NAT, and RFCs 1517, 1518, and 1519 define CIDR.

Open Shortest Path First (OSPF)

7

Terms you'll need to understand:

√ Neighbors

√ Adjacency

√ Hellos

√ Areas

√ Multiaccess versus non-broadcast multiaccess (NBMA) networks

√ OSPF neighbor discovery

√ OSPF network discovery

√ Area types

√ Router types

√ Virtual links

Techniques you'll need to master:

√ Understanding why OSPF is better than Routing Information Protocol (RIP)

√ Configuring OSPF for operation in a single-area environment

√ Understanding changes necessary to expand OSPF to a multi-area environment

√ Configuring route summaries

√ Verifying configurations with **show** commands

√ Configuring virtual links

With this chapter, we begin discussing the features, use, and configuration of advanced routing protocols. OSPF, which was developed in the 1980s specifically to overcome the limitations of RIP, is one of the more advanced routing protocols. This chapter explores why OSPF is better than RIP and how to deploy OSPF in the network if you have determined that OSPF provides a better fit than RIP for your network. We'll look at how OSPF works in a single-area (small) network as well as in a much larger, multi-area network. We'll discuss detailed configurations for OSPF in both types of deployments. We'll also explore how OSPF locates other routers, how OSPF obtains and maintains its database, and how the routing table is generated.

OSPF Vs. RIP

OSPF (a link-state protocol) was designed to improve upon RIP (a distance-vector protocol). First specified as OSPF version 1 in RFC 1131, later as version 2 in RFC 1247, and most recently in RFC 2328, OSPF has become a worthy standards-based replacement for RIP, which has severe limitations. OSPF's primary features include:

➤ **Fast convergence** Because of RIP's holddown timer, it is quite slow to converge, or adapt to topology changes: It takes minutes to age and purge defunct routes. Slow convergence is a big issue in today's networks—your internetwork must be able to adapt quickly to changes in routing pathways and reachability. OSPF spreads updates quickly and is much faster at healing the network after an outage.

➤ **No hop count limits** RIP has a maximum hop count of 15. This limitation is necessary for eliminating routing loops in distance-vector protocols. OSPF has no limit based on hops, allowing it to support much larger networks.

➤ **Supports Variable Length Subnet Masks (VLSMs)** RIP version 1 does not allow VLSMs because it does not advertise subnet masks. RIP learns the subnet mask associated with a class A, B, or C network by using an address within that network number found on one of the router's interfaces. RIP's summarization is done by another router's including only the classful A, B, or C network address, not subnets, in its updates. Summarization in RIP is limited to inclusion of the shortest hop-count path to a non-attached full class A, B, or C network address in the routing table. OSPF allows the use of VLSMs to create hierarchical routing environments. The size of the routing table can be reduced (a must considering we're using OSPF for very large networks).

➤ **Path selection metric is bandwidth based** RIP uses hop count as its metric, but is blind to the link's speed. Originally, this was adequate because everything in the local area network (LAN) was very fast (for example, 10Mbps). In addition, everything in the wide area network (WAN) was fairly homogeneous at 56Kbps or so. Hop count was great when all links were considered identical because the only difference between one route and another was how many routers (hops) were in between the two networks. OSPF may use a metric related to the inverse of the bandwidth, that is, the higher the speed of the circuit, the lower the metric. Cisco's default begins with 100Mbps divided by the bandwidth of the circuit (for example, 10Mbps Ethernet would have the metric of 10).

➤ **Update efficiency** RIP simply copies its entire routing table (except as limited by split horizon) out of every interface periodically, whether or not changes are necessary. In a large network, this could be a burden. OSPF normally sends only changes, and then only when the change happens. In a large, stable network, the update traffic from OSPF should be negligible.

Overview Of OSPF

Once the router is configured for OSPF, it must initiate the process of learning its environment. OSPF goes through several phases of initialization.

> *Note: OSPF is complex, and it is easy to get bogged down in the details. This overview uses OSPF terms defined later in the chapter and saves most of the explanation for later. We do this because if you have already confronted OSPF, you're ready for an overall view. If this is the first time you've heard of OSPF, you'll probably need to read this section once quickly, read the rest of the single-area part of the chapter, and then re-read this section.*

Identifying Neighbors With Hellos

The first step in the initialization process is that the OSPF router must identify other routers who are its neighbors—that is, other routers who share subnets with it. OSPF routers learn about neighbors using multicast Hellos from their OSPF-configured interfaces. These Hellos identify neighbors and keep the OSPF router aware of the neighbor's up/down status.

OSPF Hellos happen by default every 10 seconds. If a router doesn't hear its neighbor before its own dead timer fires (usually, four times the Hello timer), the router can assume the link (and maybe the router) is down. This fact leads to a common misconception about OSPF. OSPF does reconverge after an outage very quickly, but OSPF cannot start the reconvergence until it knows its neighbor has gone away. Either the layer 2 Keepalive or the Hellos could declare the link down. If it is from the Keepalives that the router notices the problem, it will take an average of 25 seconds to miss three Keepalives. Then the flooding and recalculation of the routing table (described below) begins. It is usually assumed that OSPF will take 30-42 seconds to notice a failure and reconverge.

Developing Adjacencies

After identifying and tracking neighbors with Hellos, OSPF learns network information in two distinct ways. First, they use the neighbor information to establish adjacencies with each other. An *adjacency* is a relationship that provides the basis for exchanging routing update information. We're willing to share our innermost secrets with adjacent neighbors. The adjacency means that I'll give you a copy of my entire routing database (not routing table) as soon as the adjacency is created. Each router adds database details it learns from its partner in the *adjacency* to its own database. On point-to-point links, adjacencies are established with all neighbors (there is only one neighbor). On multi-access networks, OSPF has a mechanism to limit the number of adjacencies, and therefore the amount of update traffic. A designated router (DR) and a backup designated router (BDR) are elected, and all neighbors establish adjacencies with them only. The second way OSPF learns network information is by running the Shortest Path First (SPF) algorithm to produce a graph from which to extract the routing table.

> Building the routing table is relatively simple. The routing table contains destination network, outbound interface, next hop address, and cost to that network. If a router has 4 neighbors on its attached interfaces and 1,000 destinations, all 1,000 destinations have one of the 4 attached routers as its next hop (except for those on connected routes).

Flooding

After the initial exchange of database information, OSPF learns of and integrates network changes by using a very different mechanism called *flooding*. As soon as a router learns of a state change on one of its own connected links, it immediately floods an update that contains information on only the changed link—not the entire database—to all of its adjacent neighbors. The neighbors change their local databases and continue flooding the change.

The flooding should take only a couple seconds, but that time and the SPF calculation time depend on the network's size. SPF is a computationally intense algorithm. On small routers with lower-speed processors, flooding can take a relatively long time and use a relatively large amount of memory. We'll see that one of the reasons for using a multi-area OSPF is to hold down the processing load, memory volume, and the eventual routing table search time.

As soon as the database is changed, a new SPF update must be run. As you will remember with distance-vector protocols, there was a problem with freshness of the information. OSPF uses sequence numbering and reliable transfers (they must be acknowledged) to make certain the flooded information is current.

Multiple routers may report one change to a link (depending on how things are connected). If the network has slow update paths, it is possible (read "likely") that if we run the SPF update immediately upon receiving the flooded change, other changes come in during the SPF cycle, resulting in an immediate recalculation. Essentially, we might get into a continuous flurry of SPF updates (this happened in earlier versions). The solution is to dampen the update frequency or delay of the beginning of the first SPF calculation (the Cisco default is five seconds). In addition, we'll delay between consecutive SPF calculations (a default of 10 seconds). As a result, reconvergence is delayed, but it is usually a good tradeoff.

> *Note:* Remember that a feature of OSPF is that all routers recalculate for every change no matter how minor (another reason for multi-area operation for larger networks).

Link-state protocols such as OSPF also flood link-state updates periodically (the default is 30 minutes) to make certain, even with all the reliability features in place, that every router's tables are correct. This periodic update is known as a *paranoid update*.

> *Note:* Neither the ACRC class nor the NP test go into every detail of OSPF operation. You may want to read the RFC, all 200+ pages, and visit the Cisco Web site for more detail.

OSPF Single-Area Operation

An OSPF network consists of nodes (routers) and the links that connect them. OSPF maintains a database (not the routing table) of all neighbor routers and all active links in its universe. The total amount of information could grow without end if there weren't separate areas. *Areas* allow you to create subsets of the OSPF network. Each router in an area must maintain an identical database to that of every other router in the area. In small networks, with up to 70 routers, you can use a single area referred to as *Area 0*. Figure 7.1 illustrates the terminology used in an OSPF network.

Links connect *nodes*. Each link exists as a router-link in the database. Each link has a *cost* associated with it that the OSPF routers use as a metric (least-cost sum) to determine the best path to each destination network. Cisco has traditionally used a cost related to bandwidth (using the formula 100,000,000/BW). For example, a 56Kbps link has a cost of 1,785 associated with it, whereas a 100Mbps Fiber Distributed Data Interface (FDDI) link has a cost of 1. Link speeds have grown rapidly (for example, much faster than 100Mbps), so Cisco has added a command to allow you to increase the 100Mbps figure, thereby allowing for higher-bandwidth links to be handled correctly.

Learning Initial Database Information

The first phase of network learning starts with routers learning of each other and performing immediate, initial exchanges of their current databases. Neighbor router discovery starts with Hellos. As soon as all the routers know about all other routers, they begin the exchange protocol—the way they learn initial routing database information.

OSPF issues a number of differing packets. These packets, shown in Table 7.1, are function-specific entities, each with its own special mission.

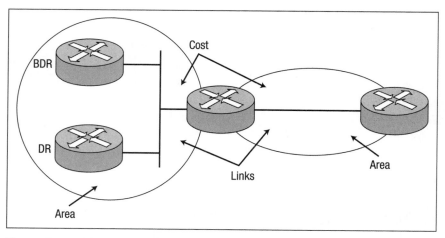

Figure 7.1 OSPF terminology.

Table 7.1 OSPF packet types.	
Type Code	**Description**
1	Hello
2	Database Description (DD or DBD or DDP)
3	Link-State Request (LSR)
4	Link-State Update (LSU)
5	Link-State Acknowledgment (LSA)

The Hello Protocol

OSPF uses a Hello protocol to discover other routers and decide how to interact with them. Once the relationships have been established, OSPF uses Hellos as Keepalives to learn when other routers go away. Hello messages are used to discover neighbors (routers that share links with *this* router) and are sent to the IP multicast address 224.0.0.5, an address to which all OSPF routers (and only OSPF routers) respond. Hellos contain the following fields:

➤ **Router-ID** A 32-bit value that uniquely identifies a router. It is chosen by looking at all interfaces and choosing the IP address with the highest numeric value. If a loopback interface has been configured with an IP address, it overrides the value of any physical interface and the highest value on any loopback interface is chosen. To be selected as router-id, the interface does not need to be one that OSPF itself uses. Once that value is chosen, it remains even if another interface with a higher value is activated later.

➤ **Hello/Dead Intervals** Hello intervals represent the time between Keepalive messages. If a router doesn't receive a Hello from a neighbor within the dead interval, the silent router is declared down and loses status as a neighbor. The typical Hello interval (10 seconds) and the dead interval are four times the Hello frequency (40 seconds).

➤ **Neighbors** Routers that share the same link. Actually, routers go through several stages before they become full partners (develop an adjacency).

➤ **Area-ID** A numeric value shared by all routers in an area.

➤ **Router Priority** A number that may be used to select a DR. The normal selection is done by router priority, with router-id being used as a tiebreaker. If no priority were chosen, the DR would become the router with the largest router-id and the BDR would be the router with the second highest router-ID.

➤ **DR IP Address** The router that acts as distributor of information for this multi-access segment. Essentially, it is used to hold down the number of adjacencies on multiaccess links.

➤ **BDR IP Address** The backup for the DR. It waits for half a second to hear DR flooding updates. If the DR doesn't do its job, the BDR pre-empts and passes the updates to all adjacent routers. A new BDR is then elected.

➤ **Authentication Type** Used to provide secure updates (optional).

➤ **Authentication Password** Authentication password (if used).

➤ **Stub Area Flag** An area with only one point of contact with the rest of OSPF and no connections to outside routing protocols. We will expand on this description later in this chapter.

A router starts out the state by saying Hello to the multicast 224.0.0.5 (all OSPF routers) which lists all neighbors it has heard Hellos from in the last dead interval. If things are just starting, the router is in a down state and no neighbors are in the Hello message.

As soon as a router hears a Hello from another router, the state machine of *this* router moves to *Init*, which means "I've heard from you within the last dead interval but we're not truly neighbors yet." This router's Hello packets include the list of all neighbors from whom it has heard Hellos within the last dead interval.

Listing 7.1 shows an EtherPeek display of a basic Hello packet. The high-lighted fields in the Hello packet must be identical for any routers you wish to be neighbors.

> *Note:* *You may change all of the timers. However, often you may not know the full impact of these changes (immediately), causing strange and unpredictable results.*

Listing 7.1 EtherPeek display of a basic Hello packet.

```
IP Header - Internet Protocol Datagram
   Version:            4
   Header Length:      5
   Precedence:         6
   Type of Service:    %000
   Unused:             %00
   Total Length:       64
```

```
Identifier:              0
Fragmentation Flags:     %000
Fragment Offset:         0
Time To Live:            1
IP Type:                 0x59  OSPF
Header Checksum:         0xce9a
Source IP Address:       10.0.0.6
Dest. IP Address:        224.0.0.5
No Internet Datagram Options
OSPF - Open Shortest Path First Routing Protocol
Version:                 2
Type:                    1  Hello
Packet Length:           44
Router IP Address:       172.16.64.6
Area ID:                 0
Checksum:                0x1088
Authentication Type:     0  No Authentication
Authentication Data:
--------          00 00 00 00 00 00 00 00
Network Mask:            0xff000000
Hello Interval:          10  seconds
Options:                 %00000010
        No AS External Link State Advertisements
Router Priority:         1
Dead Interval:           40  seconds
Designated Router:       0.0.0.0  No Desgntd Rtr
Backup Designated Router: 0.0.0.0  No Backup Desgntd Rtr
```

Neighbors

When your router sees its own Router-ID listed in the neighbor list of the Hello packet from one of its neighbors, the state of their relationship moves to *two-way*. The routers on a broadcast multiaccess network elect a DR and a BDR.

The election proceeds as follows: Each router's Hello packet lists the interface address of the router that the Hello-sending router believes to be the DR. Priority values start at 0 (never a DR), to 1 or more. The router with the numerically highest priority value wins the DR election. The router with the second highest priority is the BDR. If no priorities have been specified, the router with the largest Router-ID wins. The router ID is defined as the numerically highest IP address on any active interface on a router. It is possible to hard code the router's ID. To force the router's ID to be a certain address always, create a logical loopback interface and assign an IP address (no matter how high or low).

The election finishes when all the routers have settled on a DR and BDR. Now the router is ready to begin creating adjacencies, meaning we're ready to swap initial database information.

DR election is not necessary on point-to-point networks because both routers form an adjacency. The purpose of the DR/BDR scheme is to minimize the number of adjacencies on multi-access networks.

Adjacencies

On point-to-point links, each router can share with its neighbor (there is only one neighbor). However, on a multiaccess network such as Ethernet, the number of connections (adjacencies) would be too large. As a result, with this initial database exchange and with the flooding of network changes later on, you would require far more bandwidth, far larger databases, and more recalculation time. Electing the DR and BDR solve the problem of many adjacencies. Figure 7.2 shows how using a BDR allows you to have fewer adjacencies.

The number of connections between n devices is $(n \times (n - 1)) / 2$. So, if 10 routers shared a LAN segment (a large number before LAN switching), we would need $(10 \times 9) / 2$, or 45, adjacencies. If we established adjacencies with only the DR and BDR, the same number of devices would need only $2 \times (n - 1)$, or 18, adjacencies.

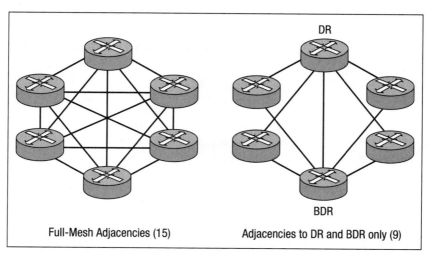

Full-Mesh Adjacencies (15)   Adjacencies to DR and BDR only (9)

Figure 7.2   Adjacencies with and without DR and BDR.

Listing 7.2 shows the router interface as well as some of the more interesting details of OSPF. The command used to generate this response is **show ip ospf interface Ethernet 0**.

Listing 7.2   OSPF interface parameters.

```
Ethernet0 is up, line protocol is up
  Internet Address 10.0.0.1/8, Area 0
  Process ID 1, Router ID 172.16.32.1, Network Type BROADCAST,
Cost: 10
  Transmit Delay is 1 sec, State DROTHER, Priority 1
  Designated Router (ID) 172.16.64.8, Interface address 10.0.0.8
  Backup Designated router (ID) 172.16.64.7, Interface address
    10.0.0.7
  Timer intervals configured, Hello 10, Dead 40, Wait 40,
    Retransmit 5
  Hello due in 00:00:07
  Neighbor Count is 7, Adjacent neighbor count is 2
    Adjacent with neighbor 172.16.64.7  (Backup Designated Router)
    Adjacent with neighbor 172.16.64.8  (Designated Router)
  Suppress hello for 0 neighbor(s)
```

Some of the things of particular interest in this listing include the IP address of the router's Ethernet 0 interface, the Router-ID and Area, the Hello and Dead intervals, and the Router Priority. This is a good example of the concept of OSPF using a DR to limit the adjacencies on a multiaccess network. Look at the Neighbor Count and the Adjacent neighbor count, then look below that line to see who is adjacent: only the DR and BDR. The network is a broadcast network, not a point-to-point or NBMA network configuration. Examples of NBMA networks are frame relay, X.25, Integrated Services Digital Network (ISDN), and Asynchronous Transfer Mode (ATM).

 NBMA versus the other types of networks is an important concept to grasp. Essentially, you select the DR and BDR with the router priority. In addition, periodic Hellos are replaced with less frequently transmitted polls.

ExStart

Once the adjacencies are established, the routers move to *ExStart* state in order to prepare for the initial database exchange. The router over each adjacency decides a master/slave relationship. This decides which router transfers and which router listens. The master is the router with the highest interface address. At this same time, the sequence numbers that will be used to exchange the databases are decided.

Exchange

The master sends and the slave acknowledges the Database Description (DD or sometimes DBD) packets. The DD packets contain summary information of the entire master router's database. After the master finishes, the slave member of the adjacency dumps all of its database in DD packets to the master. Both routers use Link State Acknowledgements (LSAs) to verify that things have gone as expected. Otherwise, retransmissions take place.

Loading

At this time, the routers enter the *Loading* state and may begin sending Link State Requests (LSRs) to any neighbor. They may also receive Link State Updates (LSUs) from any neighbor in the Exchange state asking about more recent information on routes learned in the summary exchange. Of course, the LSUs are carried in LSAs.

> **Note:** *Be aware that the LSA can also mean Link State Announcement and that there are several kinds of Link State Announcements.*

Full

Eventually, when the databases of both routers are identical, the routers show the state between them as *Full*.

Route Calculation And Cost

At this stage, all routers have identical databases. The routers run (actually have been running) the SPF calculation and build the forwarding database. OSPF uses cost as a metric, so the SPF algorithm builds a loop-free topology using the costs stored for each interface in the router-links database. To see a summary listing of the neighbors, use the command **show ip ospf neighbors**. Listing 7.3 shows a list of routers and their states summarized.

Listing 7.3   Neighbor status summary.

```
Neighbor ID   Pri State          Dead Time   Address       Interface
172.16.32.2   1   FULL/BDR       00:00:37    172.16.32.2   ATM0.9
172.16.32.4   1   FULL/DR        00:00:30    172.16.32.4   ATM0.9
172.16.32.2   1   2WAY/DROTHER   00:00:37    10.0.0.2      Ethernet0
172.16.64.7   1   FULL/BDR       00:00:36    10.0.0.7      Ethernet0
172.16.64.6   1   2WAY/DROTHER   00:00:36    10.0.0.6      Ethernet0
172.16.64.5   1   2WAY/DROTHER   00:00:30    10.0.0.5      Ethernet0
172.16.32.4   1   2WAY/DROTHER   00:00:30    10.0.0.4      Ethernet0
172.16.64.8   1   FULL/DR        00:00:39    10.0.0.8      Ethernet0
10.0.0.3      1   2WAY/DROTHER   00:00:39    10.0.0.3      Ethernet0
```

Listing 7.3 includes nine routers. If even one of the routers had been configured with a Dead timer that was 39 seconds (rather than the default 40 seconds), that router could never become a neighbor (or adjacent, which is the basis for continuing the process). The routers must agree on the Dead timer. The best advice is don't change anything. If you must, make certain that the parameter being changed is set to the same value in all routers that share the area.

Maintaining The Routing Table

Now that the routers have formed their adjacencies and shared their routing databases initially, it's time to move on to the normal operation of the network. The routers continue their Hellos and monitor their links. As soon as the state of a link changes, the attached router needs to tell every other router as soon as possible. The technique used is referred to as flooding.

Flooded Updates

For the rest of the lifetime of these routers, they send LSUs, which indicate changes to a link to which they are attached. LSUs are also known as Link State Advertisements (LSAs). In other words, phase one is over; we have complete databases. Now in phase two, we use flooding to maintain the databases.

When a router notices a change in one of its links, it generates an LSU and forwards it to the DR and BDR using the 224.0.0.6 (known as "all designated routers") address. The DR then sends the LSU to every adjacent OSPF router on the link using the 224.0.0.5 (all OSPF routers) multicast address. Each router must send an LSA (Link State Acknowledgment—LSAck) back to the DR; otherwise, the LSU goes into a retransmission queue.

The BDR heard the original message to the DR and sets an internal timer (.5 second default). Should the timer fire before the DR starts sending the LSU back to everyone, the BDR takes over the update process and a new BDR election is held. If a router that had been DR comes back up after a failure, does it become DR again? No—if the DR goes down, the BDR is promoted to DR, then an election for a new BDR is initiated. Should the original DR come back online, it does not get its job back, even though it may have a higher priority. If the new DR goes down, the new BDR is promoted into its place. Another election is forced, and the original DR gets the BDR job. At this point, it takes a DR failure for the original router to regain the DR title. Confused? In short, the DR role is not dynamically maintained. It loses its job if it cannot perform its function. It does not get it back unless the new DR fails and then the new BDR (which moves into the DR position and forces a new election for BDR) fails once it has been promoted (in that order). Only a BDR can become the DR if a DR fails.

All routers that receive the LSU flood it out of each interface to all of their adjacent neighbors on other OSPF-configured interfaces. Thus, the change packet is carried to all routers in the area quickly.

Maintaining The Topology Database

Flooding essentially consists of LSUs being spread around to every router in the area. This flooding happens when a link changes state, or every 30 minutes, whichever comes first. When an LSU is received, the router immediately compares it with the contents of the topology database. The resulting action depends on the state of the database as described below:

➤ If the entry already exists but contains same information, the aging timer is reset and an LSA is sent back to the DR. The router determines the information is the same by examining the sequence number.

➤ If the entry exists but the received LSU contains new information or if the entry doesn't exist, the router sends an LSR that asks for details about the entry to the original sender of the LSU. As a result, another LSU is sent to back to the router asking for the update from the original sender.

➤ If the entry exists but contains older information, the router sends an LSU with the newer information back to the source of the original LSU.

Link-State Announcement Types

There are several types of LSAs, each of which represents a different kind of information. They represent the information that will be held in the OSPF database. Be sure not to confuse them with OSPF packet types, which are not the same thing. Table 7.2 lists the LSA types.

Table 7.2	LSA types.
Type Code	**Description**
1	Router LSA (Router Link-States)
2	Network LSA (Net Link-States)
3	Network Summary LSA (Summary Link-States)
4	ASBR Summary LSA (not shown in Listing 7.4 later in this chapter)
5	AS External LSA (not shown)
7	NSSA External LSA (not shown)

For example, Router LSAs (Type 1) contain information about the links in the network. A link is identified by a combination of Router-ID and link identifier; both identifiers look like IP addresses. You can view these records as well as the rest of the LSAs by using the **show ip ospf database** command. Listing 7.4 shows a part of an OSPF database.

Listing 7.4   OSPF database.

```
OSPF Router with ID (172.16.32.1) (Process ID 1)

                Router Link States (Area 0)

Link ID          ADV Router      Age     Seq#        Checksum Link count
10.0.0.3         10.0.0.3        231     0x80000003 0xAF3E   1
172.16.32.1      172.16.32.1     229     0x80000003 0x3618   1
172.16.32.2      172.16.32.2     231     0x80000003 0x3417   1
172.16.32.4      172.16.32.4     226     0x80000003 0x3015   1
172.16.64.5      172.16.64.5     226     0x80000003 0xEB16   1
172.16.64.6      172.16.64.6     232     0x80000003 0xE915   1
172.16.64.7      172.16.64.7     232     0x80000003 0xE714   1
172.16.64.8      172.16.64.8     230     0x80000003 0xE513   1

                Net Link States (Area 0)

Link ID          ADV Router        Age       Seq#        Checksum
10.0.0.8         172.16.64.8       227       0x80000002 0xFD53

                Summary Net Link States (Area 0)

Link ID          ADV Router        Age       Seq#        Checksum
172.16.32.0      172.16.32.1       109       0x80000003 0x2F50
172.16.32.0      172.16.32.2       85        0x80000001 0x2D53
172.16.32.0      172.16.32.4       113       0x80000003 0x1D5F
172.16.64.0      172.16.64.5       70        0x80000001 0xD864
172.16.64.0      172.16.64.6       61        0x80000001 0xD269
172.16.64.0      172.16.64.7       79        0x80000003 0xC870
172.16.64.0      172.16.64.8       75        0x80000003 0xC275

                Router Link States (Area 1)

Link ID      ADV Router      Age       Seq#        Checksum Link count
172.16.32.1 172.16.32.1     122       0x80000004 0xDCD7   1
```

The Router LSAs are generated by routers that describe links to which they are attached. Network LSAs are generated by DRs.

Later in this chapter, we'll look at the difference between single- and multi-area OSPF operation and configuration. At that time, we will discuss the other LSAs shown as well as Area 1 in Listing 7.4. Summary LSAs are generated by Area Border Routers (ABRs), which describe links in areas to which they are attached. LSA Type 4 and Type 5 are generated by Autonomous System Boundary Routers (ASBRs); Type 7 LSAs provide information about external connections through Not So Stubby Areas (NSSAs).

Configuring Single-Area OSPF

It's quite simple to set up OSPF for single-area operation. The OSPF configuration is almost identical to the configuration for RIP and other routing protocols. The statements to do so are illustrated in Listing 7.5.

Listing 7.5   Single-area OSPF configuration.

```
interface Ethernet 0
ip address 10.0.1.1 255.255.255.0
!
interface Ethernet 1
ip address 10.0.2.1 255.255.255.0
!
interface Serial 0
ip address 172.16.5.1 255.255.255.0
!
interface Serial 1
ip address 172.16.6.1 255.255.255.0
!
router ospf 1
network 10.0.0.0 0.255.255.255 area 0
network 172.16.5.1 0.0.0.0 area 0
```

Listing 7.5 shows that an OSPF routing process has been created. It listens and advertises routes on interfaces Ethernet 0 and 1 and Serial 0. The **network** statement in OSPF differs from that of other protocols (RIP, Interior Gateway Routing Protocol—IGRP—and Enhanced Interior Gateway Routing Protocol—EIGRP) by using a wildcard mask (the same technique as that used with access lists) to select one or more interfaces. The statement for **network 10.0.0.0** includes any subnet and any host. If the router's interface matches the pattern, the interface belongs to OSPF.

Notice how the statement for 172.16.5.1 must match the interface address exactly. This specific selection of interfaces from a single IP address is unique to OSPF.

Each interface must be assigned to an area by including the area number with each **network** statement. In this example, the first area is Area 0. Area 0 is the backbone area to which all other areas must attach. In a single-area deployment, you have only Area 0 in your internetwork. You must therefore specify all OSPF interfaces using a **network** statement.

One final item to note—the 1 in **router ospf 1** is a process ID number. It is arbitrary and is not advertised between routers but can be used to allow more than one OSPF routing process running in a single router.

OSPF Multi-Area Operation

Single-area OSPF is simple to configure. If your network has fewer than 70 routers (opinions vary—some say that between 30 and 70 is a good number), don't bother creating a multi-area environment unless you have some specific issues that we will mention later. The concept of an area is simply your ability to create a subset of the network routers to reduce processing or complexity. Areas allow use of VLSM to form routing hierarchies to limit detail while maintaining reachability.

Why Multiple Areas?

Now we'll examine the reasons why multiple areas for OSPF networks might be desirable when not indicated specifically by the number of routers. Proper design of a network can make even RIP work very well up to a fairly large number of routers. OSPF was designed for very large networks with hundreds or potentially thousands of networks. Keep this concept of "large" in mind as we discuss the issues below.

Too Many Routes

The fewer the number of routes in the routing table, the faster the router can look up destinations for datagrams. In addition, having fewer routes means:

➤ Less memory dedicated to routing tables

➤ Less bandwidth for passing routing updates

➤ Less processing to produce correct routes

If it were possible to summarize the information, providing a single summary address to represent a group of subnets, reachability would be maintained. However, by losing the subnet detail updates, memory usage and overall processing would be reduced.

Slow Updating Portions Of The Network

In some networks, even though the LSAs are flooded, SPF calculations can become out of synchronization with each other. For example, in parts of your internetwork where slow paths exist to remote networks, an SPF calculation in a router might run without having received all of the update information.

The resulting network routing tables are broken (for example, not fully converged, but unaware of that fact) because OSPF believes it has perfect knowledge of the network and calculates its tables based on the concept of its seemingly perfect information. The best-case scenario is that the routing table would be fixed by running SPF again (after a 10-second delay); the worst-case scenario is that the network might become partitioned (isolated from the rest of the internetwork).

Thrashing Due To Rapid Network Changes

Another reason to form areas is to keep network changes from thrashing all of the routers. For example, a flapping interface or maybe dial-on-demand routing (DDR) to other OSPF routers (for more information on DDR, see Chapter 13) would cause a flood of updates to all routers requiring that they run the SPF calculation over and over again in a never-ending cycle to form a new routing table. Each time the link went up or down, *every single router* in the area would go through the SPF calculation. Effectively, the routing of data comes to a halt in this type of situation.

Area Types

With multiple areas, the OSPF configuration becomes much more complex. One of the first topics of concern is the separation of areas into types and the assignment of roles to individual routers. In the multi-area model, a number of variations are possible for each area. OSPF has several types of areas, which are illustrated in Figure 7.3.

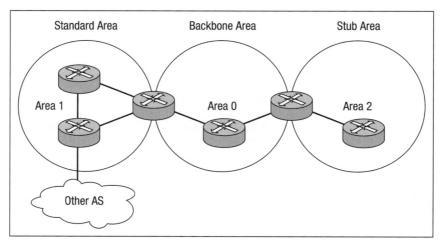

Figure 7.3 OSPF area types.

Backbone

The *backbone*, known as a *transit* area, is always Area 0. As mentioned earlier, all OSPF networks must have an Area 0. All traffic between other areas must flow through the backbone area. All kinds of routes (all LSA types) are present in Area 0.

Address summaries collect in the backbone and are either advertised to other areas or not advertised (depending on the type of area involved). We'll discuss the route advertisement or lack of route advertisement in just a bit.

Standard Areas

Areas other than Area 0 are referred to as *standard areas*. They receive all types of routing summary and external route information (unless you can fit them into one of the other area types). The other area types provide hierarchical routing because they limit the types of routes (LSAs) they'll accept.

Stub Areas

Areas that connect to the backbone and do not connect to other Autonomous Systems (ASes) are referred to as *stub areas*. It is possible to reach all routes external to this AS with a default route. ABRs attached to stub areas block the external route information, injecting a default route instead. Summary routes are sent into stub areas. All routers in a stub area still have full knowledge of intra-area routes.

Totally Stubby Areas

Cisco uses a special term for stub areas that connect to Area 0 with only one router: *totally stubby areas*. In this case, even summary routes are blocked. The routers in a totally stubby area do not see external routes or summary routes; only the default route is available to reach the rest of the world. Besides the default route, they know only their intra-area routes.

> **Note:**   *There is one more kind of area, the Not So Stubby Area (NSSA). It is not significantly covered in ACRC and will not be on the test. Therefore, we will not cover it here.*

Router Types

To support all of the differing area types, you specify specific router roles. These different router types provide different kinds of services to each area type. OSPF assigns routers roles based on where the individual routers fit into the hierarchy both physically and logically. Figure 7.4 illustrates OSPF router types and their relationship with areas. Note that a router can fit the description of multiple roles.

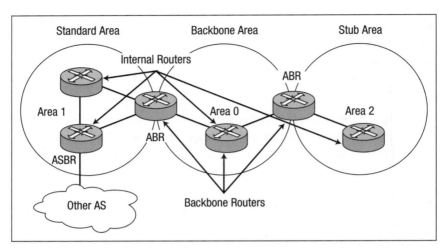

Figure 7.4 OSPF router types.

Internal Routers

An *internal router* has all of its interfaces in a single area. The area can be a backbone, standard, stub, or totally stubby area.

Backbone Routers

A *backbone router* has at least one interface in Area 0. It is can also be an internal router, which means that all of the interfaces in this router are in Area 0.

ABRs

ABRs have at least one interface in Area 0 but have interfaces in one or more other areas. ABRs are the only source of OSPF inter-area routes and route summaries.

It is important to keep the concept of a summary route separate from the concept of a summarized route. All OSPF inter-area routes are generated in ABRs and are called *summary routes*. In the ABR, you can also create a *summarized route*, which is a single route with a shorter prefix (subnet mask) to represent routes to all of the included subnets. This summarized route is advertised to other standard areas and stub areas but not to totally stubby areas.

ASBRs

An ASBR connects to other ASes. An ASBR may be in the backbone or a standard area, but not in a stub or totally stubby area. An ASBR is the source of external routes and external route summaries.

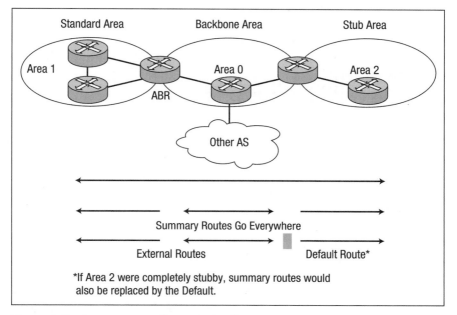

Figure 7.5   Inter-area traffic and LSA flows.

The flow of routing updates between differing types of areas and differing router roles can be complex. Only specific types of LSAs can flow into and out of particular areas. Figure 7.5 specifies which types of LSAs can flow into and out of areas.

Configuring OSPF For Multiple Areas

Initially configuring multiple areas is almost identical to doing so for single areas. Listing 7.6 shows how to configure multiple areas and stub areas. Notice the entry for Serial 0 points to a regular area, Serial 1 points to a stub area, and Serial 2 points to a totally stubby area. Looking at the statements for stub area 2, you can see an example of assigning a default cost for all routes being redistributed into the area.

Listing 7.6   OSPF multiple-area and stub-area configuration.

```
interface Ethernet 0
ip address 10.0.1.1 255.255.255.0
!
interface Ethernet 1
ip address 10.0.2.1 255.255.255.0
!
interface Serial 0
ip address 172.16.5.1 255.255.255.0
```

```
!
interface Serial 1
ip address 172.16.6.1 255.255.255.0
!
interface Serial 2
ip address 172.16.7.1 255.255.255.0
!
router ospf 1
network 10.0.0.0 0.255.255.255 area 0
network 172.16.5.1 0.0.0.0 area 1
network 172.16.6.1 0.0.0.0 area 2
area 2 stub
area 2 default-cost 10
network 172.16.7.1 0.0.0.0 area 3
area 3 stub no-summary
```

Configuring Route Summarization

Figure 7.6 shows route summarization. In it, we'll assume that there are several subnets in Area 1 that use the 172.31.0.0 private Class B address. Furthermore, assume that because you planned the network properly, the subnets are contained in the range of addresses from 172.31.32.0 to 172.31.63.0. Notice in Figure 7.6 that all subnets in the desired range share the high-order bits in the third octet. By shortening the prefix (subnet mask length), you can represent the whole range of subnets with a single entry. Route summarization is covered in more detail in Chapter 6.

You must keep all subnets in the same range within a single area (for example, they must be contiguous) in order to effectively deploy summarization. OSPF is a classless protocol and finds rogue subnets that are within your summary but are placed in other areas. This makes it difficult to summarize. Be aware that you will find unpredictable results. It is important to remember that one of the most influential reasons for choosing OSPF as your routing protocol in the first place was its ability to perform this summarization function. In many cases, organizations converting to OSPF readdress all or most of the internetwork before taking on the formidable task of internetwork conversion to OSPF.

Starting Subnet:	172.31. 00100000.0
Ending Subnet:	172.31. 00111111.0
Default Prefix:	255.255.11111111.0
Summary Prefix:	255.255.11100000.0
Binary	

Figure 7.6 Route summarization.

It is essential to note that you must configure summarization in both direc-tions (for example, into Area 0 and into the non-Area 0 areas). In Listing 7.7, we've summarized the routes for both Area 0 and Area 1. Remember also that OSPF does not automatically summarize any routes at any time. If you don't manually configure summarization, you see every possible network in each router's routing table.

In Listing 7.7, notice the summary for the Class C address. The prefix is exactly the natural subnet mask for a Class C address. RIP, IGRP, and EIGRP would automatically generate a Class C network address and redistribute that as the route. With OSPF, you must lay out the network correctly and you must do any summarization manually. Listing 7.7 shows route summarization manually.

Listing 7.7   Route summarization.

```
router ospf 1
network 192.168.1.0 0.0.0.255 area 0
network 172.16.0.0 0.0.255.255 area 1
area 1 range 172.16.32.0 255.255.224.0
area 0 range 192.168.1.0 255.255.255.0
```

External Routes And Summarization

External routes are learned from another AS or another routing protocol within the same AS whose routes have been redistributed. These routes require manual redistribution (see Chapter 9), and you need to apply appropriate metrics for the redistributed routes. OSPF provides for Type 1 (E1) and Type 2 (E2) ex-ternal routes—the difference being that E1 metrics include both the internal, OSPF-generated cost, and the external cost from the redistribution point. The E2 metric, which is the default, uses only the external cost. The idea is that you use E1 metrics if you have multiple external contact points and you need to find the closest one.

You can choose to redistribute individual routes or route summaries from the ASBR. The summarization for an external route is shown in Listing 7.8.

Listing 7.8   OSPF external route summaries.

```
!
router ospf 1
network 10.0.0.0 0.255.255.255 area 0
redistribute rip subnets
address-summary 172.24.0.0 255.255.0.0
!
router rip
network 172.25.0.0
network 172.24.0.0
```

The address summary shows the command used with external routes. The area range statement shown in Listing 7.7 deals with OSPF native routes. Listing 7.8 shows a summary to some of the 172.24.0.0 subnets. The **subnets** statement for 172.25.0.0 indicates that there are probably multiple ASBRs and you need to keep track of which subnets are reached via which ASBR (note that in a real situation, you would probably also use distribute lists, covered in Chapter 9).

Virtual Links

So far, the discussion has been about point-to-point, multi-access, NBMA, and links. In addition, we've mentioned that all areas must connect directly to Area 0. There are times when this requirement is just not convenient. OSPF provides a *virtual link* for the purpose of extending Area 0 to an attachment point across a transit area. Figure 7.7 shows a scenario where you use virtual links. Listings 7.9 and 7.10 detail the configuration necessary for the virtual link.

Listing 7.9   Configuring Router A.

```
router ospf 1
network 172.16.0.0 0.0.255.255 area 0
network 172.17.0.0 0.0.255.255 area 2
area 2 virtual-link 172.18.44.211
```

Listing 7.10   Configuring Router B.

```
router ospf 1
network 172.17.0.0 0.0.255.255 area 2
network 172.18.0.0 0.0.255.255 area 4
area 2 virtual-link 172.17.220.5
```

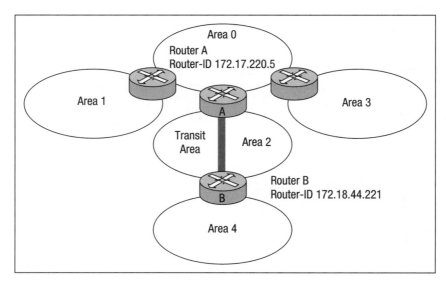

Figure 7.7   Virtual links.

Notice that the **virtual-link** statement connects the router IDs of the routers at the ends of the link. Also take note that the area number specified in the **virtual-link** statement is the transit area (for example, the area the virtual link must traverse to reach Area 0). Finally, remember that one of the routers must to be connected to Area 0.

Practice Questions

Question 1

What are some of the reasons OSPF is better than RIP in a large network? [Choose the three best answers]

- ❏ a. No hop count limit
- ❏ b. Bandwidth-based metrics
- ❏ c. Lower processor utilization
- ❏ d. Faster convergence

Answers a, b, and d are correct. Lack of hop limitations, the use of cost based on bandwidth as a metric, and faster convergence make OSPF a great choice for larger internetworks. Answer c is incorrect because SPF calculation takes much more processing than does RIP.

Question 2

What is an internal router?

- ○ a. A backbone router.
- ○ b. A router that connects multiple areas together.
- ○ c. A router that connects to an external AS.
- ○ d. A router that has all interfaces in a single OSPF area.

Answer d is correct. All interfaces must be within a single area. Although an internal router can also be a backbone router, that is not the only factor (being a backbone router is possible without being an internal router). Therefore, answer a is incorrect. Answer b is incorrect because a router that connects multiple areas together is an ABR. Answer c is incorrect because a router that connects to an external AS is an ASBR.

Question 3

What databases does OSPF use? [Choose the three best answers]

❑ a. IP host database

❑ b. Adjacencies database

❑ c. Topology database

❑ d. Routing table or forwarding database

Answers b, c, and d are correct. OSPF keeps an adjacencies database that lists neighbor routers, a topology database that gives it a map of the network, and a routing table on which to base forwarding decisions. Answer a is incorrect because IP host entries in the router have nothing to do with OSPF.

Question 4

What is contained in the topology database?

○ a. Neighbors

○ b. All routes

○ c. Best routes

○ d. Address of the designated router

Answer b is correct. All possible routes to all destinations are kept in the topology table. Answer a is incorrect because neighbor information is kept in the adjacencies database. Answer c is incorrect because the best routes are kept in the routing table or forwarding database. Answer d is incorrect because the DR is used with multi-access networks to limit the number of adjacencies and the amount of traffic.

Question 5

What are the different phases OSPF uses to learn information for its topology database? [Choose the two best answers]

❑ a. Exchange protocol

❑ b. Hellos

❑ c. Flooding protocol

❑ d. Link State Acknowledgements

Answers a and c are correct. OSPF routers initially identify neighbors and exchange or trade their entire databases to that point. After this is finished, OSPF moves on to the normal operation phase, where changes are flooded to all routers in the area. Answer b is incorrect because the Hellos are just part of both phases. Answer d is incorrect because the LSA is just part of the flooding process.

Need To Know More?

 Doyle, Jeff. *CCIE Professional Development: Routing TCP/IP Volume 1*. Macmillan Technical Publishing, Indianapolis, IN, 1998. ISBN 1-57870-041-8. Chapters 11 through 13 discuss related topics.

 Huitema, Christian. *Routing in the Internet*. Prentice-Hall, Englewood Cliffs, NJ, 1995. ISBN 0-13132-192-7. This is an excellent protocol book. Read Chapters 4 through 6 for more information on routing protocols.

 Perlman, Radia. *Interconnections: Bridges and Routers*. Addison-Wesley, Reading, PA, 1992. ISBN 0-201-56332-0. Chapter 9 provides a discussion of link-state and distance-vector protocols. Chapter 10 is about OSPF by one of the senior players in the history of protocol development.

 Stevens, W. Richard. *TCP/IP Illustrated: The Protocols*. Addison-Wesley Publishing Company, Reading, MA, 1994. ISBN 0-20163-346-9 v. 1). Chapter 10 covers the routing protocols.

 Cisco's Web site, **www.cisco.com**, includes white papers and router documentation about bridging and its logical extension, switching.

Enhanced IGRP

Terms you'll need to understand:

√ Hybrid routing protocol

√ Autonomous system

√ Neighbor router

√ Neighbor table

√ Topology table

√ Routing table

√ Current successor

√ Feasible successor

√ Route summarization

Techniques you'll need to master:

√ Configuring Enhanced Interior Gateway Routing Protocol (EIGRP) for IP

√ Configuring EIGRP route summarization

√ Configuring EIGRP for Internetwork Packet eXchange (IPX)

In this chapter, we will discuss the Cisco proprietary hybrid routing protocol Enhanced Interior Gateway Routing Protocol (EIGRP). EIGRP was developed to overcome many of Routing Information Protocol's (RIP) limitations such as the 15-hop limitation or the inability to support VLSM and/or route summarization. Unlike the other routing protocols discussed at different points throughout this book, EIGRP was not designed as a strictly IP routing protocol. EIGRP can also take the place of Internetwork Packet eXchange (IPX) RIP. In many ways, EIGRP acts as a link state routing protocol. In other ways, it resembles a distance vector routing protocol. To that end, it is also known as an "advanced distance vector" routing protocol.

EIGRP Basics

EIGRP was developed to provide a single routing protocol solution in a multiprotocol environment. You can use EIGRP, designed by Cisco as a proprietary routing protocol, to provide reachability to remote networks in IP, IPX, and AppleTalk environments. Rather than using three separate routing protocols to manage these three routed protocols, EIGRP provides a single solution to meet the network's needs.

Where Did It Come From?

The principle behind EIGRP is based on distance vector technology. Each router does not necessarily need to know all the router/link relationships for the entire network. Individual routers advertise destinations with a corresponding distance. Every router that hears the information adjusts the distance and propagates the information to neighboring routers. The distance information in IGRP is represented as a composite of available bandwidth, delay, load utilization, link reliability and maximum transmittable unit (MTU). This allows fine-tuning of link characteristics to achieve optimal paths.

How Does It Work?

EIGRP uses the Diffusing Update Algorithm (DUAL) to achieve a loop-free network at every instant throughout route computation. DUAL allows all routers involved in a topology change to synchronize at the same time. Routers that are not affected by topology changes are not involved in the recomputation of updated routing information. EIGRP has been extended to be independent of layer 3 protocols, thereby allowing DUAL to support other protocol suites.

EIGRP has four main components in its operation:

➤ Neighbor discovery/recovery

➤ Reliable transport protocol

➤ DUAL finite state machine

➤ Protocol-dependent modules

Neighbor discovery is the process of instigating a "hello" protocol outbound on each active interface in order to discover routers that are directly connected to the same networks. It is also used to learn if those routers have dropped off the network for whatever reason.

The *reliable transport protocol* is responsible for guaranteed and ordered delivery of EIGRP packets to all neighbors. For efficiency, reliability is provided only when necessary.

The *DUAL finite state machine* represents the intelligence of the decision process for all route computations. It tracks the routes that all neighbors advertise. DUAL uses the distance information, known as a *metric*, to select efficient loop-free paths.

The *protocol-dependent modules* are responsible for each specific network-layer protocol. For example, the IP-EIGRP module is responsible for sending and receiving EIGRP packets for IP operations. There is an additional module for IPX and one more for AppleTalk. These processes are completely independent of each other. The routing of multiple protocols in an environment where one routed protocol has no effect whatsoever on another is known as "ships in the night" routing.

Dynamic Routing Protocols

EIGRP is known as a hybrid routing protocol. In other words, it doesn't fall under the descriptions of traditional routing protocols. Traditional routing protocols are either distance vector or link state. EIGRP is neither. In creating EIGRP, Cisco has taken the parts we like best about both types of protocols.

Distance Vector Protocols

Distance vector protocols tend to be relatively slow when it comes to convergence; however, they also tend to consume a much lower amount of overall router resources (RAM, CPU, and so on). Distance vector devices view the network from the point of view of their directly connected neighbors. They have very little first-hand information. They obtain all information (except that which deals with directly connected networks) from their neighbors, who obtained it from their neighbors, and so on. This type of information sharing is sometimes known as *routing by rumor*. Distance vector protocols operate on update timers and triggered updates. When the update timer expires, the routing table is broadcast out of each active interface. If there are no changes in the routing table, updates are still broadcast out. The end result of this is wasted bandwidth.

Link State Protocols

Link state protocols tend to be extremely fast when it comes to convergence. That sounds great until you look at the amount of additional resources the link state routing process requires in the router. Link state protocols tend to be quite taxing on system resources, because they are keeping so much information in memory. As a result, link state protocols, such as OSPF, can waste memory space. Unlike distance vector routing protocols, link state routing protocols send updates only when necessary. When a network change is detected, a routing update is triggered and only the changes are flooded out of the interfaces. This flood of packets, known as *link state advertisements (LSAs)*, goes to every router in the area.

Getting To The Point

EIGRP, being neither distance vector nor link state, is actually a combination of the things we like best about both types of protocols. It combines very fast convergence with lower memory requirements and less processor utilization. It gets its speed and efficiency by acting as a link state protocol to its neighbors and a distance vector protocol to the rest of the internetwork. Consider Figure 8.1, which shows an example of an EIGRP network. If Router A found it

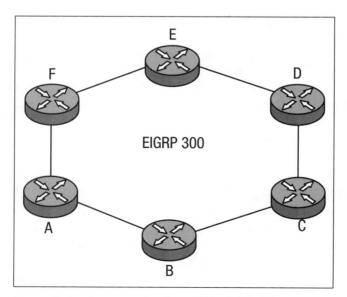

Figure 8.1   An example of an EIGRP network.

necessary to send an update, to which routers would it go? With a link state protocol, all routers would receive the update and forward it to their neighbors in a flooding pattern. EIGRP is no different from a link state protocol in that it sends the update instantly to its neighbors. However, EIGRP does not use the flooding concept. When a routing change is necessary, EIGRP simply updates the directly connected neighbors, who then update their neighbors. The result is a better behaved update process.

EIGRP knows about all of the routers' directly connected neighbors. It knows about all the networks in the internetwork through those neighbors. EIGRP is basically distance vector to the rest of the network. The only information it knows is the distance to get to that network and to which neighbor to forward packets destined for a particular network.

Route Calculation Considerations

As we mentioned earlier, EIGRP uses the concept of distance as a metric. This distance is derived through a composite calculation. The values used in this computation are known as *k values*. The values are, in order of precedence, as follows:

➤ Bandwidth

➤ Delay

➤ Reliability

➤ Load

➤ MTU

By default, all *k* values except bandwidth and delay are set to zero unless they are needed. This method of calculation using a composite metric gives bandwidth the priority over all other values in route calculation. The faster the links between source and destination, the better the route.

> ***Note:*** *Bandwidth is the primary metric for route determination, so it is imperative that all interfaces, especially serial interfaces, know their bandwidth. The default bandwidth of a serial interface is 1.544Mbps. In other words, if you have a 64Kbps link, you must issue the command **bandwidth 64**. Otherwise, the EIGRP route calculations will be incorrect. The bandwidth command is illustrated in the figures within this chapter.*

As mentioned above, distance is the product of the route calculation. The lower the distance representation, the better the route.

In order to support these processes and keep them efficient, EIGRP keeps three tables in memory at any given time. These tables are as follows:

➤ Neighbor table

➤ Topology table

➤ Routing table

 By default the route calculation uses Bandwidth and Delay. It will use the remaining values when necessary to serve as tie-breakers.

Neighbor Table

The *neighbor table* is very similar to what it sounds like. It is a listing of directly connected neighbors. When a router learns about new neighbors, it records each neighbors' address and interface. This information is stored in the neighbor data structure. Listing 8.1 shows output of the **show ip eigrp neighbors** command.

Listing 8.1 show ip eigrp neighbors command.

```
R1#show ip eigrp neighbors
IP-EIGRP neighbors for process 100
H   Address         Interface Hold Uptime   SRTT  RTO Q  Seq
                              (sec)              (ms)  Cnt Num
1   10.0.0.2        Et0        12 00:02:45    1   200 0  1
0   144.254.100.2 AT0.1       10 00:02:46    0  4500 0  2
```

The Address column indicates the address of the directly connected neighbor. The Interface column designates the outbound interface to get to that particular neighbor. When a neighbor sends a hello, it advertises a HoldTime. The *HoldTime* is the amount of time for which a router treats a neighbor as reachable and operational. In other words, if a hello packet isn't heard within the HoldTime, the HoldTime expires. When the HoldTime expires, DUAL is informed of the topology change. Sequence numbers are employed to match acknowledgments with data packets. The receiving router records the last sequence number it received from the neighbor so that it can detect out-of-order packets.

Topology Table

The *topology table* contains all destinations that neighboring routers advertise as well as the interfaces through which to dispatch packets destined for those networks. Notice that each of the routes in Listing 8.2 (which shows the **show** ip eigrp topology command) is designated as a successor. We will discuss the meaning of successors later on in this chapter.

Listing 8.2   show ip eigrp topology command output.

```
R1#sh ip eigrp topology
IP-EIGRP Topology Table for process 100

Codes: P - Passive, A - Active, U - Update, Q - Query, R - Reply,
       r - Reply status

P 144.254.100.0/24, 1 successors, FD is 18944
        via Connected, ATM0.1
P 10.0.0.0/8, 1 successors, FD is 281600
        via Connected, Ethernet0
P 192.168.1.0/24, 1 successors, FD is 146944
        via 144.254.100.2 (146944/128256), ATM0.1
        via 10.0.0.2 (409600/128256), Ethernet0
P 144.254.0.0/16, 1 successors, FD is 18944
        via Summary (18944/0), Null0
```

Associated with each entry are the destination address and a list of neighbors that have advertised the destination. For each neighbor, the advertised metric is recorded. This is the metric that the neighbor stores in its routing table. If the neighbor is advertising this destination, it must be using the route to forward packets. The output specifies the destination network followed by the number of routes the router has that can get packets to that network. Also noted in Listing 8.2 is feasible distance (FD). Feasible distance is the total distance from R1 (this router) to the listed destination network. We will discuss feasible distance in further detail along with successor routes, later in this chapter.

Routing Table

The *routing table* is the listing of the calculated "best" routes to known destination networks. This routing table reads the same as any other routing table for other routing protocols. Listing 8.3 shows the **show ip route** command.

Listing 8.3   show ip route command output.

```
R1#show ip route
Codes:C-connected, S-static, I-IGRP, R-RIP, M-mobile, B-BGP
      D-EIGRP, EX-EIGRP external, O-OSPF, IA-OSPF inter area
      N1-OSPF NSSA external type 1, N2-OSPF NSSA external type2
      E1-OSPF external type 1, E2-OSPF external type 2, E-EGP
      i-IS-IS,L1-IS-IS level-1,L2-IS-IS level-2,*-candidate default
      U - per-user static route, o - ODR
```

```
Gateway of last resort is not set

C 10.0.0.0/8 is directly connected, Ethernet0
D 192.168.1.0/24 [90/146944] via 144.254.100.2, 00:22:51, ATM0.1
  144.254.0.0/16 is variably subnetted, 2 subnets, 2 masks
C    144.254.100.0/24 is directly connected, ATM0.1
D    144.254.0.0/16 is a summary, 00:22:51, Null0
  172.30.0.0/24 is subnetted, 1 subnets
C    172.30.1.0 is directly connected, Loopback0
```

Listing 8.3 shows a legend of various routing protocols and codes that go with them. This is to show how the particular route shown in the listing was derived, because it is possible and common to run multiple routing protocols on a single router. The code in the legend matches the letter in the far left-hand column. The codes we have in this table are C and D. The C denotes a directly connected network. The D denotes an EIGRP-derived route. If you read the table left to right, you learn the following information:

➤ How this route was derived.

➤ Destination network address followed by the prefix (subnet mask for that destination address in bit format—the designation of /24 denotes a subnet mask of 255.255.255.0 because the first 24 bits are set to one).

➤ Administrative distance/metric distance (in brackets)

➤ Next hop address

➤ Age of this route

➤ Outbound interface

The routing table is the key to the entire operation of your internetwork. You should monitor it regularly to assure its accuracy.

EIGRP can keep up to six redundant pathways at any given time. This sounds like a typical capability of any routing protocol. However, these six paths do not have to be equal-metric pathways. If an administrator configures a *variance* value under the router EIGRP configuration, it is possible to configure which paths should be used. The variance is a multiplier for traffic sent across sub-optimal routes. For example, if under the router EIGRP configuration, we set the variance to four, the router would send four times the amount of traffic over the best route as it does over the sub-optimal routes. This feature allows for additional load-sharing capabilities and more granular traffic engineering potential that exists in a RIP network.

You will need to know the exact commands to show the information included in the above three sections relating to the neighbor, topology, and routing tables. Review these a few times before taking the exam.

Rights Of Succession

As we saw in Listing 8.3, some routes are designated as successors. A *successor route* is the best route based on available information to this point. The successor is the only route actually kept in the routing table. A secondary route may be kept in the topology table along with the current successor route. This secondary route is known as a *feasible successor*. The criteria for selecting a feasible successor is quite strenuous. Figure 8.2 shows an example of network topology.

The router in question is Router A. Let's view this scenario from the perspective of Router A as the source, and the 172.16.31.0/24 network as the destination network. The distances of each link are listed. The distances listed in the figure are false and are for demonstrative purposes only.

The route with the shortest feasible distance, as noted earlier, is the best route. This route is known as the *current successor*. The current successor is listed in the routing table as the preferential pathway to the destination network.

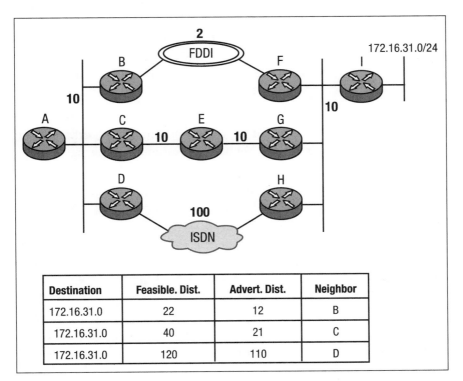

Destination	Feasible. Dist.	Advert. Dist.	Neighbor
172.16.31.0	22	12	B
172.16.31.0	40	21	C
172.16.31.0	120	110	D

Figure 8.2   An EIGRP topology scenario.

Notice that two values are associated with each route. Once is feasible distance, and the other is advertised distance. Recall that in our discussion of hybrid routing protocols, we decided that EIGRP is a little bit link state and a little bit distance vector. Distance vector works on the assumption that Router A's neighbor (Router B) is a certain distance away; therefore, the distance for Router A to get to a destination must be Router B's distance from that destination plus the distance from Router A to Router B. That is precisely the premise we're dealing with when the EIGRP feasible and advertised distances are calculated.

What Is Distance?

Advertised distance is the distance that my neighbors are advertising as their own distance to get to a particular destination, in this case 172.16.31.0. Once Router A has received distance information from all neighbors, it can add the distance to each particular neighbor to those advertised distances to create feasible distance. Therefore, feasible distance is the distance calculated for Router A to reach 172.16.31.0 as a destination network.

Now that we have crowned the best route, it is time to determine if there is a suitable route to fill the role of backup route. This backup route is known as the *feasible successor*. Even though multiple routes may lead to a single destination, as shown in Figure 8.2, a feasible successor is not always selected. In Figure 8.2, the route to network 172.16.31.0 through neighbor B is the current successor because it has the shortest feasible distance. The route through neighbor C is the next best, followed by the route through neighbor D.

Look at the advertised distance of 21 via neighbor C, the second-best route. With that in mind, look at the feasible distance of 22 via neighbor B, the best route. If the advertised distance of the second-best route is shorter than the feasible distance of the best route, the second-best route is designated as the feasible successor.

Should Router B fail, the route via Router C would be immediately updated to the status of current successor. It is important to mention that if the Fiber Distributed Data Interface (FDDI) network goes down, neighbor B sends out to all of its neighbors a routing update concerning only that network. Now that the best route is no longer available, and the feasible successor has been promoted to current successor, it is time to select a new feasible successor if possible. Figure 8.3 shows the new topology of the network.

Apply the rules for crowning a feasible successor to this scenario now. In order for a feasible successor to be selected, the advertised distance of the second-best route must be shorter than the feasible distance of the new best route. The

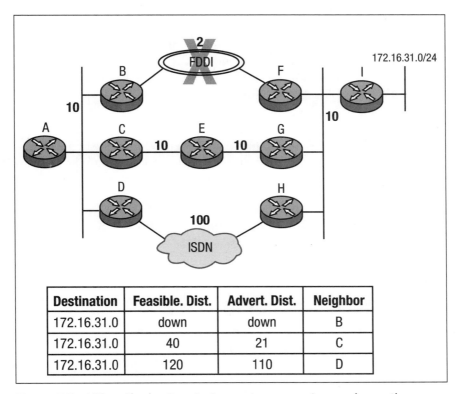

Destination	Feasible. Dist.	Advert. Dist.	Neighbor
172.16.31.0	down	down	B
172.16.31.0	40	21	C
172.16.31.0	120	110	D

Figure 8.3 When the best route (current successor) goes down, the next-best route (feasible successor) is promoted to current successor.

criterion is not met in this case, so the route via neighbor D is not selected as feasible successor. Should the route via neighbor C disappear for some reason, the route via neighbor D is the only alternative. Even so, it is not a feasible successor in the eyes of the algorithm.

If the router cannot find a feasible successor, it issues a route request to its neighbors for a feasible successor route to that specific destination network. If the neighbors can provide the information, the route is installed as feasible successor. Otherwise, the router goes on without a feasible successor.

 Route selection criteria for the current and feasible successors is critical to the overall topology of the network.

Configuring EIGRP For IP

Configuring EIGRP for IP is quite simple. The procedure for basic configuration is the same procedure used in configuring IGRP and RIP. The configuration consists of selecting an Autonomous System (AS) number as well as networks to send updates to. The AS simply consists of all the routers under a common administration. All of the routers in your network that are exchanging route information have the same Autonomous System number. In order to share route information between dissimilar AS numbers, you must configure redistribution. Figure 8.4 shows a basic EIGRP configuration example and Listing 8.4 displays the configuration commands necessary to configure the R1 router in the figure.

Listing 8.4 Configuration commands for Figure 8.4.

```
Interface ethernet 1
ip address 172.16.2.2 255.255.255.0
!
interface ethernet 2
ip address 172.16.5.1 255.255.255.0
!
interface serial 0
ip address 10.12.4.1 255.255.255.0
bandwidth 64
!
router eigrp 400
network 10.0.0.0
network 172.16.0.0
```

Even though there are three interfaces, the configuration requires only the two network statements listed. EIGRP configuration, like that for RIP and IGRP, requires that you specify only the natural network number.

 The AS number must be the same on all routers in the AS. It is important to understand the network statements and their use.

Route Redistribution

Although we address route redistribution in Chapter 9, it is appropriate to address it here to a degree. Redistribution is usually a manual configuration. It is automatically done for you in specific cases. EIGRP encompasses most of those instances.

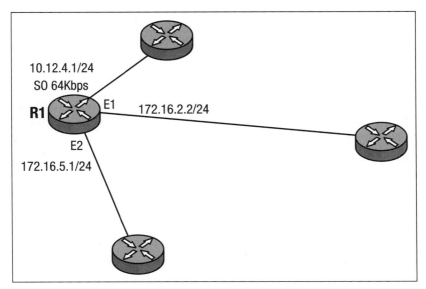

Figure 8.4   Basic EIGRP IP configuration.

In cases where EIGRP and IGRP are being run together on a single router, automatic redistribution is performed if, and only if, the Autonomous System numbers for both routing protocols have been configured identically. Listing 8.5 shows an example of when automatic redistribution between EIGRP and IGRP occurs if both protocols a to be implemented on R1 in Figure 8.4.

Listing 8.5   IGRP and EIGRP together.

```
interface serial 0
ip address 10.12.4.1 255.255.255.0
bandwidth 64
!
router igrp 400
network 10.0.0.0
network 172.16.0.0
passive-interface e1
!
router eigrp 400
network 172.16.0.0
passive-interface e2
```

 If the AS numbers for EIGRP and IGRP are identical, route redistribution between the two protocols is done automatically. If the AS numbers are different, redistribution has to be manually configured.

The code in Listing 8.5 shows that **passive-interfaces** have been implemented. The configuration for EIGRP and IGRP uses the natural network numbers for any given network, so it is necessary to keep each protocol from sending updates out unnecessarily through interfaces where no neighbors are listening for those updates. In this case, we have configured IGRP to be sent out of interfaces Ethernet 0 and Ethernet 2. There is no reason to send IGRP updates out of interface Ethernet 1 if the neighboring router is not an IGRP router. The end result of using passive interfaces is bandwidth conservation.

Route Summarization

EIGRP was designed with some scalability in mind. Route summarization is one of the key elements in scalability. EIGRP is not building a hierarchy in the same manner as Open Shortest Path First (OSPF) does (discussed in Chapter 7). However, it is capable of routing-table reduction. Reducing the overall number of routes in a routing table has the following benefits:

➤ Less memory utilization

➤ Faster routing table lookups

➤ Reduction in delay through the router

When left to its default settings, EIGRP automatically summarizes to the boundaries of natural class. In other words, the summary routes are advertised at the class A, B, or C boundaries. This means that, by default, EIGRP does not support Variable Length Subnet Masks (VLSMs). You can manually override the automatic summarization feature in the EIGRP configuration by using the **no auto-summary** command and placing a summary route. You typically perform such physical configuration of summary route information on the outbound interface on an edge router between two autonomous systems. Figure 8.5 shows an example of EIGRP route summarization. Listing 8.6 details the commands necessary for configuring a summary route.

Listing 8.6 R1 Route summarization configuration.

```
router eigrp 400
network 10.0.0.0
network 172.16.0.0
no auto-summary
!
interface serial 0
ip address 10.1.27.5 255.255.255.0
bandwidth 64
ip summary-address eigrp 400 172.16.0.0 255.255.0.0
```

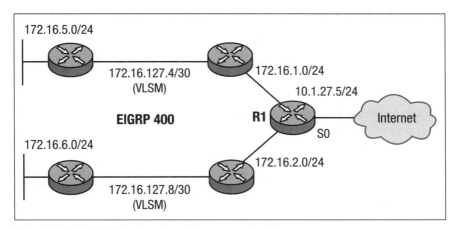

Figure 8.5   EIGRP manual route summarization.

In the above example, all of the 172.16.0.0 networks are advertised out as a single route to the rest of the world. Rather than keeping all of its routes in the external routing tables, the router keeps only a single route that can generalize all of Autonomous System 400's networks. The result is an overall reduction in the number of entries in external routing tables. The reverse scenario could be true. In Autonomous System 400, it is likely that the many routes that may find their way into the internal routing tables are not welcome. Therefore, you can manually force a reduction in the overall number of routes. Route summarization is only one tool that you can use to reduce the size of routing tables. You can also implement default routes and route filtering. Again, the benefits of a correctly summarized routing table tend to far outweigh the consequences.

EIGRP For IPX

EIGRP is a very functional and feature-rich routing protocol for IP. However, it was developed with a layer 3-independent attitude. In other words, it was made to not care what protocol it routes. At this point, Cisco has implemented EIGRP for IP, AppleTalk, and IPX only. We discussed IP in Chapter 3, and AppleTalk is beyond the scope of our discussions in this book.

IPX Basics Revisited

Internetwork Packet eXchange (IPX) is a protocol developed by and for Novell. Novell NetWare environments are exceedingly common in the corporate internetwork infrastructure. Novell implemented IPX as a proprietary communications protocol suite to enable client-server communication in NetWare environments. Recently, Novell has announced a move away from IPX as its core protocol in favor of IP. However, there is a huge number of IPX implementations out there, and it is important to know how to deal with those environments.

IPX functionality rests squarely on two protocols—IPX Routing Information Protocol (RIP) and IPX Service Advertising Protocol (SAP), which are the foundation of any Novell implementation. Without RIP and SAP, Novell clients cannot find the network resources they require for day-to-day operation. However, it is this dependency on RIP and SAP that causes a large number of issues in internetworks.

IPX RIP

Novell's implementation of RIP is almost identical to that of its IP counterpart. Recall that IP RIP is a distance vector routing protocol that broadcasts updates out of all configured interfaces at 30-second intervals. IP RIP uses a hop count as the primary metric. IPX RIP is similar in that it is a distance vector protocol that broadcasts routing updates out of all configured interfaces. However, IPX has a 60-second update interval.

The metric that IPX RIP uses is known as ticks. A *tick* is a measurement of time, specifically 1/18 of 1 second. The use of ticks as a means of route calculation gives IPX RIP an advantage over IP RIP. IPX RIP has an idea of how much time is involved with sending data over a particular pathway, so it can have some notion of bandwidth and delay. If a high-bandwidth link with low delay is traversed, the overall amount of time to get to the destination should also be low. In other words, the result is lower a number of ticks for that specific pathway. Should two pathways be equal with regard to ticks, the number of hops to the destination serves as a tiebreaker to select one as the better route.

IPX SAP

Novell developed SAP to propagate and advertise network server entities. SAP, like RIP is on a 60-second update timer. Novell servers (file servers, print servers, and so on) periodically broadcast information about the services that they provide by broadcasting this information onto their connected local area network (LAN) or wide area network (WAN) interfaces. Routers are required to propagate SAP updates through an IPX network so that all clients can see the service messages. These updates, along with RIP, consume large amounts of bandwidth.

EIGRP For IPX Operations

Cisco developed its implementation of EIGRP for IPX to overcome the amount of bandwidth that IPX RIP and SAP waste. EIGRP can quiet RIP and SAP traffic. By default, on serial interfaces, EIGRP sends RIP and SAP updates only when there is an update to send. If an update is necessary, only the change is sent across the link. In other words, routing updates are sent across the link only when there are routing changes. SAP updates occur only when a new service is added or an existing one is taken out of the table.

Although updates are incremental (only when necessary) on serial links, they continue on the 60-second update interval on LAN interfaces. This is done for the simple reason that on serial links, no NetWare clients or servers need to hear the updates. On LAN interfaces, it is highly possible that there are NetWare clients and/or servers that need to take advantage of those services. NetWare servers are expecting to hear those updates every 60 seconds.

EIGRP For IPX Configuration

Configuring IPX and EIGRP is somewhat similar to configuring IP, discussed earlier. You must select an AS number that is completely independent of the IP AS number. These numbers can be the same, but they don't have to be. You must select the networks that you wish to send EIGRP updates to. Finally, you have to disable IPX RIP on those networks. Figure 8.6 shows a sample configuration of EIGRP for IPX. Listings 8.7 and 8.8 specify the command configurations for the routers in Figure 8.6.

Listing 8.7   R1 configuration.

```
ipx routing
!
interface serial 0
bandwidth 64
ipx network 20
!
interface ethernet 0
ipx network 30
!
ipx router eigrp 500
network 20
!
ipx router rip
no network 20
network 30
```

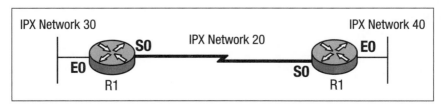

Figure 8.6 Sample EIGRP for IPX configuration.

Listing 8.8   R2 configuration.

```
ipx routing
!
interface serial 0
bandwidth 64
ipx network 20
!
interface ethernet 0
ipx network 40
!
ipx router eigrp 500
network 20
!
ipx router rip
no network 20
network 40
```

The configuration shows the networks configured under **ipx router rip**. In your configuration files, you do not see the commands for the **ipx router rip** configuration. They are default settings. When you enter the **ipx routing** command, **ipx router rip** is automatically turned on and configured for interfaces to which you have assigned IPX network numbers. It is necessary to turn off RIP on those interfaces to stop the 60-second updates from being broadcast out. The configuration of RIP in this manner automatically assumes that the same parameters are to be used for SAP updates. Therefore, no manual SAP configuration is necessary.

As noted earlier, by default, all serial interfaces on which EIGRP is configured are set to incremental updates. In other words, update only when there is a change. LAN interfaces continue on in periodic update manner on a 60-second timer. It is possible to force LAN interfaces onto the same incremental update scheme. Using the **ipx sap-incremental** command forces RIP and SAP updates to cease on specific interfaces. Referring back to Figure 8.5, the use of the command on R1 is shown in Listing 8.9.

Listing 8.9   R1 configuration.

```
ipx routing
!
interface serial 0
bandwidth 64
ipx network 20
!
interface ethernet 0
ipx sap-incremental eigrp 500
ipx network 30
!
```

```
ipx router eigrp 500
network 20
!
ipx router rip
no network 20
network 30
```

> *Note:*   *You should take care when using the **IPX sap-incremental** command. If entities on the network are expecting to hear RIP and SAP at periodic intervals, using this command in effect sabotages reachability and/or services for that particular network.*

Once configured, IPX creates three tables. These tables are the same tables that we discussed in the "Route Calculation Considerations" section earlier in this chapter: the neighbor, topology, and routing tables.

IPX EIGRP Neighbor Table

The neighbor table for IPX, again, is nearly identical to that for IP. Listing 8.10 shows an example.

Listing 8.10   show IPX EIGRP neighbors command output.

```
R1#show ipx eigrp neighbors

IPX EIGRP Neighbors for process 500
H  Address              Interface   Hold Uptime   SRTT  RTO  Q   Seq
                                    (sec)         (ms)       Cnt Num
0  400.0000.0000.0002 AT0.4         10 00:06:05   517  3102  0   5
```

The neighbor information includes the *next hop* address of the neighbor, the interface through which to depart this router, as well as HoldTime for this entry. The "next hop" address is the address on the interface directly connected to the same logical network as is this router.

IPX EIGRP Topology Table

The topology table for IPX includes the same basic information as the IP version of the table. Note that the same terminology has been used in route selection. Feasible successors are listed along with each destination network. Listing 8.11 shows the IPX topology table as constructed by EIGRP.

Listing 8.11   show IPX EIGRP topology command output.

```
R1#show ipx eigrp topology
IPX EIGRP Topology Table for process 500
```

```
Codes: P - Passive, A - Active, U - Update, Q - Query, R - Reply,
       r - Reply status

P 400, 1 successors, FD is 18944
        via Connected, ATM0.4
P 10, 1 successors, FD is 128256
        via Connected, Loopback0
P 20, 1 successors, FD is 146944
        via 400.0000.0000.0002 (146944/128256), ATM0.4
```

IPX EIGRP Routing Table

The IPX routing table includes all of the information you would expect from a routing table. Note that the table now includes the letter E to indicate an EIGRP-derived route. Listing 8.12 shows the IPX routing table as constructed by EIGRP.

Listing 8.12   show IPX route command output.

```
R1#show ipx route
Codes:C-Connected primary network, c-Connected secondary network
      S-Static, F-Floating static, L-Local(internal), W-IPXWAN
      R-RIP, E-EIGRP, N-NLSP, X-External, A-Aggregate
      s-seconds, u-uses

3 Total IPX routes. Up to 1 parallel paths and 16 hops allowed.

No default route known.

C         10 (UNKNOWN),       Lo0
C         400 (SNAP),         AT0.4
E         20 [146944/0] via       400.0000.0000.0002, age 00:09:34,
                            1u, AT0.4
```

The route selection process for IPX is identical to the process discussed in the "Rights of Succession" section earlier in this chapter. A current successor is selected, as is a feasible successor (should a secondary route meet the requirements).

IPX Route Redistribution

Route redistribution for IPX routes is automatic. None of the features we've discussed requires manual configuration, with the exception of forcing incremental updates on LAN interfaces. See Figure 8.7 for an example of the *ipx sap-incremental* command usage.

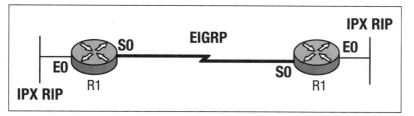

Figure 8.7 IPX EIGRP Automatic Redistribution Example.

As shown in Figure 8.7, IPX RIP and SAP information is automatically redistributed across the EIGRP portions of the network. Should you wish to limit the information being passed through the network, you'll need to configure route filters and/or SAP filters. Route filtering is discussed in detail in Chapter 9.

How Do I Know What Is Going On?

We recommend that some type of monitoring be in progress on any internetwork. Whether it is done through the use of traditional Simple Network Management Protocol (SNMP) implementations or through manual monitoring, management is an essential part of the internetwork. Table 8.1 lists various commands that will assist the monitoring of individual routers.

Table 8.1   EIGRP useful show commands.

Command	Description
show ip eigrp neighbors	Displays the EIGRP p neighbor table.
show ip eigrp topology	Displays the EIGRP ip topology table.
show ip route	Displays the IP routing table.
show ip protocols	Displays a detailed listing of all active routing protocols.
show ip eigrp traffic	Monitors EIGRP packets sent and received.
show ipx eigrp neighbors	Displays the EIGRP ipx neighbor table.
show ipx eigrp topology	Displays the EIGRP ipx topology table.
show ipx route	Displays the IPX routing table.

Practice Questions

Question 1

> EIGRP is which type of routing protocol?
>
> ○ a. Distance vector
>
> ○ b. Link state
>
> ○ c. Hybrid
>
> ○ d. None of the above

Answer c is correct. EIGRP does not fall in the category of either answer a or b. However, it does have some of the characteristics of both types of protocols. It is considered to be link state to its neighbors and distance vector to the rest of the network. Answer d is incorrect because a correct answer is given.

Question 2

> EIGRP, like OSPF, is a standardized routing protocol defined by an official RFC.
>
> ○ a. True
>
> ○ b. False

Answer b is correct, False. EIGRP is a Cisco proprietary routing protocol.

Question 3

> Which of the following tables does EIGRP keep? [Choose the three best answers]
>
> ❑ a. ARP table
>
> ❑ b. Routing table
>
> ❑ c. Neighbor table
>
> ❑ d. Topology table

Answers b, c, and d are correct. EIGRP keeps routing, neighbor, and topology tables for each of the protocols for which it is configured. Answer a is incorrect because the router keeps an ARP cache in active memory; however, EIGRP does not maintain the table.

Question 4

The best route to any specific network is known as a successor.

○ a. True

○ b. False

Answer a is correct, True. The best route is known as the successor or current successor. The next-best route, if it meets specific criteria, is known as the feasible successor.

Question 5

When a network topology change occurs, routing updates are sent to which of the following?

○ a. All routers in the internetwork.

○ b. All routers in the area.

○ c. All directly connected routers.

○ d. None of the above

Answer c is correct. Because EIGRP is not considered a "hierarchical" routing protocol, it creates a large flat network (such as non-hierarchical). In a flat network, all updates must be propagated to all routers. Answer a is incorrect because that type of update propagation is known as flooding. EIGRP does not cause link state advertisement flooding. Answer b is incorrect because EIGRP does not use an area hierarchy as does OSPF. Answer d is incorrect because a correct answer is given.

Question 6

EIGRP uses which of the following in route metric calculation? [Choose the three best answers]

❑ a. Hop count

❑ b. Cost

❑ c. Delay

❑ d. Load

❑ e. Bandwidth

Answers c, d, and e are correct. Bandwidth is the primary metric value followed by delay. Should additional information be necessary to calculate a tiebreaker between two routes, load, reliability and MTU size will be added into the calculation. Answer a is incorrect because hop count is used by RIP for route calculation. EIGRP does not include hop count in its calculations. Answer b is incorrect because cost is used by OSPF in route calculation, not by EIGRP.

Question 7

Examine the image below. What is the correct configuration commands to correctly configure the EIGRP process?

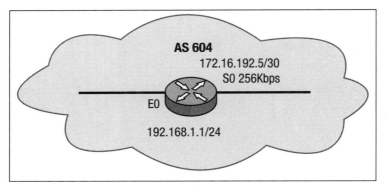

Build an EIGRP configuration.

The correct code command is as follows:

```
interface ethernet 0
ip address 192.168.1.1 255.255.255.0
!
interface serial 0
ip address 172.16.192.5 255.255.255.252
bandwidth 256
!
router eigrp 604
network 192.168.1.0
network 172.16.0.0
```

The EIGRP configuration required the configuration of an AS number as well as appropriate network statements.

Question 8

Which command represents the correct use of the EIGRP summarization command for the Serial 0 interface configuration in Question 7?

○ a. **ip summary 172.16.192.0 255.255.240.0**

○ b. **ip summary-address eigrp 604 192.168.0.0 255.255.0.0**

○ c. **summary 192.168.1.0 255.0.0.0**

○ d. None of the above

Answer b is correct. This statement advertises that all networks contain **192.168** as the first two decimal values, regardless of the values of the last two. Answer a is incorrect because both the syntax and the network address being summarized are not correct. Answer c is incorrect due to syntax. Answer d is incorrect because a correct answer is given.

Question 9

Which code designator appears next to EIGRP-derived routes in the IPX routing table?

○ a. R

○ b. D

○ c. E

○ d. B

Answer c is correct. According to the legend that appears when the command **show ipx route** is used, E designates an EIGRP-derived route. Answer a is incorrect because R is the designation for a RIP route. Answer b is incorrect because there is no D in the IPX routing table legend. D is the designation for EIGRP-derived routes in the IP routing table. Answer d is incorrect because B is the IP routing table designation for a Border Gateway Protocol BGP-derived route.

Question 10

> What is the correct command to force EIGRP incremental updates (such as, updates only when necessary) on a router's interface Ethernet 0 for autonomous system 350?

The correct code command is as follows:

```
interface ethernet 0
ipx sap-incremental eigrp 350
```

The ipx sap-incremental command is used to force updates only when necessary on an LAN segment. Normal operation in EIGRP defaults to periodic updates on LAN interfaces. This command changes that setting and assumes the absence of NetWare servers and the presence of other Cisco routers on this specific LAN segment.

Need To Know More?

Cisco IOS Solutions for Network Protocols, IP Vol. 1, Cisco Systems, Indianapolis, IN, 1998, ISBN 1-578-70049-3. It covers in depth IP and routing protocol documentation.

Huitema, Christian. *Routing in the Internet*, Prentice Hall, Jersey City, NJ, 1995. ISBN 0-13-132192-7. It focuses on basic internetwork architecture and addressing. It is a well-written book for a basic level to an advanced level audience.

For more information on Cisco Certification tracks, visit **www.ccieprep.com**.

For more information on EIGRP, visit **www.cisco.com** and perform a search with "Enhanced IGRP" as keywords.

Optimizing Routing Updates

9

Terms you'll need to understand:

√ Static routes

√ Passive interfaces

√ Default routes

√ Route filtering

√ Redistribution between different routing protocols

Techniques you'll need to master:

√ Configuring and using static routes

√ Understanding and configuring passive interfaces

√ Configuring and using default routes

√ Understanding and applying IP and Internetwork
   Packet eXchange (IPX) route filters

√ Applying route redistribution to multiple routing
   protocols

√ Using various techniques to prevent loop development
   when redistributing

So far in this book, we've seen how various routing protocols propagate routing update information through the network. Sometimes, however, you may want to prevent routing information from flowing into or out of a router. For example, when a low-bandwidth wide area network (WAN) link connects two parts of a network, there may be no useful information to gain by filling the bandwidth with routing updates. Therefore, you shouldn't send them—use static or default routes instead. In this chapter, we will explore update optimization through the use of passive interfaces, route filters, and route redistribution.

Controlling Routing Information

How you design your WAN network profoundly affects your ability to manipulate routing updates as well as network reachability. At the same time, a good design makes configuration and troubleshooting significantly easier. A combination of static routes, passive interfaces, default routes, and route filters can provide full reachability while eliminating redundant routing information. Two of the tools for manipulating routing information include static routes that are permanent and hand-coded routes used to override normal routing protocol-learned routes. Default routes are just a special case of static routes used when a large number of routes may be left out of the routing table without sacrificing reachability. The best example of a default route is the path from your company's network to the Internet. There is no value gained by having thousands of extra routes in each of your company's routers when all of your company's data goes through a single router on its way to the Internet. Route filters, implemented with the **distribute-list** command, are used to hide routes by blocking their inclusion in routing updates in or out of interfaces and other routing protocols.

All of these tools may also be used with other protocols such as IPX.

Network Topology

The network's topology (the physical layout) is a key concern in your design. How you implement your WAN links profoundly affects the internetwork's operations. Cisco uses a three-tier hierarchy as its network model. At the bottom of the hierarchy are access routers, which are small routers with features used in controlling single LANs or dial-access. The distribution routers occupy the middle tier in the hierarchy. Their function is to shape traffic and to steer traffic toward the appropriate backbone or access router. Access lists might be used in access or distribution routers to eliminate useless traffic or keep undesirable traffic away from the core routers (backbone). The third and highest tier contains the core routers. These are usually very large machines connected over very fast links in a meshed pattern (distribution and access routers are not meshed) for redundancy and to provide for quality of service and differentiation of paths across the network. Switching may be used at the access and core levels to speed network operation but, routers are required to give the network form (hierarchy) and scalability. (Remember, switching is bridging—there are limits to how many devices may be successfully bridged). While this isn't a design course, remember that correct design will allow the tools to work properly. One quick, good example of the kind of problem you encounter if you mesh access routers might be "Where to put the access lists?" If the hierarchy is well laid out and maintained, your traffic is always flowing toward or away from the backbone. If it's meshed, there are many possible directions, thus you need more and longer access lists to keep the traffic where you want it.

Full-Mesh Networks

Full-mesh networks are those networks in which all hosts have a direct connection to all other hosts across the WAN. This type of layout is not very common because it is very expensive to maintain the full mesh. To calculate the number of circuits you'll need to facilitate the full mesh network, use the formula $n(n-1)/2$. In other words, for a 20-router full mesh network, you will need to configure 190 circuits—a significant amount of time and other resources. Some degree of meshing is common in the core where the need for redundancy overrides cost.

Hub And Spoke Networks

Possibly the most common WAN topology is known as *hub and spoke*. In this layout, the central hub router connects to multiple spoke networks (sometimes referred to as *stub networks*). The magic of this design is that no alternate routes exist to the remote sites. Although this may mean a loss of service when the network fails, it alleviates any fear of routing loops. One issue that arises with this type of implementation is, of course, redundancy. What if a link fails? In that case, you can implement a technology known as *dial backup*. We'll discuss a way to get redundancy with one form of dial backup known as dial-on-demand routing (DDR) in Chapter 13. Figure 9.1 shows a hub and spoke layout.

Notice in Figure 9.1 that all spoke sites connect only to the central hub. As a result, a spoke site's only path to the rest of the world is through the hub. In this scenario, there is no benefit in filling the bandwidth between the central hub and spoke site with routing updates. The reason is simply reachability. To get to any remote network, the spoke router must forward all traffic to the hub router. The hub router knows about all routes in each spoke router. These routes are wasted resources because they point to the hub router for all destinations except for those that are local.

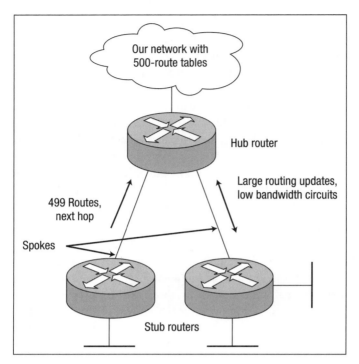

Figure 9.1 A hub and spoke network.

Static Routes And Passive Interfaces

If you don't want your spoke routers to hold all known routes in the internetwork, you do have a number of alternatives. One of them is static routes, that is, permanent, hand-coded routes that are used to preclude the need for routing updates. The problem is: How do the routers in the main network cloud find the correct router to forward traffic to the stub networks. You configure static routes to remote stub networks in the hub router that point to the appropriate spokesite as a next hop address. The static routes in the hub are added to its outgoing routing updates via route redistribution (covered later in this chapter) and are propagated to all other routers in the main part of our network cloud.

Just because you use static routes doesn't mean the routing protocol will not try to advertise routes out of an interface; for that we need either an outbound route filter (distribute list) or a **passive-interface** command. The **passive-interface** command keeps the routing protocol that is running in the hub router from wasting the bandwidth by sending the routing updates to the stub sites.

The effect of this command differs depending on the routing protocol with which it is used. For RIP and IGRP, it has a "listen, but don't talk" effect. In other words, it accepts, but does not send, updates from that interface. For OSPF and EIGRP, it has a "don't talk, don't listen" effect. In other words, these two protocols require a neighbor relationship to be established before they can exchange updates. The router cannot accept these routing updates because the neighbor relationship cannot be established through a passive interface. You can use the **passive-interface** command with all routing protocols.

 When you are using the **passive-interface** command with OSPF and EIGRP, the "don't talk" prevents even Hellos from being sent. See Chapters 7 and 8 for more information on Hello operation with OSPF and EIGRP.

Figure 9.2 illustrates the use of static routes and passive interfaces, and Listing 9.1 details their configuration.

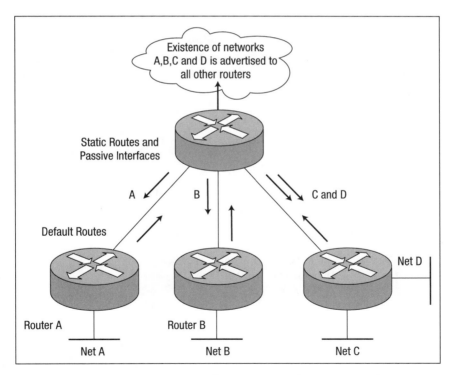

Figure 9.2 Using static routes and **passive-interface** commands.

Listing 9.1 Hub router configuration.

```
interface Serial 0
ip address 172.16.4.1 255.255.255.0
!
interface Serial 1
ip address 172.16.3.1 255.255.255.0
!
ip route 172.16.5.0 255.255.255.0 Serial 0
ip route 172.16.7.0 255.255.255.0 Serial 1
ip route 172.16.8.0 255.255.255.0 Serial 2
ip route 172.16.9.0 255.255.255.0 Serial 2
!
router rip
network 172.16.0.0
passive-interface Serial 0
passive-interface Serial 1
passive-interface Serial 2
```

> *Note:* *You do not need to use a redistribute static command because the static routes point to interfaces on the local router and have the administrative distance of a connected route. You must redistribute static routes when they do not point to an interface on this router because the administrative distance would be greater than zero (the administrative distance of a connected route) and would therefore not automatically be redistributed.*

Static Route Command Syntax

Static routes have several interesting features. The static route syntax and the parameter definitions are shown in Listing 9.2.

Listing 9.2 Static route command syntax.

```
ip route destination-network [network-mask]
       {next hop ip address | interface}
       [administrative distance] [permanent]
```

The following are the parameter definitions from Listing 9.2:

➤ **destination-network** and **network-mask** point to the final destination. The parameters indicate the direction in which packets should be forwarded. If the next step is a Serial interface or sub-interface, specifying the outbound interface on this router does the trick. If the outbound interface is a multiaccess network (such as Ethernet or Token Ring), you must indicate exactly which address on the multiaccess network represents the next hop for the packet on its way to the end destination network.

➤ **administrative distance** (which we discuss in the next section) allows you to position a route above others to the same destination. If multiple routes to the same destination network are available for insertion into the routing table (such as a dynamic routing protocol and one or more static routes to the same destination that point to different interfaces), the route with the lowest numeric value for its administrative distance will be selected.

➤ The **permanent** keyword is used to keep the route active even if the next hop becomes unavailable. Normally, if an attached route goes down, the router removes the static route from consideration as the route for the forwarding database. Using the **permanent** keyword forces the router to keep the route in the forwarding base, causing any packets for that destination to be dropped. This might be useful in an encryption device being used on a very secure path. Should the encryption device or the path become unusable, the permanent static route will not allow the packets to follow another less secure path.

Administrative Distance

The router must decide what routes should be included in its forwarding database. "Forwarding database" is a new term that has moved into the Cisco vernacular. The term "routing table" is not specific enough when many sources of routing information exist simultaneously. For example, we might have a static route or two, a Routing Information Protocol (RIP) route, an Enhanced Interior Gateway Routing Protocol (EIGRP) route, and an Open Shortest Path First (OSPF) route to the same destination network. Which route should be inserted into *the* routing table? The problem is that each protocol creates its own set of routes to all destinations and thus can be considered to have a routing table. To remove some of the confusion, Cisco uses the term "forwarding database," which is the component that the routed protocol uses to forward actual traffic.

 You may find the terms "routing table" and "forwarding database" used at different times.

The forwarding database is constructed from the best routes that each protocol offers. Which route actually ends up in the forwarding database depends upon the believability—or quality—of the route based on its administrative distance. Cisco uses an internal value called **administrative distance** to judge the relative believability of the route. When more than one route to a single destination network is available from multiple routing sources, the route with the lowest administrative distance is preferred. Administrative distance is covered in Chapter 5, but it is important to understand what happens when the wrong route is chosen.

You can alter administrative distances for individual routing protocols or individual routes when a less believable protocol offers a better path. Remember that routing is similar to the situation in statistics: What is true for the population in general (the relative believability or quality of a particular routing source) is not necessarily true when you look at a single case (one route). Figure 9.3 shows administrative distance selecting the wrong path.

Router A advertises Network A to both Routers B and C. Let's assume that Router C advertises Network A to Router B (before Router B was advertising it to Router C). Router B installs the Interior Gateway Routing Protocol (IGRP) route to Router C as being the next hop for Network A (the destination). You can remedy this problem by making Router C's interface passive, or by filtering information from Router C. However, by filtering the IGRP route to Network A, you remove the IGRP alternate path if the primary path to Network A through Router A fails.

The best long-term solution is to alter the administrative distance so that the router's routing protocol can fix the network after a failure. A way to adjust administrative distance is by using the **distance** command. Listing 9.3 shows its syntax.

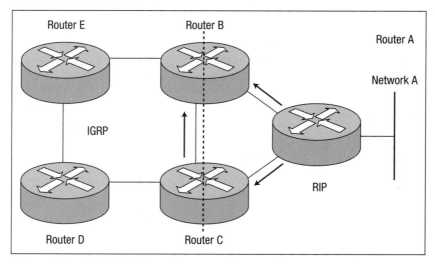

Figure 9.3 Administrative distance selecting the wrong path.

Listing 9.3   Distance Syntax Command

```
distance weight [address wildcard-mask
       [access-list number | name]]
```

The parameters used with the distance command are shown below:

➤ **weight** Administrative distance with a range of 10 through 255 (0 through 9 are reserved for internal use)

➤ **address** IP address in dotted-decimal notation; this is optional

➤ **wildcard-mask** Wildcard mask; this is optional

➤ **access-list number | name** Standard IP access list used to select the routes that will use the **weight** parameter

Listing 9.4 shows how you can use the **distance** command to alter the routing table.

Listing 9.4   Using the **distance** command to change a route's believability.

```
router igrp 200
network 172.31.0.0
redistribute rip
default-metric 100 400 255.1 1500
distance 130 0.0.0.0 255.255.255.255 99
!
access-list 99 permit 172.16.5.0 0.0.0.255
```

Use of the 0.0.0.0 255.255.255.255 in the **distance** command allows **access-list 99** to select which networks need changes.

 | Adjusting administrative distance is a good technique for correcting single route problems because it provides for an automatic alternate path if the primary path fails.

Default Routes

If your network has a large number of routes, static routes may not buy you much due to the tradeoff between simplifying the routing updates and the constant manual changing of the static routes as the network configuration changes in each router. If you don't want to use static routes, default routes—which are known as *gateways of last resort*—present another option. If the routing table does not have a route to a destination network, the default route will be used. For example, going back to our hub and spoke scenario, to enable a default route, simply define in each spoke router a default route that points back to the hub router for unknown traffic. Listings 9.5 and 9.6 show how to configure each spoke router shown in Figure 9.2 to have an Internet Protocol (IP) (or other protocol) address on its local area network (LAN) segment, but it uses a default route that points in the direction of the bigger cloud. Notice the configurations of the spoke sites.

Listing 9.5   Configuring the router attached to Network A.

```
interface Serial 0
ip address 172.16.4.2 255.255.255.0
```

Listing 9.6   Configuring the default route that points toward the hub.

```
ip route 0.0.0.0 0.0.0.0 Serial 0
```

Note that the other router configurations are identical to this router's configuration except for the addresses on the Serial interfaces.

A default route is actually a static route to network 0.0.0.0 with a 0.0.0.0 mask. This 0.0.0.0 form of default route is used with RIP and OSPF to indicate a "none of the above routes" path. If no routes exist in the forwarding database for the destination IP address in the datagram, the router forwards it in the direction of the default route.

Referring back to Figure 9.2, the default route of Router A points to an interface on the local router. This configuration works on links where nothing further is required to indicate the next hop address. The default route of Router B—although not required in Figure 9.2—shows a configuration that you could use on a multi-access network segment where you needed to point to a specific router. The form of the default route for IGRP and EIGRP is **ip default-network x.x.x.x**, where *x.x.x.x* is the actual network address. Obviously, you must have a valid route to the destination network. In all other ways, the default routes of Routers A and B work the same way.

Let's walk through how traffic would flow from Network A to Network D in Figure 9.2. The router attached to Network A attempts to match the packet's destination IP address with that of one of the destinations in its forwarding database. If it can't find a matching entry, the router forwards the packet upstream along the default path toward the hub (but only if the default route is present). The hub has a next hop address for Network D due to the static route included in the configuration and forwards the traffic properly. The return traffic follows the same path in the reverse order.

Deciding When To Use Static Or Default Routes

Because static and default routes (a default is a special case of the static route) don't change even when the network breaks, it is important to point out that the best use of static routes is when only one path exists between source and destination. Since no alternate path exists (due to the network design), no confusion will result when the primary, actually the only, path goes down. Notice in Listings 9.5 and 9.6 that the static route is more specific and points from the "big" cloud to the "little" cloud. The placement decision is easy because all routers in the bigger cloud need to learn the route to the stub network (or networks) and the stub router will intentionally not be advertising its connected routes. We'll add a static route pointing to the stub into the router at the edge of the larger cloud and redistribute the static routes to provide the necessary information. The default route, being the "none of the above" choice, points from the "little" cloud toward the "big" one. This approach keeps the size of the stub router's forwarding database to a minimum while providing full connectivity and minimizes the routing overhead. If we use default routes, we will probably use two defaults: one from the stub site to the rest of the organization and the other in the "big" cloud pointing to the Internet. An Internet Service Provider (ISP) would likely use a static route to our organization's network to allow the rest of the Internet to find us.

For more information on ISPs, see Chapter 10.

Remember that RIP and IGRP are *classful* routing protocols. It is often necessary to use the **ip classless** command if you are planning to reach destinations of unrecognized subnets of directly connected Networks. By default, the IOS will discard the packets received for a subnet that numerically falls within its subnet if there is no such subnet number in the routing table and there is no default route. When the **ip classless** command is used, the IOS will forward these packets to the best supernet route or the default route.

Distribute Lists

Passive interfaces are great for blocking all routing updates from departing through a specific interface. However, you may want to limit distribution of only some specific routes. To accomplish specific route filtering, use distribute lists (also known as route filters, which are simply access lists that are used on

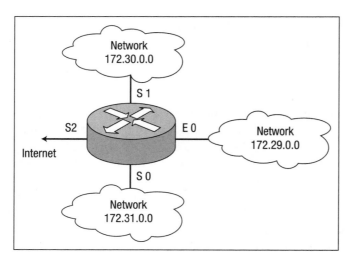

Figure 9.4 Hiding routes.

routing updates rather than on traffic). For more information on access lists, see Chapter 3. Notice in Figure 9.4 that you can decide to hide routes from one part of our network or another because default and static routes may make having all routes in a forwarding database undesirable. Listing 9.7 details the configuration of a route filter.

Listing 9.7   Route filtering.

```
interface Ethernet 0
ip address 172.29.5.1 255.255.255.0
!
interface Serial 0
ip address 172.31.14.1 255.255.255.0
!
interface Serial 1
ip address 172.30.3.1 255.255.255.0
!
interface Serial 2
ip unnumbered Ethernet 0
!
ip route 0.0.0.0 0.0.0.0 S2
!
router rip
network 172.29.0.0
network 172.30.0.0
network 172.31.0.0
```

```
distribute-list 99 out Serial 0
distribute-list 98 out Serial 1
!
access-list 99 permit 172.30.0.0 0.0.255.255
!
access-list 98 permit 172.31.0.0 0.0.255.255
```

The listing illustrates that every device can reach the Internet from the router shown in Figure 9.4; but the 172.29.0.0 network will remain unknown to the 172.30.0.0 and 172.31.0.0 networks. The forwarding databases of the routers within 172.30.0.0 and 172.31.0.0 would be reduced in size, providing faster routing table lookups, a smaller forwarding database, and smaller routing updates. However, with the default route going through the router shown in Figure 9.4, traffic would still flow to and from the 172.29.0.0 cloud because the router actually knows all of the routes for all networks plus the default route to the Internet. If security—not the size of the routing tables—is your primary concern, you need access lists to block traffic. You can code standard IP access lists exactly the same way you did in Chapter 3. This time, however, use the **access-list** command with the **distribute-list** command to filter routing update traffic.

Syntax Of The **distribute-list** Command

Listing 9.8 shows the full syntax and parameter descriptions of the **distribute-list** command.

Listing 9.8 Syntax of the **distribute-list** command.

```
[no] distribute-list {access-list | name} in [ interface-name]

[no] distribute-list {access-list | name} out [ interface-name ]
| routing-process | autonomous-system number ]
```

The parameter descriptions are as follows:

➤ **access-list number | name** Associates an IP access list with this statement.

➤ **out | in** Describes the direction in which the filter acts. Notice that inbound distribute lists apply only to interfaces.

➤ **interface-name | routing-process | autonomous-system number** Describes what routing destination is to be filtered. If this parameter is not specified, the default is for all interfaces.

Redistribution And Filtering With IPX

Up to this point in this book, we've talked only about redistribution and filtering between IP protocols (except for a brief discussion of IPX in Chapter 8). In recent years, new routing protocols have been developed for the Novell proprietary layer 3 protocol, IPX. The good news is that for Novell Link Services Protocol (see the "NLSP" section in Chapter 11) and Cisco's Enhanced IGRP (see the "EIGRP" section in Chapter 8), redistribution between either one and IPX RIP (the default Novell routing protocol) is automatic. This means that you do not have to configure anything.

However, it is useful to be able to block IPX routing updates. Figure 9.5 shows how you can also use **distribute-list** commands with Novell IPX. Listing 9.9 details the configuration for you.

Listing 9.9 Novell IPX **distribute-list** code sample.

```
ipx router eigrp 200
network 1c
network 1d
network 40e
network 35
distribute-list 899 out s0
access-list 899 permit 40e
```

 When you are filtering IPX routes, a side effect is that routes are filtered to destination networks. Depending on your particular scenario, this can be good or bad. Novell SAP information is not distributed if the route to the required destination network does not exist. This may be exactly what you intended or the side effect may unwanted. For example,

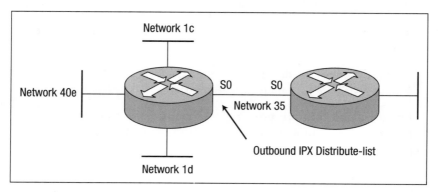

Figure 9.5   Novell IPX **distribute-list**.

if a server issued SAP information regarding a particular service to a client, then the client returned a service request message for that service to the server providing it, the router would have no choice but to drop the traffic because the server does not have a route to the server's location.

Using More Than One Protocol

The real power of routers is found in the dynamic routing protocol, where lost routes can be circumvented and newly added routes can be discovered and added to the forwarding database. It is better—and easier—to support only one routing protocol per routed protocol; however, you must sometimes run multiple routing protocols in the same router at the same time.

Situations where you run multiple routing protocols in one router are primarily the following:

➤ You are migrating or converting your network from one routing protocol to another.

➤ Two organizations share common routers and need to share certain routes to each other; however, for political reasons, the organizations want to keep most of the network's routes separate and private.

➤ There are multiple vendor interoperability issues or incompatible protocols.

➤ You have some application-specific need. For example, you might need to convert from RIP to OSPF to gain convergence fast enough to support IBM Systems Network Architecture (SNA) traffic.

➤ You need to support legacy protocols. Unix systems commonly run RIP, but you want your core backbone routers to run EIGRP or OSPF.

Route Redistribution

Redistribution is the term used to describe the action of a routing protocol when the routing protocol advertises (redistributes) its routing information to another routing protocol running on the same router. When two or more protocols are running simultaneously in the same router, each protocol learns and maintains its own routes. The router must build a single forwarding database from multiple sources of routing information. If only one route exists (for example, only one of several routing protocols is reporting that route) to a destination, that route is installed in the forwarding database. If more than one choice for a route to a particular destination exists (that is, more than one routing source has a route to it), which route should be used? A vendor may simply write code to select the "best" route from the multiple sources. Cisco uses *administrative distance* as a way to grade routes on their "believability".

The router has access to each protocol's routes but only the most believable routes are added to the forwarding database. When it comes time to redistribute the routes, each individual routing protocol advertises only routes it has learned. A protocol will not include routes from another routing protocol unless you specifically tell the other routing protocol to share or redistribute its routes. The metrics that the routing protocols use are completely different and incompatible (the notable exception being IGRP and EIGRP). Therefore, you need to help the routing protocol by telling it what metric values to use when redistributing routes from another source of routing information

Route redistribution must be done with care considering issues related to the mixing of routes from different routing sources. For example consider that each part of the network will reconverge at a different rate which results in routes that are aging out and being replaced at different rates. If you connect the network parts with a single router even though you might be using a protocol that converges quickly in one part of the network, its new source of information may not be correct (current enough). The problem is much worse if routes are being shared from multiple routers. Redistribution adds a great opportunity to share conflicting information throughout your internetwork. That is what this chapter is about.

A single routing protocol has features to produce consistent, loop-free topologies. The fact to keep in mind is that when redistributing, you—the administrator—are the one who must keep things straight, both logically and physically to prevent loops.

Routing Metrics

Metrics extract the best pathway to a specific destination. They vary based on the routing protocol(s) active on the router. Incompatible route selection information is one problem that occurs with route distribution. RIP, OSPF, and EIGRP/IGRP all have different ideas as to what a good metric is. As a result, we must set *seed metrics* (the metrics used when routes are redistributed) when redistributing. In addition, because the router uses administrative distance to rate the believability of different routing sources, you have a good source for misunderstanding about what the *real* route into and out of the internetwork should be. There is no way to directly map either the hop count metric of RIP to the cost routing metric that OSPF uses, or the composite metrics that IGRP and EIGRP use. You must manually plug in metric values for the redistributed routes.

Each protocol begins building its metric from the Autonomous System Boundary Router (ASBR) (any router that connects two routing protocols), which is based on the initial seed value. It is a good idea to set the seed metric for a redistributed route to a larger value than the metric value derived locally for a route to the same destination. This way, if routes from your network are redistributed back at you (route feedback, discussed later in this chapter), they will be perceived as being farther away than any local protocol metric and therefore not used.

 This technique of setting the seed metric higher for redistributed routes than any local metric has a very big advantage over filtering routes to prevent route feedback. If your local route to a network fails, that backup route through the non-local protocol may still be available. If the routes were simply filtered, no alternative path would be available.

Figure 9.6 shows how using a low value for the seed metric produces suboptimal paths.

Notice at the lower left what happens when the routes come back through. Assume that 1 is the seed metric for IGRP routes (which are, in actuality, the earlier redistributed RIP routes the route update information is looping) being redistributed into the RIP cloud. RIP begins growing the metric value as if the RIP-> IGRP-> RIP (again) routes are one hop from the ASBR. The lower left

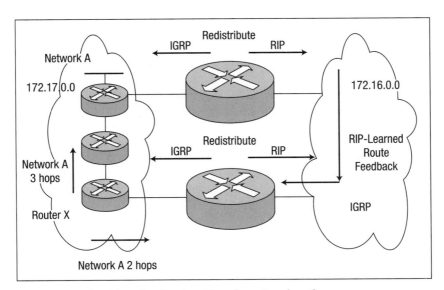

Figure 9.6 Routing feedback with sub-optimal paths.

router sees Router X as being three hops along the internal path. However, because we have attached a low metric value coming back from the IGRP cloud, Network X appears to be closer via the IGRP cloud. The result is an inaccurate routing decision.

What are possible solutions to the problem? One approach is to always apply a metric higher than the maximum in the local cloud. For example, if the maximum diameter in the RIP cloud is 5 hops, assign a metric of 6 to routes coming from the IGRP cloud. Doing so keeps RIP feedback originating within the IGRP cloud from seeming to provide better paths than natural RIP paths. Manipulating seed metrics is better than filtering routes because if Router X became unreachable through the normal RIP cloud and if a real path did exist through the IGRP cloud, it would become the pathway of choice through normal route selection. If the routes are filtered, no alternative paths through the other network are available.

The primary command used to establish the seed metric is **default-metric**. There are two versions of the command's syntax. Listing 9.10 shows the syntax for RIP and OSPF; Listing 9.11 shows that for IGRP and EIGRP.

Listing 9.10   Configuring **default-metric** for RIP and OSPF.

```
[no] default-metric <number>
```

For RIP, we must provide a hop count. For OSPF, we need to provide a path cost, which is simply a number based on the link's bandwidth.

Listing 9.11   Configuring **default-metric** for IGRP and EIGRP.

```
[no] default-metric <bandwidth> <delay> <reliability> <load> <mtu>
```

For IGRP and EIGRP, we need to use the more complex components used for them (see Chapter 8). Refer to Listing 9.13 for a good example of **default-metric** usage.

You can tune routes using other strategies such as route mapping and policy routing. These are not covered in ACRC and will not be on the test, but if you are interested in learning about them, go to Cisco's Web site.

Single Router Between Two Networks

Several distinct scenarios exist for the use of a single router with multiple networks. There are also several tools available to aid you in the configuration of those scenarios. Some solutions fit better than others in given situations. Figure 9.7 illustrates a simple, but common, problem of having one router between two different routing clouds.

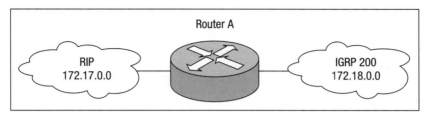

Figure 9.7   Multiple routing protocols in one router.

On the left is an RIP cloud, and on the right is IGRP. Router A's forwarding database contains routes from both RIP and IGRP. As a result, all networks are reachable from Router A. The RIP process in Router A advertises only RIP-learned routes (only those not learned through the interface that is directly connected to the RIP cloud) back into the RIP cloud due to split horizon. *Split horizon* is a loop-avoidance technique that prevents distance-vector protocols from advertising a route back to the router interface from which it was learned.

The IGRP routing process in Router A advertises only IGRP's route information, again taking split horizon into account for outbound updates. To make the routing processes advertise each other's routes, you must configure additional statements (one for each protocol that needs redistribution) that specifically authorize each protocol to redistribute routes learned from the other protocols.

 Split horizon is an important concept. You must understand that split horizon does affect the outcome of passing routing updates from a router.

Listing 9.12 and 9.13 shows how to handle redistribution for the scenario shown in Figure 9.7.

Listing 9.12   IGRP configuration.

```
router igrp 200
network 172.17.0.0
redistribute rip
default-metric 10000 2000 255 1 1500
```

Notice the IGRP/EIGRP-style seed metric. The 10000 represents the bandwidth in K (for example, 10000K is 10Mbps), the 2000 is the approximate serialization delay for an Ethernet frame at 10Mbps. Serialization delay is simply how long it takes to put the bits onto the circuit at a given speed. For example, an 8000 bit record being sent on a 64Kbps link would take 8000/64000 of a second to leave the router's interface. The 255 represents the link's reliability as a ratio with 255 as the denominator so a 100 percent reliable link would be 255/255. The 1 represents the current load factor again as a ratio with 1/255 indicating a not-busy link. Finally the 1500 represents the MTU size for the link.

Listing 9.13 RIP configuration.

```
router rip
network 172.18.0.0
redistribute igrp 200
default-metric 3
```

The seed metric for RIP is in hops.

The statements authorize each protocol to advertise routes from the forwarding database that the other protocol originally learned. Notice that the **default-metric** statements provide values in each protocol's native metric format to allow the routing protocol to compare routes. This method of providing a metric is necessary because RIP and IGRP use totally different metric types. There is no realistic way to translate RIP's hop count to IGRP's complex metric. Therefore, you must provide the **default-metric** before any information can be passed between the two protocols.

Note that there is only one point of connection between the two networks. In this situation, you would gain little by redistributing all routes in both directions. Rather than adding additional entries into all routing tables on both sides of the cloud, consider redistributing all routes into one protocol (into either the core or the surviving protocol during a conversion) and injecting a default route into the other side. Listings 9.14 through 9.16 show such a scenario.

Listing 9.14 Redistributing routes in one network and using the default in the other.

```
router igrp 200
network 172.18.0.0
redistribute rip
default metric 10000 2000 255 1 1500
```

Listing 9.15 Configuring a static route that points to the RIP side of the network.

```
ip route 0.0.0.0 0.0.0.0 Serial 0
```

Listing 9.16 RIP configuration.

```
router rip
network 172.16.0.0
redistribute static
default-metric 3
```

We didn't need to show the **redistribute** command for static routes in this case, but we included it for clarity. Notice that we sent the default route into only the RIP side of the network. There is really no effective way to generate a default route into both protocols from within the same router unless a common default route exists for both. Figure 9.8 shows an example of a default route to a third network, in this case the Internet.

In Figure 9.8, you could send a default route to both the RIP and OSPF routing domains because they both want to reach destinations on the Internet. This scenario works because the router that runs the multiple protocols is also the router that connects to the Internet. If, for example, another router were the default to the Internet, redistribution in one direction with a default route in the other direction, is more typical.

Redistributing in one direction and using a default route in the other is a good strategy when you have a single router between two clouds. When multiple points of redistribution (multiple routers) between two or more clouds exist, the problem requires you to combine route filtering, metric, or administrative distance manipulation strategies.

Route Feedback

Redistributing routes in one direction and employing a default route in another direction works well in the situation shown in Figure 9.7. Unfortunately, a new problem arises—routing feedback, which causes sub-optimal paths and/or routing loops. Figure 9.9 shows route feedback. We've discussed feedback in earlier sections. However, additional detail is warranted.

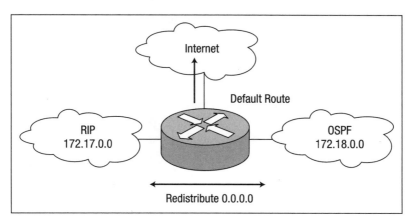

Figure 9.8 Default route to a third network.

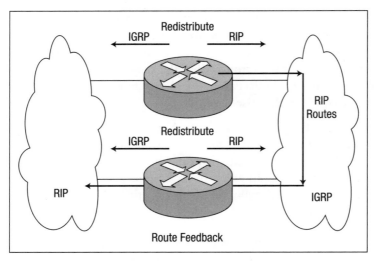

Figure 9.9 Route feedback.

We have two (or more) connections between the clouds, so routes redistributed originally from the RIP cloud to the IGRP cloud attempt to return to the RIP cloud from IGRP. The more connections there are, the bigger the problem. We highly recommend that you avoid having multiple equal-cost routes out of your Autonomous System (AS). If your traffic is departing your network via one router and returning via a different router, you have created a routing loop that could cause massive instability in your internetwork. This problem is troublesome, causing routing loops and "funny" routes that provide strange paths to the destinations. You can use the following strategies (alone or in combination) to handle route feedback:

➤ Redistribute in one direction only using a default route in the other cloud.

➤ Redistribute in both directions but filter routes in both directions.

➤ Redistribute but make certain the seed metric is higher than any local metric. For example if the maximum number of hops in the RIP cloud is 7, set the default metric to 8. This approach provides a backup through the "other" cloud if all paths through this network are down.

➤ Redistribute and change metrics or administrative distance on specific routes.

Configuring Redistribution

The best of all worlds would be to run only one routing protocol, but when you must redistribute, keep the following in mind:

➤ Don't run overlapping protocols.

➤ Decide where a new protocol should be added.

➤ Try to always have a sharp, distinct border, an edge, between sections of the network that are running different protocols. Usually the edge is a short-term position. The edge is just a way for you to better visualize the redistribution situation.

➤ Determine which protocol will be the edge (the one being eliminated) and which will be the core (the one to remain). A good strategy is to redistribute into the core (or backbone) and filter or use default routes to reach the core from the edge protocol.

➤ Select the ASBR(s) carefully. Decide which routes will be injected in which direction and the strategy for blocking their return.

Designating the edge device may be permanent due to necessity, as with a group of Unix machines running RIP (not capable of any other protocol) and connecting to a backbone that runs OSPF. It is feasible, however, that the edge might be temporary and movable for a migration. Figures 9.10, 9.11, and 9.12 show what we mean by keeping a defined edge.

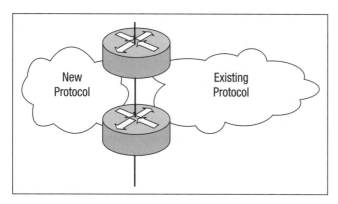

Figure 9.10   Keeping an edge.

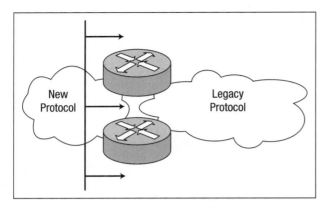

Figure 9.11 | Moving the edge in discrete steps.

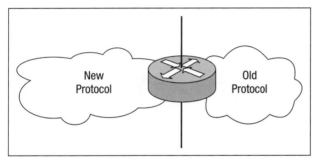

Figure 9.12   Establishing the end position.

Testing The Configuration

The commands of most use in this section deal with the forwarding table. But all of the following commands will be useful:

➤ **show ip route** Shows the content of the forwarding database including the next hop, metric, routing source (such as RIP, OSPF, EIGRP, and IGRP), administrative distance, and route aging information.

➤ **show [ip | ipx | •••] protocols** Displays which protocols are currently running in the router, what the routing update sources are (other routers), and the default administrative distance for the protocol. The "•••" represent the name of the routed protocol whose information you want to see.

➤ **trace** Shows the path taken by traffic for a particular destination.

Cisco tests are beginning to ask you to type in a command to show some information rather than just pick from a list of commands. Practice using these commands as much as possible before taking the test. Remember that ALL characters must be correctly specified, not just the abbreviations.

Migration Strategies

Plan migrations from one network form and routing protocol to another carefully. Sometimes you can do a small network conversion as a one-shot conversion (flash cut), where there is no edge. Often, however, you must plan the migration to occur over several steps. When you plan it, it is important to have in mind a good idea of what you expect to happen. Nothing can replace what you know about your current network. Study the network extensively and carefully; then plan the steps. Use one or more of these strategies to keep things working:

➤ If you have access to planning tools, such as Cisco NetSys, or if you have a lab where you can try a pilot implementation of the solution before putting it into a live network, by all means do so.

➤ Show your design to everyone you can. Sometimes, someone—too often a guy on the job for fewer than two weeks—will see a problem you missed. Even if the other members of your team don't notice a problem, they'll all understand what's about to happen and when; if something goes a little off the mark, they'll be more prepared to help.

➤ When you make the changes, be ready to reinstall the original-configuration network. One way could be TFTP servers with original configurations. Another approach is to simply make changes to running RAM only, not saving the changes to NVRAM. That way, a reload will fix the problem.

➤ Hopefully, you can make any necessary changes in other than prime time.

Some other issues you may face include special statements for dealing with IGRP and EIGRP. These protocols employ a different kind of default route coding than other protocols.

Watch for problems with discontiguous networks when working with distance-vector protocols. Distance-vector protocols cannot deal with discontiguous networks because they cannot distinguish between a subnet from a single classful network and differing subnet masks. See Chapter 6 for more information.

Practice Questions

Question 1

> Why would two routing protocols be used in the same router? [Choose the three best answers]
>
> ❑ a. During a conversion or migration from one protocol to another.
>
> ❑ b. When you need to support legacy routing protocols.
>
> ❑ c. Because of political boundaries within the organization.
>
> ❑ d. Due to multi-vendor interoperability or host-based routers.

Answers a, b, c, and d are correct. All answers provide possible scenarios when you may need or want to consider using multiple protocols.

Question 2

> What is an ASBR?
>
> ○ a. A type of route used to connect ASes.
>
> ○ b. A router that runs OSPF.
>
> ○ c. A router that runs two different routing protocols simultaneously.
>
> ○ d. A different vendor's router.

Answer c is correct. An ASBR is a router that runs two different routing protocols at the same time, although the definition is usually expanded to include that the protocols share the routes. Answer a is incorrect because ASBR is not a route. Answer b is incorrect because although the term ASBR is commonly used with OSPF, the definition of an ASBR is more general. Answer d is incorrect because with ASBR, no differentiation is made regarding another vendor's router.

Question 3

What is an administrative distance?

- ○ a. A Cisco-specific mechanism for deciding which protocol is more believable or has a better-quality route.
- ○ b. A metric used by OSPF.
- ○ c. An identifier that describes routers under common administration.
- ○ d. A type of access list used to filter routes.

Answer a is correct. An administrative distance is used when more than one routing source has a route single destination. The route associated with the lowest numeric value administrative distance is the one inserted into the forwarding database. Answer b is incorrect because the OSPF metric is known as cost. Answer c is incorrect because an identifier that describes routers under common administration defines an AS. Answer d is incorrect because the access list used to filter routes is called a distribute list.

Question 4

What is the command to display the administrative distance associated with an IP route?

- ○ a. show ip route
- ○ b. show ip protocols
- ○ c. show interface
- ○ d. show administrative distance

Answer a is correct. The routing table lists for each non-connected route the metric, administrative distance, age, next hop, and outgoing interface. Although **show ip protocols** shows the administrative distance for the protocol, it does not show if a route has had its administrative distance changed. Therefore, answer b is incorrect. Answer c is incorrect because it doesn't show administrative distance at all. Answer d is incorrect because this command doesn't exist.

Question 5

What is a disadvantage of using a route filter or filters to eliminate a route from the routing table?

- ○ a. There are no disadvantages; using a route filter is the best way to avoid route feedback.

- ○ b. A route filter becomes almost the reverse of a static route. If the route you're filtering represents a possible alternative route, filtering it prevents it from ever being an alternate route.

- ○ c. It changes the administrative distance on the route.

- ○ d. It changes the seed metric associated with a route.

Answer b is correct because a route filter will not adapt just because the network changes. It works like a static route that won't allow the network to heal because you're overriding the ability of the routing protocol to fix itself. Answer a is incorrect because although a route filter is one way to avoid route feedback, there are better ways to avoid it. Although you can use an access list to select traffic for these types of changes, the route filter allows (**permit**) or blocks (**deny**) routing update contents. Therefore, answers c and d are incorrect because they have nothing to do with route filters.

Need To Know More?

 Cheek, Andrea, H. Kim Lew, and Kathleen Wallace. *Cisco CCIE Fundamentals: Network Design and Case Studies*, Cisco Press, Indianapolis, IN 1998. ISBN 1-57870-066-3. This is a great book for even more information on CCIE fundamentals.

 Doyle, Jeff. *CCIE Professional Development: Routing TCP/IP Volume I*. Macmillan Technical Publishing, Indianapolis, IN, 1998. ISBN 1-57870-041-8. Chapters 11 through 13 discuss related topics.

 Cisco's Web site, **www.cisco.com**, includes white papers and router documentation about bridging and its logical extension, switching.

Connecting To An Internet Service Provider

10

. . . .

Terms you'll need to understand:

√ Internet Service Provider (ISP)

√ Autonomous System

√ Default route

√ Interior Gateway Protocol (IGP)

√ Exterior Gateway Protocol (EGP)

√ Border Gateway Protocol (BGP) neighbor

√ Internal Border Gateway Protocol (IBGP)

√ External Border Gateway Protocol (EBGP)

Techniques you'll need to master:

√ Finding the right Internet Service Provider (ISP)

√ Configuring a default route

√ Configuring BGP neighbors

√ Configuring Internal BGP

√ Configuring External BGP

This chapter presents how to connect a company to an Internet Service Provider (ISP) and the ordeals and issues that may arise in doing so using Border Gateway Protocol (BGP) version 4 (the current version). BGP is the protocol of choice for most ISPs, so we don't have much choice in the matter when it comes to deciding how to connect to them. ISPs have the resource we want—the Internet—so we have to agree to abide by their policies. BGP gives them the power to affect Internet Protocol (IP) routing policy throughout the networks that attach to their systems. By the same token, National Access Providers (NAPs) are implementing policy above ISPs in the grand scheme of things. ISPs must therefore adhere to policies handed down to them as well.

Internet Service Providers

Selecting an ISP is a rather painful process at times. Many factors come into play, including the size of your company, the spectrum of user types, and the points of presence you will need. Points of presence refer to the geographic diversity of your Internet connection points. The placement of these points will have a profound effect on the flow of your Internet traffic. The size of your company weighs in heavily because it provides the basis for your Internet plan. Here are some questions you should ask about your own network prior to beginning your ISP quest:

➤ How many users in the company require Internet access (presumably all)?

➤ How many of these users are connected to your company's local area network (LAN)?

➤ How many of these users require mobile accounts?

➤ How much bandwidth is sufficient to support all of the above?

➤ How do you handle electronic mail?

➤ If your company is nationwide, do you require multiple points of presence on the Internet? That is, does the New York office have to go through the San Francisco office to get to the Internet, or is there a separate local connection in each location within the network?

➤ How do you connect to your ISP? Via a serial link? At what speed?

➤ Is this Internet connection mission critical? If so, you should provide some redundancy for your Internet access.

Redundant links to an ISP will require the use of BGP to affect routing policy. Without routing policy, there is a high likelihood of routing loops or other routing inconsistencies. BGP policies will flow down from the top tiers of the Internet backbone. You must also be sure to filter the IP network space reserved for private use on your side of the link so that those addresses do not leak out into the Internet. The potential result there is routing loops and/or other inconsistency.

These are only a few of the questions that you need to answer. A small ISP, although inexpensive, may not be the answer for a nationwide company. Once you've selected an ISP that can meet your needs, it's time to start thinking of how you will be sending data to and receiving data. You have a number of data-forwarding alternatives. This chapter explores these differing methods.

Your Autonomous System And You

What is an Autonomous System? The term alone sounds intimidating. *Autonomous System (AS)* is simply a generic term that defines all the devices under a common administration. In other words, all of the routers that your company owns and operates (such as administrators) are part of the same AS. In some routing protocols, it is necessary to define a numeric value (or name) for this AS. If you're not connecting to the public data network, you can simply make up a number for use in every router.

Be careful with Autonomous System Numbers. If your routing protocol requires the number to be defined as part of the configuration, it must be the same on all routers. Examples of routing protocols that require this are Interior Gateway Routing Protocol (IGRP), Enhanced Interior Gateway Routing Protocol (EIGRP), and Border Gateway Protocol (BGP). Routers that are not configured as part of the same AS do not exchange network reachability updates (such as routing updates).

Within your AS, you run a dynamic routing protocol. A routing protocol that runs within an AS is known as an *Interior Gateway Protocol (IGP)*. Examples of IGPs are Routing Information Protocol (RIP), Open Shortest Path First (OSPF), IGRP, EIGRP, and a few others. It is possible to run multiple routing protocols within a single AS. If you do so, you have to redistribute the routing information between the protocols. Usually, this is a manual process that you must do on the router that borders both ASes. However, if you are running

IGRP and EIGRP with the same AS number, the routing process automatically does the redistribution for you. If your protocols require manual redistribution, then you must accomplish that on your own before any updates can pass between the two dissimilar protocols. We covered route redistribution in Chapter 9, so we won't revisit that topic here except where relevant.

At times, it becomes necessary to connect your AS to another AS. This would be the case as you connect to your ISP. You must advertise reachability to the Internet's networks throughout your private network. You can accomplish this in a number of ways. The first thing we need to look at is how we connect our AS to the ISPs. Connecting two ASes is done via an *Exterior Gateway Protocol (EGP)*. The most common EGP is known as BGP. We will discuss BGP in some more detail later in the chapter.

Connection Options

When you connect to your ISP, you have a number of options. These options are key points to consider in how you configure reachability propagation to the Internet itself within your company. Who chooses the options? Well, you are connecting to the ISP's network. Therefore, the ISP can choose what options to implement based on your network's size. Now, you can define your network's size in two ways. First, how many nodes do you have on your internal internetwork? Second, how spread out geographically are these nodes? The answers to these questions point to the method of connection. The options available are *static routes* between your company and the ISP, and *dynamic routes* between you and your ISP. Static routes are route table entries that an administrator has placed into service. Dynamic routing protocols advertise and generate routing tables. Let's look at these more closely.

Static Routing

At the ISP's discretion, you may be allowed to run static routes in order to connect to its network. If this is the case, your job can be difficult or easy, depending on how you choose to administer your static routes. In every router, you can set static routes that point back to the ISP's network. Doing so becomes cumbersome and is quite error prone. The ISP gives you the appropriate information that is necessary to create the static routes. Figure 10.1 shows a sample network scenario.

To specify the next hop address to get our data traffic out to the ISP's edge router, use the following:

```
ip route 10.0.0.0 255.0.0.0 172.16.4.6
```

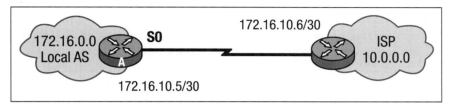

Figure 10.1   A sample network scenario.

To specify the interface through which our data traffic should leave our edge router to get to the ISP's edge router, use the following:

```
ip route 10.0.0.0 255.0.0.0 Serial 0
```

Static routing can be a chore—administrative nightmare is possibly a more accurate term. You must inform each router in your network about the pathway to the ISP. Rather than going through the pain of making manual entries on every router, consider using a default route. You can set a default route on the edge router and force it to inject backwards into your network. Network 0.0.0.0 with the mask of 0.0.0.0 is considered to be a default network. If you set this to route to exit interface serial 0, the router assumes that 172.16.10.4 (the network address of the serial link) is now the IP default network. This route is propagated along with your regular routing updates. The following code is an example of the use of a static default route using Figure 10.1 as a reference scenario:

```
ip route 0.0.0.0 0.0.0.0 s0
```

Set a default static route at the edge router of your AS. Be sure to give it an outbound interface, not a next hop address. When a static route has an outbound interface, it is automatically re-distributed throughout your network. All routers then have a gateway of last resort set automatically; they will therefore know how to get to your ISP's network with little configuration on your part.

Dynamic Routing

Your ISP can decide, with your input of course, to run dynamic routes across the connection between your network and its network. The choice here is what type of dynamic routing protocol to use. You can use IGPs and EGPs, as mentioned earlier.

Interior Gateway Protocols

IGPs include all of the traditional routing protocols you would use in your private internetwork. These protocols include, but are not limited to, RIP, OSPF, IGRP, and EIGRP. We discuss all of these protocols at various points in this book. However, we don't cover RIP and IGRP in great detail because they are not part of the ACRC exam criteria. For information on OSPF and EIGRP, see Chapter 7 and Chapter 8, respectively.

Whatever protocol you run internally, the ISP may determine that it is in your mutual best interests to use an IGP. If so, you simply configure your edge router(s) to redistribute the ISP's networks into your own. You will probably wish to filter out many of the routes that will then come pouring into your routing tables. See Chapter 9 for more information on route redistribution.

Exterior Gateway Protocols

EGPs are protocols designed with the purpose of connecting two dissimilar autonomous systems. This almost sounds much like what we are attempting here. EGPs include Exterior Gateway Protocol (EGP)—yes, that is its name— and BGP. EGP is not widely used these days, so we will focus on BGP version 4.

BGP offers some capabilities that other dynamic routing protocols lack. A particular specific ability has made BGP the most popular protocol among ISPs and their big brothers, the NAPs: being able to affect routing policy at a high level and to have it flow down through all of the connected ASes. This feature allows the NAPs to set rules and regulations regarding route propagation at the highest levels of the Internet hierarchy. NAPs can also know that all ASes connecting to them, however far down the chain, are subject to those rules and regulations. Figure 10.2 depicts the basic Internet hierarchy.

In Figure 10.2, you can see that there are a number of connection options. You are not limited to connecting to a single ISP. For the purposes of redundancy, you may wish to connect to multiple ISPs. The geography of your company may also be a deciding factor. If your ISP does not have coast-to-coast points of presence, multiple ISPs may be your only option.

BGP Basics

BGP has a relatively short history in the grand scheme of internetworking technologies. The protocol itself is connection oriented. It relies on Transmission Control Protocol (TCP) for connectivity before it begins communication with a neighboring device. Configuring BGP, RIP, or IGRP are similar processes. You simply start the process in the router and define the networks you wish to advertise. Unlike with RIP and IGRP, you do not simply configure the directly connected networks on which you want to send updates. You must

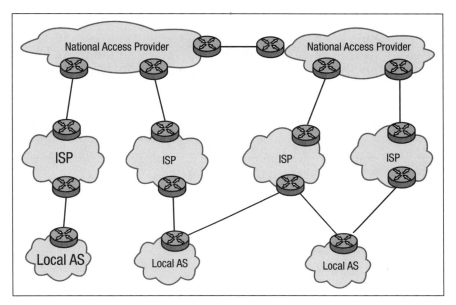

Figure 10.2 The basic hierarchy of the Internet.

configure all of the networks—directly connected or not—that you wish BGP to advertise. Once the network statements are in the configuration, your work is not done. You must define the neighbor to which the BGP process on this router connects at the ISP side of the connection.

Although configuring BGP can be complex in large internetwork situations, it can also be relatively simple. Figure 10.3 shows the basic BGP configuration that you must know for the ACRC exam. Listing 10.1 shows the basic configuration necessary for router A to connect to the ISP router. This connection is also known as *"peering."*

Listing 10.1 The basic BGP configuration for Router A.

```
router bgp 100
network 172.16.0.0
neighbor 172.16.10.6 remote-as 200
```

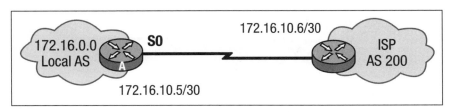

Figure 10.3 The basic BGP configuration.

The peering of routers in dissimilar ASes is an example of External BGP (EBGP) configuration. EBGP is simply a connection to a remote AS. The "neighbor" statement establishes router A as a peer to the ISP router. Would you ever want to peer two routers in your internal network? Certainly the case may arise. Configuring such a connection, known as Internal BGP (IBGP), is very similar to configuring the external peer connection. Figure 10.4 shows an IBGP configuration. Listings 10.2 and 10.3 show the basic configuration commands necessary to create the internal peer connection. Note that the **remote-as** is the same as the local AS number defined by the **router bgp 100** command. This tells the router that the connection is internal.

Listing 10.2   Neighbor 1 configuration.

```
router bgp 100
network 172.16.0.0
neighbor 172.16.1.1 remote-as 100
```

Listing 10.3   Neighbor 2 configuration.

```
Router bgp 100
Network 172.16.0.0
Neighbor 172.16.3.1 remote-as 100
```

Note that Figure 10.4 shows two pathways. We've specified 172.16.1.1 as the neighbor address. What would happen if that particular interface were lost? The answer is that BGP would lose the connection, even in the presence of another route to that particular router. To avoid such a situation, you should create a logical loopback interface and then configure an IP address on this logical interface. In the BGP configuration, set the neighbor IP address to that of the loopback interface. Doing so forces BGP to use both available pathways to get to the logical network, shown in Figure 10.5. Listing 10.4 shows the

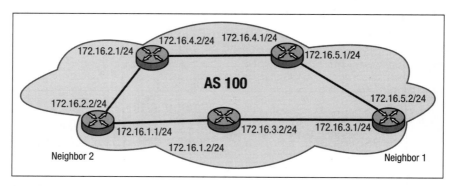

Figure 10.4   An IBGP configuration.

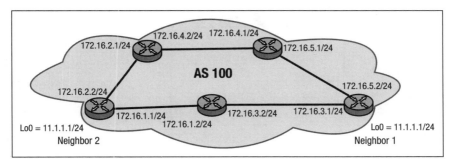

Figure 10.5 Forcing BGP to use both available pathways to get to the logical network.

creation of a logical loopback interface and the change in code on the Neighbor 1 router.

Listing 10.4 New Neighbor 1 configuration.

```
Interface loopback 0
Ip address 10.1.1.1 255.255.255.0
!
Router bgp 100
Network 172.16.0.0
Network 10.0.0.0
Neighbor 11.1.1.1 remote-as 100
```

Listing 10.5 shows the similar changes on the Neighbor 2 router.

Listing 10.5 New Neighbor 2 configuration.

```
Interface loopback 0
Ip address 11.1.1.1 255.255.255.0
!
Network 172.16.0.0
Network 11.0.0.0
Neighbor 10.1.1.1 remote-as 100
```

Practice Questions

Question 1

Routing Information Protocol is an example of an Exterior Gateway Protocol.

○ a.   True

○ b.   False

Answer b is correct, False. RIP is an IGP, defined as any of the commonly used protocols to facilitate the dissemination of private internetwork reachability information. An EGP serves to connect dissimilar autonomous systems.

Question 2

Which of the following can you use to connect to your ISP?

○ a.   BGP

○ b.   Static routes

○ c.   RIP

○ d.   All of the above

Answer d is correct. You can use any method the ISP chooses to connect the two internetworks. Propagation of routes to the ISP is your responsibility within your own internetwork.

Question 3

Using the image below, what is the correct use of the BGP neighbor command to connect your router to the ISP? Use R1 as the edge router for your network and R2 as the edge router of the ISP.

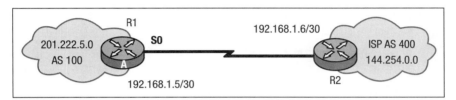

A BGP scenario.

The correct answer is **Neighbor 192.168.1.6 remote-as 400.**

Question 4

Which protocol does BGP depend on for neighbor connectivity?

○ a. UDP

○ b. IPX

○ c. TCP

○ d. None of the above

Answer c is correct. BGP is TCP connection-oriented. Answer a, UDP (User Datagram Protocol), is a connectionless protocol and is therefore incorrect. Internetwork Packet eXchange (IPX) is a separate layer 3 protocol suite and has nothing to do with IP or IP routing protocols. Therefore, answer b is incorrect. Answer d is incorrect because a correct answer is given.

Question 5

Which of the following scenarios requires BGP routing? [Choose the two best answers]

❑ a. Need to make decision based on source and destination of internal traffic within an AS.

❑ b. Connections to different Internet Service Providers.

❑ c. Security concerns require that you must filter all but three networks from the Internet.

❑ d. The ISP you connect to uses BGP.

Answers b and c are correct. When connecting to different providers, it is necessary to configure BGP to select the appropriate pathway to the Internet. You must also filter the private internetwork addresses to keep them off of the Internet. Answer a is incorrect because your internal traffic will be forwarded based on your IGP, not BGP. Answer d is incorrect because your ISP will be using BGP at some points within the network. The fact that they are using BGP does not dictate that you will have to use it. It is still a matter of discretion on the ISP's part.

Need To Know More?

 Halabi, Basam. *Internet Routing Architecture*, Cisco Press, Indianapolis, IN, 1997. ISBN 1-56205-652-2. This book is an authoritative guide to BGP configuration.

 Stewart, John W. *BGP4: Inter-Domain Routing in the Internet*, Addison-Wesley, New York, NY, 1998. ISBN 0-02013-7951-1. This is a must-read for more information on Inter-Domain Routing in the Internet.

 Check out **www.cisco.com** and perform a search on "BGP". You will get numerous hits on that search. There is one particular document known as the "BGP Design Guide." Check it out.

NetWare
Link Services
Protocol (NLSP)

Terms you'll need to understand:

√ Distance-vector protocol

√ Link-state protocol

√ Tick

√ Hop

√ Cost

√ NetWare Link Services Protocol (NLSP) level

√ Area

√ Adjacency

√ Pseudonode

√ Logical designated router (DR)

√ Internetwork Packet eXchange (IPX) internal network number

Techniques you'll need to master:

√ Configuring NLSP

√ Removing IPX Routing Information Protocol (RIP)

√ Verifying the configuration

This chapter introduces Novell's NLSP, a link-state routing protocol created to propagate reachability for Internetwork Packet eXchange (IPX) networks. NLSP was designed to replace IPX RIP and SAP, which we will briefly review here. Novell originally created NLSP to run on its Multiprotocol Router product, an add-on application for NetWare servers. Recently, however, Novell has announced the cessation of further development for NLSP. This chapter will present an overview of Cisco's support for NLSP.

IPX RIP Review

In Chapter 5, we spent a lot of time on distance-vector routing protocols with regard to Internet Protocol (IP)-specific protocols. In Chapter 8, we discussed the specifics of IPX RIP, a distance-vector protocol that utilizes ticks and hops as a metric. A *tick* is a measure of delay on a network. In other words, it measures the time it takes to traverse a link. The higher the link's bandwidth, the lower the delay and therefore the lower the link's tick count. Should two routes to a single destination end up with the same tick count, IPX RIP uses the hop count as a tiebreaker to select the better route.

IPX RIP utilizes a periodic update cycle to propagate routing information. Every 60 seconds, the entire IPX routing table is broadcast out of every active IPX interface. The broadcast is sent out on 60-second intervals—whether or not the routing updates are needed—resulting in inefficient bandwidth utilization. In environments where IPX RIP must be used in conjunction with NLSP, IPX RIP will be automatically redistributed within the internetwork.

IPX Service Advertising Protocol (SAP) Review

Novell developed SAP to propagate and advertise network entities. SAP, like RIP, is on a 60-second-update timer. Novell servers (file servers, print servers, and so on) periodically broadcast information about the services that they provide by broadcasting this information onto their connected local area network (LAN) or wide area network (WAN) interfaces. Routers are required to propagate SAP updates through an IPX network so that all clients can see the service messages. These updates, along with RIP, consume large amounts of bandwidth.

NLSP Basics

NLSP is a link-state routing protocol for IPX networking. It was designed to solve many of the issues caused by using RIP and SAP in large IPX internetworks. Novell released NLSP Version 1.0 in late 1994 for use in NetWare file servers. In early 1995, NLSP was released for use in the Novell

Multiprotocol Router (MPR) software addition for NetWare servers (to enable routing of various layer 3 protocols). Cisco first introduced support for NLSP in version 10.3 of the Internetwork Operating System (IOS).

Hierarchy

NLSP is designed for use in a hierarchical routing environment, in which networked systems are grouped into routing areas. Routing areas can then be grouped into routing domains, and domains can be grouped into an internetwork. NLSP routers are divided into three *levels*. Level 1 routers connect networked systems within a given routing area. Areas connect together via Level 2 routers. Dissimilar routing domains are connected together via Level 3 routers.

The router at each level of the topology stores complete information for its level. For instance, Level 1 routers store complete link-state information about their entire area. This information includes a record of all the routers in the area, the links that connect them, the operational status of the devices and their links, and other related parameters. For each point-to-point link, the database records the end-point devices and the state of the link. For each LAN, the database records which routers are connected to the LAN. Similarly, Level 2 routers store information about all the areas in the routing domain, and Level 3 routers store information about all the domains in the internetwork.

Although NLSP is designed for hierarchical routing environments that contain Level 1, 2, and 3 routers, only Level 1 routing has been defined in a specification.

Operation

NLSP is a link-state protocol, meaning that every router in a routing area maintains an identical copy of the Link-State Database that contains all information about the area's layout. All routers communicate, synchronizing their views of the databases in order to keep their copies of the link-state database consistent. NLSP has the following three major databases:

➤ **Adjacency Database** Tracks the router's immediate neighbors and the operational status of the directly attached neighbor by exchanging Hello packets.

➤ **Link-State Database** Tracks the connectivity of a routing area by merging the immediate neighbor information from all routers into link-state packets (LSPs). LSPs contain lists of adjacencies that each router knows.

➤ **Forwarding Database** Is calculated from the adjacency and link-state databases using Djykstra's shortest path first (SPF) algorithm.

 It's important for you to understand both the different databases that NLSP keeps and their basic functions.

NLSP operates similar to other link-state protocols. When the NLSP process initializes on the router, a Hello protocol is initiated on every NLSP configured interface. When Hello responses are received, a neighbor relationship is formed. This is known as an *adjacency*. If a link or router goes down, adjacencies time out and are deleted from the database.

When the adjacency in place, the neighboring routers exchange link-state databases, which are synchronized with all neighbors. In the event of a topology change, a link state advertisement (LSA) is sent out of every NLSP interface. When a router receives an LSA, it looks at the inbound update and verifies that it is in fact a new update (such as one that it hasn't already seen and processed). Once the router determines that the LSA is valid, it enters it into the link-state database and forwards it out of every interface to all neighbors. The LSPs are flooded to all other devices with every link-state change. LSPs are refreshed every two hours by an update known as a *paranoid update*. In other words, if no changes have occurred, an update is sent just to keep in touch with the neighbor routers. To keep the size of the link-state database reasonable, NLSP uses fictitious identifiers known as *pseudonodes* (which represent the LAN as a whole) and DRs (which originate LSPs on behalf of the pseudonode).

Once the new entry is in the link-state database, the SPF algorithm is run against the database, resulting in a SPF tree that depicts a map of the internetwork structure. The routing table is then constructed from the SPF tree. The entire process is repeated with every LSA received from any source on the network. If the network remains stable (such as no routing updates are flooded through the network) for up to two hours, NLSP devices send out paranoid updates. Figure 11.1 illustrates the basic routing update process.

DRs

NLSP was fashioned, to a degree, after Open Shortest Path First (OSPF). With that in mind, it is important to discuss the role of DRs. They are selected only on broadcast media segments. In implementations of non-broadcast media such as Serial encapsulations (X.25, Frame Relay, ATM, and so on), no DRs exist.

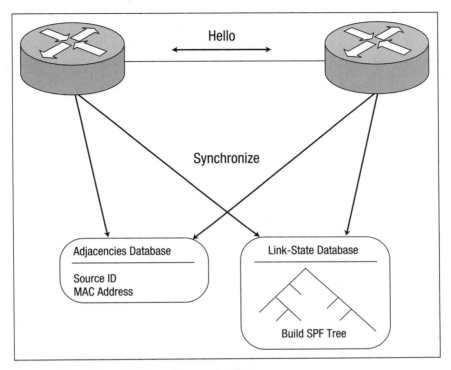

Figure 11.1 The NLSP routing update process.

Consider an Ethernet segment on which four NLSP routers co-exist. They all know about each other because they send and receive Hello packets. In NLSP, a DR is not a physical device (unlike OSPF). If these four routers were to create a full mesh of adjacencies, 12 adjacencies would be formed, one from each router to the other three routers. That scenario would require an unnecessarily high amount of system resources.

To combat the amount of overhead needed to run NLSP, a logical DR is created in between the four physical routers. Each physical router need only peer with the logical DR to establish a relationship and have full connectivity on the network. Figure 11.2 illustrates this concept.

The logical DR is designed to cut down on the amount of overall traffic on the shared network segment.

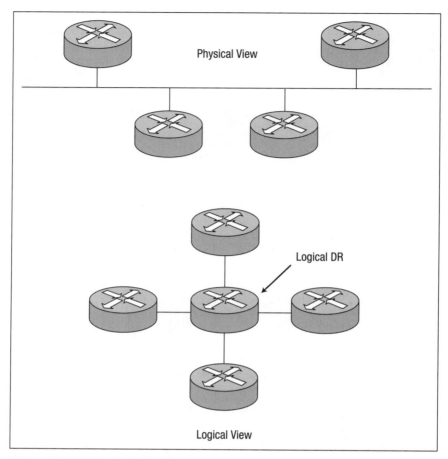

Figure 11.2 The logical DR concept.

Configuration

NLSP configuration obviously depends on how you configure IPX routing on the router. To turn on the IPX routing functionality, issue the **ipx routing** command. You must then activate NLSP and deactivate IPX RIP, which is turned on by default.

It's important for you to define an IPX internal network number for the router. This is used as a unique identifier for the router. To set an internal network number for NLSP to use, use the **ipx internal-network** global configuration command. It is also necessary to disable IPX RIP for those networks on which you wish to configure NLSP. Figure 11.3 illustrates a simple NLSP configuration. Listing 11.1 details the configuration parameters necessary to implement NLSP on R1, and Listing 11.2 details the configuration parameters necessary to implement NLSP on R2.

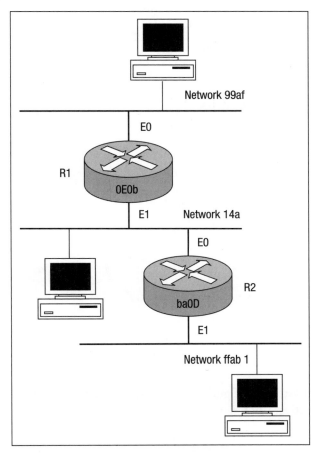

Figure 11.3 A simple NLSP network.

Listing 11.1 The configuration for R1.

```
!
ipx routing
ipx internal-network 0e0b
ipx router nlsp
area-address 0 0
!
ipx router rip
no network 99af
no network 14a
!
interface Ethernet 0
ipx network 99af
ipx nlsp enable
!
```

```
interface Ethernet 1
ipx network 14a
ipx nlsp enable
!
```

Listing 11.2   The configuration for R2.

```
!
ipx routing
ipx internal-network ba0d
ipx router nlsp
area-address 0 0
!
ipx router rip
no network 14a
no network ffab1
interface Ethernet 0
ipx network 14a
ipx nlsp enable
!
interface Ethernet 1
ipx network ffab1
ipx nlsp enable
!
```

Listings 11.1 and 11.2 illustrate configurations that include the activation of IPX routing. After you activate IPX routing, take the following steps:

1. Configure each router's IPX internal network number using the **ipx internal-network** command.

2. Activate NLSP in the global configuration mode using the **ipx router nlsp** command at the global configuration mode.

3. Define an area definition using the **area-address** command (the global configuration portion of the NLSP configuration is now complete).

4. Activate NLSP on each interface using the **ipx nlsp enable** command.

It's important to know the command syntax for the configuration parameters necessary to provide basic NLSP functionality.

Practice Questions

Question 1

> Write the command that enables NLSP on a given interface. [Fill in the blank]
>
> _____

ipx nlsp enable is the correct answer. This command enables NLSP functionality for the interface on which it is entered.

Question 2

> Which of the following was NLSP designed to replace? [Choose the two best answers]
>
> ❑ a. OSPF
>
> ❑ b. RIP
>
> ❑ c. SAP
>
> ❑ d. IPX RIP

Answers c and d are correct. Hopefully, you read all the answers before making your selections. NLSP was designed to replace IPX RIP and SAP. Answers a and b are incorrect because OSPF and RIP are IP routing protocols, which cannot route IPX traffic. While OSPF is a link state protocol, it is not capable of understanding the forwarding of IPX traffic. RIP is a distance vector protocol. The trick in this question is a demonstration of a potential pitfall that lies in testing. That potential pitfall comes in not reading the question carefully. When you see RIP, you may have a tendency to pick it and go on without reading all of the answers and noticing IPX RIP. Don't forget to read every answer, even if you think you know the correct one already.

Question 3

> What commands are necessary for NLSP configuration but not necessary for basic IPX routing functionality with IPX RIP? [Choose the three best answers]
>
> ❑ a. ipx internal-network
>
> ❑ b. ipx network
>
> ❑ c. area-address
>
> ❑ d. ipx nlsp enable

Answers a, c, and d are correct. For NLSP to function, you must define an IPX internal network number and an area address as well as enable NLSP on each interface. Answer b is incorrect because you must assign an IPX network number in the configuration of NLSP and IPX RIP. In basic IPX routing configurations, you must enable IPX routing and assign network numbers to each interface that should participate in IPX traffic forwarding. It is not specific to NLSP.

Question 4

> Which are databases that NLSP routers keep? [Choose the three best answers]
>
> ❑ a. Adjacency Database
>
> ❑ b. Routing Database
>
> ❑ c. Forwarding Database
>
> ❑ d. Link-State Database

Answers a, c, and d are correct. The Adjacency Database keeps track of an NLSP router's neighbors. The Forwarding Database (also known as the routing table) is a listing of the best pathways to individual destinations. The Link-State Database tracks connectivity and the status of each individual pathway to destinations. Answer b is incorrect because there is no Routing Database in NLSP.

Question 5

> What is the command to configure this router's area membership designation. [Fill in the blank]
>
> _____

Area-address 0 0 is the correct answer. Cisco's support for NLSP only includes a single level of hierarchy. So, Area 0 is the only area in which NLSP routers may be configured. Since Novell is not going to be engaging in further NLSP development, Cisco will also not be developing IOS support for NLSP any further. Therefore, if you are going to use NLSP, you will be using a single area.

Need To Know More?

 Cisco Systems. *Cisco IOS Solutions For Network Protocols Volume II: IP, IPX, AppleTalk, and More*. Cisco Press, Indianapolis, IN, 1998. ISBN 1-57870-050-7. This book covers Network-layer protocols as well as addresses NLSP configuration.

 For more information on NLSP, visit Novell's Web site at **http://support.novell.com** and search using the keyword "NLSP".

 For more information on NLSP, visit **www.cisco.com** and search using the keyword "NLSP".

Introduction
To WANs

Terms you'll need to understand:

√ Wide area network (WAN)

√ Point-to-Point Protocol (PPP)

√ Dedicated circuits

√ Switched networks

√ Frame Relay

√ Switched Multi-Megabit Data Services (SMDS)

√ Asynchronous Transfer Mode (ATM)

√ High-Level Data Link Control (HDLC)

Techniques you'll need to master:

√ Selecting the correct WAN connectivity option for your network

√ Selecting the correct encapsulation

This chapter introduces WANs and contrasts using them with operating local area networks (LANs) used inside buildings or on campuses. We'll also review some of the features of each type of connection. For certification, you will need to be able to describe the key features that differentiate the kinds of WAN services and when to use each one.

LANs Vs. WANs

LANs and WANs each have a place in the network. Before we discuss each WAN service offering, let's review the differences between LANs and WANs. Throughout this book, we have discussed LAN implementations (Ethernet, Token Ring, and so on) and deployment. We have touched on WAN implementation, but not in the detail necessary to deploy a WAN. Instead, we have focused on what you need to know to do well on the exam.

LAN Overview

There are a number of LAN implementations—Ethernet (10Base2, 10Base5, 10BaseT, 10Base100, Gigabit Ethernet), Token Ring (4Mbps or 16Mbps, Switched Token Ring)—and the list goes on. While topologically different, these various types of connections share characteristics, including the following:

➤ **They connect local devices** Local may mean in this room, on this floor, in this building, on this campus, or even in this department.

➤ **You own and control them** The organization that owns the LAN determines the speed limit and the types of protocols. You need not feel that any external body must approve the decisions you've made for your LAN because LANs are private and not subject to public scrutiny and tariffs. If you need faster throughput, you can simply upgrade the technology currently in use. Other than ongoing maintenance and support costs, you don't generally have to pay any periodic- or volume-related charges for the bandwidth.

➤ **Speeds are high to very high** It's easy and relatively inexpensive to send data at multi-megabit or even gigabit speeds, because you have control of the equipment.

➤ **Connections to local devices are full-time** That is, you are not being charged based on usage, so you don't need to implement any sort of bandwidth-on-demand scenario.

WAN Overview

WANs are usually somewhat more difficult to implement than LANs. When WAN links come into the big picture, you must rely on external parties to provide many of the *long-haul services*, simply another name for long distance. If you have offices separated by geography, WAN deployment is a viable choice. In general, WANs can be characterized as follows:

➤ **WANS connect remote devices** Your organization may purchase the use of facilities based on a number of factors including: connectivity duration, distance involved, volume, and immediacy of connection. These connections are typically point-to-point in nature. However, some point-to-multi-point services as offerings from your local carrier with— some Frame Relay and/or ATM installations, IBM Synchronous Data Link Control (SDLC), and also some newer multicast services—are available. Whereas LAN facilities are typically broadcast multi-access, shared links (the signal is placed on the wire and every active node receives it), WANs are known as non-broadcast multi-access (we want to be very selective in choosing which nodes get the transmission).

➤ **An international government agency or a public carrier owns and controls the facility** You have to go through a telephone carrier to obtain a WAN. Costs to use facilities are based on tariffs, not competitive prices. In other words, the owner charges basically whatever it wants to charge, to a degree. WAN users pay charges related to speed, duration of use, time of use, amount of traffic generated and exclusivity of use. Public (federal government) policy—not your organization's desire and ability to pay for a service—limits a service's availability. In the United States, service availability sometimes used to depend on (and often still does) the local telephone operating company's political desires.

➤ **Speeds are low to very high** Technology has rapidly converged the speeds available in WANs with those available in LANs. In the past, you could assume that the slower part of the network, or the *bottleneck*, was at the WAN interfaces. This is becoming less the case with the advent of technologies such as ATM.

 Ensure that you know the different characteristics of LANs and WANs.

WAN Service Offerings

WAN links come in several service types that may be appropriate in various scenarios (you're concerned with speed, costs, amount of traffic and so on). Cisco offers many services—each with advantages and disadvantages, mostly advantages—that satisfy every need. As is the case with any technology, it is still evolving. Each of the standards bodies responsible for these different WAN functions is constantly tweaking the standards in an attempt to perfect them. Basic types of connections include:

➤ Dedicated lines, using synchronous Serial interfaces

➤ Asynchronous dial-ins made from PCs or other low-volume terminal devices

➤ Dial-on-demand routing (DDR) connections, using Integrated Services Digital Network (ISDN), traditional analog, or asynchronous facilities to make temporary, circuit-switched connections between routers

➤ Packet-, frame-, and cell-switched services like X.25, Frame Relay, SMDS, and ATM

Dedicated Circuits

Dedicated circuits, also referred to as *leased lines* or *private lines*, provide full-time synchronous connections. Almost all Cisco router models provide the possibility for non-broadcast point-to-point connections as opposed to the broadcast multi-access connections found in LAN connections over Serial interfaces. The universal input/output (I/O) Serial interfaces are capable of speeds of up to E1 speeds (2.048Mbps).

Dedicated circuits are generally used in high-traffic environments where the traffic flow must be constant. A disadvantage of dedicated circuits is that tariffs are expensive compared to the cost of other services (such as Frame Relay) unless the connection is used heavily.

Synchronous dedicated lines, also referred to as leased or private lines, provide full-time connectivity between two routers. Often, synchronous dedicated lines are deployed to reach speeds of 56Kbps, 64Kbps, or a multiple of 64Kbps. Because the bandwidth is always available, these connections provide the best functionality for constant, high-volume traffic. The tariffs for dedicated circuits are quite expensive, thus making dedicated circuits useful only when the benefits of the service outweigh the costs incurred.

In a private lab environment, you can also directly attach the routers using a synchronous cable for short distances (such as across a computer room but not the campus). Figure 12.1 illustrates the typical dedicated line connection.

In Figure 12.1, notice the use of the Channel Service Unit/Digital Service Unit (CSU/DSU). CSU/DSUs are additional pieces of hardware normally required for digital circuits. They can be external (which is usually the case) or, depending on the type of interface, they may be integrated with the router. If the circuit you are using is analog, the device is likely to be a modem.

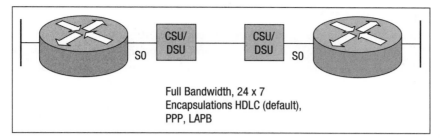

Figure 12.1 Dedicated line connection.

Asynchronous Dial-In Access

A specific type of connection is required for dial access using asynchronous modems. Many short-duration users typically call into a pool of telephone lines. Typically, these applications are PCs being used to access email or other data from central sites. Cisco offers several router models (such as 2509/10/11/12 and the AS-5x00 series access servers) that offer a group of asynchronous ports to support dial-in access by remote client devices. Today, the client machines are mostly desktop PCs or laptops. Security authentication for dial access may be provided through PPP authentication (Password Authentication Protocol [PAP] or Challenge Handshake Authentication Protocol [CHAP], both of which are discussed in Chapter 13) or by router participation with security applications such as Cisco's Terminal Access Control Access Control Server plus (TACACS+). An example of asynchronous connectivity is shown in Figure 12.2.

Asynchronous dial-in access connections have been around for a long time, so many terminal access services are available. We will briefly discuss each one.

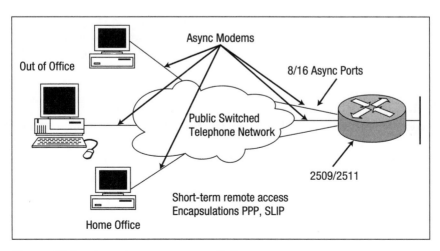

Figure 12.2 Asynchronous connectivity.

Remote-Node Services

Remote-node services are sometimes referred to as Remote Access Services (RAS) and are normally used to connect home or mobile users with centralized LAN services such as databases and email. This implementation can be performed using routers or external third-party servers (Windows NT, modem sharing devices, communications servers, and so on).

Terminal Services

Terminal services allow the router to support a large variety of terminal types and protocols without requiring that the terminal have particular functions built in. These services include:

➤ **Telnet and rlogin** Both provide virtual terminal access between two systems. The router provides a reliable connection to simple asynchronous terminals and many PC terminal emulation software packages, allowing them to provide a much less expensive alternative to dedicated lines. These devices get the necessary functionality without the need to run more complex software (such as IP addresses, which are not necessary because they are part of the router, not part of the terminal or PC).

➤ **X.25 Packet Assembler/Disassembler (PAD)** X.25 provides services for guaranteed sequential delivery across the network. Non-PC devices previously did not contain the functionality to provide the X.25 features. Today, even with PCs, it is not common to provide all of these features in the terminal emulation software. All of Cisco's routers can function as X.25 PAD devices in place of or along with other terminal services.

➤ **TN3270** TN3270 is a service that runs on top of the Telnet service to provide access to IBM 3270 terminal emulation controllers. The 3270 protocol is a popular screen-formatting service that has been used to access IBM mainframes for almost 30 years. The router allows normal Telnet terminals to connect to the mainframe applications invisibly without additional software.

Protocol Translation

Protocol translation allows the routers to provide conversion of one terminal protocol into another. The translation services supported are TN3270, X.25 PAD, Telnet, and DEC Local Area Transport (LAT)—a Digital virtual terminal service.

Vty-Async

These services are capable of translating a call from X.25 to PPP. X.25 is found all over the world and is a popular dial access protocol. This router service makes connecting to IP applications easier.

Asynchronous Routing Services

Asynchronous routing services provide DDR services over asynchronous links. You can use this feature for backup or limited-volume services, but it's much more efficient to use synchronous connections using ISDN.

DDR

For situations when fixed locations do not require full-time connectivity or exceed low-volume, periodic traffic, DDR is a good option. These connections use standard public switched networks with either analog or digital connections. Most commonly today, the connections are made with ISDN. The big difference between DDR and asynchronous dial-in devices is that routers calling routers complete DDR. It is normally—but not always—synchronous.

> *Note:*   *This discussion does not provide the necessary detail to implement and deploy DDR. DDR is covered in detail in Chapter 13, so we will spend very little time on it here.*

DDR is very useful in two specific cases:

➤ **Low-volume, periodic traffic** *Interesting traffic*, as defined by an administrator, causes the dialed connection to be initiated automatically as traffic is routed to the DDR-configured interface in the calling router. Periodic messages such as routing updates, client-server watchdog messages, and the like should not be included as interesting. As long as the connection is up, the routing updates and so on are forwarded over the link. However, these routing updates are not considered important enough to force the call to stay active or to trigger the call setup again once the call has been torn down.

➤ **Dial backup** For situations that require backup circuits, DDR allows administrators to support critical connections by initiating a call to replace a downed or overloaded circuit.

An example of DDR routing is shown in Figure 12.3.

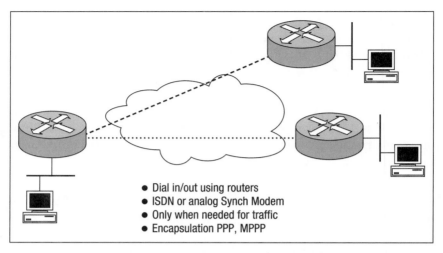

Figure 12.3 The use of DDR in the routing environment.

ISDN

ISDN is the technology of choice for DDR, and many of Cisco's router models enhance ISDN's features. Some of these features are used in a number of differing ways. There are many ways to deploy the DDR functionality including:

➤ Multiprotocol traffic transport. ISDN functions exactly the same way as a dedicated circuit after the call has been set up.

➤ PPP, with compression and authentication options, is supported.

➤ Many router models support ISDN either as Basic Rate Interface (BRI) or Primary Rate Interface (PRI).

➤ Bandwidth on demand is supported. At pre-configured utilization levels, the router will automatically make additional calls to the same destination to share the load.

➤ Connections are made only when necessary. This feature saves money and facilities by providing services only when interesting traffic desires to cross the link by using DDR.

➤ Simple Network Management Protocol (SNMP) management is supported via the ISDN Management Information Base (MIB) group in the routers.

➤ Multiple bearer channels (B channels) are an ISDN offering that the routers support. They may be used independently or combined (multilink PPP (MPPP)—see Chapter 13) for bandwidth on demand. Administrators can configure the speeds on the B-channels for 56K or 64K operation.

➤ If the carriers along the dial path support it, the routers have the option of using inbound caller identification as a means of enhancing security. The receiving router is pre-configured with acceptable inbound phone numbers, and the router answers only if the call arrives from a valid source number. This feature is not universally available from the carriers and may not be useable.

 Ensure that you know and understand the functions and features of the various types of circuits discussed in the above sections.

Packet- And Cell-Switched Service Offerings

In addition to the more traditional WAN offerings, the routers may provide various packet-, frame-, or cell-switched connection alternatives. These services use the concept of a virtual circuit (VC) to provide an end-to-end path.

Packet-switched networks are most often provided by commercial carriers; however, you can create your own packet-switched network by configuring your own routers to act as switches. The data is carried in packets (X.25), frames (Frame Relay), or cells (SMDS/ATM). The switching of the packets is invisible to the user. As far as the routers are concerned, the switched networks are multi-access networks. Figure 12.4 shows an example of a packet-switched network.

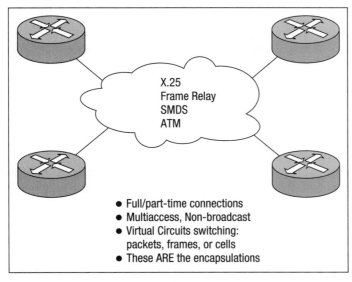

Figure 12.4   The packet-switched network.

X.25 Packet Switching

X.25 networks are common around the world, but not so prevalent in the United States. They were created to be carrier-provided services that support *permanent virtual circuits (PVCs)*, the packet network version of dedicated connections, and *switched virtual circuits (SVCs)*, which play the role of dial access calls. The telco providers originally assumed that customers would have two lines into each house or business: normal telephones for voice and, if needed, an X.25 connection for data. Normally, a corporate user would not attach a modem to a voice telephone line. Most likely, there would be two networks.

Bandwidth was provided via mostly analog facilities, and the quality of the circuit was assumed to be limited. Consequently, the protocols built into the X.25 network at both layer 2 and layer 3 were reliable. That is, each switch is capable of retransmitting damaged or missing packets or frames. This reliable connection technique provided high-quality service levels; however, due to the overhead associated with re-transmissions, speeds were typically limited. As digital circuit quality and speed have improved, so have the speeds associated with X.25. Today, access speeds range from dial terminal rates up to 1.5/ 2.048Mbps (T1/E1).

X.25 is more common than it might first appear. Telephone carrier equipment in most cases does not use SNMP management; instead, it uses X.25 packets to carry alert/alarm information.

Today, most dial access is done by PCs using PPP protocol. However, many of the Internet Service Providers (ISPs) and public networks still provide *dumb terminal* (an unintelligent access device utilizing only a keyboard and display with no local processing) access via X.25. An ASCII device would send asynchronous characters to a PAD function that is typically contained in a router. The PAD would assemble the characters into packets, and the VC's operation would guarantee that they would be delivered in order to the far end of the network.

Frame Relay Networks

As network quality has improved due to digital circuitry and because we have moved network reliability to the Transport layer, a lighter-weight service was created to carry data. Because of this, Frame Relay switches no longer need to have the ability to retransmit individual frames within the network. The switches can simply rely on the end station protocol to retransmit data as needed. Frame Relay originally provided only PVCs, but Cisco today supports SVCs. At the time of this writing, however, most Frame Relay networks still do not offer SVC support, except in a small number of test markets. The service is connection oriented because the path through the network is created before the data flows and because the frames (if they arrive) all arrive in sequence.

The main difference between Frame Relay PVCs and those offered by X.25 is that, with Frame Relay, the network does not notify you of errors, nor does it retransmit dropped or damaged frames. The flow-control and error-detection functions have been moved to the Transport layer with Transmission Control Protocol (TCP) or equivalent logic.

Due to the use of digital circuits, the error rate on the circuits is lower than the rate the X.25 developers originally expected and planned for. As a result, the circuits may operate at much higher speeds (up to E3/T3—34/45Mbps, respectively) than X.25. Frame Relay does include a *frame check sequence (FCS)*, also called a *Cyclic Redundancy Check (CRC)*, to allow damaged frames to be dropped. Retransmission is done outside of the Frame Relay cloud. Flow control is limited to fairly basic congestion notification.

SMDS

SMDS is connectionless service that uses cell-switching technology. Each record is a datagram. That is, each record transmitted must carry the addressing necessary to reach its destination. The datagrams are forwarded to a central connectionless server device, which then routes the data on to the destination. A nice feature of this type of connectionless server is that administrators can use multicast (group) addressing to reach several devices with a single message. The source device addresses and forwards the packet to the multicast group and the server does the replication. Figure 12.5 shows an illustration of the SMDS network components.

The SMDS Interface Protocol (SIP) is based on the IEEE standard protocol for metropolitan area networks (MANs). The 4000 and 7000 series routers can provide a direct SIP interface to SMDS via an ATM interface board.

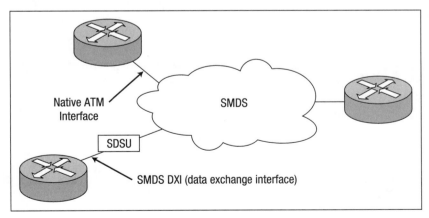

Figure 12.5 SMDS network devices.

Another approach would be to use a regular serial interface that connects to a special CSU/DSU-like device by using the SMDS data-exchange interface (SMDS DXI).

ATM Networks

ATM is a high-speed, cell-switching environment. It is available in the United States and Europe and is the basis for the new telephone switching systems in China. ATM supports both PVCs and SVCs as a connection-oriented service. End-to-end error checking and retransmission are done at layer 4. Although the basic technology is around 10 years old, most of the standards are still evolving. The interface specifications for routers and other "edge" devices (those devices that represent the outer boundary of your network as well as the boundary of the carrier network) are referred to as the *User Network Interface (UNI)*. All traffic—whether voice, video, or data—is sent across the network as 53-byte (5 bytes of header and 48 bytes of data) fixed-length cells.

You can use ATM for WAN connections at a wide variety of speeds generally anywhere from quite low (64Kbps) to very high (9.6Gbps). Typical speeds today range from one or more T1 (1.5Mbps) circuits used together up through 155Mbps to around 622Mbps.

 Ensure that you know the basic characteristics of packet-, frame-, and cell-switched technologies well enough to be able to distinguish among them.

Cisco WAN Service Offerings

Several IOS features and/or hardware interfaces provide the types of service offerings we have mentioned. Table 12.1 summarizes service requirements and Cisco features.

Table 12.1   Service requirements and Cisco features.

Service Required	Cisco Features
Private (dedicated/leased) line	Serial interfaces
Async dial service	Access servers
Router to router dial	ISDN and DDR
Packet and Cell switched services	X.25, Frame Relay, SMDS, and ATM

WAN Encapsulations

Each WAN service type uses a different encapsulation to carry the traffic across the provider network. These are a few of those encapsulations:

➤ **HDLC** A Cisco proprietary encapsulation that is used only between Cisco routers to support multi-protocol point-to-point circuits. HDLC is the default encapsulation on Serial links.

➤ **PPP** A standardized protocol encapsulation that is used synchronously to connect routers of different types. PPP supports multi-protocol circuits. PPP may also be used on dial circuits in asynchronous mode (such as PC Internet access).

➤ **Serial Line Internet Protocol (SLIP)** A standard that is used for IP access only. It is used only on dial circuits.

➤ **Link Access Procedure Balanced (LAPB)** An encapsulation that is used as the layer 2 protocol between routers when X.25 is configured at layer 3. LAPB performs error detection, flow control, or retransmission at layer 2. You can specify LAPB between the routers without X.25 if the circuit is unreliable. Doing so allows the retransmissions to take place at the Data Link layer rather than at the Transport layer.

➤ **SDLC** An IBM protocol that is seen in Cisco environments only where the connection is between a Cisco router and either an IBM front-end processor or IBM terminals.

➤ **Frame Relay** An encapsulation that is used only on connections to or between Frame Relay switches and customer premise equipment (CPE).

Choosing The Right Connection Type

Choosing the correct service type can make a big difference in the overall cost of your WAN deployment. When you are deciding on the WAN service type, you need to evaluate six issues: availability of services, the type of application traffic, bandwidth, routing protocol characteristics, ease of management, and cost. Usually when you look at a scenario, one of the issues outweighs the others. Let's look at each of these more closely.

Availability Of Services

You cannot take the availability of services for granted. Not all service providers offer all services. For example, ISDN is still not available in some areas.

ATM is still considered a new technology may not be readily available from all carriers. It is important to determine that the speed and types of circuits you need will be available when and where you need them.

Type Of Application Traffic

You may need to categorize and prioritize traffic. For example, you may have large amounts of high-volume (such as a large-packet) traffic that may be lower priority. In contrast, you may have lower-volume, smaller packets that are high-priority traffic.

Some traffic types may need fast responses. Highly interactive traffic may require prioritization should a congestion occur. For example, consider a situation where your local servers cache transactions during the day (usually for uploading in the middle of the night). Local devices would need to look up information locally because connectivity with the core site is established only at night. For this example, a bandwidth-on-demand or dial-on-demand deployment may be appropriate. On the other hand, you may also need constant access to several different, widely dispersed servers within the internetwork, so full-time connection would more useful in meeting your needs in this situation.

Bandwidth

Bandwidth is expensive. We're literally "renting" it, so the cost of full-time versus part-time connectivity is a large issue. The traffic may arrive intermittently throughout the day or in big bursts. The transactions may come frequently or very rarely. All of these issues affect the decisions about the appropriate type of circuit (such as dial or dedicated and if dedicated, Frame Relay or a leased line).

Dedicated lines are very expensive, but the constant nature of the traffic may require them. Dial access lines are a good choice if the traffic is within the dial circuit's bandwidth limitations. The connect time charges based on the amount of time necessary for the data transfers should be low enough to justify using DDR circuits. Frame Relay provides constant availability but with lower maximum volume and lower cost when compared with dedicated facilities.

Routing Protocol Characteristics

Routing protocols have an impact on the circuit type you select. Some routing protocols, such as Routing Information Protocol (RIP), send constant, periodic updates. This periodic update cycle can contribute to increased traffic volume as well as slow connect times. For example, if it were necessary to dial a call every 30 seconds, as with RIP, the cost to exchange routing updates would likely exceed what a full-time connection costs. Several options exist to help with this problem. They include snapshot routing (discussed in detail in Chapter 13) for distance-vector protocols, Open Shortest Path First (OSPF, discussed in Chapter 7), and Enhanced Interior Gateway Routing Protocol (EIGRP discussed in Chapter 8).

Ease Of Management

This is a big issue. It may be difficult to install (initial startup) and maintain (ongoing costs) the desired connections. You can often make it easier to manage your network by using a carrier's packet-switching, frame-switching, or cell-switching-based services. You may leave the provisioning of new equipment and facilities—as well as some of the troubleshooting and possibly even maintenance—to the vendor. In some cases, you can outsource the entire network service. Using contract labor may allow you to avoid much of the cost of training your own personnel in some new technology.

Cost

You must take all of the above considerations seriously. In the end, if all services are available, it eventually comes down to cost. You must look at both the network's initial startup and ongoing costs. Functionality and features that you *want* for the network may be trimmed down to only functionality and features that are *essential* for the network.

With many services having similar features, the right choice comes down to availability and cost. Can I get it and how hard will it hit my budget? The other factors discussed will play into the decision, however, they will not have as large an impact on your decision as cost and availability. Watch for clues (such as high volume, long duration, or frequent access) that indicate some sort of full-time connection is needed. Infrequent access and lower-volume needs lend themselves more to dial services.

Practice Questions

Question 1

> What is the default encapsulation used on dedicated facilities between Cisco routers?
>
> O a. Frame Relay
>
> O b. HDLC
>
> O c. LAPB
>
> O d. PPP

Answer b is correct. Cisco's proprietary version of HDLC is the default encapsulation on Serial interfaces. Answers a, c, and d are incorrect because they are valid encapsulations but not the default one.

Question 2

> Which protocol is a standard designed to connect routers of different manufacture?
>
> O a. Frame Relay
>
> O b. HDLC
>
> O c. LAPB
>
> O d. PPP

Answer d is correct. PPP is used on synchronous WAN links to connect routers. Although you may use Frame Relay, PPP was specifically designed to support multiple-protocol virtual circuits between routers. Therefore, answer a is incorrect. Answer b is incorrect because Cisco's HDLC is proprietary and is therefore not supported by other vendors. At the same time, Cisco does not support the proprietary protocols of other vendors. Answer c is incorrect because basic LAPB has no protocol or type field that makes the circuit a single-protocol circuit.

Question 3

> What protocol is most-often used for asynchronous dial access?
>
> ○ a. SLIP
>
> ○ b. HDLC
>
> ○ c. LAPB
>
> ○ d. PPP

Answer d is correct. PPP is used on asynchronous WAN links to connect PCs or workstations and routers. Although SLIP is the predecessor to PPP and although it may be used on asynchronous dial circuits, it supports only IP. Therefore, answer a is incorrect. Answer b is incorrect because Cisco's HDLC is a proprietary, synchronous protocol unknown to PC vendors. Answer c is incorrect because LAPB is a synchronous, connection-oriented protocol used between routers.

Question 4

> DDR refers to what form of communication?
>
> ○ a. Routers dialing other routers when traffic arrives for destinations supported by the other router.
>
> ○ b. PCs or workstations dialing routers or other PCs or workstations.
>
> ○ c. Frame Relay-connected routers.
>
> ○ d. PPP

Answer a is correct. Specifically, DDR refers to router-to-router dialing. Answers b and c are incorrect because they are not router-to-router dialing. Answer b is referred to as asynchronous dial access, usually using PPP. Answer c is incorrect because Frame Relay is not a DDR-capable technology. Answer d is incorrect because it is a line protocol; although it is used for both DDR and asynchronous dial access, PPP is not the name for the service.

Question 5

An application typically generates very frequent, high-volume traffic all day and all night. What type of WAN service is appropriate?

- ○ a. DDR
- ○ b. Frame Relay
- ○ c. Dedicated circuit
- ○ d. ATM

Answer c is correct. Dedicated circuits are available at all times. Answer a is incorrect because very frequent traffic would work against DDR; it would either constantly be bringing the circuit up and down, or the circuit would stay up all the time and the cost would be prohibitive. Answer b is part of the trick in this question. It is incorrect because high-volume traffic would indicate a dedicated circuit over Frame Relay because dedicated circuits provide 100 percent of the bandwidth on a full-time basis. The issue about all day and all night would indicate either Frame Relay or dedicated service; however, the comment regarding the volume of traffic would more likely indicate dedicated. Answer d is also possibly a part of the trick in this question. You can set up ATM for PVC service (static and always available) or SVC service (initiates a call to the destination). There is a bit of ambiguity in the question, which you should expect when taking the exam.

Question 6

An application typically generates very frequent, high-volume traffic all day and all night. Which service selection criterion is appropriate for consideration in planning a network deployment? [Check all correct answers]

- ❑ a. Availability of services
- ❑ b. Application traffic characteristics
- ❑ c. Bandwidth
- ❑ d. Routing protocol characteristics
- ❑ e. Ease of management
- ❑ f. Cost

Answers a, b, c, d, e, and f are correct. All answers are appropriate.

Need To Know More?

 Flanagan, William A. *The Guide to T1 Internetworking*. Miller Freeman Books, London, United Kingdom, 1998. ISBN 0-93664-826-0. This book goes in-depth about T1 and other digital technologies.

 For information on WAN services, check out the Cisco site at **www.cisco.com** and perform a search using the keywords "WAN", "ISDN", "HDLC", or other encapsulations and protocols covered in the chapter.

 For information on IBM-related WAN services such as SDLC, visit **www.networking.ibm.com** and search with the keyword "SDLC".

 For information on ATM services, visit **www.atmforum.com**. You can download any completed specification and view upcoming specifications in progress.

 For information on Frame Relay services, visit **www.frforum.com**. You can download any of the completed Frame Relay specifications.

Internetworking With ISDN

Terms you'll need to understand:

√ Basic Rate Interface (BRI)

√ Dial-on-demand routing (DDR)

√ Interesting traffic

√ Password Authentication Protocol (PAP)

√ Challenge Handshake Authentication Protocol (CHAP)

√ Multilink Point-to-Point Protocol (PPP)

√ Dialer profile

√ Rotary group

√ Dial backup

√ Snapshot routing

Techniques you'll need to master:

√ Understanding the use of Integrated Services Digital Network (ISDN)

√ Configuring dial-on-demand routing

√ Defining Interesting Traffic

√ Configuring PPP authentication

√ Configuring dialer profiles

√ Configuring rotary groups

√ Configuring dial backup

√ Configuring snapshot routing

This chapter introduces Integrated Services Digital Network (ISDN) as an internetworking technology and addresses its related technologies. We focus on the Point-to-Point Protocol (PPP), various dialing configuration parameters, and the configuration of secure authentication procedures. Although the information contained in this chapter may not be sufficient to adequately configure ISDN services in a production environment under varying circumstances, it will give you a solid understanding of ISDN fundamentals as they pertain to the ACRC exam.

Integrated Services Digital Network Basics

You may already be somewhat familiar with ISDN as a technology—it has been around the internetworking realm for a number of years. ISDN refers to a set of digital services that are becoming available to end users. It involves digitizing the telephone network so that providers can provide end users with multiple services from a single end-user interface over existing telephone wiring. ISDN is an effort to standardize subscriber services, user/network interfaces, and network and internetwork capabilities. The ultimate goal of standardizing subscriber services is to give some level of international compatibility. At the same time, this standardization facilitates multivendor interoperability.

The ISDN community would like to ensure that ISDN networks communicate easily with one another. ISDN was developed with the idea that it would be used to transport voice calls, data traffic, and video traffic. The evolution of ISDN as a viable technology moves forward with the needs of those very different traffic types in mind. ISDN applications include high-speed image applications, additional telephone lines in homes to serve the telecommuting industry, high-speed file transfer, and video conferencing. ISDN is also becoming very common in home-based offices as many corporations extend their offices into the residential arena.

Basic Rate Interface

The Basic Rate Interface (BRI) refers to the most typical type of ISDN connection. BRI refers to a native ISDN interface on a router. The basic rate connection consists of two Bearer (B) channels and one *Delta* or *Digital subscriber service* (you may have come across both depending on how much you work with this stuff) (D) channel. Each B channel has 64,000 bits per second (bps) of bandwidth available to it. When both B channels are active, the aggregate bandwidth reaches 128,000 bps. You can purchase ISDN service with two, one, or zero B channels. Typical deployments use two B channels, implementations of one B channel may have to do with cost reduction, and zero B channel implementations are possible when you wish to run another technology (such as X.25) across the D channel. We will not discuss deployments of zero B channels because such implementations are not typical in most internetworks.

The D channel is used to convey signaling requests to an ISDN switch. In essence, it provides a local loop to the telephone company's central office. Such requests are the equivalent of picking up your telephone handset and dialing a phone number. The router uses the D channel to dial destination phone numbers. The bandwidth of the D channel is 16,000 bps, which is more than adequate for ISDN's needs. Our discussion will focus on the most typical implementation of ISDN: two B channels and one D channel.

You can configure ISDN interfaces for High-Level Data Link Control (HDLC), Frame Relay, Link Access Procedure Balanced (LAPB), Point-to-Point Protocol (PPP), and X.25 encapsulation. When you configure PPP encapsulation, you can specify the use of Password Authentication Protocol (PAP) or Challenge Handshake Authentication Protocol (CHAP). We will discuss these options later in this chapter.

Installing ISDN

When you have an ISDN line installed, the telephone company (telco) places a Category 5 unshielded twisted-pair (UTP) cable at your site. The telco runs the cable to whatever location you specify. Many times, the base installation charge covers only bringing the line into your premises. In that case, you must decide if you want to extend the cable into your wiring closet or server room. We've found that it is well worth the negligible additional charge to allow the telco installer to extend it to a point that is easy to reach from the router with another cable. Make your support of the network as easy as possible. Once you have decided where to put the cable and have had it put in place, the installer will place an eight-pin modular (RJ-45) jack to the cable and attach it to the wall.

The installer should label the jack with your Service Profile Identifiers (SPIDs) and a circuit identifier number. You'll need these if you call for service at a later time. This jack is the *Point of Demarcation (demarc)*, where responsibility for the line changes hands. The equipment on your side of the point of demarc is known as *customer premise equipment (CPE)*. The jack that the telco installs is a direct interface from the local central office switch to your customer premise equipment.

ISDN Equipment

A key piece of equipment that you need in your ISDN installation is a network termination 1 (NT1). The NT1 is a device similar to a Channel Service Unit/Digital Service Unit (CSU/DSU), used in serial connections. The NT1 has at least two interfaces: a Subscriber (S)/Trunk (T) interface jack and a User (U) interface. The S/T interface is where you plug into the router's BRI interface. The U interface plugs into the telco jack. Many of Cisco's BRI-capable routers are now available with an integrated NT1. If you don't have this feature, you'll need an external NT1. The NT2 is a more complicated device that performs layer 2 and 3 protocol functions and concentration services. The native ISDN interface is known as the terminal equipment 1 (TE1) interface.

From time to time, you may find that you must install ISDN, but you have no native BRI interface on your router. In such cases, can you still use ISDN, or do you have to go with a more expensive T1 or fractional T1 solution? The answer is quite simple. Yes, you can still use ISDN; however, you need another piece of hardware known as a *terminal adapter*. The terminal adapter is a device that contains the BRI that your router is missing. In the recent ISDN hype, telecommunications manufacturers marketed terminal adapters as ISDN modems. Terminal adapters are *not* modems. They do not modulate and demodulate signals. What they do is interface your router's universal I/O serial port. The terminal adapter interfaces the NT1 with a native BRI.

The non-native ISDN is known as the terminal equipment 2 (TE2) interface. The interface between the TE2 and the TA is known as the Remote (R) interface. It is important to note that a non-native ISDN interface (more specifically, any solution that lacks a D channel) requires that you use the **dialer in-band** command in order to issue signaling requests to the ISDN switch. Using the **dialer in-band** configuration, each B channel, in effect, loses 8,000 bps of available bandwidth for signaling. Therefore, the bandwidth available per B channel becomes 56,000 bps. In some cases, ISDN facilities are available only at 56,000 bps per B channel, whether or not the interface is native ISDN. Check with your provider for details on your particular installation. Figure 13.1 depicts the details of the ISDN equipment interfaces.

Dial-On-Demand Routing

Dial-on-demand routing (DDR) is a feature available on ISDN-capable Cisco routers. It was created to allow users to save money on usage-based ISDN. If you are being charged for every minute of connect time on your ISDN circuit, your deployment is usage-based. Obviously, when you're being charged by the minute, you want to be able to bring the connection down during low-volume traffic times. DDR provides that ability. DDR offers a wide array of commands and differing command configurations. We will cover many of those configuration options in the remainder of this chapter. In addition, we will address how we may need to manipulate our dynamic routing protocols in order to stop periodic or incremental updates from keeping an ISDN call up unnecessarily.

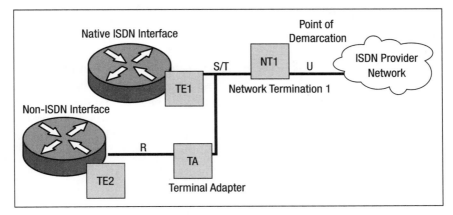

Figure 13.1   Examples of the ISDN interfaces and their positions in the network.

Interesting Traffic

The entire configuration of DDR depends on how you define the traffic types that cause a call setup to occur. This traffic is known as *interesting traffic*. Cisco's implementation of DDR allows for as much or as little specificity as is deemed necessary. Interesting traffic is defined by the creation of dialer-lists. *Dialer-lists* can specify that an entire protocol suite, no matter the level of traffic, causes a call setup. They can also be associated with standard or extended access lists in order to be specific to various traffic types. We covered access lists in Chapter 3. We'll use the same syntax to define the access lists; however, rather than associating the access list with an interface, we'll associate the access list with a dialer-list.

Figure 13.2 shows a basic configuration in which all Internet Protocol (IP) traffic has been deemed interesting. The line that defines the interesting traffic

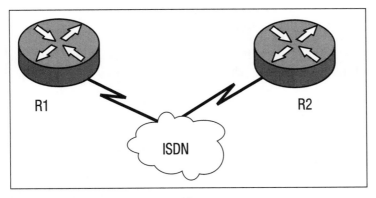

Figure 13.2   A basic DDR configuration.

is the *dialer-list* line. This dialer-list is associated with the proper interface using the *dialer-group* line, as shown. Note the list number and the group numbers are identical. This number is what ties the dialer-list and dialer-group together. You may not re-use any of these list or group numbers in the same router. Another command of interest in this configuration is the **dialer idle-timeout** command, which specifies the length of time in minutes that the link should stay up if there is no interesting traffic. Once the idle timer reaches zero, the call is disconnected. Listings 13.1 and 13.2 show basic DDR configurations for each of the routers in Figure 13.2.

Listing 13.1   R1 basic DDR configuration.

```
isdn switch-type basic-5ess
!
interface BRI0
 ip address 10.1.0.1 255.255.0.0
 encapsulation ppp
 dialer idle-timeout 180
 dialer map ip 10.1.0.2 5552222
 dialer-group 1
!
dialer-list 1 protocol ip permit
```

Listing 13.2   R2 basic DDR configuration.

```
isdn switch-type basic-5ess
!
interface BRI0
 ip address 10.1.0.2 255.255.0.0
 encapsulation ppp
 dialer idle-timeout 180
 dialer map ip 10.1.0.1 5551111
 dialer-group 1
!
dialer-list 1 protocol ip permit
```

The configuration is not always so straightforward. Usually, you'll want to make certain types of traffic initiate the call, as well as restrict other types.

Listing 13.3 shows the command line parameters for a more detailed DDR configuration.

It is imperative that you fully understand the basics of the DDR configuration.

RIP will not be moving across the link, so it is important that you use static routes in place of RIP updates. You must do so to provide bi-directional reachability between the two sites in the absence of routing protocol traffic. Also note that on the R2 configuration, any IP traffic that needs to cross the link has been defined as interesting. What is anticipated in this example is a heavier data flow from R1 to R2 than the reverse. Do not confuse this with security. DDR defines only what types of traffic initiate a call. Once a call has been established, any type of traffic that has been configured to traverse the link can do so. Therefore, you should make an additional change to the RIP routing protocol configuration to make the BRI interface passive. As a result, RIP is not allowed to send updates out of that interface.

ISDN Switch Types

Certain configurations require additional commands. The telco provides you with the type of switch to which you are connecting. Manufacturers of ISDN central office switches (also known as *local exchange equipment*) divide the local exchange into two functions: *local termination* and *exchange termination*. The local termination function primarily deals with the transmission facility and termination of the local loop. The exchange termination function deals with the switching portion of the local exchange.

The AT&T 5ESS and the Northern Telecom DMS-100 are the two principal ISDN switches used in North America. The recent release of National ISDN-1 software has corrected most incompatibility issues between the AT&T and Northern Telecom switches. Prior to the release of this software, for example, you could not use AT&T ISDN products with a Northern Telecom switch.

AT&T introduced the 5ESS switch in 1982. It can provide up to 100,000 local loops. Approximately 1,600 5ESS switches are in use worldwide, serving close to 40 million lines. In the United States, approximately 85 percent of the BRI lines in service connect to a 5ESS-equipped central office.

By comparison, the Northern Telecom DMS-100 switch family is intended to deliver a wide range of telecommunication services. The DMS-100, introduced in 1978, can terminate up to 100,000 lines. Although AT&T and Northern Telecom have deployed the most ISDN switches, there are other ISDN switch manufacturers.

Other types of ISDN-capable switches are used in Australia, Europe, Japan, and New Zealand and are usually country-specific. Use *the* **isdn switch-type** command to configure the router for the type of switch to which the router connects. Your telco provides you with this information.

Additional Command Configuration Options

Most ISDN configurations require you to specify a Service Profile Identifier (SPID), the way you identify your router to the central office switch. The telco can associate a variety of features with your SPID. (Those features are beyond the scope of this book because they don't apply to the router's configuration.) The telco gives you one SPID for each of your B channels. You must configure both SPIDs on the interface. Use the **isdn spid1** command. You may also need to use the **isdn spid2** command to configure both B channels if you'll be using both. These commands also allow you to specify the local directory number (LDN), which is a seven-digit number assigned by the service provider that is part of the incoming setup message. The LDN is not necessary for establishing ISDN-based connections, but it you must specify it if you want to receive incoming calls on B channel 2. The LDN is required only when two SPIDs are configured.

> *Note:* *There is no standard format for SPID numbers. Therefore, your SPID numbers may vary from installation to installation depending on the switch vendor and telephone carrier. Contact your telco for the exact format to use at each site.*

 The SPID numbers will play an integral role in your DDR configuration.

You may want to enable features such as caller identification in order to decide whether or not to accept an ISDN call. You can configure **isdn answer** commands to tell the router from which phone numbers to accept calls. Listings 13.3 and 13.4 show the DDR configurations of each router with SPID numbers and **isdn answer** commands added.

Listing 13.3 R1 SPID and ISDN answer configuration.

```
isdn switch-type basic-5ess
!
Interface ethernet 0
ip address 9.0.0.1 255.0.0.0
!
Interface ethernet 1
ip address 10.2.0.1 255.255.0.0
!
interface BRI0
 ip address 10.1.0.1 255.255.0.0
 encapsulation ppp
```

```
dialer idle-timeout 180
isdn spid1 21455511110101 2145551111
isdn spid2 21455511120101 2145551112
isdn answer 2145552222
isdn answer 2145552223
dialer map ip 10.1.0.2 2145552222
dialer map ip 10.1.0.2 2145552223
dialer-group 1
!
access-list 101 deny rip any any
access-list 101 permit tcp any any eq telnet
access-list 101 permit tcp any any eq ftp
access-list 101 permit tcp any any eq ftp-data
!
dialer-list 1 list 101
!
router rip
network 10.0.0.0
network 9.0.0.0
passive-interface BRI0
!
Ip route 11.0.0.0 255.0.0.0 BRI0
```

Listing 13.4   R2 SPID and ISDN answer configuration.

```
isdn switch-type basic-5ess
!
Interface ethernet 0
ip address 11.0.0.1 255.0.0.0
!
interface BRI0
 ip address 10.1.0.2 255.255.0.0
 encapsulation ppp
 dialer idle-timeout 180
 isdn spid1 21455522220101
 isdn spid2 21455522230101
 isdn answer 2145551111
 isdn answer 2145551112
 dialer map ip 10.1.0.1 2145551111
 dialer map ip 10.1.0.1 2145551112
 dialer-group 1
!
dialer-list 1 protocol ip permit
!
no router rip
!
Ip route 9.0.0.0 255.0.0.0 BRI0
```

Point-To-Point Protocol (PPP)

PPP, described in RFC 1661, encapsulates network-layer protocol information over point-to-point links. Although it can be configured on a variety of interfaces, our focus remains on the ISDN-capable interface. In order to establish communications over an ISDN link, each end of the PPP link must first send Link Control Protocol (LCP) packets to configure and test the data link. After the link has been established and optional facilities have been negotiated as needed, PPP must send Network Control Protocol (NCP) packets to choose and configure one or more network-layer protocols. Once each of the chosen network-layer protocols has been configured, datagrams from each network-layer protocol can be sent over the link. The link remains configured for communications until explicit LCP or NCP packets close the link down, or until some external event occurs (for example, an inactivity timer expires or a network administrator intervenes). In other words, PPP is simply a pathway opened for multiple protocols simultaneously. The call setup is initiated by interesting traffic as defined using access lists and terminated by an external event such as manual clearing or idle timer expiration.

PPP Authentication

The PPP with CHAP authentication or PAP is often used to inform a central site about the remote routers that are connected to it. With this authentication information, if the router or access server receives another packet for a destination to which it is already connected, it need not place an additional call. CHAP and PAP were originally specified in RFC 1334, and CHAP is updated in RFC 1994. These protocols are supported on ISDN interfaces.

When using CHAP or PAP authentication, each router or access server identifies itself by a *name*. This identification process prevents a router from placing another call to a router to which it is already connected, as well as prevents unauthorized access. Access control using CHAP or PAP is available on all serial interfaces that use PPP encapsulation. The authentication feature reduces the risk of security violations on your router or access server. You can configure either CHAP or PAP for the interface.

When CHAP is enabled on the BRI interface and a remote device attempts to connect to it, the local router or access server sends a CHAP packet to the remote device. The CHAP packet requests or "challenges" the remote device to respond. The challenge packet consists of an ID, a random number, and the hostname of the local router.

The required response consists of two parts:

➤ An encrypted version of the router's ID, a secret password (or *secret*), and the random number

➤ The hostname of the remote device

When the local router or access server receives the response, it verifies the secret by performing the same encryption operation as indicated in the response and looking up the required hostname. The secret passwords must be identical on the remote device and the local router. By transmitting this response, the password is never transmitted in clear text, preventing other devices from stealing it and gaining illegal access to the system. Without the proper response, the remote device cannot connect to the local router. CHAP transactions occur only when a link is established. The local router or access server does not request a password during the rest of the call. (The local device can, however, respond to such requests from other devices during a call.)

When PAP is enabled, the remote router that is attempting to connect to the local router or access server must send an authentication request. If the username and password specified in the authentication request are accepted, the router sends an authentication acknowledgment. All PAP operations are performed in clear text across the link. PAP authentication is accomplished with a similar configuration. The only difference lies in the **ppp authentication pap** interface command for PAP and the **ppp authentication chap** interface command for CHAP. To configure authentication, you must define the remote hostname (or username) and password. These usernames and passwords are case sensitive. Password encryption is available as needed for PAP and CHAP passwords in your router configurations. Once you have configured usernames and passwords, you must configure the interface. The **ppp authentication** command is used to select the appropriate authentication. Listings 13.5 and 13.6 show an example of CHAP configuration.

Listing 13.5   R1 CHAP configuration.

```
hostname R1
isdn switch-type basic-5ess
username R2 password secret21
username R1 password secret21
!
interface BRI0
ppp authentication chap
 ip address 10.1.0.1 255.255.0.0
 encapsulation ppp
 ppp multilink
 dialer load-threshold 110
 dialer idle-timeout 180
 dialer map ip 10.1.0.2 5552222
```

```
dialer-group 1
!
dialer-list 1 protocol ip permit
```

Listing 13.6   R2 CHAP configuration.

```
hostname R2
isdn switch-type basic-5ess
username R1 password secret21
username R2 password secret21
!
interface BRI0
ppp authentication chap
 ip address 10.1.0.2 255.255.0.0
 encapsulation ppp
 ppp multilink
 dialer load-threshold 110
 dialer idle-timeout 180
 dialer map ip 10.1.0.1 5551111
 dialer-group 1
!
dialer-list 1 protocol ip permit
```

Multilink PPP

Multilink PPP is a specification that allows the bandwidth aggregation of multiple B channels into one logical pipe. More specifically, the Multilink PPP feature provides load-balancing functionality over multiple wide area network (WAN) links, while providing multivendor interoperability, packet fragmentation and proper sequencing, and load calculation on both inbound and outbound traffic. Cisco's implementation of Multilink PPP supports the fragmentation and packet sequencing specifications in RFC 1717. Multilink PPP allows packets to be fragmented and the fragments to be sent at the same time over multiple point-to-point links to the same remote address.

The multiple links come up in response to a dialer load-threshold that you define. The load can be calculated on inbound traffic, outbound traffic, or on either, as needed for the traffic between the specific sites. Multilink PPP provides bandwidth on demand and reduces transmission latency across WAN links. For example, consider a sample configuration including the activation of Multilink PPP and the dialer load-threshold of 110. Load is a value in the range of 1 through 255. It's calculated based on the utilization of the interface. You can see the current load of the interface by using a **show interface** command. With our setting of 110, we've specified that at approximately 60 percent utilization, the second B channel should be dialed and brought up to the destination to provide for fragmentation and load balancing across the link.

Dialer Profiles

Dialer profiles allow you to configure physical interfaces to be separated from a logical configuration required for a call. Profiles may also allow the logical and physical configurations to be bound together dynamically call by call.

A dialer profile consists of the following elements:

➤ **Dialer interface configuration** A logical interface created by an administrator. It includes one or more dialer strings (also known as *ISDN phone numbers*), each of which is used to reach one destination.

➤ **Dialer map-class** A single group of commands that defines all the characteristics for any call to the specified dial string (ISDN phone number).

➤ **Dialer pool** A pool of physical interfaces ordered on the basis of the priority assigned to each physical interface.

All calls going to or from the same destination subnetwork use the same dialer profile. A dialer interface configuration includes all settings needed to reach a specific destination router. You can specify multiple ISDN destination phone numbers for the same dialer interface, each phone number being associated with a different dialer map-class. For example, the map-class for one destination might specify a 56K bps ISDN speed whereas the map-class for a different destination might specify a 64K bps ISDN speed.

Each dialer interface uses a dialer pool. A physical interface can belong to multiple dialer pools, contention being resolved by priority. On ISDN interfaces, you can set a limit on the number of B channels that any dialer pools have reserved. A channel that a dialer pool has reserved remains idle until traffic is directed to the pool. When dialer profiles are used to configure DDR, a physical interface has no configuration settings except encapsulation and the dialer pools to which the interface belongs.

Figure 13.2 shows the same basic network we've worked with throughout this chapter. The configuration shows that we've associated the physical interface BRI0 with a logical dialer interface. Although our configuration will show only a single physical interface associated with the dialer interface, you can associate multiple BRI interfaces with a single logical interface. You'll notice that there is a minimal configuration on BRI0. We've simply set the encapsulation, authentication and told this interface that it is to be a member of dialer pool 4, and set its priority to 255. The priority parameter is used to specify the order of use for the interfaces.

You can make a single physical interface a member of multiple dialer pools by simply repeating the configuration on the physical interface to assign a new pool and, of course, configuring another dialer interface. In Figure 13.2, the dialer interface configuration is below the physical interface configuration. On this logical dialer interface, we've configured protocol attributes for IP, and set the encapsulation to PPP. The **dialer remote-name** command specifies the name to expect for CHAP authentication, if CHAP is to be used. Next, we've configured the ISDN phone number to use in order to connect to the other side of the ISDN network. Also included in the dial string command is the application of a map-class. The **map-class** command is used to allow you to specify different characteristics for different types of calls on a per-call-destination basis. For example, you can specify higher priority and a lower wait-for-carrier time for an ISDN calls map-class than for a modem calls map-class. You can also specify a different speed for some ISDN calls than for others.

Now that we've defined destination information and authentication parameters, we need to tell the logical dialer interface which physical interfaces it has at its disposal. We accomplish this with the **dialer pool** command, which specifies that any BRI interface that has been made a member of dialer pool 4 can be used to make ISDN calls to any destination. With all of these configuration commands completed, we cannot overlook the most important aspect of DDR: interesting traffic. We've configured a dialer list and associated a dialer-group with the logical dialer interface. Listings 13.7 and 13.8 show CHAP authentication along with the use of dialer profiles with dialer pools on each router.

Listing 13.7 R1 dialer profile with dialer-pool configuration.

```
isdn switch-type basic-5ess
username R1 password cisco
username R2 password cisco
!
interface BRI0
 no ip address
 encapsulation ppp
 dialer pool-member 4 priority 255
 no fair-queue
 ppp authentication chap
!
interface Dialer1
 ip address 10.1.0.2 255.255.255.0
 encapsulation ppp
 dialer remote-name R2
 dialer string 5552222 class toR2
 dialer pool 4
 dialer-group 1
 ppp authentication chap
```

```
!
map-class dialer toR2
 dialer idle-timeout 180
 dialer isdn speed 56
!
dialer-list 1 protocol ip permit
```

Listing 13.8 R2 dialer profile with dialer-pool configuration.

```
isdn switch-type basic-5ess
username R2 password cisco
username R1 password cisco
!
interface BRI0
 no ip address
 encapsulation ppp
 dialer pool-member 4 priority 255
 no fair-queue
 ppp authentication chap
!
interface Dialer1
 ip address 10.1.0.1 255.255.255.0
 encapsulation ppp
 dialer remote-name R1
 dialer string 5551111 class toR1
 dialer pool 4
 dialer-group 1
 ppp authentication chap
!
map-class dialer toR1
 dialer idle-timeout 180
 dialer isdn speed 56
dialer-list 1 protocol ip permit
```

The use of correct configuration parameters for dialer pools will give you great flexibility in your network.

Rotary Groups

ISDN *rotary groups* are similar to dialer pools. One primary difference is the lack of map-class capabilities in rotary groups. Note that we are creating a logical dialer interface in the same manner as we did with dialer-pool configuration. However, the interface designation of the dialer interface is an important detail. Listing 13.9 shows all of our physical BRI interfaces associated with **dialer rotary-group 2**. We used the number 2 as our rotary group number, so we must use the number 2 as our dialer interface number designator. The only protocol or configuration attributes we are configuring on the physical interface are the single command that makes the BRI interface a part of the rotary group and the encapsulation. On dialer-pool interfaces, we had the option of setting a priority in order to specify the order in which the interfaces will be used. With rotary groups, we don't have that granularity. You configure all protocol attributes in the logical dialer interface. Listings 13.9 and 13.10 show the routers' configuration with rotary groups enabled.

Listing 13.9   R1 rotary group configuration.

```
hostname R1
!interface BRI0
no ip address
encapsulation ppp
dialer rotary-group 2
!
interface BRI1
no ip address
encapsulation ppp
dialer rotary-group 2
!
interface BRI2
no ip address
encapsulation ppp
dialer rotary-group 2
!
interface Dialer2
ip address 10.1.0.1 255.255.255.0
encapsulation ppp
dialer map ip 10.1.0.2 name R2 5552222
dialer-group 1
!
dialer-list 1 protocol ip permit
```

Listing 13.10   R2 rotary group configuration.

```
hostname R2
!
interface BRI0
no ip address
encapsulation ppp
dialer rotary-group 2
!
```

```
interface BRI1
no ip address
encapsulation ppp
dialer rotary-group 2
!
interface BRI2
no ip address
encapsulation ppp
dialer rotary-group 2
!
interface Dialer2
ip address 10.1.0.2 255.255.255.0
encapsulation ppp
dialer map ip 10.1.0.1 name R1 5551111
dialer-group 1
!
dialer-list 1 protocol ip permit
```

Routing Protocol Operations With Dialer Interfaces

Routing updates have undoubtedly come to mind while you've been reading this chapter. What about RIP, Interior Gateway Routing Protocol (IGRP), or other dynamic protocols? Won't they keep the link up once it's been established? The answer is yes. If I define all IP as interesting traffic, does that mean a routing protocol update forces a call to initiate? Again, yes, it does. At this point, we need to discuss how to deal with unwanted routing updates. The answer to this situation is simple: static routes and passive interfaces.

The issue is this: Routing updates are causing unwanted uptime on my ISDN circuit. To stop these updates, you need to define a static route to the destination network at the remote site. In creating this static route, you have two options. The first option includes defining the static route using an outbound interface. By defining the outbound interface, we are telling the router to treat the destination network as if it were a directly connected network.

According to Cisco, the static route is a required piece of information in a DDR scenario. You can specify either the next hop address or the outbound interface through which to depart the router. When a next hop address is specified you must manually redistribute static routes. When an outbound interface is specified redistribution is automatic and the router treats the route as a directly connected network. More on redistribution in Chapter 9.

Our other option is to define the static route using the next logical hop address. Once we've got the static routes in place, we need to tell our routing protocol not to send updates out of the BRI interface. We accomplish this by telling the routing protocol that this particular interface is *passive*, which is simple to do. We have configured R1 with a static route to the network on the other side of R2, network 11.0.0.0. Note the use of BRI0 as the outbound interface for the static route. We've set a static route to the 11.0.0.0 network, so we've also gone into the **router rip** configuration and told it to make interface BRI0 passive so that no routing updates can go out across the link as broadcasts. We have configured R2 with a static route back to network 9.0.0.0; we have not configured any routing protocol. R1 is the only router that R2 connects to, so the static routes suffice for traffic flow between the two routers.

Sometimes, R1 may have additional networks (to which R2 may need to forward traffic) connected to it. If that is the case, you may need to configure additional static routes. If doing so becomes cumbersome due to a large number of networks, consider using a default network. We have configured R2 with a default network instead of numerous additional static routes. A *default network* is simply a way of telling the router, "If it's not here, then go there (such as across the ISDN network)." Using this command is similar in function to giving a workstation a default gateway. Any traffic destined for a network other than the local network should be sent to this device. The static route defined on R2 simply serves to provide destination information so that R2's traffic knows how to reach the default network. Listings 13.11 and 13.12 show the use of passive interfaces to stop routing updates from leaving BRI0, the use of the **ip default-route** command and static routes to reach remote networks in the absence of routing updates.

Listing 13.11 R1 passive interface and static route configuration.

```
isdn switch-type basic-5ess
!
Interface ethernet 0
ip address 9.0.0.1 255.0.0.0
!
interface BRI0
 ip address 10.1.0.1 255.255.0.0
 encapsulation ppp
 dialer idle-timeout 180
 dialer map ip 10.1.0.2 5552222
 dialer-group 1
!
dialer-list 1 protocol ip permit
!
router rip
```

```
network 10.0.0.0
network 9.0.0.0
passive-interface BRIO
!
Ip route 11.0.0.0 255.0.0.0 BRIO
```

> *Note:*   *R1 passive interface and static route are the core site and the location of the default network, so it does not need the default network statement.*

Listing 13.12   R2 static route and default route configuration.

```
isdn switch-type basic-5ess
!
Interface ethernet 0
ip address 11.0.0.1 255.0.0.0
!
interface BRIO
 ip address 10.1.0.2 255.255.0.0
 encapsulation ppp
 dialer idle-timeout 180
 isdn spid1 21455522220101
 isdn answer 5551111
 dialer map ip 10.1.0.1 5551111
 dialer-group 1
!
dialer-list 1 protocol ip permit
!
no router rip
!
Ip default-network 9.0.0.0
Ip route 9.0.0.0 255.0.0.0 BRIO
```

> *Note:*   *Since RIP has not been enabled, there is no need at the remote site for passive interface configuration.*

Custom Dial-On-Demand Routing Operations

Up to this point, DDR has served as a means of providing a data pathway between physically separate facilities. In the remainder of this chapter, we'll explore some of DDR's other capabilities: dial backup and snapshot routing.

Dial Backup

Dial backup is a means of providing redundancy for WAN links. Although the ISDN connection may not provide the same amount of bandwidth as a primary link, dial backup provides a maintenance path if a primary link fails. Once the down condition of the primary link is detected, the dial-on-demand configuration is placed into service. Figure 13.3 depicts a typical use of dial backup. Listings 13.13 and 13.14 show the configuration of dial backup for use in primary interface overload and/or failure.

Listing 13.13   R1 dial backup configuration for load and failure.

```
isdn switch-type basic-5ess
!
Interface Serial 0
ip address 11.1.0.1 255.255.255.0
encapsulation hdlc
backup interface BRI0
backup delay 5 60
backup load 90 5
!
interface BRI0
 ip address 10.1.0.1 255.255.0.0
 encapsulation ppp
 dialer idle-timeout 180
 dialer map ip 10.1.0.2 5552222
 dialer-group 1
!
dialer-list 1 protocol ip permit
```

Listing 13.14   R2 configuration for load and failure.

```
isdn switch-type basic-5ess
!
Interface Serial 0
ip address 11.1.0.2 255.255.255.0
encapsulation hdlc
backup interface BRI0
backup delay 5 60
backup load 90 5
!
interface BRI0
 ip address 10.1.0.2 255.255.0.0
 encapsulation ppp
 dialer idle-timeout 180
 dialer map ip 10.1.0.1 5551111
 dialer-group 1
!
dialer-list 1 protocol ip permit
```

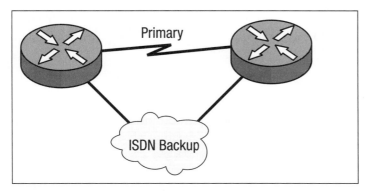

Figure 13.3   A sample dial backup configuration.

The primary data pathway across the WAN exists between each router's Serial 0 interface. You can implement dial backup in two ways. The first, and most obvious, manner is that dial backup can function if a primary link fails. When a "down" condition is detected on the primary interface, the secondary, or backup, link is changed to an "up" state and a connection is established.

The backup pathway is used in the absence of the primary, obviously. But how does the backup link know when it's time to return to the backup state? You must configure the parameters of the "up"/"down" state for the backup link. In Listing 13.14, notice the **backup delay 5 60** command. It specifies that if there is a failure, the system should wait five seconds to bring up the backup link. Once the failure has passed, the system should wait 60 seconds to bring the link back down.

Implementation of these timers is an attempt to compensate for a "bouncing" interface. In other words, the timers exist to compensate for an interface that drops momentarily and then comes right back up. Is the instance of a failure the only time the backup interface initializes? No. Note the **backup load 90 5** command. It specifies that the router should monitor the load on the primary interface and bring the link up at times when the load is particularly heavy. The first number represents the load of the interface as shown by a **show interface** command. Load is a number between 0 and 255. The second number is a measurement of aggregate load. Once the primary link is up, the router brings the secondary link back down when, in this case, the load of the two interfaces combined reaches a value of 5. So, we can use dial backup for link redundancy to partially compensate for failure. We can also use it provide load sharing capabilities to alleviate congestion on the WAN link.

Command parameter options for dial backup is an extremely common use of ISDN installation to provide for backup data flow in the event of the loss a of a primary link.

Snapshot Routing

Snapshot routing was developed to save bandwidth utilization across dial up interfaces. With snapshot routing, the router's routing table is frozen. The routing table is not updated during the *quiet period*, the amount of time that the routing table remains frozen. When the quiet timer expires, a dialer interface initiates a call to a remote router. The *active period* is the amount of time the call remains up in order for the two routers to exchange routing updates. It is important to note that snapshot routing is designed for use only with distance vector routing protocols. You can configure the router to exchange routing updates each time the line protocol goes from "down" to "up" or from "dialer spoofing" to "fully up."

A router can play two roles in a snapshot relationship: server and client. The *client* router is in charge of decrementing the quiet timer and dialing the *server* router once the quiet timer has reached zero. Snapshot routing allows dynamic distance vector routing protocols to run over DDR lines. Usually, routing broadcasts (routes and services) are filtered out on DDR interfaces and static definitions are configured instead.

With snapshot, normal updates are sent across the DDR interface for the short duration of the active period. After this, routers enter the quiet period, during which time the routing tables at both ends of the link are frozen. Snapshot is therefore a triggering mechanism that controls routing update exchange in DDR scenarios. Only in the active period do routers exchange dynamic updates. During the quiet period, no updates go through the link (up or down) and the routing information previously collected is kept unchanged (frozen) in the routing tables.

Snapshot routing is useful in two command situations:

➤ Configuring static routes for DDR interfaces

➤ Reducing the overhead of periodic updates sent by routing protocols to remote branch offices over a dedicated serial line

In Figure 13.4, we've defined R1 as the server router and R2 as the client router. The quiet timer is slowly counting down to zero, the end of the quiet period. Once the quiet period timer expires, the client router dials the server router. The quiet period we've defined is 12 hours (actually 720 minutes). Once

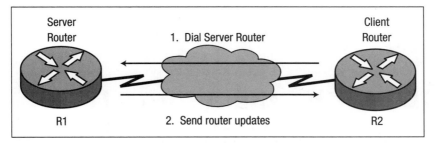

Figure 13.4   A sample snapshot routing configuration.

the 12 hours have elapsed, the client and server routers unfreeze their routing tables and exchange updates for the duration of the active period, in this case, 5 minutes. Listings 13.15 and 13.16 show the server and client configurations respectively.

Listing 13.15   R1 Snapshot server configuration.

```
isdn switch-type basic-ni1
!
interface BRI0
snapshot server 5 dialer
!
dialer map snapshot 1 name R2 5552222
```

Listing 13.16   R2 Snapshot client configuration.

```
isdn switch-type basic-ni1
!
interface BRI0
snapshot client 5 720 dialer
!
dialer map snapshot 1 name R1 5551111
```

The active period must match on both server and client routers. Five minutes is the minimum active period you can configure for any snapshot configuration. We should note here that although the routing tables are frozen, routing updates are still sent at their regular intervals out of any LAN interfaces on the router. For example, if there is an Ethernet segment on the opposite side of a snapshot router, the routing updates still broadcast out of that interface at the normal update interval, while remaining dormant on the BRI interface. It is possible to force the quiet period to expire and start the active period manually using the **clear snapshot quiet-time** command. In order to monitor snapshot routing processes, use the **show snapshot** command.

Snapshot routing is a seemingly insignificant topic, but Cisco is a big proponent of this type of configuration. It is only for use with distance vector routing protocols.

DDR With Other Protocols

You can configure DDR with any routable protocol. Our discussions to this point have focussed on IP only. However, in some instances, IP is not the only protocol that needs to traverse the network. Internetwork Packet eXchange (IPX) is in widespread use around the world. We need to be able to provide support for Novell network workstations that may be implemented in the enterprise internetwork. In the following sections, we'll take a look at IPX configuration parameters with regard to DDR.

DDR And IPX

When IPX routing is enabled and IPX network numbers are configured on interfaces, the IPX RIP and the Service Advertising Protocol (SAP) are also enabled for those interfaces. When one of those interfaces happens to be a BRI interface, we need to take into account some configuration parameters. IPX RIP and SAP are broadcast updates for routing table information and network service propagation, respectively. These broadcasts are on independent 60-second timers. You may or may not wish for this traffic to go across your ISDN link. To avoid this traffic, you can simply not include RIP and SAP in your interesting traffic definitions. At this point, RIP and SAP go across the link only as long as the link is up due to the transfer traffic that fits the interesting parameters. You can also define IPX static routes and static SAP entries. If you define static routes for IPX traffic, you should change the automatically configured parameters under the **ipx router rip** configuration to turn off RIP and SAP for specific interfaces. To do so, make them passive interfaces in the same manner as we discussed for IP passive interfaces (see the "Routing Protocol Operations With Dialer Interfaces" section earlier in this chapter).

IPX works on the premise of constant communication between clients and servers. A constant stream of keepalive traffic traverses the network to keep connections viable. Novell's NetWare structure uses the concept of *SPX Keepalives* to stay in constant communication with each client on the network. When communication via SPX Keepalives stops for some reason, the connection is presumed dead and should be dropped. IPX employs the *watchdog* to monitor these connections. If a connection is dormant for an extended period of time, the *watchdog* clears the connection on the NetWare server. This is done because Novell has implemented a server licensing scheme that allows you to have only the number of connections to the server for which you have purchased licensing. For example, if you purchase a five-user license and a sixth person tries to log in to the server, the connection is denied based on licensing, or the lack thereof. To that end, connections to a server can be a point of contention in a growing network. The watchdog packets monitor those connections and get rid of the ones that have not been active, allowing more users to log in to the NetWare server.

If we're going to implement a DDR solution, we must be able to satisfy these SPX Keepalive packets as well as the watchdog packets. In order to accomplish that task, we simply lie—or *spoof.* We must configure the routers at both sides of the ISDN link to spoof these packets. In other words, the router needs to know how to talk to the server as well as send the SPX Keepalives and keep the watchdogs happy on behalf of clients on the other side of the ISDN network. If the router cannot accomplish these tasks, none of these packets can flow when the link is down. If we don't spoof them, the connections will die. When we configure these options on the router, we enable the router to monitor the connections. The router is now in charge of watchdog and keepalive traffic, so we need to specify an amount of time to wait before clearing a connection that has gone dormant. We've turned off *IPX route caching* as well as enabled SPX Keepalives and watchdog spoofing. We've also specified that we allow only 300 seconds (five minutes) to pass before clearing a connection. Listings 13.17 and 13.18 show a basic IPX DDR configuration.

Listing 13.17   R1 IPX DDR configuration.

```
isdn switch-type basic-5ess
!
ipx routing 0000.0000.0001
!
interface BRI0
 encapsulation ppp
 ipx network 100
 dialer idle-timeout 180
 dialer map ipx 100.0000.0000.0002 5552222
 dialer-group 1
 no ipx route-cache
 ipx watchdog-spoof
 ipx spx-spoof
 ipx spx-idle-time 300
!
dialer-list 1 protocol ipx permit
```

Listing 13.18   R2 IPX DDR configuration.

```
isdn switch-type basic-5ess
!
Ipx routing 0000.0000.0002
!
```

```
interface BRI0
encapsulation ppp
ipx network 100
dialer idle-timeout 180
dialer map ipx 100.0000.0000.0001 5551111
dialer-group 1
no ipx route-cache
ipx watchdog-spoof
ipx spx-spoof
ipx spx-idle-time 300
!
dialer-list 1 protocol ipx permit
```

> *Note:* *Although we can spoof SPX Keepalives and watchdogs to maintain server connections, we have no working method of spoofing NetWare Directory Services (NDS) traffic. Therefore, we recommend that you do not implement DDR with any NetWare implementation in which NDS is used. Using DDR in this type of environment results in NDS synchronization errors and unpredictable results.*

 It is important for you to understand the commands to implement DDR for IPX.

ISDN-Related Commands

This section is dedicated to **show** and **debug** commands related to ISDN, because it is sometimes necessary to troubleshoot ISDN issues. You should use the commands and brief descriptions that accompany them often in order to keep yourself familiar with the way things are supposed to look when everything works well. If you know how it's supposed to look, then you'll have an easier time sorting out what's wrong when it does not work so well.

The **show** Commands

You use the **show** commands to give you realtime statistics and the status of the varying conditions in the router. They are useful to monitor traffic flow, packet drops, dialer interface status, and possible reasons for failures. Here are only a few of the many **show** commands available in the router:

➤ **show dialer**—Displays the current status of the link, including how long the link has been active for this call

➤ **show isdn active**—Displays the call status while in progress

➤ **show isdn status**—Display the status of the ISDN interface

As we mentioned earlier, it takes practice to become proficient when using these commands. It takes time to get comfortable with the command output. You'll need to be able to pick out just the right information at the right time. Play with these and explore the other available commands.

| As always is the case, abbreviated commands are not allowed on the exam.

The **debug** Commands

The **debug** commands are extremely useful in monitoring the realtime operations of call setup, status, and disconnect. They are most useful in troubleshooting. Note that **debug** output by default goes to the console port. If you're accessing the router via Telnet, you should enter the **terminal monitor** command at the privileged exec mode prompt. You should be extremely careful in debugging. **debug** has an extremely high priority in the router. If the output is too intense, you could lose keyboard interrupt capabilities. In other words, you cannot turn off the **debug** commands and therefore the output will continue to scroll across the screen. The eventual outcome may be the use of all available resource in the router causing it to crash. If you lose keyboard interrupt capabilities, try to Telnet into the router and type **no debug all** from the privileged exec mode. If this does not work, the only alternative is to power cycle the router. OK, now that you're sufficiently warned about **debug** dangers, here are some ISDN-related **debug** commands:

➤ **debug isdn q921**—Shows call setup and teardown activities. This is useful in monitoring call failures. It can point you to the possible causes of the failure.

➤ **debug isdn q931**—Shows the ISDN network layer operations. This command too is useful in monitoring call failures.

➤ **debug dialer**—Shows dialing events as well as responses, if any, from the other side of the link.

Practice Questions

Question 1

In the image below, what are the appropriate ISDN interface designations?

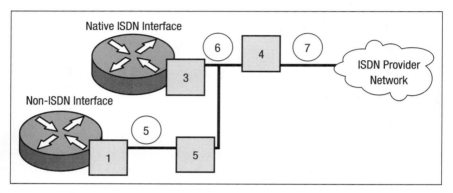

ISDN interface names

See Figure 13.1 at the beginning of the chapter for the picture detail to check your answers.

Question 2

Which piece of equipment is necessary to connect to your ISDN-capable router to the telephone company switch?

- O a. Modem
- O b. NT1
- O c. CSU/DSU
- O d. None of the above

Answer b is correct. The NT1 is the device that interfaces the U interface from the telco and the S/T interface to your router. Answer a is incorrect because traditional modems are not used in ISDN networks. They cannot perform required tasks such as authentication. Answer c is incorrect because CSU/DSUs are used only in T1 and fractional T1 networks, not ISDN. Answer d is incorrect because a correct answer is given.

Question 3

Which of the following are possible encapsulations for an ISDN-capable interface? [Choose the four best answers]

❑ a. Frame Relay

❑ b. LAPB

❑ c. PPP

❑ d. HDLC

❑ e. ATM

Answers a, b, c, and d are correct. ISDN was designed to provide a transport for other technologies including Frame Relay, LAPB, PPP and HDLC. ISDN is also capable of supporting X.25 encapsulation. Answer e is incorrect because Basic Rate Interfaces are not capable of providing Asynchronous Transfer Mode (ATM) services. Specialized ATM interfaces are required for utilization of ATM technology.

Question 4

Which of the following is the correct use of the command to tell the router that it is connecting to an AT&T 5ESS switch?

○ a. **isdn switch-type basic-5ess**

○ b. **switch-type basic 5ess**

○ c. **isdn switch 5ess**

○ d. **isdn type 5ess**

Answer a is correct. Again, the telco should provide the switch type to you. You need tell the router only the switch to which it connects. The remaining answers are incorrect syntax for the Cisco IOS and cannot be understood by the router. Therefore, answers b, c, and d are incorrect.

Question 5

> Which feature of the Point-to-Point-Protocol allows the bonding of multiple B channels?
>
> ○ a. PPP authentication
>
> ○ b. Multilink PPP
>
> ○ c. **dialer idle-timeout**
>
> ○ d. **dialer-group**

Answer b is correct. Multilink PPP was created with the intention of aggregating the bandwidth of multiple Bearer channels. Cisco has an extension of the Multilink strategy that allows the aggregation of B channels from physically separate chassis. Answer a is incorrect because PPP authentication is the process of verifying identity of a calling party to a called router. Answer c is incorrect because the **dialer idle-timeout** command tells the router how long to keep the dialed circuit active after interesting traffic has ceased flowing across the link. Answer d is incorrect because the **dialer-group** command is used in defining that interesting traffic by associating a dialer-list with a particular interface.

Question 6

> Password Authentication Protocol uses encrypted passwords for identity verification on an ISDN circuit.
>
> ○ a. True
>
> ○ b. False

Answer b is correct, False. Challenge Handshake Authentication Protocol uses encryption, whereas Password Authentication Protocol uses clear text. Stick with CHAP; you will be much more secure.

Question 7

> Rotary group configuration requires the creation of a logical dialer interface.
>
> ○ a. True
>
> ○ b. False

Answer a is correct, True. The rotary group configuration hinges squarely on the creation of this logical dialer interface. Without it, the configuration does not work.

Question 8

Which of the following defines all the characteristics for any call to the specified dial string?

- ○ a. PPP authentication CHAP
- ○ b. dialer-group
- ○ c. passive-interface
- ○ d. dialer map-class

Answer d is correct. Map-class configuration allows you to set up one profile for all calls to a specific destination rather than having to type the same commands time after time to get the desired configuration. Answer a is incorrect because authentication has nothing to do with a dial string. Answer b is incorrect because, as mentioned above, **dialer-group** is used in defining interesting traffic. Answer c is incorrect because the **passive-interface** command is used to control routing updates.

Question 9

Which technology allows redundancy for serial links?

- ○ a. Dial backup
- ○ b. Snapshot routing
- ○ c. Multilink PPP
- ○ d. Terminal adapter

Answer a is correct. Dial backup was designed to provide emergency redundancy for other serial links. Dial backup can provide load-reduction backup or a fallback measure if the primary link fails completely. Answer b is incorrect because snapshot routing is used to keep routing updates off of ISDN links, not to provide redundancy. Answer c is incorrect because Multilink PPP is used to aggregate the bandwidth of multiple channels, not to provide backup services. Answer d is incorrect because a terminal adapter is a physical piece of hardware used in connecting a non-native ISDN interface to an NT1.

Question 10

Which roles can a router perform in snapshot routing? [Choose the two best answers]

❑ a. Snapshot server

❑ b. Snapshot client

❑ c. Dialer-list

❑ d. Dialer-map

Answers a and b are correct. You must configure these roles so that you can tell the routers who is doing the calling and who is being called. The Snapshot Client and Server also serve to define quiet and active timers for the routing updates. Answer c is incorrect because it deals with defining interesting traffic for a particular interface, not routing updates. Answer d is incorrect because the dialer-map statements are used to map a next logical hop layer 3 address to a specific phone number that should be dialed to initiate the connection.

Need To Know More?

 Flanagan, William A., *"The Guide to T1 Internetworking"*, Miller Freeman Books, London, U.K.,1998. ISBN 0-936648-26-0. This book is in depth detail on T1 and other digital technologies.

 Kessler, Gary C. and Peter V. Southwick. *ISDN: Concepts, Facilities, and Services*, McGraw-Hill, 1998. ISBN 0-07034-437-X. This book covers ISDN exclusively and in great detail.

 For more information on internetworking with ISDN, check out **www.cisco.com**.

 For a great library of technology overviews and details, check out **www.techguide.com**.

Bridging

Terms you'll need to understand:

√ Repeater

√ Bridging

√ Transparent bridging (TB)

√ Encapsulated bridging

√ Integrated routing and bridging (IRB)

√ Concurrent routing and bridging (CRB)

√ Source-route bridging (SRB)

√ Source-route transparent bridging (SRT)

√ Source-route translational bridging (SR/TLB)

Techniques you'll need to master:

√ Configuring transparent bridge groups

√ Configuring IRB

√ Configuring SRB

√ Configuring SRT

√ Configuring SR/TLB

This chapter introduces repeaters as well as some of the various bridging technologies in use today. Repeaters are mentioned here only as a reference. Bridging, which is the process of forwarding traffic based on a Media Access Control (MAC) address, has been around quite a long time, but the use of bridges has evolved well beyond the scope that the designing engineers imagined. Bridging is necessary because not all protocols have layer 3 addresses, thereby making them non-routable. Layer 2 protocols lack a network address, so each media segment appears to be a single LAN segment or broadcast domain. If you want to handle bridging for those protocols without layer 3 addresses, you can configure Cisco routers to do so.

Repeaters

Repeaters are devices that simply regenerate the physical signal. You can use them to extend the physical layer. Repeaters serve to extend a segment at layer 1 (the physical layer), at layer 2 (the data link layer), or at layer 3 (the routing layer). However, you are limited to the number of repeaters you can use in sequence (due to signal degradation, for which repeaters cannot compensate).

Repeaters function at layer 1, so they cannot understand the concept of a layer 2 or layer 3 protocol. The collection of segments attached with repeaters acts as a single wire. Hence, in the Ethernet realm, the Carrier Sense Multi-Access/Collision Detection (CSMA/CD)-layer protocol presents a single collision domain made up of all wires that have been connected together. Poorly created or even damaged frames are copied onto all segments because the repeater is not aware of the concept of a *frame*, the entity usually associated with layer 2; it knows about bits only.

A repeater creates new reshaped bits, allowing the distance between devices to be longer. This bit reshaping is its only function. It is not capable of understanding anything beyond the physical regeneration of the signal. One of the limiting factors in Ethernet is the number of collisions present on the wire over time. Repeaters really cannot do anything about collisions. Excessive collisions can cause the eventual shutdown of the Ethernet segment because no end nodes can place new data on the wire (due to jamming that is performed when collisions are detected). During the jamming time, none of the end nodes is allowed to transmit data. Collisions will remain a major issue with repeaters in place.

Repeaters are the least expensive way to extend the LAN environment because the hardware is cheap and no configuration is required. Repeaters work fine in small networks, but have minimal value—larger networks.

Bridges

Bridges forward frames at layer 2 (the data link layer). They require more configuration than a repeater, but far less configuration than a router. They make data-forwarding decisions based on the layer 2 Media Access Control (MAC) address. In order for bridges to function, they must have a basic understanding of the frame. Frames include information on the source and destination MAC address as well as a Cyclic Redundancy Check (CRC).

Bridges break up a physical wire segment. In Ethernet implementations, they reduce the number of collisions on the wire by segmenting the area in which collisions can occur, known as a *collision domain*. A bridge does not break up the area in which broadcasts occur, known as a *broadcast domain*.

Bridges have layer 1 interfaces, so they can regenerate the bits that comprise the frame, as do repeaters. However, because bridges understand the concept of a frame format, bridges can detect invalid information and do not pass bad frames. You can define a bad frame in a number of ways. For instance, in Ethernet technologies, *runts* are frames that consist of fewer than 64 bytes in total length (which violates the minimum transmittable unit size defined by the Ethernet specifications). *Giants* are frames whose size is greater than 1,518 bytes (which violate Ethernet's maximum transmittable unit specification). Bridges also detect and discard frames with bad frame check sequences as needed.

Because bridges understand CSMA/CD, devices on one segment don't necessarily interfere with those on another. For example, a bridge "listens" before forwarding a frame onto a new segment so as not to violate the rules of conversation on that CSMA/CD segment. You can equate the rules of conversation for CSMA/CD segments to the rules of speaking on a Citizen's Band (CB) radio. When no one else is talking, you are free to talk. If someone talks at the same time as you do, no one hears either of you properly. Therefore, conversing must be an orderly process or it does not work as intended. Figure 14.1 illustrates the use of a repeater, a bridge, or a router to attach LANs.

The Bridging Process

The bridging process is somewhat similar to the routing process. A bridge table lookup is performed based on a layer 2 MAC address and traffic is forwarded based on the result of the table lookup.

Forwarding

Each device attached to a segment has a unique MAC address. Bridges can identify devices based on the frames that these devices have transmitted. The bridge learns on which segment a device exists by keeping its source MAC

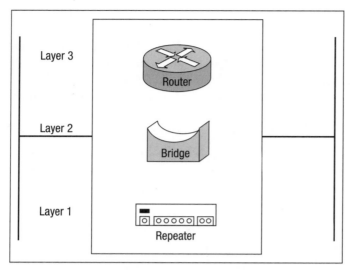

Figure 14.1 Repeaters, bridges, and routers.

address in a *bridge table*. The bridge doesn't forward traffic out of any interface if it determines that the destination interface is the one through which the traffic entered the bridge. In other words, it won't send traffic out of the interface from which it received the traffic. It forwards traffic only when the destination MAC address has been associated with another interface. In this way, the bridge can block or filter not only the invalid frames but also those frames forwarded between devices on the same physical side of the bridge.

Blocking

In order for this blocking and/or filtering procedure to work, the bridge must listen to traffic and record the source MAC addresses in a table associated with the port from which the bridge saw that MAC address. The learning process is illustrated in Figures 14.2, 14.3, and 14.4. In Figure 14.2, Device A transmits a frame, which the bridge sees. The bridge then enters Device A's MAC address in the bridge table.

In Figure 14.3, you can see that Device C has transmitted frames, which the bridge saw and learned also. Again, an entry is made in the bridge table and associated with the port through which it was learned.

Figure 14.4 illustrates how the bridge table should look once all devices have transmitted traffic. If all devices have transmitted, the bridge has learned all devices' source MAC addresses and made an appropriate entry in the bridge table.

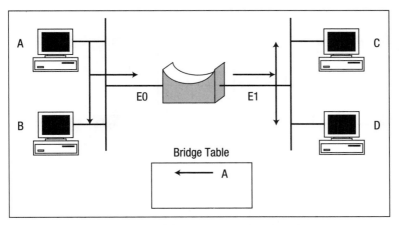

Figure 14.2   A bridge that is learning MAC addresses.

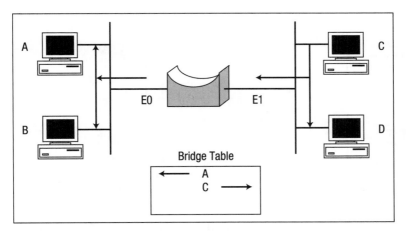

Figure 14.3   The beginning construction of a bridge table.

Once the devices have all spoken and the bridge has constructed a table on which to base forwarding decisions—it decides whether a frame should be forwarded or filtered (dropped)—the bridge can function properly on the network. As frames arrive at the bridge interfaces, the bridge checks the destination MAC address against the contents of the bridge table. If that destination address matches a MAC address associated with the same side of the bridge, the frame is filtered. In Figure 14.5, notice that the frame from A to C was forwarded because Device A was not on the same side of the bridge as Device C. On the other hand, the frame from C to D was filtered because the destination (Device D) is on the same side of the bridge as Device C.

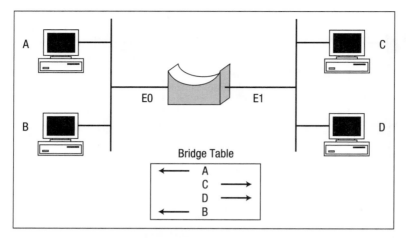

Figure 14.4 A completed bridge table.

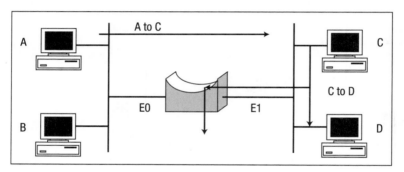

Figure 14.5 Forwarding and filtering.

This procedure works beautifully most of the time and is a very fast method of data forwarding. However, if multiple, redundant paths to the same destination segment exist, bridge loops result. The easiest way to see this effect is to watch the effects of broadcasts. A *broadcast* is a transmission destined for all MAC addresses. The bridge forwards it out of every interface. Figures 14.6, 14.7, and 14.8 illustrate the problem of bridge loops.

Figure 14.6 shows a transmission that originates from Device A. The broadcast is meant to go to all active nodes on this network segment. The bridge does not break up the broadcast domain; it serves only to break up the collision domain.

Figure 14.7 shows the bridge taking the broadcast and forwarding it on to the second bridge that has been added to the scenario.

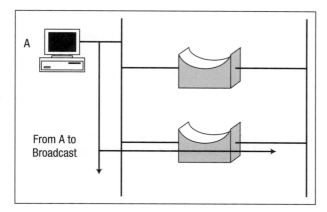

Figure 14.6   The beginning of a bridge loop.

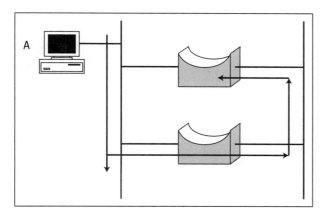

Figure 14.7   The loop begins to grow.

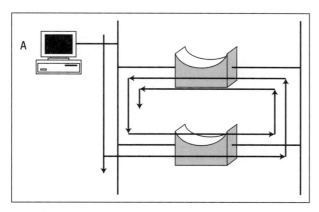

Figure 14.8   The loop continues to grow out of control.

Figure 14.8 shows the inevitable result of the bridge loop. The broadcast has now become something that resembles a whirlpool. This phenomenon is known as a *broadcast storm*.

> **Note:** *Although these illustrations show the bridge loop as a uni-directional occurrence, please understand that they are completely bi-directional. In other words, it is twice as bad as it looks. What one bridge does with the broadcast, the other bridge does as well. The uni-directional nature of these illustrations is simply to make it easier to understand the explanation of the loop principle.*

Avoiding Loops

As you can see in Figures 14.6, 14.7, and 14.8, some sort of protocol to prevent such loops needs to be included in the bridging intelligence. To that end, a Digital Equipment Corporation (DEC) engineer named Radia Perlman invented the *spanning tree protocol* (*STP*). Although the detailed operation of STP is beyond the scope of this book, we'll spend a few sentences on it here. Essentially, the bridges send each other messages that are called Bridge Protocol Data Units (BPDUs). By using a special multicast address used only by other bridges, each bridge can begin to communicate with its peers. Figure 14.9 illustrates the spanning tree algorithm, which disables a redundant interface between two LAN segments.

Initially, all bridges believe themselves to be the primary bridge in the network (known as the *root bridge*). A root bridge exists at the top of the bridging

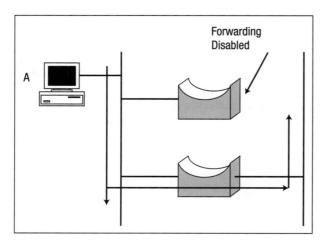

Figure 14.9 Spanning tree operation.

hierarchy. Each bridge has a bridge identifier. The most significant part of the bridge-id is a *priority field*, which is configurable. The remaining portion of the bridge-id contains the lowest numerical value MAC address on the bridge. The spanning tree protocol selects the root bridge based on the lowest bridge-priority. If the bridge priorities are equal, the MAC identifier is the tiebreaker.

Table 14.1 shows a piece of an EtherPeek display of a BPDU (the fields of interest are in bold). We've left details about some of the fields for you to study on your own because they are beyond the scope of our discussions.

Calculating A Path

Every two seconds, a bridge claims that it is the root (until it hears from another bridge that claims to know that there is a root bridge with a lower bridge-id than that bridge is advertising). In addition to knowing the identity of the root bridge, it is important for the bridge to pick the best pathway possible to reach the root. Therefore, there must be a way to measure what should be defined as the best path.

Part of the BPDU is the accumulated port cost from the advertising bridge's port back to the root. At any point in which two bridge ports are claiming the best path to the root, one of them (the one with the highest cost) is put into a blocking state. In other words, no forwarding of packets is performed via this

Table 14.1   A BPDU breakdown.

BPDU	Contents
802.1	Bridge spanning tree
Protocol Identifier	0
Protocol Version ID	0
Message Type	0 Configuration Message
Flags	%00000000
Root Priority/ID	**0x8000 / 00:c0:1d:81:8c:8e**
Cost Of Path To Root	**0x00000000 (0)**
Bridge Priority/ID	**0x8000 / 00:c0:1d:81:8c:8e**
Port Priority/ID	0x80 / 0x14
Message Age	0/256 seconds (exactly 0 seconds)
Maximum Age	5,120/256 seconds (exactly 20 seconds)
Hello Time	512/256 seconds (exactly 2 seconds)
Forward Delay	3,840/256 seconds (exactly 15 seconds)

blocked port. However, the blocked port continues to send BPDUs in order to stay in communication with the other bridges on the network. Should the blocked port realize that due to some failure it now needs to become the active port that services a pathway, reconfiguration messages are flooded around the network, causing a recalculation of the paths to the root bridge.

Even with just a few bridges, this re-convergence can still take a relatively long time. To improve convergence, bridges do respond to a number of varying configuration commands. You can alter the port cost and the bridge's priority.

Remember that there may be redundant paths to a LAN but they cannot be active at the same time. No load sharing (possible with routers) is possible with bridges. Only one path can exist to each LAN; otherwise, a bridge loop results.

 You must understand the basic premise behind the selection of the root bridge as well as the relation between the root bridge and the path selection criteria that the bridge uses.

Routers

Routers forward packets, or datagrams, at layer 3 (the network layer) based on the addressing scheme of a specific network-layer protocol. They require considerable configuration but they can provide several features that make them more valuable than bridges. For example, routers break up a collision domain (similar to what bridges accomplish). However, routers also break up broadcast domains, a task that bridges cannot perform. Bridges forward all broadcasts out of all active interfaces; by default, routers do not forward broadcasts. With routers, broadcasts are limited to the subnet or network number on a single wire.

Routers view separate wires as separate networks or subnets, so they can decide what to do with the broadcast information based on a network node protocol address. They could cache it and provide added value by furnishing the cached information on demand (such as Address Resolution Protocol (ARP)—caches). Another alternative would be for the router to offer a point of control in re-advertising the information (such as Service Advertising Protocols (SAPs)—and routing updates), allowing a reduction in the amount of network traffic. In general, routers do not forward layer 2 broadcasts. To enable forwarding of selected broadcasts, use IP and/or IPX helper addresses. For more information on helper addresses and the **ip forward-protocol** command, see the "Helper Addresses" section in Chapter 4.

As we have mentioned, protocols without layer 3 addresses must be bridged. Protocols with layer 3 addresses (routable protocols) may be bridged. If the router has not been configured to route a specific protocol, the traffic generated by that protocol can simply be forwarded based on its layer 2 address. With bridging enabled on an interface, all protocols are bridged by default. It is possible to have routing and bridging running on the same router at the same time. Figure 14.10 shows how you decide whether a protocol is routed or bridged.

Transparent Bridging (TB)

TB, usually associated with Ethernet bridging applications, is one of the most basic bridging implementations. Configuring a Cisco router to function as a bridge is a simple procedure. The steps are as follows:

1. Select an STP. The DEC implementation is the original, but the Institute of Electrical and Electronic Engineers (IEEE) 802.1D is the standard and is available with all bridges. The two versions are not compatible, but Cisco supports both versions. Remember that all bridges that are expected to participate in the same spanning tree must be using the same version of the algorithm.

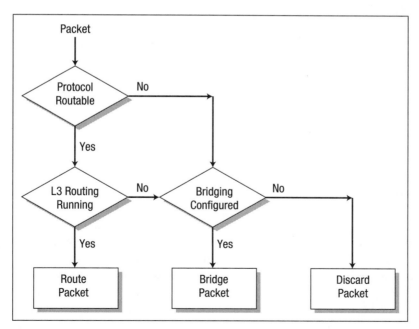

Figure 14.10 The decision to route or bridge.

2. Assign a priority to the bridges. Bridge priority is used to select the root bridge. It is important to select the root bridge to help the spanning tree properly converge. Spanning tree operations are significantly slower than similar operations performed by routers unless you help the process in some way. The help can be in the form of hierarchical design but is most often added by using **priority-value** and **path-cost** values. The bridge with the lowest **priority-value** is considered to be the highest-priority bridge and therefore the root bridge. The priority defaults are 32768 for IEEE and 128 for DEC. You can also designate a backup root if the root bridge fails. To do so, assign a **priority-value** that is numerically higher than that assigned for the root bridge but lower than the default value. You may assign optional **path-cost** commands to interfaces in the bridge group. Bridges calculate the cost back to the root bridge, so lower-than-default costs will create preferred paths and vice versa. The default is 1Gbps divided by the bandwidth of the circuit involved.

3. Assign the interface to a spanning tree with the **bridge-group** command. Router interfaces not assigned to the spanning tree will not forward bridge traffic.

Figure 14.11 shows the configuration of a basic transparent bridge. All interfaces that should participate in the bridging functions are assigned to a bridge group. Listing 14.1 details the necessary configuration parameters.

Listing 14.1   A sample transparent bridge configuration.

```
bridge-group 1 protocol ieee
!
interface Ethernet 0
bridge-group 1
!
interface Ethernet 1
bridge-group 1
!
interface Ethernet 2
bridge-group 1
```

In Listing 14.1, the device bridges all traffic that comes into any of the three configured interfaces. To configure it, simply assign an instance of an STP (in this case, the IEEE version) and assign the interfaces to a bridge group. You can also define a priority to manipulate the selection of the root bridge as well as assign a path cost to an interface. Figure 14.12 shows a more sophisticated bridged environment; the configuration details are shown in Listings 14.2 and 14.3.

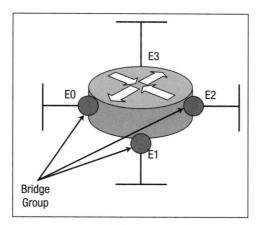

Figure 14.11 Transparent bridge configuration.

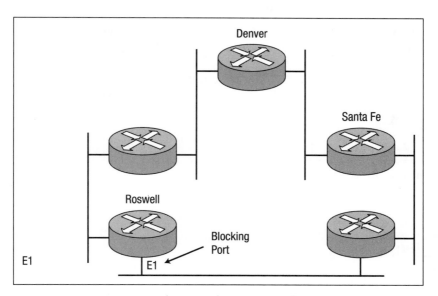

Figure 14.12 A more sophisticated transparent bridged environment.

Listing 14.2 The transparent bridge configuration of the Denver device.

```
bridge 1 protocol ieee
bridge 1 priority 1
!
interface Ethernet 0
bridge-group 1
!
interface Ethernet 1
bridge-group 1
```

Listing 14.3 The transparent bridge configuration of the Santa Fe device.

```
bridge 2 protocol ieee
bridge 2 priority 64
!
interface Ethernet 0
bridge-group 1
bridge-group 1 path-cost 10
!
inteface Ethernet 1
bridge-group 1
bridge-group 1 path-cost 10
```

In verifying your bridging configuration, use these commands:

➤ **show bridge** Shows the current status of the bridge interfaces

➤ **show span** Shows the current status of a particular bridge in the spanning tree structure

 You will need to know the proper command to activate TB on an interface (*bridge-group <number>*) and to understand the correct configuration in a given example.

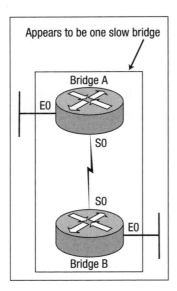

Figure 14.13 Encapsulated bridging.

Encapsulated Bridging

It is often necessary to extend the network to different locations within your organization's campus or possibly even across wide geographical spans. You may also need to extend the reachability of your network for both layer 2 and layer 3 protocols. Encapsulated bridging is a means of extending TB across such distances. The configuration is not difficult or complex; you simply assign serial interfaces to the transparent bridge group. Figure 14.13 shows encapsulated bridging, and Listing 14.4 details the configuration.

Listing 14.4   An encapsulated bridging configuration for Bridge A.

```
bridge 1 protocol ieee
!
interface Ethernet 0
bridge-group 1
!
interface Serial 0
bridge-group 1
```

Listing 14.5 shows an example of an encapsulated bridging deployment.

Listing 14.5   An encapsulated bridging configuration for Bridge B.

```
bridge 1 protocol ieee
!
interface Ethernet 0
bridge-group 1
!
interface Serial 0
bridge-group 1
```

The Ethernet frame is encapsulated in the specific frame type used on the connecting Serial interface. In this instance, you would use the Cisco default encapsulation of High-Level Data Link Control (HDLC). The local and remote bridge, along with all interfaces that belong to the bridge group configured on each device, appear as a single bridge logically. The Serial encapsulation is removed at the remote end of the connection, and the Ethernet frame continues in its original form from that point toward its destination as if it had passed through a single bridge. Another version of encapsulated bridging uses Fiber Distributed Data Interface (FDDI) as the connecting transport. The FDDI version functions in the same manner as described earlier in this section. Figure 14.14 shows this concept of encapsulated bridging over FDDI.

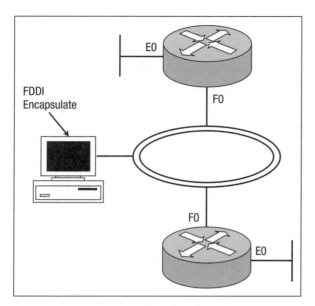

Figure 14.14   Encapsulated bridging across an FDDI backbone.

It is possible for transparent bridging to take place between Ethernet and FDDI devices. An alternative is to use the FDDI ring as a *transit* segment, in which case the hosts on the FDDI ring cannot be sources or destinations for bridged traffic. The decision about the encapsulation depends on FDDI interface card version. If your FDDI connection supports the translation and the other end doesn't, use the **fddi encapsulate** command on your end of the configuration.

Integrated Routing And Bridging (IRB)

For years, the routing world has competed with the bridging world. The two have long clashed to be crowned the best technology. Although the eventual outcome is unknown, it is thought that the outcome will be the merger of the two technologies. With the advent of Ethernet switching, layer 2 bridging has taken on a whole new life. At the same time, the development of layer 3 switching (routing at switching speeds) has added a new twist to the game. IRB is one of the first steps toward the next evolution. With IRB, you can forward out of a bridged interface traffic received via a routed interface and vice versa. This technology is not to be confused with concurrent routing and bridging (CRB). CRB and IRB, although similar, are completely different technologies. We briefly discuss CRB later in this chapter. Figure 14.15 shows an IRB configuration.

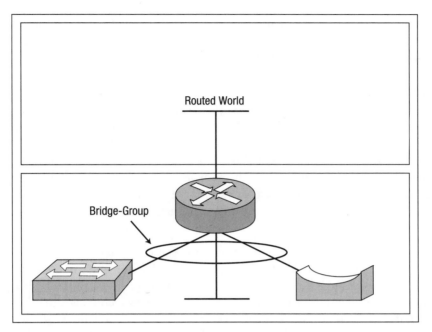

Figure 14.15 Use IRB to forward traffic between routed and bridged environments.

Figure 14.15 shows that a bridging interface would probably do better bridging the traffic back out of one of the other bridged interfaces rather than dispatching the traffic via a routing interface. However, it is important to be flexible and route traffic if necessary. Before IOS version 11.2, a routable protocol could be bridged or routed—but not both simultaneously on the same router. In IOS version 11.2, Cisco supports routing of IP, Internetwork Packet eXchange (IPX), AppleTalk, and the simultaneous bridging of the same protocols in the same router.

How Does It Work?

The key to IRB's operation is yet another logical software interface called the Bridged Virtual Interface (BVI). There are several variations, but essentially, the real interfaces are configured for bridging, and the virtual interface is configured with the routing parameters. The MAC address that the BVI uses is one of those from an interface in the bridge group. The BVI acts as a liaison between the routed and bridged domain.

The BVI has two uses. First, it connects the routed and bridged domains to increase performance by bridging local traffic and breaking up a local collision domain. Second, it conserves network addresses, providing a more complete utilization of larger address space (because the bridge group is considered to be a single subnet). You don't need to deploy additional subnets unnecessarily.

Bridge Or Route?

The inevitable question is: "How does the device decide whether to route or bridge the arriving traffic?" We need to explore the answer a bit. Consider a normal IP-capable PC workstation on a network segment. It is configured with an IP address, a subnet mask, and a default gateway. (The default gateway is the address of the router to which the workstation should forward traffic destined for locations off the local subnet.) If data traffic is to be moved from one subnet to another, a router must make a forwarding decision based on the layer 3 address.

When the workstation determines that it must send traffic to the default gateway, it must broadcast an ARP request (if it doesn't have an entry in the ARP cache already). An ARP entry serves to map a layer 3 address to the layer 2 address. This is a necessary step in almost any networking technology. In other words, the traffic destined for a remote subnet is destined for the MAC address of the router. When the router sees inbound traffic with a destination MAC address that matches that of the BVI, it knows that this traffic must be routed. If the traffic arriving at the device includes a destination MAC address of any device other than that of the BVI, the traffic must be bridged.

Figure 14.16 illustrates the concept of IRB. Listing 14.6 details the basic configuration of IRB.

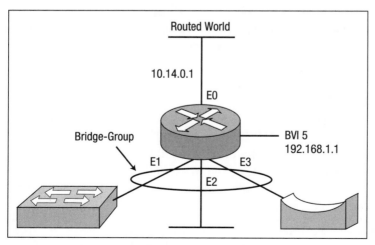

Figure 14.16   The IRB concept.

Listing 14.6   A basic IRB configuration.

```
interface Ethernet 0
ip address 10.14.0.1 255.255.255.0
!
bridge irb
bridge 5 protocol ieee
!
interface Ethernet 1
bridge-group 5
!
interface Ethernet 2
bridge-group 5
!
interface Ethernet 3
bridge-group 5
!
interface BVI 5
ip address 192.168.1.1 255.255.255.0
!
```

The BVI appears to the 192.168.1.0 network to be a normal router's interface. Bridged traffic accesses the routed domain by addressing frames to the MAC address of the BVI. The end stations learn the MAC address of the BVI in IP by issuing an ARP request for the MAC address to IP address mapping, as discussed earlier in this section.

The BVI's configurations can be quite sophisticated. In Listing 14.7, we refer to back to Figure 14.16 but add more to it. In this example, we're routing IP, bridging and routing IPX, and routing all other protocols.

Listing 14.7   A more sophisticated IRB configuration example.

```
ipx routing
bridge irb
bridge 5 protocol ieee
bridge 5 route ipx
bridge 5 route ip
no bridge 5 bridge ip
!
interface Ethernet 0
ip address 10.14.0.1 255.255.255.0
ipx network 1000
!
interface Ethernet 1
ip address 10.15.0.1 255.255.255.0
```

```
bridge-group 5
!
interface Ethernet 2
ip address 10.16.0.1 255.255.255.0
bridge-group 5
!
interface Ethernet 3
ip address 10.17.0.1 255.255.255.0
bridge-group 5
!
interface BVI 5
no ip address
ipx network 2000
```

There are several points to keep in mind when you are configuring IRB:

➤ Remember to review the Maximum Transmittable Unit (MTU) size. You may need to modify it.

➤ IRB bridges by default. Explicitly configure routing for the protocols that need it.

➤ Don't configure any routing protocol attributes on the bridge interfaces when doing both routing and bridging.

➤ Don't configure bridging attributes on the BVI.

In verifying the operation of IRB, use the **show interface <type> <number> irb** command. With this command, you can see what the *router* believes you've configured regarding the bridging and routing of various protocols.

Be able to choose the correct lines in a basic IRB configuration example similar to those noted in this section.

Concurrent Routing And Bridging (CRB)

CRB was introduced in IOS 11.0 and has been replaced by IRB. The difference between CRB and IRB is that CRB allowed routing and bridging of the same protocol on the same interface. However, no path was possible between the routed and bridged domains. In other words, bridged traffic could not be routed out of the router. Bridged traffic had to be dispatched via a bridged interface. By the same token, routed traffic had to be dispatched via a routed interface. IRB allows such a combination of routing and bridging.

CRB is not covered on the exam; therefore, we will not spend any more time on the subject.

Source-Route Bridging (SRB)

TB is not the only form of bridging available. As we mentioned in the "Transparent Bridging (TB)" section, TB is usually associated with Ethernet implementations. IBM created a different kind of bridge for its Token Ring-based LANs. SRB picks a path through the bridged environment by finding the best path and using it for the duration of communication. Table 14.2 provides a bit of background information by showing the fields of a Token Ring frame.

Table 14.2   A field-by-field detail of a Token Ring frame.
Token Ring Frame Fields
Source MAC Address–The source of the transmission.
Destination MAC Address*–The final destination of the transmission
RIF (the RIF is detailed below)
Routing Control (RC)
Type (3 bits)
0XX Specific route (normal traffic)
10X All rings, all routes TEST (explorer) frame
11X Spanning route TEST frame
Length (5 bits)
Used to determine how many RDs are currently in the frame
Direction (1 bit)
"0"   Interpret the RDs in a forward direction
"1"   Interpret the RDs in a reverse direction
Largest Frame (3 bits)
(516, 1,500, 2,052, 4,472, 8,144, 11,407, 17,800, 65,535)
Route Designator (RD)
LAN/Ring Number (12 bits)**
Bridge Number (4 bits)**

* *The Routing Information Field (RIF) field is present if the first bit of the source address is set to 1. This position would be the multicast bit—referred to as the Routing Information Indicator (RII)—in the destination address but is normally unused.*

** *The bridge number doesn't need to be unique, but the ring/bridge combination must be.*

Locating The Destination

The source device needs to determine a path to the destination. Device A sends a TEST frame, also referred to as an *explorer frame*, around the local ring. By not setting the first bit of the source MAC address (the RII), the bridges do not copy the local TEST frame to other rings. If the destination device sees its MAC address in the destination MAC portion of the frame and the frame is undamaged, the destination device indicates its successful reception of the frame by turning on the "address bit" in the "frame status" field following the "end delimiter" of the frame. If the destination is on the same ring as the source, the frames can simply be forwarded.

If the destination is not found on the local ring, the source device creates an *all rings, all routes* TEST frame. The first bit in the source address tells the bridges to copy the frame to other rings. As this is done, the local ring number and bridge number are added to the RIF in the frame. This procedure is repeated as the TEST frame flows toward its destination. Upon reaching the destination device, the direction bit is reversed (set to 1) and the frame is forwarded along the path in the reverse direction, traversing the path back to the original source.

The first frame that arrives back at the source is assumed to have taken the best path (for example, it traverses the fewest and fastest rings and bridges). From this point on in the session, all traffic follows this selected path only. The RIF header, if present, follows the destination-address field in an IEEE 802.5 frame format. The presence of the RIF field is signaled by an RII, which is the first bit of the Source Address field of the Token Ring frame. The RIF field contains an RC field and one or more RDs.

The RC field contains five fields:

➤ **Frame Type** This is used to differentiate data frames from two kinds of explorer or TEST frames. A zero in the first bit position indicates that this is not a TEST frame; it is essentially carrying data. The other two frame types indicate that the frame is either an *all rings, all routes* explorer or a *single route* (sometimes referred to as an *all rings, spanning routes*) explorer. The all rings, all routes type is allowed to find the best path to the destination. The "best" route is normally indicated by the frame that returns first because, as mentioned earlier, it followed the fastest, shortest, or least busy path. Other choices for the path could be a path that provides the longest MTU or some other specific descriptor.

The spanning explorer would pass through only those interfaces that the spanning tree algorithm marked in the forwarding state.

➤ **Length** This is 5 bits and grows in length as the RDs are added to the RIF field.

➤ **Direction bit** When this is set to zero, it indicates a forward interpretation of the RD entries. A one bit indicates the reverse path.

➤ **Largest-frame (essentially layer 2 MTU)** This is used to select the largest frame size that may traverse the path. As each bridge adds a new

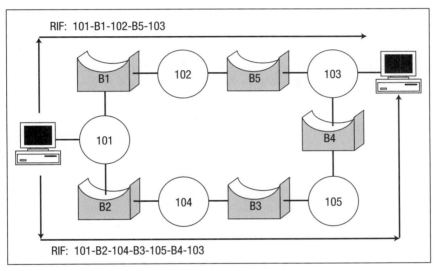

Figure 14.17   SRB locating the destination.

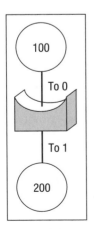

Figure 14.18   A classic SRB configuration.

routing descriptor, the bridge reduces the size of the largest-frame if the interface on the new ring has a smaller largest-frame than currently indicated in the explorer frame. This helps the efficiency of the protocol. According to the standard, bridges cannot fragment frames. Ethernet is limited to 1,500 bytes. The choice would be to cripple the token rings by configuring the largest-frame to 1,500 bytes or never allowing an Ethernet segment to be in the path. This discovery of the largest-frame allows token rings to be both efficient (if the paths have large largest-frames) and compatible (if Ethernets or other limited interface largest-frames are encountered). The eight values that may be represented in the 3-bit field are 516, 1,500, 2,052, 4,472, 8,144, 11,407, 17,800, and 65,535.

➤ **Routing descriptor** This contains a 12-bit ring number and a 4-bit bridge number. The bridge number does not need to be unique, but the ring-bridge-ring combination must be. Unique ring numbers provide a method for the bridges to trim the number of frames and keep them from looping. A bridge does not copy an outgoing TEST frame onto a ring it has already traversed. In addition, the IBM version of the RIF field supports 7 bridges and 8 rings; the IEEE version increases that to 13 bridges and 14 rings. So the RDs define a limit just as the Time To Live (TTL) field does in IP routing.

Figure 14.17 depicts an example of the construction of the RIF and, of course, the route from source to destination.

Configuring SRB

It's usually quite simple to configure SRB. You must define the ring numbers for the Token Ring interfaces as well as a bridge number to represent the source-route bridge being crossed. Configuration of SRB is shown in Figure 14.18 and detailed in Listing 14.8. Note the use of a two-ring configuration, which represents a classic source-route bridge.

Listing 14.8   A simple SRB configuration.

```
bridge 3 protocol IBM
!
interface Token-Ring 0
source-bridge 100 1 200
source-bridge spanning 3
```

At the top of Listing 14.8, two separate **source-bridge spanning** commands have been issued. The use of these commands is an either/or relationship. Use the **source-bridge spanning** command if you are constructing the spanning tree manually. Most people would rather not do that, so there is the **source-bridge spanning 3** command, which starts an automatic STP for SRB group 3. If you're going to use an automatic STP, you must define which one to use. In this case, we have issued the **bridge 3 protocol IBM** command to specify the use of the IBM STP for SRB group 3.

The interface commands shown in Listing 14.9 declare that SRB traffic is bridged between the ring number on the first interface and another ring attached to the same bridge. The command at the interface defines simply the source ring number, bridge number, and destination ring number in each direction to make the forwarding decision. The bridge number ranges from 1 through 9.

Optionally, you can set path cost to help create the automatic spanning tree. Changing the path cost facilitates the election of a root bridge in the network. The path cost ranges between 0 and 65,535, with the default of 16.

Classic IBM bridges have only two ports. When using the router as a bridge, we want to do a couple of things. First, we want to be able to use more than two interfaces per router to perform bridging functions. Second, we want to preserve our organization's investment in network management software that expects two-port bridges. The solution to accomplish both goals is known as a *virtual ring* (referred to as a *ring-group*) and is illustrated in Figure 14.19. Listing 14.9 lists the configuration commands to accomplish virtual ring configuration.

Listing 14.9   A sample virtual ring configuration.

```
bridge 3 protocol IBM
source-bridge ring-group 20

interface Token-Ring 0
source-bridge 100 3 20
source-bridge spanning 3
!
interface Token-Ring 1
source-bridge 200 3 20
source-bridge spanning 3
!
interface Token-Ring 2
source-bridge 300 3 20
source-bridge spanning 3
!
```

The virtual ring number (which ranges from 1 through 4,095) shows up in the RIF and in every way appears to be a real ring. The commands in Listing 14.10 illustrate the basic multiport source-route bridge. Routers are very versatile and capable devices. They support flexible configuration features that improve the operation of SRB by extending the classic two port bridge.

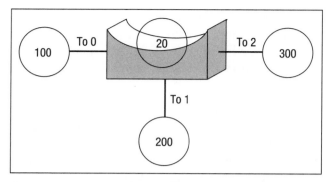

Figure 14.19 Virtual Ring illustration.

Additional Functionality Of SRB

SRB has existed in the internetworking arena for a number of years. It, along with every other technology, has evolved into a more functional tool over time. A problem with SRB's operation is the potential impact of explorer traffic on the network. If two devices on the same ring need to reach the same destination, they must both generate explorer traffic to find that destination.

One valued addition to SRB is **source-bridge proxy explorer**. Essentially, the statement is put on the bridge's inbound interface from a ring. When the first host dispatches explorers for a particular destination, the router/bridge caches the RIF entry in the returning explorer frames. That way, for popular locations, the search through the whole network occurs only once. Once the second host dispatches explorer frames to find the same destination, the bridge can block that traffic and reply with the cached RIF entry.

One problem could be that all traffic follows the same route, resulting in that pathway becoming congested. Another is that a ring could fail, rendering the route unusable. To avoid such scenarios, the cache holding time is short, 15 minutes (contrast that with the default 240 minutes for an IP ARP cache). In this way, the problems cure themselves within a few minutes. Another solution is to clear the bridge's RIF cache if a problem occurs. You can, of course, do this

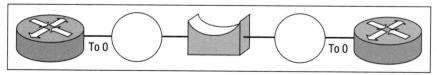

Figure 14.20 Configuring the **multi-ring** command.

manually if you set Simple Network Management Protocol (SNMP) traps correctly. It is simple to create an automatic script to clear the cache quickly and automatically when it occurs.

Another possible problem happens when routed protocols path must traverse more than one ring to reach the next hop. Essentially, we need a way to cause the router to add an RIF to first search for, and later simply find, the next hop router's MAC address. An example of this configuration is shown in Figure 14.20. Listing 14.10 shows how to configure the **multi-ring** command.

Listing 14.10 A multi-ring configuration example.

```
!
interface Token-Ring 0
ip address 172.16.5.1 255.255.255.0
multi-ring ip
!
```

Ensure that you can recognize the **multi-ring** command in its correct form.

Source-Route Transparent Bridging (SRT)

The concept of SRT is quite simple. The router simply transparently bridges any frames that don't contain an RIF and source-route bridges those frames that do contain an RIF. The use of SRT implements the traditional IEEE spanning tree algorithm just as described in the Transparent Bridging (TB) section earlier in this chapter. The router decides to use bridging based on

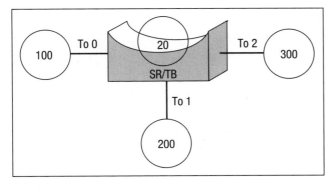

Figure 14.21 SRT bridging.

whether or not an RIF field exists. Figure 14.21 illustrates the concept of SRT, and Listing 14.11 details the command line configuration.

Listing 14.11 A sample SRT configuration.

```
bridge 1 protocol IEEE
source-bridge ring-group 20
!
interface Token-Ring 0
bridge-group 1
source-bridge 100 3 20
source-bridge spanning 3
!
interface Token-Ring 1

bridge-group 1
source-bridge 200 3 20
source-bridge spanning 3

interface Token-Ring 2
bridge-group 1
source-bridge 300 3 20
source-bridge spanning 3
!
```

The configuration simply consists of starting the TB function and the SRB function simultaneously. The commands you use are the same ones described in the "Transparent Bridging (TB)" and "Source-Route Bridging (SRB)" sections earlier in this chapter. You are simply implementing both on the same device simultaneously.

> **Note:**   As we have mentioned, TB is usually associated with Ethernet bridge implementations. However, that is not always the case. You can use TB with Token Ring implementations that do not support the use of an RIF. Even though we're using the TB algorithm, the frame encap-sulations differ between Ethernet and Token Ring. SRT does not allow the traffic to pass between the Token Ring interfaces and the Ethernet interfaces. In order for Ethernet-to-Token-Ring traffic to pass between the differing media types, you must configure source-route translational bridging (SR/TLB).

Source-Route Translational Bridging (SR/TLB)

Throughout their evolution, the bridging standards have stated that the frame format may not—and must not—be changed. This makes sense if you buy an inexpensive bridge. Routers already know how to handle differing layer 2 encapsulations. This built-in media independence allows the use of a very useful feature in being able to move from Transparent Bridged environments to Source Route Bridged environments (in this case Ethernet to Token Ring and back again.

In many environments, it would be very useful to be able to bridge between Ethernet and Token Ring environments. However, until the advent of SR/TLB, this was not feasible. If your routers could provide an interim solution until you needed to replace your current PCs, you would have to be doing only one conversion rather than two (converting from Token Ring to Ethernet and reconfiguring all bridges in the network to support the new topology). It would be an advantage to let the router convert the traffic until you could coordinate moving to a new local attachment mode (such as a switched Ethernet and so on) with another upgrade. Figure 14.22 illustrates SR/TLB. Listing 14.12 details the command line parameters to implement SR/TLB on a Cisco router.

Listing 14.12   An example of configuring SR/TLB.

```
bridge 1 protocol IEEE
source-bridge ring-group 20
source-bridge transparent 20 30 3 1
!
interface Token-Ring 0
source-bridge 100 3 20
source-bridge spanning 3
!
interface Token-Ring 1
source-bridge 200 3 20
source-bridge spanning 3
!
interface Ethernet 0
bridge-group 1
!
interface Ethernet 1
bridge-group 1
```

You will note that the command to pull both domains together is **source-bridge transparent** even though we're doing SR/TLB.

The **source-bridge transparent** part of the statement must be followed by the numeric parameters in sequence:

➤ The number of the ring-group (virtual or dummy ring)

➤ The ring (pseudo ring) number used to represent the transparent-bridged devices to the source-routed domain

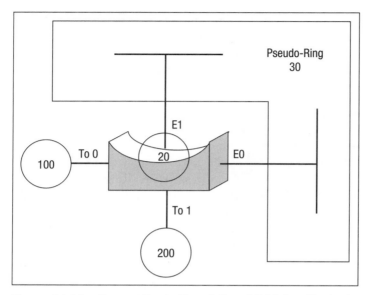

Figure 14.22 Source-Route Translational Bridging illustration.

➤ The number of the source-routed bridge that leads to the TB domain

➤ The number of the translational bridge that ties to the source-routed domain

Translation Issues

If you want TB to be successful, you must handle a couple issues. You must strip the RIF field and cache it when going from the SRB domain to the TB domain. (Obviously, you need to add it back in the reverse direction.) In addition, when you are creating the RD entries, the software needs to handle Ethernet's 1,500-byte limitation. Usually, no manual configuration is necessary. Another issue to consider is that the bit transmission sequence for Ethernet is least-significant-bit first, whereas with both Token Ring and FDDI, the sequence is most-significant-bit first. The bridging standards for these token-passing technologies specify that the first two bits *transmitted* have special meaning. The first bit on the link (in the destination address) has the value of zero when it is an individual address and a value of one when it is a group address. The second bit transmitted represents the global/local nature of the address.

If you re-examine the transmission sequence, you'll note that when the bridge reads the Ethernet MAC address, the group address bit is on the right side of the first octet (for example, 000000ba—where a is the individual/group bit and b is the local/global bit). The router handles this situation for you.

Cisco routers can bridge traffic for one or more protocols while simultaneously routing traffic for others. In addition to the two basic flavors, TB and SRB, Cisco provides several variations of basic bridging to add value to the network. SR/TLB connects the transparent-bridged and source-routed domains of Ethernet and Token Ring respectively.

As you can see in Listing 14.13, the **source-bridge transparent** command speci-fies all of the pieces that must come together for SR/TLB to work properly. You will have to specify a number for the virtual ring (in this case 20) so that the multiport SRB can function. You have to give the Token Ring side of the configuration a way to view the Ethernet side. The configuration creates a pseudo ring (with a ring number of 30) so that SRB hosts simply view the Ethernet destinations as another Token Ring. You must configure a **source-bridge group** for automatic spanning in SRB (in this example, we used 3 as our **source-bridge group**). Finally, you have to configure TB for the Ethernet in-terfaces by assigning them all to a bridge group (in this case, group 1). The **source-bridge transparent** command employs all of these differing numbers to create the logical picture of the network within itself and to be able to make the transition between Ethernet and Token Ring segments.

Practice Questions

Question 1

What is the factor that determines whether a protocol is routable?

○ a. A network-layer address

○ b. A MAC address

○ c. An 802.3 frame format

○ d. A layer 2 address

Answer a is correct. The single determining factor of whether a protocol is routable or not is the presence of a network-layer address. Answers b and d are incorrect because all layer 2 LAN frames contain a MAC address. Answer c is incorrect because the 802.3 frame format doesn't matter; only the layer 3 address determines routability.

Question 2

Assuming that a router is configured for bridging, what factors determine whether traffic will be bridged or routed? [Choose the two best answers]

❑ a. The presence of a network-layer address.

❑ b. The presence of a MAC address.

❑ c. The routing protocol must be enabled.

❑ d. A **bridging-enabled** statement needs to be included.

Answers a and c are correct. Not only does the protocol need a layer 3 address, but the routing protocol also needs to be turned on and enabled on the interfaces where that type of routable traffic arrives at the router. Answer b is incorrect because layer 2 MAC addresses are part of any LAN frame whether it is routable or not. Answer d is incorrect because no such statement exists.

Question 3

To pass traffic between Ethernet and Token Ring what statement is true?

- ○ a. You cannot do so; the frame formats are different.
- ○ b. The traffic must be routable.
- ○ c. Use SRB. Simply load the source-route software on the LAN hosts.
- ○ d. Use SR/TLB.

Answer d is correct. You will have to use Source-Route Translational Bridging to move traffic from Ethernet to Token Ring and back again. The router can handle the encapsulation and bit ordering problems. Answer a is incorrect because it is just not true; you can pass traffic between Ethernet and Token Ring. Answer b is incorrect because although routable traffic may be transferred between LAN segments of different encapsulations, that is not the limiting factor. Answer c is incorrect because SRB is simply a Token Ring bridging technology.

Question 4

Which of the following protocols are routable? [Choose the two best answers]

- ❑ a. DECnet
- ❑ b. SNA
- ❑ c. AppleTalk
- ❑ d. IPX

Answers c and d are correct. AppleTalk and IPX have network-layer addresses and are routable. Answers a and b do not have layer 3 addresses and must be bridged. Therefore, they are incorrect.

Question 5

What prevents looping in transparent bridging networks?

- ○ a. The maximum number of RD entries.
- ○ b. The spanning tree algorithm.
- ○ c. The shortest path first algorithm.
- ○ d. The source device.

Answer b is correct. The spanning tree protocol was developed specifically to guarantee a loop free bridging environment. Answer a is incorrect because the RD is part of SRB, not TB. Answer c is incorrect because the shortest path first protocol is used as a basis for routing, not bridging, protocols. Answer d is incorrect because the source device in a bridged network believes the whole network to be one link.

Question 6

> Which bridging technology is used to break up Ethernet LAN segments?
>
> ○ a. SRB
>
> ○ b. SR/TLB
>
> ○ c. IRB
>
> ○ d. TB

Answer d is correct. Transparent bridging is invisible to the end stations. It breaks up the collision domain. It doesn't break up the broadcast domain. Answer a is incorrect because SRB is a Token Ring technology. Answer b is incorrect because SR/TLB is used to translate between Ethernet and Token Ring. Answer c is incorrect because IRB is used to move traffic between bridged and routed network environments.

Question 7

> Which three pieces of information must be known in order to configure SRB? [Choose the three best answers]
>
> ❑ a. RIF
>
> ❑ b. Source ring number
>
> ❑ c. Bridge number
>
> ❑ d. Destination ring number

Answers b, c and d are correct. You must configure the pathway that traffic will follow in getting through the bridge. You must define source and destination ring numbers and the bridge number. Answer a is incorrect because the RIF is the entity that holds the Ring and Bridge numbers between the source and destination stations.

Question 8

What is the code command to make interface Ethernet 0 a member of the transparent bridging group number 4? [Fill in the blank]

The correct answer is **bridge-group 4**. In transparent bridging, you simply define interface membership on a one-by-one basis at the interface configuration level.

Question 9

Which technology allows routed protocol traffic to be transported across a bridged environment?

○ a. IRB

○ b. SR/TB

○ c. Encapsulated Bridging

○ d. Multiring

Answer d is correct. Multiring is the technology that allows the transport of routed traffic across a bridged network. Answer a is incorrect because IRB allows the routing traffic that entered the device through a bridged interface and the bridging of traffic that entered via a routed interface. This is the tricky part of the question. Note that the wording of the question specified "traffic to be transported". Answer b is incorrect because SR/TB allows SRB clients and TB clients (both must be Token Ring) to communicate through the bridge. The bridge adds and removes the RIF as necessary. Answer c is incorrect because encapsulated bridging is meant to move bridged traffic across a Serial technology or provide connectivity between FDDI and Ethernet clients.

Question 10

The part of the Token Ring frame that holds pathway information in SRB is know as what?

○ a. RII

○ b. IRB

○ c. RIF

○ d. SNA

Answer c is correct. The RIF holds the routing information for the communication traffic between a source and destination host. Answer a is incorrect because the RII is meant to signify the existence or absence of an RIF in the Token Ring frame. Answer b is incorrect because IRB is the technology that allows the mixture of routing and bridged traffic. Answer d is incorrect because SNA is one of the layer 2 protocols that we must bridge.

Need To Know More?

 Cheek, Andrea, Lew, H. Kim and Wallace, Kathleen, *Cisco CCIE Fundamentals: Network Design and Case Studies*, Cisco Press, Indianapolis, IN 1998 ISBN 1-57870-066-3. This is a great reference for more information on network designs.

 Perlman, Radia. *Interconnections: Bridges and Routers*. Addison-Wesley, Reading, PA, 1992. ISBN 0-201-56332-0. Chapter 3 of this book, written by the woman who invented the spanning tree algorithm, details bridging. Chapter 12 has a good discussion talking about the future of bridging.

 For more information on bridging and switching, visit Cisco's Web site, **www.cisco.com**, and you'll find white papers and router documentation about bridging and its logical extension, switching.

Configuring T1, E1, And PRI Options

Terms you'll need to understand:

√ Alternate Mark Inversion (AMI)

√ Bipolar with Eight Zero Substitution (B8ZS)

√ High Density Bipolar 3 (HDB3)

√ Superframe

√ Extended Superframe (ESF)

√ Digital signal level 0 (DS-0)

√ Primary Rate Interface (PRI)

Techniques you'll need to master:

√ Configuring framing type and line coding

√ Configuring T1 Controller

√ Configuring Primary Rate Interface

In this chapter, we will discuss T1/E1 and Primary Rate Interface (PRI) options. T1, first introduced as a viable technology in the early 1960s, is an extremely common technology. From its humble roots in Chicago in 1965—when the first commercial T1 lines were installed—to the massive install base it has today, T1 hasn't changed all that much. It is the basis of digital technology.

> **Note:**   *Knowing a little background information on T1 will help you to understand the configuration parameters.*

T1 Basics

What does the "T" in T1 stand for? That question has been posed and answered incorrectly for years. Is it "Transmission" or "Terminal"? No. The "T" stands for "Terrestrial." When T1 was introduced, most lines were land-based lines, therefore terrestrial-based lines. We also saw the emergence of satellite communications capabilities. However, satellite communications are beyond our scope and therefore will not be covered in this book.

T1 was originally developed as a digital transport for voice traffic. In the early 1930s, there was a very large amount of innovation in digital technology. We credit most of what we now know to a brilliant technician, Harry Nyquist, the pioneer of the digital voice field. To understand his ideas, we need to cover some background information.

What's This Funny Squiggle?

Normal everyday telephone conversations that you hold with friends, family, or anyone else are transported as analog waves. Analog is simply a waveform without discrete states. In other words, analog waveforms are simply funny looking squiggles when viewed on an oscilloscope. Figure 15.1 shows an example of an analog wave. Although the wave represented here is not characteristic of a voice wave, it demonstrates our point.

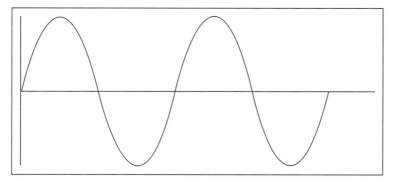

Figure 15.1   An analog waveform.

Now that we have produced the analog wave, we can explore how it is manipulated. If an analog wave is left alone, it shrinks in height until it disappears, a phenomenon known as *attenuation*. So, we must amplify it. However, a certain amount of noise, caused by interference, attenuation, and many other sources, is always present. Noise consists of additional waveforms, (such as waves we don't want) that piggyback along with the wave that the speech created (the wave we do want). When we amplify the wave, the noise is amplified also. Unfortunately, it seems that the noise tends to amplify better (and with greater magnitude) than the desired waveform. Eventually, the noise distorts our wave beyond recognition.

A New Kind Of Squiggle

The solution to the attenuation, amplification, and noise issue is to convert the analog waveform to a digital signal. A *digital signal* is simply a string of ones and zeros. Only two states are possible, so noise is no longer an issue. To create this digital signal, you measure the height of the analog waveform over time. Each of these measurements, known as *samples*, is represented by an 8-bit value. Figure 15.2 shows a picture of the wave as it is being sampled.

Each of these measurements is precisely the same distance apart. The sampling rate, developed by Harry Nyquist, is 8,000 samples per second.

Do The Math

At this point, we have the basic information to put together the basis of transmission for T1. This basic unit of transmission is known as a *timeslot*. However, as you are about to see, you already know it by another name.

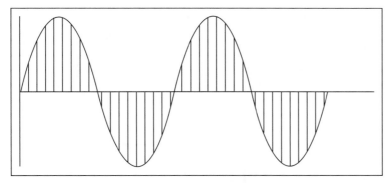

Figure 15.2   Sampling an analog waveform facilitates digital encoding.

Put it together: 8,000 samples per second. Each sample is represented by an 8-bit code. The total comes to 64,000-bits per second (bps), one DS-0.

A T1 circuit consists of 24 of these DS-0s. The total aggregate throughput is: $64,000 \times 24 = 1,536,000$ bps. It is a well-known fact that the bandwidth of a T1 is 1,544,000 bps. Where are the missing 8,000 bps?

When you put together one timeslot (or sample) from each of the 24 channels of the T1, you have what is called a *T1 frame*. One single frame represents one-eight thousandth of one second. Therefore, we have 8,000 frames in one second. There must be a way to tell where one frame stops and the next one starts. An additional bit that is added to each frame represents this frame delineation. Twenty-four 8-bit samples comes to a grand total of 192-bits. One additional bit is added for framing (an additional 8,000 bps), so that number becomes 193-bits.

When the additional bit per frame is added in, $64,000 \times 24 = 1,536,000 + 8,000$ framing bits = 1,544,000 bps.

The process of sampling the analog wave and creating a digital signal is known as *Pulse Code Modulation (PCM)*. The resulting digital signal is similar to that shown in Figure 15.3.

You will be required to know that a T1 has 24 channels and an E1 has 30 channels. It is important that you know primary differences between the two.

What Do We Do With It?

Each timeslot, which represents one sample, is transmitted across the network and put back together on the remote end. Figure 15.4 shows what happens

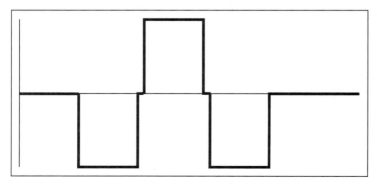

Figure 15.3 A view of a digital signal.

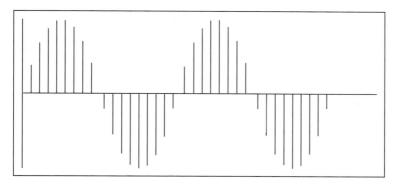

Figure 15.4   When the samples are placed back into their original analog positions, you can construct the waveform.

when the samples are put back together in order to construct the original wave-form where it can be forwarded on to the destination telephone. Looking at the figure, you can see the representation of the waveform. All that is left is to connect the dots.

T1 Framing And Line Coding

T1 providers have developed specific methods of transporting the digital bitstream across long distances. Transmitting the signal requires specific framing and coding procedures. The provider (telco) specifies the type of framing and coding to use for your particular implementation.

In North America, two framing types are commonly used. These are known as Superframe (SF or D4) and Extended Superframe (ESF). Superframe was the first to be developed. One T1 frame consists of one sample from each of the 24 timeslots in a T1. When 12 of these frames are put together, they create a single Superframe. When 24 of these frames are put together, they create a single ESF.

The telco also provides you with the type of line coding that is required to interface its equipment. The *line coding* is the physical bit transmission method. There are two types of line coding used in North America: Alternate Mark Inversion (AMI) and Bipolar with Eight Zero Substitution (B8ZS).

AMI was the first line coding method used in T1 implementation. As its name implies, AMI uses pulses of alternating polarity (such as if one is positive, the next will be negative) on the line (refer back to Figure 15.3 for an example of this). In binary language, a *mark* is a one. Only marks cause the T1 line to pulse. These pulses are necessary to keep the clocking precise. If you introduced a long string of zeros, the clocking mechanism of the network would begin to drift, causing errors. In voice transmission, density of ones is not an issue because the analog wave is a continuously varying entity. However, with data, density of ones is highly likely when you are working with various types of data such as an assembler or a machine language. To combat this problem, the *ones density rule* was introduced. Ones density states that there must be a concentration of at least 12.5 percent ones on the line. In other words, there can be no more than 15 consecutive zeros on the line.

To enforce this rule, AMI changes the value of the least significant bit of every timeslot to a one. In effect, that bit is lost, or *stepped on*. This stepping-on of bits occurs only in data transmission. Therefore, AMI does not lend itself as well to data transmission as it does to voice transmission. Effectively, we have only 7-bits per timeslot now. We still get 8,000 samples per second. If each one is 7-bits, the effective throughput becomes 56,000 bps.

> **Note:** *AMI was developed for voice and provides 64,000 bps for voice traffic. Only when data is transmitted does using AMI decrease your effective transmission rate to 56,000 bps.*

In an attempt to provide the full 64,000 bps for voice as well as data traffic, a new line coding method, B8ZS, was devised. As its name implies, it substitutes out a string of eight contiguous zeros in any particular timeslot. Any timeslot that contains eight zeros has all of its bits changed to ones because zeros are a problem (since they do not pulse the clock), and because we must meet the requirements of the ones density rule. In communicating to the remote end, a *bipolar violation* is inserted into the bitstream. In other words, the first two ones in the timeslot pulse in the same direction, thereby violating the alternating mark pattern. Figure 15.5 demonstrates a bipolar violation. The result is that it is no longer necessary to step on any bits to enforce ones density. Therefore, B8ZS is also known as *clear channel*.

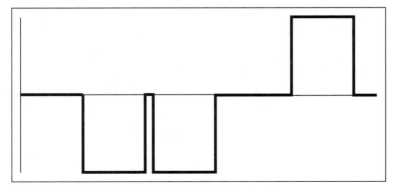

Figure 15.5 A B8ZS bipolar violation.

The AMI and B8ZS coding techniques that you will configure on the router must match what the telco has specified for your particular leased line situation. Also, ensure that you know whether to use superframe (SF) or extended superframe (ESF) to match the telco configuration.

E1 Framing And Line Coding

Most countries (except the United States and Canada) do not implement T1. Instead, a similar technology known as E1 is in place. E1 uses much the same implementation as T1—with a few exceptions. Rather than 24 channels, E1 uses 32 channels. However, not all of these channels are used for data. E1 uses a full DS-0 for framing and another full DS-0 for signaling. The result is 30 DS-0s, for a total throughput capacity of 2,048,000 bps.

E1 implementers are capable of using AMI, as described above. However, there is a different evolution for E1 line coding. For T1, the evolution of AMI was B8ZS. With E1, the evolution is known as High Density Bipolar 3 (HDB3). HDB3 implements a bipolar violation, similar to B8ZS, if it detects three consecutive zeros on the line.

E1 implementations make use of Cyclic Redundancy Check 4 (CRC4) and non-CRC4 framing. These framing types are sometimes specific to a particular country. For instance, if you are installing E1 in Australia, you must add the word "Australia" to the end of the framing configuration command.

Router Configuration

The Channel Service Unit/Digital Service Unit (CSU/DSU) is the device that understands the framing and line coding. You need to configure it with the setting that that telco provides. A number of options are available with regard to the CSU/DSU. Many implementations require an external CSU/DSU whereas others have an integrated CSU/DSU in the hardware. Most of Cisco's router models, from 12000 down to 760, are available with integrated CSU/DSUs.

If the CSU configuration is integrated, you must configure it as part of the router's Internetwork Operating System (IOS) configuration. Otherwise it is simply an additional piece of hardware with vendor-specific configuration command parameters. Our discussion will focus, of course, on the router IOS configuration.

To configure T1 or E1 access on a router, you must configure the controller to create associations of DS-0s to interfaces. The controller configuration is actually the CSU/DSU configuration. Therefore, you must set the framing and line coding at this point as well. Again, the T1/E1 carrier should provide the framing and line coding parameters. Figure 15.6 shows a sample T1 controller configuration, as well as the interface configuration for the defined group associations. Listing 15.1 shows a sample configuration for channeling a T1 circuit to use groups of DS0's for specific services.

Listing 15.1 Configuration for the router in Figure 15.6.

```
controller t1 4/1
framing esf
line code b8zs
clock source line
channel-group 0 timeslots 1
channel-group 8 timeslots 6-11
!
interface serial 4/1:0
ip address 10.1.1.1 255.255.255.0
encapsulation ppp
!
interface serial 4/1:8
ip address 10.2.2.1 255.255.255.0
```

Ensure that you know how to pick out a proper T1 configuration similar to the one above and how to configure for T1 framing and line coding, as well as the clock source.

In the above configuration, we have set the framing to ESF and line coding to B8ZS. We set the router to receive clocking from the network by using the **clock source line** command.

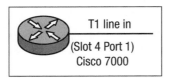

Figure 15.6 A sample router configuration.

The channel-group configuration is the actual channelization of the DS0s. DS0s (timeslots) 1 through 11 have been placed into service for data purposes. The first timeslot is associated with channel-group 0. Timeslots 6 through 11 have been associated with channel-group 8.

The channel-group configurations allow you to create logical interfaces to which you can assign protocol attributes such as IP address, Internetwork Packet eXchange (IPX) network address, and so on. Notice the configuration designates interface Serial 4/1:0. The 0 in that command ties this logical interface back to channel-group 0, with which we associated only a single DS0. In addition, we created interface serial 4/1:8. The 8 in the command ties back to channel-group 8, with which we associated six DS0s. The aggregate bandwidth available to that logical interface is the number of timeslots assigned multiplied by 64,000 bps.

 If you are planning to use Open Shortest Path First (OSPF), Interior Gateway Routing Protocol (IGRP) or Enhanced Interior Gateway Routing Protocol (EIGRP), you must set the bandwidth statements on each interface in order for the route calculation to be correct.

PRI Options

Primary Rate Interface (PRI) is an ISDN technology. Basic Rate Interface (BRI) consists of two B channels and a single D channel. PRI consists of 23 B channels and a single D channel. The D channel is used for signaling requests. To facilitate the D channel's needs, 1 of the 24 DS0s is set aside for these signaling requests. ISDN is discussed in detail in Chapter 13, so we won't discuss it in detail here.

The framing and line coding for PRI are identical to those for T1. T1 PRI requires that you use the last DS0 as a D channel for communication with the provider switch. To that end, you must tell the router to which type of switch it is connecting. The carrier should provide the switch type. Refer back to Figure 15.6 as an example of a PRI configuration. Listing 15.2 shows the actual configuration commands.

Listing 15.2   A basic PRI example.

```
isdn switch-type primary-4ess
!
controller t1 4/1
```

```
pri-group timeslots 1-23
framing esf
linecode b8zs
!
interface serial 4/1:23
ip address 10.1.1.1  255.255.255.0
```

Practice Questions

Question 1

> From where is the line coding and framing information obtained?
>
> O a. You make it up.
>
> O b. You get it from the telco.
>
> O c. You use the defaults of the CSU/DSU.
>
> O d. None of the above.

Answer b is correct. You must obtain the proper line coding and framing information from the telco provider. Answers a and c are incorrect because you must match your configuration to that of the provider equipment to which you are attaching. Although you could get lucky and match the settings, the information should still come from the provider. Answer d is incorrect because a correct answer is given.

Question 2

> You have purchased a Cisco 7500 router with at least one T1 interface. It is now time to configure the controller and the interfaces. If the T1 card is in slot 1 and the port to which the T1 is attached is number 1, what are the appropriate configuration commands? Use the first 12 DS0s for channel-group 1 and the remaining 12 DS0s for channel-group 2. Use line coding B8ZS and ESF framing. Configure the router to receive clocking from the provider network. Use IP addressing of your choice.

The correct answer is:

```
controller t1 1/1
framing esf
line code b8zs
clock source line
channel-group 1 timeslots 1-12
channel-group 2 timeslots 13-24
!
```

```
interface serial 1/1:1
ip address 10.1.1.1 255.255.255.0
!
interface serial 1/1:2
ip address 10.2.2.1 255.255.255.0
```

Question 3

In T1 Primary Rate Interface installations, how many Bearer channels are provided?

○ a. 2

○ b. 24

○ c. 23

○ d. 64

Answer c is correct. T1 PRI consists of 23 B channels and 1 D channel. Answer a is incorrect for PRI, but it is correct for BRI implementations. Answer b is incorrect because all 24 channels are not available in a PRI installation. One is set aside for signaling and framing. Answer d is incorrect because these technologies do not support 64 channels.

Question 4

What is the command to set the integrated CSU/DSU to get clocking from the telco network?

The correct answer is **clock source line**.

Question 5

E1 is used primarily in North America.

○ a. True

○ b. False

Answer b is correct, False. E1 is used primarily in European nations.

Need To Know More?

 Flanagan, William A., *"The Guide to T1 Internetworking"*, Miller Freeman Books, London, U.K.,1998. ISBN 0-93664-826-0. This book provides in-depth detail on T1 and other digital technologies.

 Minoli, Daniel and Minoli, Emma, *"Delivering Voice of Frame Relay and ATM"*, Wiley Computer Publishing, New York, NY, 1998. ISBN 0-47125-481-9. This book focuses on voice-over frame relay and ATM technologies. However, the first four chapters are an in depth discussion of T1 and E1 encoding technologies.

 For more information on T1 and E1, visit **www.cisco.com** and perform a search on the these keywords.

Sample Test

In this chapter, we provide pointers to help you develop a successful test-taking strategy, including how to choose proper answers, how to decode ambiguity, how to work within the Cisco testing framework, how to decide what you need to memorize, and how to prepare for the test. At the end of the chapter, we include 72 questions on subject matter that pertains to Cisco Exam 640-403, "Advanced Cisco Router Configuration" (ACRC).

Questions, Questions, Questions

There should be no doubt in your mind that you are facing a test full of specific and pointed questions. The version of the ACRC exam that you will take is fixed-length, so it will include 72 questions and you will be allotted 90 minutes to complete it. You will be required to achieve a score of 70 percent or better to pass the exam.

For this exam, questions belong to one of six basic types:

➤ Multiple-choice with a single answer

➤ Multiple-choice with multiple answers

➤ Multipart with a single answer

➤ Multipart with multiple answers

➤ Simulations (that is, you must answer a question based on a picture of a network scenario)

➤ Fill in the blank (you must type out your answers without using the abbreviations that so many Cisco administrators are used to using)

Always take the time to read a question at least twice before selecting an answer, and always look for an Exhibit button as you examine each question. Exhibits include graphics information that is related to a question. An exhibit is usually a screen capture of program output or GUI information that you must examine to analyze the question's contents and to formulate an answer. The Exhibit button brings up graphics and charts used to help explain a question, provide additional data, or illustrate page layout or program behavior.

Not every question has only one answer; many questions require multiple answers. Therefore, it's important to read each question carefully, to determine how many answers are necessary or possible, and to look for additional hints or instructions when selecting answers. Such instructions often occur in brackets immediately following the question itself (as they do for all multiple-choice, multiple-answer questions). Unfortunately, some questions do not have any right answers and you are forced to find the "most correct" choice.

Picking Proper Answers

Obviously, the only way to pass any exam is to select enough of the right answers to obtain a passing score. However, Cisco's exams are not standardized like the SAT and GRE exams; they are far more diabolical and convoluted. In some cases, questions are strangely worded, and deciphering them can be a real challenge. In those cases, you may need to rely on answer-elimination skills. Almost always, at least one answer out of the possible choices for a question can be eliminated immediately because it matches one of these conditions:

➤ The answer does not apply to the situation.

➤ The answer describes a nonexistent issue, an invalid option, or an imaginary state.

➤ The answer may be eliminated because of the question itself.

After you eliminate all answers that are obviously wrong, you can apply your retained knowledge to eliminate further answers. Look for items that sound correct but refer to actions, commands, or features that are not present or not available in the situation that the question describes.

If you're still faced with a blind guess among two or more potentially correct answers, reread the question. Try to picture how each of the possible remaining answers would alter the situation. Be especially sensitive to terminology; sometimes the choice of words ("remove" instead of "disable") can make the difference between a right answer and a wrong one.

Only when you've exhausted your ability to eliminate answers, but remain unclear about which of the remaining possibilities is correct, should you guess at an answer. An unanswered question offers you no points, but guessing gives you at least some chance of getting a question right; just don't be too hasty when making a blind guess.

 Since you're taking a fixed-length test, you can wait until the last round of reviewing marked questions (just as you're about to run out of time or out of unanswered questions) before you start making guesses. Guessing should be your technique of last resort!

Decoding Ambiguity

Cisco exams have a reputation for including questions that can be difficult to interpret, confusing, or ambiguous. In our experience with numerous exams, we consider this reputation to be completely justified. The Cisco exams are tough, and they are deliberately made that way.

The only way to beat Cisco at its own game is to be prepared. You'll discover that many exam questions test your knowledge of things that are not directly related to the issue that a question raises. This means that the answers you must choose from, even incorrect ones, are just as much a part of the skill assessment as the question itself. If you don't know something about most aspects of ACRC, you may not be able to eliminate obviously wrong answers because they relate to a different area of ACRC than the one that the question at hand is addressing. In other words, the more you know about the software, the easier it will be for you to tell right from wrong.

Questions often give away their answers, but you have to be Sherlock Holmes to see the clues. Often, subtle hints appear in the question text in such a way that they seem almost irrelevant to the situation. You must realize that each question is a test unto itself and that you need to inspect and successfully navigate each question to pass the exam. Look for small clues, such as the mention of times, group permissions and names, and configuration settings. Little things like these can point at the right answer if properly understood; if missed, they can leave you facing a blind guess.

Another common difficulty with certification exams is vocabulary. Be sure to brush up on the key terms presented at the beginning of each chapter. You may also want to read through the Glossary at the end of this book the day before you take the test.

Working Within The Framework

The test questions appear in random order, and many elements or issues that receive mention in one question may also crop up in other questions. It's not uncommon to find that an incorrect answer to one question is the correct answer to another question, or vice-versa. Take the time to read every answer to each question, even if you recognize the correct answer to a question immediately. That extra reading may spark a memory or remind you about a Cisco router Internetwork Operating System (IOS) feature or function that helps you on another question elsewhere in the exam.

Since you're taking a fixed-length test, you can revisit any question as many times as you like. If you're uncertain of the answer to a question, check the box that's provided to mark it for easy return later on. You should also mark questions you think may offer information that you can use to answer other questions. On fixed-length tests, we usually mark somewhere between 25 and 50 percent of the questions on exams we've taken. The testing software is designed to let you mark every question if you choose; use this framework to your advantage. Everything you will want to see again should be marked; the testing software can then help you return to marked questions quickly and easily.

For fixed-length tests, we strongly recommend that you first read through the entire test quickly, before getting caught up in answering individual questions. This will help to jog your memory as you review the potential answers and can help identify questions that you want to mark for easy access to their contents. It will also let you identify and mark the really tricky questions for easy return as well. The key is to make a quick pass over the territory to begin with, so that you know what you're up against; and then to survey that territory more thoroughly on a second pass, when you can begin to answer all questions systematically and consistently.

Deciding What To Memorize

The amount of memorization you must undertake for an exam depends on how well you remember what you've read, and how well you know the software by heart. The tests will stretch your recollection of the router's commands and functions.

At a minimum, you'll want to memorize the following kinds of information:

➤ The basics of Enhanced Interior Gateway Routing Protocol (EIGRP) and how it selects routes.

➤ The basic functions and configuration of Open Shortest Path First (OSPF). Know how to spot a bad configuration example.

➤ The role of dial-on-demand routing (DDR) and its various deployment possibilities.

➤ The various **show** commands that allow you to see the status of the subjects mentioned throughout the book.

If you work your way through this book while sitting at a Cisco router (actually you may need a group of routers, and try to manipulate this environment's features and functions as they're discussed throughout, you should have little or no difficulty mastering this material. Also, don't forget that The Cram Sheet at the front of the book is designed to capture the material that is most important to memorize; use this to guide your studies as well.

Preparing For The Test

The best way to prepare for the test—after you've studied—is to take at least one practice exam. We've included one here in this chapter for that reason; the test questions are located in the pages that follow (and unlike the preceding chapters in this book, the answers don't follow the questions immediately; you'll have to flip to Chapter 17 to review the answers separately).

Give yourself 90 minutes to take the exam, keep yourself on the honor system, and don't look at earlier text in the book or jump ahead to the answer key.

When your time is up, or you've finished the questions, you can check your work in Chapter 17. Pay special attention to the explanations for the incorrect answers; these can also help to reinforce your knowledge of the material. Knowing how to recognize correct answers is good, but understanding why incorrect answers are wrong can be equally valuable.

Taking The Test

Relax. Once you're sitting in front of the testing computer, there's nothing more you can do to increase your knowledge or preparation. Take a deep breath, stretch, and start reading that first question.

There's no need to rush; you have plenty of time to complete each question and to return to those questions that you skip or mark for return. If you read a question twice and remain clueless, you can mark it. Both easy and difficult questions are intermixed throughout the test in random order. Since you're taking a fixed-length test, don't cheat yourself by spending too much time on a hard question early on in the test, thereby depriving yourself of the time you need to answer the questions at the end of the test.

On a fixed-length test, you can read through the entire test, and before returning to marked questions for a second visit, figure out how much time you've got per question. As you answer each question, remove its mark. Continue to review the remaining marked questions until you run out of time, or you complete the test.

That's it for pointers. Here are some questions for you to practice on.

Practice Questions

Question 1

RIP supports VLSM.

○ a. True

○ b. False

Question 2

OSPF supports VLSM.

○ a. True

○ b. False

Question 3

What is the principle on which routers make forwarding decisions?

○ a. Classless routing

○ b. VLSM

○ c. Longest match

○ d. None of the above

Question 4

Where in the internetwork is summary routing generally performed?

○ a. On the edge routers between dissimilar networks

○ b. On all routers

○ c. Nowhere

○ d. On point-to-point Serial links

Question 5

What is the process of mapping private internal addresses to registered public addresses known as?

○ a. Network Address Translation

○ b. Subnet masking

○ c. Address summarization

○ d. Classless Interdomain Routing

Question 6

What command shows all interfaces configured for IPX?

○ a. **show interfaces ipx**

○ b. **show ipx interfaces**

○ c. **display ipx**

○ d. **show protocol ipx**

Question 7

What command displays the IPX SAP table with all learned services? [Write your answer without abbreviation]

Question 8

Which statements are true regarding EIGRP? [Choose the two best answers]

❑ a. It supports areas.

❑ b. It supports VLSM.

❑ c. It requires considerably more configuration than OSPF.

❑ d. It keeps all protocols in one table.

❑ e. It sends notifications to only the systems that are affected by a change.

Question 9

If your network uses RIP, how do you prevent distribution of routes without using access lists?

○ a. Default routes

○ b. Passive interfaces

○ c. Static routes

○ d. Routing update filters

Question 10

What command enables IPX on a router? [Fill in the blank]

_____

Question 11

Why is OSPF better than RIP in a large network? [Choose the two best answers]

❑ a. OSPF has virtually no reachability limits.

❑ b. OSPF is less complex than RIP.

❑ c. OSPF has fewer tables to manage.

❑ d. OSPF selects the best path using cost based on bandwidth as a metric.

Question 12

How many Class Cs can be summarized with the route 192.12.172.0/20?

○ a. 4

○ b. 8

○ c. 16

○ d. 20

○ e. 32

Question 13

Which statements are true regarding the command **source-bridge transparent 20 23 1 4**? [Choose the two best answers]

❑ a. Virtual SRB ring is defined as ring 20.

❑ b. Pseudo ring 23 is the transparent domain.

❑ c. The 1 removes this virtual interface from the spanning tree.

❑ d. The bridge group number is 1.

Question 14

Which of the following situations would require BGP routing? [Choose the two best answers]

❑ a. You need to make a decision based on the source and destination of internal traffic within an AS.

❑ b. You need to make connections to different Internet Service Providers.

❑ c. Security concerns require that you filter all but three networks from the Internet.

❑ d. The ISP you connect to uses BGP to connect to the NAP.

Question 15

Which problems can be associated with a high number of routers in an OSPF area? [Choose the two best answers]

❑ a. Excess LSA traffic

❑ b. Frequent table recalculation

❑ c. Frequent adjacency table recalculation

❑ d. More reachability errors

Question 16

How would you control SAP traffic across a WAN link?

○ a. Disable GNS on some Novell servers.

○ b. Spoof SPX watchdog traffic.

○ c. Use EIGRP for SAP updates.

○ d. None of the above

Question 17

Which options are available on IP extended access lists, but are not available for standard access lists? [Choose the three best answers]

❑ a. Session-layer information

❑ b. Destination IP

❑ c. Application port number

❑ d. Source host IP

Question 18

Which of the following is true about non-routable protocols?

○ a. There is no FCS in the header.

○ b. There is no network-layer addressing.

○ c. They use broadcasts to determine the best route.

○ d. They should not be used with WAN links.

Question 19

In what situation would you use a null interface instead of an access list?

○ a. When an access list does not provide the necessary functionality.

○ b. When you want to use hostnames rather than IP addresses.

○ c. When you need to conserve CPU resources.

○ d. When you cannot filter non-routable protocols.

Question 20

Which address ranges are private? [Choose the two best answers]

❏ a. 192.167.2.0

❏ b. 172.16.0.0

❏ c. 172.68.0.0

❏ d. 192.168.1.0

Question 21

What command specifies generic route encapsulation to carry traffic through an IP tunnel? [Write your answer without abbreviation]

_____

Question 22

Which statement about EIGRP is true?

○ a. It keeps a copy of its neighbors' tables.

○ b. It uses forward broadcasts to discover routers.

○ c. Adjacencies exist between master routers (MRs).

○ d. It provides support for other network-layer protocols such as IPX AppleTalk and IP.

Question 23

Which of these descriptions of OSPFs features are true? [Choose the three best answers]

❏ a. It can span more than 15 hops.

❏ b. Its path can be based on throughput.

❏ c. It sends a full routing table on updates.

❏ d. Its routing updates are multicast.

❏ e. It effectively replaces RTMP, IPX, RIP, and IP RIP.

Question 24

Which two are T1 framing types? [Choose the two best answers]

- ❑ a. AMI
- ❑ b. HDB3
- ❑ c. B8ZS
- ❑ d. CRC4
- ❑ e. None of the above

Question 25

Which queuing method provides automated traffic sorting based on messages and conversations?

- ○ a. Custom queuing
- ○ b. FIFO
- ○ c. Priority queuing
- ○ d. Weighted fair queuing

Question 26

As IPX networks grow, which of the following become important? [Choose the two best answers]

- ❑ a. Broadcasts
- ❑ b. Limitations of IPX
- ❑ c. Non-routable NetWare protocols
- ❑ d. IPX 16-hop limit

Question 27

What command do you use to display the routing information field of token ring frames that pass through the router? [Write your answer without abbreviation]

Question 28

Why is OSPF better than RIP in large networks? [Choose the two best answers]

☐ a. It uses less RAM on the router.

☐ b. It has no reachability limits.

☐ c. It is less complex than RIP.

☐ d. It supports VLSMs.

Question 29

What command configures source-route bridging from ring 500 to bridge 1 to ring 501? [Write your answer without abbreviation]

Question 30

What command displays both OSPF interfaces that are configured to each area and all the adjacent neighbor names? [Write your answer without abbreviation]

Question 31

Which statements are true about the following configuration? [Choose the two best answers]

```
interface Ethernet 0
ip address 172.16.1.77 255.255.255.0
ip helper-address 172.16.90.255
```

☐ a. Host 172.16.90.255 is a backup router for 172.16.1.77.

☐ b. TFTP broadcasts on interface Ethernet 0 will be forwarded to network 172.16.90.0.

☐ c. All non-routable protocol traffic will be forwarded to network 172.16.90.0.

☐ d. NetBIOS broadcasts from network 148.19.90.0 will be sent as directed broadcasts to the 172.16.90.0 network.

Question 32

What commands are necessary to configure OSPF?

○ a. **router ospf network ; <address-mask> <area-id>**

○ b. **router ospf <process id> network <address-mask> <area-id>**

○ c. **router ospf <process id>; network <address>
<wildcard-mask> <area area-id>**

○ d. None of the above

Question 33

What is the order of transmission in priority queuing?

○ a. Higher-priority queues are emptied before lower-priority queues.

○ b. All queues use a round-robin method.

○ c. Time division.

○ d. FIFO.

Question 34

What is the command to show EIGRP routing tables? [Write your answer without abbreviation]

Question 35

Through what process can a single IP represent many IP addresses?

○ a. Default routes

○ b. Static routes

○ c. Route summarization

○ d. Route expansion

Question 36

Which of the following statements regarding the sample configuration are true? [Choose the two best answers]

```
router EIGRP 100
network 12.0.0.0
network 13.0.0.0
```

☐ a. The AS 100 is invalid.

☐ b. The EIGRP process is running in Autonomous System 100.

☐ c. The network statements are missing the **netmask** statement.

☐ d. The network 12.0.0.0 is included in Autonomous System 100.

Question 37

What is the full the command to display access list 190? [Write your answer without abbreviation]

Question 38

What does the command **backup delay 5 30** signify?

○ a. When the load reaches 30, bring the secondary link up for 5 seconds.

○ b. When a failure is detected, wait 5 seconds to bring up the backup. Once the failure clears, wait 30 seconds to bring the secondary link back down.

○ c. When delay on the link reaches 5 ms, bring the backup link up for 30 minutes.

○ d. When delay on the link reaches 5 ms, wait 30 seconds to bring the secondary link up.

Question 39

What is the command to enable Multilink on a PPP link? [Write your answer without abbreviation]

Question 40

What is the interface between the NT1 and the point of demarcation?

- ○ a. R interface
- ○ b. S interface
- ○ c. T interface
- ○ d. U interface

Question 41

Which of these are tables kept by EIGRP routers? [Choose the three best answers]

- ❑ a. Protocol
- ❑ b. Topology
- ❑ c. Neighbor
- ❑ d. Routing

Question 42

If you cannot connect an OSPF area directly to area 0, what must you configure?

- ○ a. Route summarization
- ○ b. Static routes
- ○ c. Virtual link
- ○ d. Designated router

Question 43

What is the command to view EIGRP routers with which you have established neighbor relationships? [Write your answer without abbreviation]

Question 44

What is the best route to any destination in an EIGRP routing table called?

○ a. Feasible successor

○ b. Current successor

○ c. Adjacency

○ d. DUAL

Question 45

What is the command to force EIGRP to stop summarizing routes to normal classful boundaries? [Write your answer without abbreviation]

_____

Question 46

What type of traffic was ISDN developed to carry?

○ a. Voice

○ b. Video

○ c. Data

○ d. All of the above

Question 47

What is the command that both creates a dialer list with the tag number of 1 and specifies all IP traffic as interesting traffic? [Write your answer without abbreviation]

_____

Question 48

What is the RFC that defines private internetwork address space?

○ a. 1783

○ b. 1918

○ c. 1009

○ d. 2022

Question 49

Create a single summary address for the addresses consisting of the following networks:

```
172.15.168.0
172.15.169.0
172.15.170.0
172.15.171.0
172.15.172.0
172.15.173.0
172.15.174.0
172.15.175.0
```

Question 50

Which of the following are pieces of information that OSPF requires to establish and maintain a neighbor relationship? [Choose the three best answers]

❏ a. Hello/dead interval

❏ b. Routing table

❏ c. Router priority

❏ d. Designated router ID

Question 51

> What is the command under the **router rip** configuration that would stop RIP updates from leaving via interface Ethernet 3? [Write your answer without abbreviation]
>
> _____

Question 52

> What command sets a default static route via interface Serial 0? [Write your answer without abbreviation]
>
> _____

Question 53

> A standard access list is used in route filtering with distribute lists.
>
> ○ a. True
>
> ○ b. False

Question 54

> Which items must be spoofed in order for DDR to function with IPX? [Choose the two best answers]
>
> ❏ a. Watchdogs
>
> ❏ b. SPX Keepalives
>
> ❏ c. NetWare Core Protocol
>
> ❏ d. IPX SAP

Question 55

Which ISDN protocol deals with the ISDN network layer between the terminal and the switch?

○ a. Q.931

○ b. Q.921

○ c. E.164

○ d. I.100

Question 56

From the **interface Ethernet 0** configuration prompt, what is the command to enable transparent bridging? [Write your answer without abbreviation]

_____

Question 57

Which of the following is the IPX access list equivalent of the IP access list keyword **any**?

○ a. **host**

○ b. **-1**

○ c. **0.0.0.0**

○ d. **permit**

Question 58

What is the command to view the status of the snapshot routing process? [Write your answer without abbreviation]

_____

Question 59

What is the command, using group number 3, to place any IPX traffic into the low-priority queue? [Write your answer without abbreviation]

Question 60

Which command will inform a BRI ISDN router that it is conversing with a National (Ni1) switch?

○ a. **switch-type basic-ni1**

○ b. **switch-type primary-ni1**

○ c. **isdn switch-type basic-ni1**

○ d. **isdn switch-type primary-ni1**

Question 61

Which command displays all of the directly connected OSPF routers?

○ a. **show ip ospf neighbors**

○ b. **show neighbors**

○ c. **show cdp neighbor detail**

○ d. **show ip route**

Question 62

What command displays all currently active routing protocols for IP? [Write your answer without abbreviation]

Question 63

What command gets you into the virtual terminal configuration mode for all virtual terminal lines? [Write your answer without abbreviation]

_____

Question 64

What command gets you into the console configuration mode? [Write your answer without abbreviation]

_____

Question 65

Which command must be used in conjunction, specifically, with a non-native ISDN implementation?

○ a. **dialer in-band**

○ b. **dialer-list 1 protocol ip permit**

○ c. **dialer map ipx 100.0000.0000.0001 5551111**

○ d. None of the above

Question 66

What is the process of configuring dissimilar routing protocols to share information?

○ a. Summarization

○ b. ISDN

○ c. Adjacency

○ d. Redistribution

Question 67

Where should you utilize traffic prioritization?

- ○ a. On bursty WAN links (T1 and below) that experience temporary congestion.
- ○ b. On all WAN links, no matter the speed.
- ○ c. On LAN links only.
- ○ d. All of the above

Question 68

How many custom queues are available for administrator configuration?

- ○ a. 17
- ○ b. 16
- ○ c. 4
- ○ d. 1

Question 69

What is the designation given to routers at the top of your network hierarchy?

- ○ a. Distribution
- ○ b. Access
- ○ c. Primary
- ○ d. Core

Question 70

What command specifies that the second BRI B-channel should activate at a load of 110 inbound or outbound? [Write your answer without abbreviation]

_____

Question 71

Where do IPX-configured Serial interfaces obtain their node addresses? [Choose the two best answers]

❑ a. From the lowest numbered LAN interface.

❑ b. The administrator hard Codes them.

❑ c. They are assigned at random.

❑ d. They are learned from neighbors.

Question 72

Where should an IP helper address be placed?

○ a. On the outbound interface of the broadcasting router.

○ b. On the inbound interface of the broadcasting router.

○ c. On the outbound interface of the router that receives the broadcast request.

○ d. On the inbound interface of the router that receives the broadcast request.

Answer Key

1. b
2. a
3. c
4. a
5. a
6. b
7. show ipx servers
8. b, e
9. b
10. ipx routing
11. a, d
12. c
13. a, b
14. b, c
15. a, b
16. c
17. a, b, c
18. b
19. c
20. b, d
21. tunnel mode gre ip
22. d
23. a, b, d
24. e
25. d
26. a, d
27. show rif
28. b, d
29. source-bridge 500 1 501

30. show ip ospf neighbors
31. b, d
32. c
33. a
34. show ip route
35. c
36. b, d
37. show access-list 190
38. b
39. ppp multilink
40. d
41. b, c, d
42. c
43. show ip eigrp neighbors, show ipx eigrp neighbors, or show appletalk eigrp neighbors
44. b
45. no auto-summary
46. d
47. dialer-list 1 protocol ip permit
48. b
49. 172.15.168.0 255.255.248.0

50. a, c, d
51. passive-interface Ethernet 3
52. ip route 0.0.0.0 0.0.0.0 Serial 0
53. a
54. a, b
55. a
56. bridge-group <number>
57. b
58. show snapshot
59. priority-list 3 protocol ipx low
60. a
61. a
62. show ip protocols
63. line vty 0 4
64. line con 0
65. a
66. d
67. a
68. b
69. d
70. dialer load-threshold 110 either
71. a, b
72. d

Question 1

Answer b is correct, False. RIP does not support VLSM, route summarization, or classless routing in any way. It cannot include the prefix in routing updates.

Question 2

Answer a is correct, True. OSPF, unlike RIP, can pass the prefix in routing update information.

Question 3

Answer c is correct. Longest Match is based on the number of bits of a destination address that correspond to entries in the routing table. The entry that matches the most contiguous bits, should be the proper entry on which to base a forwarding decision. Answer a is incorrect because classless routing is what allows us to perform route summarization and VLSM. It does not describe the method the router uses to make a forwarding decision. VLSM is basically a type of classless routing implementation; therefore, answer b is incorrect. Answer d is incorrect because a correct answer is given.

Question 4

Answer a is correct. To get an idea of how you might use a border between dissimilar networks, consider the OSPF implementation of separate area hierarchy as a great example of where to summarize. If you summarize at the area borders, you need only a single route to provide reachability to all networks outside of the local area. Refer to Chapter 9 for more information on OSPF. Answer b is incorrect because summarization is not performed on all routers; it would be ineffective to do so. Summarization makes a difference only between dissimilar networks. If we summarize on every router, the routers in similar address space could misdirect traffic flow and create routing inconsistencies or routing loops. Answer c is incorrect because in order for summarization to work, it must be properly configured at the proper points. Answer d is incorrect—point-to-point serial links are a transport mechanism, not a summarization scheme.

Question 5

Answer a is correct. NAT is used specifically to allow access to the public Internet without an administrator having to readdress the existing network. Subnet masking is the process of dividing up the address space you have internally.

Therefore, answer b is incorrect. Address summarization, otherwise known as route summarization, is the process of reducing the routing table by aggregating addresses based on a common bit boundary. Therefore, answer c is incorrect. CIDR allows you to conserve address space by giving you as close as possible the number of addresses you need, rather than wasting addresses needlessly. Therefore, answer d is incorrect.

Question 6

Answer b is correct. **show ipx interfaces** gives you the information of all IPX-configured interfaces currently active on the router. Answers a, c, and d are incorrect because they are not valid commands.

Question 7

show ipx servers is the correct answer. This command displays all Novell NetWare servers that are being advertised to it.

Question 8

Answers b and e are correct. EIGRP does support VLSM in environments where it is necessary. In addition, when there is a change in the network, an update is sent to the directly connected neighbors because they will also be affected by the change in reachability. Answer a is incorrect because EIGRP does not support a hierarchical area structure like OSPF. Answer c is incorrect because a basic EIGRP configuration is much simpler in nature than that of OSPF. EIGRP does not require the use of a wildcard mask to specify network statements. Therefore, answer d is incorrect. EIGRP can route multiple layer 3 protocols, but it keeps separate neighbor, topology, and routing tables for each protocol.

Question 9

Answer b is correct. Passive interfaces tell RIP and other routing protocols not to send updates out of the specified interface(s). Answer a is incorrect because default routes are placed in the routing table by an administrator or by a redistribution of routing information. They do not stop RIP updates. Answer c is incorrect because static routes are placed in the routing table by an administrator and will be advertised only in certain circumstances. Answer d is incorrect because routing update filters require the use of access lists to function.

Question 10

ipx routing is the correct answer. This command initializes the IPX protocol on the router.

Question 11

Answers a and d are correct. RIP has a 15 hop reachability limitation. This is one of the reasons for the creation of OSPF in the beginning. RIP uses hop count as a metric, where OSPF's route calculation takes into account the bandwidth of the pathway to the destination. OSPF is a more intelligent routing protocol than RIP. Answer b is incorrect because RIP's configuration is actually much less complex than OSPF's configuration. Answer c is incorrect because OSPF actually builds more tables than RIP. OSPF builds a topology database, SPF tree, and a routing table. It also must build a table to track neighbor and adjacency relationships.

Question 12

Answer c is correct. A natural Class C address is automatically summarized to 24 bits. However, when we take away 4 bits from the natural network portion, we have to make a calculation of 2^4, which is 16. No other answer mathematically works out properly when we are looking at 20 bits with a Class C address.

Question 13

Answers a and b are correct. The command specifies a virtual ring (to accommodate a multiport bridge) within the bridge, a pseudo ring number (how the Token Ring clients see the Ethernet segment), bridge number (for SRB), and a transparent bridge group. These are the configuration parameters necessary to configure source-route translational bridging. Answer c is incorrect because the 1 is a bridge number; it does not remove any interfaces from the spanning tree. Answer d is incorrect because the bridge group number is 4, not 1.

Question 14

Answers b and c are correct. Connecting to multiple ISPs requires you to manipulate local preference or the multi-exit discriminator attributes in order to choose the preferred route out of your AS. It is not desirable for your traffic to leave your AS via one ISP and return via the other. In order for you to implement security in your network, you will need to be in charge of what information comes into and goes out of your network. Should you wish to filter networks, at the ISP connection, you will need to do that with the protocol that allows the two AS's to communicate, BGP. Answer a is incorrect because IGP, not BGP, should make your internal AS routing decisions. Answer d is incorrect because the method by which your ISP connects to the tier above it is irrelevant to your connection to that ISP.

Question 15

Answers a and b are correct. The reasons for creating areas are to cut down on the number of route calculations that must be made as well as to cut down on the impact of routing updates. If the area gets too big, changes in the network can have a profound effect on the router's ability to keep up with the changes. By cutting down the amount of LSA traffic, you will reduce the frequency of routing table recalculations. Answer c is incorrect because the routing table gets recalculated, not necessarily the adjacencies. Without the adjacency relationship, there is no other router to which to send LSA traffic. Answer d is incorrect because reachability is the reason for the LSA traffic. If the traffic is being received and alternative routes are available, reachability should not be affected to a great degree.

Question 16

Answer c is correct. EIGRP has the ability to silence SAP traffic across a link. Normal SAP operation has updates that broadcast every 60 seconds. EIGRP for IPX eliminates the periodic updates in favor of incremental updates. In other words, SAP updates will be sent across the link only when there is a change, and only the change is sent. Answer a is incorrect because you cannot turn off GNS functionality of a server. If that were done, no clients would connect to it. Answer b is incorrect because spoofing traffic in IPX environments is done only in DDR implementations. Answer d is incorrect because a correct answer is given.

Question 17

Answers a, b, and c are correct. IP extended access lists can filter based on the session-layer protocols TCP or UDP. They can filter based on source and destination IP address as well as an application port number. Answer d is incorrect because IP standard access lists can filter only on source address.

Question 18

Answer b is correct. Non-routable (also called layer 2) protocols do not contain network-layer information that is associated with IP/IPX/AppleTalk. In other words, there is no *network.node* relationship in a layer 2 protocol. Answer a is incorrect because the layer 2 framing does have an FCS. Answer c is incorrect because some non-routable protocols use explorer frames to find routes rather than using broadcasts. Answer d is incorrect because many times, you may have no other choice but to send these protocols across a WAN link.

Question 19

Answer c is correct. Using a null interface has a similar effect to using access lists without the additional CPU overhead associated with access lists. The router simply makes a routing decision and routes packets destined for the specified network into a non-existent logical interface. No error message is generated because the use of the null interface is a valid routing decision. Answer a is incorrect because an access list actually provides more functionality than a null interface. Answer b is incorrect because the use of hostnames has nothing to do with actual network routing decisions. In any event, a hostname must be resolved to an IP address, so you'd have to use both the hostname and the IP address. Answer d is incorrect because using a null interface is a routing decision. Non-routable protocols are not supported in these layer 3 decisions.

Question 20

Answers b and d are correct. RFC 1918 defines the private internetwork address space. The Class A range is the network 10.0.0.0 through 10.255.255.255. The Class B range is 172.16.0.0 through 172.31.255.255. The Class C range is 192.168.0.0 through 192.168.255.255. Answers a and c do not fall within any of these ranges and are therefore incorrect.

Question 21

tunnel mode gre ip is the correct answer. This is the default mode for a tunnel interface. Therefore you should not have to type it. However, it might be worth the time involved in learning the command.

Question 22

Answer d is correct. EIGRP provides routing support for IP, IPX, and AppleTalk. Answer a is incorrect because EIGRP does not keep a copy of its neighbors' routing tables. It does keep track of the destinations the neighbors know about, but not their actual routing tables. Answer b is incorrect because EIGRP does not use broadcasts to forward routing updates. Answer c is incorrect because there is no master router relationship in EIGRP.

Question 23

Answers a, b, and d are correct. OSPF does not have the limitation of 15 hops as does RIP. It uses a cost based on bandwidth to select the best routes, and all routing updates go out as multicast traffic—not broadcast traffic. Answer c is incorrect because OSPF updates go out on an as-needed basis and then only the changes are sent, not the full routing table. Answer e is incorrect because OSPF is an IP-only routing protocol.

Question 24

Answer e is correct. Answers a, b, c, and d are T1 and E1 line coding methods, not framing types. T1 framing types are Superframe and Extended Superframe.

Question 25

Answer d is correct. Weighted fair queuing gives the lower-volume traffic the priority on the link. It sorts each traffic flow into conversations in the output queue. Answer a is incorrect because custom queuing is a round-robin load-balanced traffic-output algorithm. The sorting is not automated and must be manually configured. Answer b is incorrect because the first-in-first-out method is what is used in the absence of any other queuing strategy. Traffic is sent out in the order in which it arrived. Answer c is incorrect because priority queuing uses predefined high-, medium-, normal-, and low-priority queues to sort traffic based on the administrator's configuration for prioritization. It also is not an automated queuing strategy.

Question 26

Answers a and d are correct. IPX uses broadcasts to propagate routing information. It, like IP RIP, is subject to a 15-hop limit. Answer b is incorrect because the limitations of IPX are always a factor in deployment. For example, IPX is not a manageable protocol as is IP. There is no SNMP equivalent for IPX. Answer c is incorrect because any router not configured for bridging will not forward non-routable protocols. So, the size of the network makes no difference because these protocols will not leave the broadcast domain.

Question 27

show rif is the correct answer. This command will show the information included in the Route Control and Route Descriptor fields of the RIF.

Question 28

Answers b and d are correct. OSPF is a more intelligent routing protocol than RIP. It does not suffer from the 15-hop limitation as does RIP. In addition, it supports VLSM. Answer a is incorrect because the tradeoff to having additional functionality is more resource utilization in the router. Answer c is incorrect because the OSPF configuration parameters tend to be somewhat complex, whereas RIP configuration is very simple.

Question 29

source-bridge 500 1 501 is the correct answer. You must specify the source ring number, bridge number and destination ring number in any SRB configuration.

Question 30

show ip ospf neighbors is the correct answer. You will be able to monitor neighbor relationships for the OSPF process using this command.

Question 31

Answers b and d are correct. **ip helper-address** enables the forwarding of specific broadcast traffic via unicast, multicast, or (in the case of answers b and d) directed broadcast. Answer a is incorrect because this is not a backup scenario. Answer c is incorrect because the use of **ip helper-address** is not a bridging technique. It simply enables the forwarding of selected broadcasts, not all layer 2 protocols.

Question 32

Answer c is correct. OSPF configuration requires the process to be initialized on the router by using the **router ospf <process id>** command. The **id** is a locally significant number that sets one OSPF process apart from other OSPF processes that may be running on this particular router. Answers a and b do not specify the appropriate information. Therefore, they are incorrect. Answer d is incorrect because a correct answer is given.

Question 33

Answer a is correct. Priority queuing specifies high-, medium-, normal-, and low-priority queues. The higher priority queues are serviced until they are empty. Answer b is incorrect because custom queuing uses the round-robin method to dispatch traffic. Answer c is incorrect because time division refers to a multiplexing method generally associated with physical-layer transmission. Answer d is incorrect because priority queuing is used to decide which traffic has the priority on any particular outbound interface. FIFO is the first-in-first-out method in which all traffic, no matter the type, is transmitted in the order in which it was received.

Question 34

show ip route is the correct answer. While there are EIGRP specific commands to view the topology and neighbor tables, there is still only one to view the routing table.

Question 35

Answer c is correct. Route summarization is the method by which a single address can be used in the routing table to represent any number of addresses. Answer a is incorrect because default routes serve only as gateways of last resort for traffic that cannot be adequately associated with any destination network in the routing table. Answer b is incorrect because static routes do not provide summarization. You can use static routes to override what the dynamic routing protocol has chosen for a pathway. Answer d is incorrect because route expansion is not a valid internetworking term.

Question 36

Answers b and d are correct. The commands are specifying that the EIGRP process should be a part of AS 100. They also state that any interface that includes an address of 12.X.X.X or 13.X.X.X should be included in the EIGRP routing process. Answer a is incorrect because 100 is a perfectly valid AS number for your internal private routing domain. Answer c is incorrect because EIGRP configurations do not require or make use of a netmask.

Question 37

show access-list 190 is the correct answer. This command will show only the access list lines that are part of the 190 list.

Question 38

Answer b is correct. The **backup delay** command specifies two "wait" periods. The first one (5) specifies that in the case of a failure, wait five seconds before initiating the backup link. The second one (30) states that once the primary link has recovered, wait 30 seconds before bringing the backup link back down.

Question 39

ppp multilink is the correct answer. PPP Multilink allows multiple channels to be aggregated and used as if they were a single entity.

Question 40

Answer d is correct. The U interface is considered to be the local loop between your premises' equipment and the telco. It is seen as the point where responsibility for the connectivity changes hands. The other answers are incorrect because they do not specify the appropriate interface designation.

Question 41

Answers b, c, and d are correct. EIGRP routers keep a topology table, neighbor table, and routing table for IP, IPX, and AppleTalk. Each of these tables is a separate entity. Answer a is incorrect because the router does not keep a protocol table.

Question 42

Answer c is correct. OSPF virtual links are required when a non-area 0 must connect to the network via another non-area 0. Virtual links should be avoided. Answer a is incorrect because, although route summarization takes place at area borders, it is not the connection between the two. Answer b is incorrect because static routes exist in various places throughout an area but do not connect areas. Answer d is incorrect because a designated router is an OSPF router with a high-priority and/or high-router ID on a broadcast multi-access network such as Ethernet.

Question 43

show ip eigrp neighbors, **show ipx eigrp neighbors**, or **show appletalk eigrp neighbors** are all correct answers. Each of these commands will show the EIGRP neighbors for their respective protocols.

Question 44

Answer b is correct. The current successor is the route with the lowest feasible distance. Answer a is incorrect because the feasible successor is the second best route. Answer c is incorrect because adjacency refers to the forming of a neighbor relationship. Answer d is incorrect because DUAL refers to the algorithm that EIGRP uses for route selection.

Question 45

no auto-summary is the correct answer when typed under the **router eigrp configuration** mode.

Question 46

Answer d is correct. All answers are correct. ISDN was developed to carry voice, video, and data across a WAN.

Question 47

dialer-list 1 protocol ip permit is the correct answer. This will define all IP traffic as "interesting" traffic and allow it to initiate the ISDN call.

Question 48

Answer b is correct. RFC 1918 defines the private address space and makes RFC 1597 obsolete. Answer a is incorrect because RFC 1783 defines OSPF. Answer c is incorrect because RFC 1009 defines VLSM. Answer d is incorrect because RFC 2022 defines Multicast Address Resolution Services (MARS) for ATM networks.

Question 49

172.15.168.0 255.255.248.0 is the correct answer.

Question 50

Answers a, c, and d are correct. OSPF routers must keep track of neighbors as they come up on and drop off of the network. This is done through a Hello protocol. The Hello protocol keeps track of a *dead interval*. The dead interval is how long a router will wait before purging the neighbor entry once it has ceased responding to and sending Hello packets. The router priority is used in the election of a designated router. It is important to know what the DR for a particular network segment happens to be at any point in time. Answer b is incorrect because the neighbor relationship must be maintained in order to pass routing updates so the routing table can be built. Although it is important to maintain the routing table, it is not necessary to the formation and/or maintenance of the neighbor relationship.

Question 51

passive-interface Ethernet 3 is the correct answer. This will stop the updates from leaving the router via the Ethernet 3 interface.

Question 52

ip route 0.0.0.0 0.0.0.0 Serial 0 is the correct answer. This command will set the default route and assume it to be directly connected to Serial 0.

Question 53

Answer a is correct. Standard access lists are used to define permitted or denied networks for distribute lists.

Question 54

Answers a and b are correct. Watchdog and SPX Keepalive traffic are necessary to maintain a connection between NetWare clients and servers. Answer c is incorrect because NetWare Core Protocol is part of the client/server conversation, but it is not used to monitor connectivity. Answer d is incorrect because IPX SAP is used to advertise services available on the Novell network, not to maintain a connection between client and server.

Question 55

Answer a is correct. Q.931 provides the network-layer interface between the terminal and the switch. It provides a call setup protocol. Answer b is incorrect because Q.921 deals the Link Access Procedure over the D channel (LAPD). Answer c is incorrect because E.164 is the international ISDN numbering plan standard. It doesn't necessarily deal with the interface between terminal and switch. Answer d is incorrect because I.100 deals with concepts, structures, and terminology in the ISDN network.

Question 56

bridge-group <number> is the correct answer. You will have to specify the same bridge group number for all interfaces that will be taking part in the transparent bridging function.

Question 57

Answer b is correct. **-1** in an IPX access lists specifies the permission or denial of any host, network, and so on that is not specifically noted elsewhere in the access list. Answer a is incorrect because the **host** keyword is used only in IP access lists to specify an exact host address. Answer c is incorrect because **0.0.0.0** is the IP wildcard mask that states to check and match all bits. Answer d is incorrect because **permit** or **deny** is the action that is to be performed on the entities specified by **-1**.

Question 58

show snapshot is the correct answer. This command will display the current status of the snapshot process. You can also debug the snapshot processes to watch the exchange of information.

Question 59

priority-list 3 protocol ipx low is the correct answer. This will place all IPX into the low priority queue.

Question 60

Answer a is correct. The switch type in the router to specify National ISDN type 1 switch is **basic-ni1**. Answers b and d are incorrect because they use primary rate, not basic rate. Answer c is incorrect because it uses the command incorrectly.

Question 61

Answer a is correct. OSPF keeps a table of its neighbors, and at times you need to view their status. Answer a is the only one that shows the proper use of the command. Answer b is incorrect because it does not specify what neighbors to show. It is not a valid command. Answer c is incorrect because the Cisco Discovery Protocol (CDP) neighbor commands are used to view any directly connected routers whether OSPF neighbor relations have been established or not. Answer d is incorrect because it shows the routing table, not neighbors.

Question 62

show ip protocols is the correct answer. This command will display the status of all currently active IP routing protocols.

Question 63

line vty 0 4 is the correct answer. You can use this command to configure all of the vty lines with identical settings simultaneously.

Question 64

line con 0 is the correct answer. You will use this command to configure the options of the primary router access port, the console.

Question 65

Answer a is correct. The **dialer in-band** statement must be used on the router when a non-native ISDN interface is deployed. Answer b is incorrect because, although it is a necessary part of any DDR configuration, it is not specific to non-native ISDN implementation. Answer c is incorrect because it is used to map the next-hop IPX address to a phone number to be dialed to initiate the call. Again, although they are a necessary part of the configuration, dialer maps are not specific to non-native ISDN implementations. Answer d is incorrect because a correct answer is given.

Question 66

Answer d is correct. Route redistribution is the configuration of the routers to share information learned via routing protocol processes. Answer a is incorrect because summarization is the process of aggregating routes in order to reduce the number of routing table entries. Answer b is incorrect because ISDN is simply a high tech phone call. Answer c is incorrect because adjacency refers to the establishment of a relationship between two routers running a common routing protocol.

Question 67

Answer a is correct. Traffic prioritization is necessary only when there is congestion in the network. Generally, congestion occurs on slower Serial links. Answer b is incorrect because faster Serial links will not be subject to congestion as easily as their slower counterparts. Answer c is incorrect because LAN interfaces do not usually need traffic prioritization. Answer d is incorrect because answers b and c are incorrect.

Question 68

Answer b is correct. Administrators can configure 16 custom queues. Answer a is incorrect because, although there are actually 17 queues, numbered 0 through 16, queue 0 is not configurable. Answer c is incorrect because priority queues, not custom queues, use four configurable queues. Answer d is incorrect because custom queuing can potentially use 16 queues, not 1.

Question 69

Answer d is correct. Core routers exist at the top of your routing hierarchy. They are also known as backbone routers. Answer a is incorrect because distribution routers exist just below the core routers in the hierarchy. Answer b is incorrect because access routers exist below distribution routers in the network. Answer c is incorrect because primary is not a term to denote placement in the routing hierarchy.

Question 70

dialer load-threshold 110 either is the correct answer. This command specifies that if the load in either the inbound or outbound direction reaches 110 out of 255, the second B channel should be activated.

Question 71

Answers a and b are correct. IPX node addresses are taken from the MAC address of the interface on which IPX was activated. Serial interfaces do not have burned-in MAC addresses. Therefore, they will all obtain their MAC address, when needed, from the lowest numbered LAN interface. This node address can also be hard coded when IPX routing is activated. Answer c is incorrect because node addresses are not just assigned at random. Answer d is incorrect because without the node address, no neighbor conversations are active as far as IPX is concerned; therefore, no address could be learned.

Question 72

Answer d is correct. An IP helper address forwards selected broadcasts that it receives on to a unicast of directed broadcast address specified in the command. The IP helper address should be placed on the inbound interface of the router that receives the broadcast. Answers a, b, and c are incorrect because they do not illustrate the proper placement of the IP helper address. Placing the address anywhere other than as described in answer d is ineffective.

Glossary

. . . .

ABR (Area Border Router)—In OSPF, any router that has interfaces configured to be a part of multiple areas.

access-class—A method of restricting Telnet access to and from a router using access lists.

access-group—When an access list is created, it must be associated with a physical interface. **access-group** is the association of the access list to the interface.

access-list—A method of permitting and/or denying traffic based on pre-defined criteria for a particular protocol.

access router—Any router that exists at the lowest levels of a network hierarchy.

ACK (Acknowledgment)—A response returned to a traffic source to inform that source that the transmitted data has been received.

adjacency—In a link-state or hybrid routing protocol, a relationship that is formed to facilitate the passing of routing updates.

administrative distance—A number between 0 and 255 that specifies the believability of a route derived by one routing protocol versus a route to the same destination derived by another routing protocol. It is based on the routing protocol's selection criteria (such as the metric) or manual administrator manipulation.

Advanced Distance-Vector Routing Protocol—*See* Hybrid Routing Protocol.

advertised distance—In EIGRP, the metric advertised by a directly connected neighbor for a specific destination network.

AMI (Alternate Mark Inversion)—A method of T1/E1 line coding that uses alternating positive and negative electrical pulses to transmit digital signals.

analog—A wave form of constantly varying state usually associated with voice technology components.

any—In access lists, a keyword used to specify the permission or denial of traffic no matter the source, destination, protocol, or port.

AppleTalk—A network-layer protocol developed by Apple Computer to facilitate communication between Macintosh desktop computers.

Application layer—The top layer of the OSI Model. It only generates data for transmission across a network.

area—In OSPF, a logical grouping of routers that breaks up the number of devices affected by routing changes and that thereby reduces convergence time.

area border router—*See* ABR (Area Border Router).

ARP (Address Resolution Protocol)—A protocol used in the association of a network-layer address (layer 3) to a data link-layer address (layer 2 or MAC address) to facilitate transmission of information across various media types.

AS (Autonomous System)—The collective name of the grouping of all routers under a single administration.

ASBR (Autonomous System Boundary Router)—In OSPF, a router that is a part of the area hierarchy, but that also has a connection to an external AS, such as an ISP.

ASCII (American Standard Code For Information Interchange)—A U.S. standards body that governs most of the specifications used in networking and communications within the United States.

ATM (Asynchronous Transfer Mode)—A high-speed switching technology based on the transmission of a fixed-size cell rather than variable sized frames.

B Channel (Bearer Channel)—In ISDN, a single 64Kbps link. In BRI implementations, there are two such B channels. In PRI, there are 23.

B8ZS (Bipolar With Eight Zero Substitution)—A T1 line coding scheme that utilizes intentional bipolar violations to signify that binary ones should be transmitted across a T1 circuit in place of the eight binary zeroes that were actually supposed to be coded. This is done to keep the clocking in the network consistent.

backbone router—In OSPF, any router that is connected to Area 0.

bandwidth—The total amount of throughput available on a given interface.

BDR (Backup Designated Router)—In OSPF, when multiple routers are connected to broadcast media segments (such as an Ethernet), specific routers are elected as representatives (one primary and one backup) of the network to receive and transmit routing updates on that segment. The election is based on priority and/or router ID. The BDR is the backup router on that segment.

Bellman-Ford Algorithm—The process by which distance-vector routing protocols exchange updates on a periodic timer. This process is generally characterized by low memory utilization and slow convergence time. It is also known as routing by rumor.

BGP (Border Gateway Protocol)—A dynamic routing protocol used to connect external ASes and to implement routing policy throughout the network. BGP can be implemented internally or externally.

bipolar violation—A pair of digital pulses that have the same polarity (such as positive or negative). This intentional error is introduced to inform the remote end of the link that a string of ones is being sent in place of a string of zeroes.

BootP (Boot Protocol)—A protocol used in resolving an IP address based on a layer 2 MAC address.

bottleneck—Any point in an internetwork where the amount of data being received exceeds the data-carrying capacity of the link. *See also* congestion.

BPDU (Bridge Protocol Data Unit)—A spanning tree protocol update entity used in path determination between bridges.

BRI (Basic Rate Interface)—An ISDN implementation that typically consists of two B channels and one D channel. This is a native ISDN-capable interface.

bridge—A device used to break up a collision domain and make forwarding decisions between the segments based on a MAC address.

bridge group—In transparent bridging, the designation given to a physical interface (usually Ethernet) to initiate its participation in bridging functions.

bridge priority—The criterion on which a root bridge is elected. The bridge with the lowest priority becomes the root bridge.

broadcast—A transmission sent to all nodes on a particular media segment.

BVI (Bridged Virtual Interface)—In IRB, an interface used to translate between routed and bridged traffic. This interface has both a protocol address for the protocol to be routed and a MAC address on which to base bridging decisions.

CHAP (Challenge Handshake Authentication Protocol)—An encrypted user verification algorithm that uses a mathematical riddle based on the pre-defined username and password of the calling device. The actual password is not passed over the wire.

Class A Address—Any IP address with a first octet value that is between 1 and 126.

Class B Address—Any IP address with a first octet value that is between 128 and 191.

Class C Address—Any IP address with a first octet value that is between 192 and 223.

Class D Address—Any IP address with a first octet value that is between 224 and 239. This class of address is used for multicast operations.

Class E Address—Any IP address with a first octet value that is between 240 and 247. This class of address is used for research purposes only and is not currently deployed in existing internetworks.

classful routing—Routing based on information derived from the natural boundaries of the different classes of IP addresses. Routing table information for networks that are not directly connected is kept only based on that natural network because the subnet masks of those remote networks are not contained in the routing update.

classless routing—Routing based on information derived from routing updates that includes subnet mask (such as prefix) information. Routing table information shows all known networks and their accompanying prefix information.

clear channel—The use of B8ZS line coding for T1 circuits. *See* B8ZS (Bipolar with Eight Zero Substitution).

clock source—The specification of the party responsible for providing clocking for synchronization of a circuit.

congestion—A condition that arises when the data being passed across a circuit exceeds the data-carrying capacity of that circuit.

console—A physical port used in the configuration of a router. The console is the default source for configuration information.

convergence—The exchanging of routing updates by routers that participate in dynamic routing protocol activities to form a consistent perspective of the network. When all routers know of all possible destinations in the network, the network has converged.

core router—Any router attached to the highest level of network hierarchy, usually the core backbone of the network.

cost—In OSPF, the metric used for route calculation. This calculation is based on the bandwidth of the link in question.

CPE (Customer Premise Equipment)—Any device for which an end user is responsible, as opposed to equipment for which a telco provider is responsible.

CPU (Central Processing Unit)—The core decision-making device in a router.

CRB (Concurrent Routing And Bridging)—A technology that allows the mixing of routing and bridging on a single device. However, data that arrives at the router through a bridged interface can be dispatched only via another bridged interface. The same is true for routed traffic.

CRC (Cyclic Redundancy Check)—A calculation performed on an inbound frame to verify its validity.

CSMA/CD (Carrier Sense Multi-Access/Collision Detection)—The nature of a network to be based on contention for the use of resources on a physical media segment. An example of this is Ethernet technology.

CSU/DSU (Channel Service Unit/Digital Service Unit)—A device that provides physical connectivity between telco equipment and CPE.

current successor—In EIGRP, the existing best route to a particular destination network.

custom queuing—A Cisco proprietary strategy for prioritizing traffic output from a router interface, usually a low-speed Serial interface.

D Channel—A digital subscriber service channel to facilitate communication between an ISDN-capable router and the switch to which that router is connected.

data link layer—The layer in the OSI Model at which hardware signals and software functions are converted. This is also known as layer 2 of the OSI Model. This layer is logically subdivided into two parts: the MAC sublayer and the Logical Link Control (LLC) sublayer. The MAC portion is where the burned-in hardware address is stored. The LLC discriminates between protocols to ensure proper passage of various network-layer protocol traffic types.

DDR (Dial-On-Demand Routing)—A technology generally associated with ISDN in which a data connection is established on an as needed basis. When not in use, the link automatically disconnects and returns to an idle state.

debug—Any of the many commands used in diagnosing router problems, or simply watching router operation processes.

dedicated circuit—A data circuit, generally point to point, that is available at all times between two routers.

default route—A route that signifies a gateway of last resort for traffic destined for remote networks for which a router does not have specific reachability information.

delay—A calculation based on bandwidth of the link to determine the amount of time it takes to transmit data from across that link. This value is an amount of time expressed in milliseconds.

Demarc—*See* Point of Demarcation.

deny—The process of prohibiting the passage of specific traffic.

designated router (DR)—In OSPF, the primary router elected to receive and send link-state updates to all routers that share a broadcast media segment. This election is based on the router priority then router ID as a tie-breaker.

destination protocol address—The layer 3 address of the intended recipient of a specific packet.

DHCP (Dynamic Host Configuration Protocol)—A Microsoft Corporation implementation of the BootP protocol used for dynamic assignment of IP addresses on the network.

dial backup—A DDR technology used to provide redundancy for a primary circuit to compensate for overload and/or failure of that circuit.

dialer-group—A designation that specifies the association of a dialer-list with a specific router interface. A dialer-group is usually used in the definition of interesting traffic.

dialer interface—A logical interface used in the creation of rotary groups. A dialer interface is generally in charge of one or more physical interfaces.

dialer-list—A designation used to define interesting traffic that should be allowed to initiate a DDR call to a specific destination.

dialer pool—A group of physical interfaces ordered on the basis of the priority assigned to each physical interface.

dialer profile—A configuration of physical interfaces to be separated from a logical configuration required for a call. Profiles may also allow the logical and physical configurations to be bound together dynamically call by call.

dialer string—A telephone number associated with a particular destination.

digital—In networking technologies, a string of electrical signals that take on the characteristics of one of two discrete binary states.

directed broadcast—A layer 3 term for a data transmission destined to all hosts in a specific subnet.

Distance-Vector Routing Protocol—Any dynamic routing protocol that uses of the Bellman-Ford Algorithm for routing update exchange that employs the use of metric addition to derive a measurement of a route to a particular destination network. Commonly referred to as "routing by rumor."

distribute list—A configuration option that allows the filtering of reachability (such as routing) information using **access-list** commands to permit and/or deny routes.

distribution router—Any router in your internetwork hierarchy that connects lower-level access routers to the higher-level core routers.

Djykstra Algorithm—The process that many link-state routing protocols employ to keep reachability information in a current state. Generally characterized by high memory usage and very fast convergence time.

DNS (Domain Name Service)—A service that runs on an IP-capable server that resolves IP addresses to private or registered names.

DS0 (Digital Signal 0)—A single 64,000-bit-per-second timeslot, usually associated with a T1 or fractions thereof.

DS1 (Digital Signal 1)—A grouping of 24 DS0s. DS1 refers to the framing methodology of T1 transmissions. However, DS1 is often incorrectly considered to be synonymous with T1. T1 refers to the Line Coding Methodology.

DUAL (Diffusing Update Algorithm)—The algorithm for routing update exchange and maintenance that EIGRP employs.

E1—A European implementation of digital transmission technology that consists of 30 DS0s, for a total bandwidth of 2.048Mbps.

EBGP (External Border Gateway Protocol)—A BGP implementation that connects external ASes.

EGP (Exterior Gateway Protocol)—A dynamic routing protocol that connects two external ASes.

EIGRP (Enhanced Interior Gateway Routing Protocol)—A Cisco proprietary dynamic routing protocol that attempts to combine the positive traits of distance-vector and link-state protocols. EIGRP is sometimes referred to as a hybrid routing protocol or an advanced distance-vector routing protocol.

encapsulated bridging—The encapsulation of transparently bridged frames into the framing type of a Serial link (HDLC, Frame Relay, and so on) in order to cross a WAN.

ESF (Extended Superframe)—A T1 framing convention that employs the transmission of 24 T1 frames.

Ethernet—A framing convention used in CSMA/CD networks.

explorer—An SRB term that refers to frames dispatched from a source device in order to locate a suitable pathway to a specific destination device.

extended access list—Any access list that is meant to employ more than basic functionality of traffic filtering. In IP, an extended access list can filter on source address, destination address, protocol, and port.

external route—In OSPF, a route received from any source outside of the local area.

FCS (Frame Check Sequence)—A function performed on inbound frames to determine whether or not they are valid entities and are worthy of further processing.

FDDI (Fiber Distributed Data Interface)—A dual-ring, token-passing technology that employs the use of fiber-optic cable.

feasible distance—In EIGRP, the metric associated with each piece of routing information entered into the routing table.

feasible successor—In EIGRP, the second best route to a particular destination network. The feasible successor is selected only if the advertised distance of the second best route is loweb than the feasible distance of the best route.

FIFO (First-In-First-Out)—A queuing strategy that dispatches traffic in the order in which it was received. In other words, FIFO is the absence of queuing.

flash memory—Physical storage space in a router in which the router's operating system is stored.

frame—Any entity generated at the data link layer.

Frame Relay—A Serial technology that employs the use of frame switching, usually through a telco provider switching facility.

FTP (File Transfer Protocol)—A TCP-based file upload/download protocol that allows for security and authentication procedures.

giant—An Ethernet frame in excess of the maximum transmittable unit size of 1,518 bytes.

gigabit—One billion bits.

GNS (Get Nearest Server)—A Novell IPX client request for connectivity to a NetWare server.

GNS filter—A means of filtering GNS requests to limit client connectivity to desired NetWare servers.

HDB3 (High Density Bipolar Level Three)—A line-coding technique employed by users of E1 technologies.

HDLC (High-Level Data Link Control)—A Cisco proprietary Serial framing convention that allows the use of multiple protocols across a Serial link. This is the default encapsulation for Serial interfaces on Cisco routers.

Hello Protocol—A means of communication between two hosts on a network that require constant and continued connectivity to each other. The two devices exchange these Hello messages at a specified interval.

helper address—An address used to forward selected broadcasts by converting them to unicasts or directed broadcasts.

HoldTime—A general term that refers to how long a device waits before purging an entry in a routing table, neighbor table, topology table, and so on. Once the HoldTime expires, the entry, whatever the type, is purged.

hop—The crossing of a router in an internetwork.

host—A specific end station that exists on a subnet.

HSSI (High Speed Serial Interface)—A Serial interface that must be employed in order to transmit and/or receive at a rate greater than 2Mbps, up to 52Mbps.

hub—A non-intelligent physical-layer device used in connecting Ethernet clients.

Hybrid Routing Protocol—A routing protocol that employs the characteristics of both distance-vector and link-state protocols to attempt to exploit the positive aspects of each.

IBGP (Internal Border Gateway Protocol)—An implementation of BGP between routers inside the same AS.

ICMP (Internet Control Message Protocol)—An IP status protocol that returns status, error, and message notifications to a specified host. Ping is an example of ICMP implementation.

IEEE (Institute of Electronic and Electrical Engineers)—A standards body comprised of electronic and electrical engineers charged with creating physical- and data link-layer standards.

IGP (Interior Gateway Protocol)—Any routing protocol employed within an AS.

IGRP (Interior Gateway Routing Protocol)—A Cisco proprietary routing protocol that functions on a 90-second update timer.

inter-area route—In OSPF, any route to a destination outside of the local area.

interesting traffic—In DDR, the specific traffic types that can initiate an ISDN connection to connect two remote sites.

internal router—In OSPF, any router in which all interfaces configured for OSPF operation are in the same area.

Internet—A public IP-based internetwork that facilitates communications on a global scale.

intra-area route—In OSPF, a route to a destination network within the local area.

IOS (Internetwork Operating System)—Cisco's router operating system software that provides the intelligence and functionality of Cisco routers.

IP (Internet Protocol)—A layer 3 protocol based on a 32-bit address, some portion of which is known as network and the remainder of which is known as host.

IP Address—A 32-bit address consisting of network and host portions that is used in data communications.

IPX (Internetwork Packet eXchange)—A layer 3 protocol employed by Novell NetWare clients and servers.

IPX Address—An 80-bit address that consists of network and host portions. The host portion of the address is usually the MAC address of the end station.

IPX RIP (IPX Routing Information Protocol)—A Novell NetWare distance-vector routing protocol based on delay (ticks) in the network.

IPXWAN—A Novell NetWare configuration parameter usually associated, but not always necessarily, with NLSP.

IRB (Integrated Routing And Bridging)—A technology that allows the merger of bridged and routed domains so that data can be passed between the two domains.

ISDN (Integrated Services Digital Network)—A digital telephony technology that allows the use of a dialed phone call to provide data connectivity across geographical separations.

ISP (Internet Service Provider)—A company that specializes in providing individuals, companies, and corporations with access to the public Internet.

K Values—In IGRP and EIGRP, the values of bandwidth, delay, reliability, load, and MTU.

Keepalive—A message passed across a link in order to keep an active, constant conversation with a node on the remote end.

kilobit—One thousand bits.

LAN (Local Area Network)—A network meant to interconnect physically co-located devices and to enable the sharing of local resources.

LAPB (Link Access Procedure Balanced)—A layer 3 technology associated with X.25 implementations.

LAPD (Link Access Procedure D Channel)—A technology that allows the use of a separate access path for ISDN signaling and call requests.

LAT (Local Area Transport)—A layer 2 protocol developed by the Digital Equipment Corporation.

layer 1—*See* physical layer.

layer 2—*See* data link layer.

layer 3—*See* network layer.

layer 4—*See* transport layer.

layer 5—*See* session layer.

layer 6—*See* presentation layer.

layer 7—*See* application layer.

Link-State Routing Protocol—Any dynamic routing protocol that employs the Djykstra Algorithm for passing and maintaining routing information.

load—A value between 1 and 255 that specifies the saturation level of a link.

logical AND—The process of deriving an IP network address by associating the address with a subnet mask and performing this Boolean function on the pair.

longest match—The methodology behind route selection and data forwarding decisions within the router. The more bits a router can match when comparing the destination address and the routing table, the better the chance of reaching that destination.

LSA (Link State Advertisement)—A routing update flooded through the network by routers that participate in a link-state routing protocol.

MAC Address—A layer 2 address associated with LAN interfaces. This is also referred to as a Burned In Address (BIA).

MAN (Metropolitan Area Network)—An internetwork implementation that spans across a city, not necessarily large geographic spans.

mark—In T1/E1 implementations, a binary value of 1. T1-capable devices use 1s to maintain proper clocking.

megabit—One million bits.

metric—A unit of measure to facilitate the selection of the best route to a given destination.

MIB (Management Information Base)—A network information database installed on an end station that is used and maintained by a network management protocol such as SNMP or CMIP.

MTU (Maximum Transmittable Unit)—The largest entity that can be forwarded by any given layer 2 encapsulation.

multicast—A transmission onto a network segment that is destined for multiple, but not all, hosts on a destination network. In OSPF, the means by which routing updates are passed. Only OSPF routers respond to OSPF multicasts.

Multilink PPP—A standardized implementation of PPP that allows for the bonding of multiple B channels to aggregate bandwidth for the duration of a specific call.

multiring—In bridging, the use of a bridged network to forward traffic between two layer 3 networks.

NAP (National Access Provider)—A corporation responsible for larger portions of the public Internet. NAPs are in charge of providing public Internet access to ISPs and to efficiently manage scarce IP address space.

NAT (Network Address Translation)—A technology that allows the static and/or dynamic mapping of private, internal IP addresses to registered public IP address for communication via the public Internet.

neighbor table—In non-distance-vector routing protocols, a listing of routers that share directly connected links.

NetBIOS—A connectionless, data link-layer protocol that utilizes broadcasts for communications.

network layer—The layer in the OSI Model at which path determination for layer 3 protocols (i.e., IP, IPX, AppleTalk, and so on) is performed. The network layer is the primary focus of routing operations.

NLSP (NetWare Link Services Protocol)—A dynamic, link-state routing protocol developed by Novell to replace IPX RIP, for use in IPX internetworks.

NT1 (Network Termination 1)—An ISDN device that connects the point of demarcation to the CPE.

NT2—An ISDN device that performs layer 2 and 3 protocol functions and concentration services.

null interface—A logical software interface in a router used as an alternative to access lists to deny traffic. Traditionally, a static route is configured to specify the null interface as the outbound interface for traffic destined for the denied network.

NVRAM (Non-Volatile Random Access Memory)—Static memory space in the router where the router's configuration is stored. NVRAM, as the name implies, does not require power to keep its contents in storage.

octet—One of four 8-bit divisions of an IP address.

OSI Model—A model devised by the International Standards Organization to divide the task of networking into separate modules to facilitate accelerated evolution of each individual component.

OSPF (Open Shortest Path First)—A standardized dynamic-link state routing protocol designed to overcome the limitations of RIP by utilizing a hierarchical area structure.

PAP (Password Authentication Protocol)—An authentication method that utilizes clear text usernames and passwords to permit and deny access to remote users and/or routers.

periodic update—A routing update dispatched at a specified interval.

physical layer—The lowest layer of the OSI Model. It deals with physical media and connectivity.

Point of Demarcation—In telecommunications, the point at which responsibility for the Serial link changes from the customer to the telco and vice versa.

port number—In IP, a service access point between the transport layer and the upper application layers.

PPP (Point-To-Point Protocol)—An access protocol designed for use by remote clients (such as end users and/or routers) to access the centralized network resources.

PPP Multilink—*See* Multilink PPP.

prefix—The bits in an IP address that comprise the network portion.

presentation layer—The layer of the OSI Model that deals with file format.

PRI (Primary Rate Interface)—An ISDN implementation that consists of 23 B channels and 1 D channel.

priority queuing—A Cisco queuing strategy that allows the prioritization of various traffic based on its importance in the network.

private internetwork address space—Any IP addresses that exists in space defined by RFC 1918 (consisting of network 10.0.0.0 through 10.255.255.255, 172.16.0.0 through 172.31.255.255, and 192.168.0.0 through 192.168.255.255).

protocol—A set of rules that define a method of communication.

Protocol Address—A network-layer address that consists of a network and a host portion.

pseudo ring—In source-route translational bridging, the method used to portray an Ethernet segment to token ring hosts as simply another token ring.

public internetwork address space—Any IP addresses that exist outside of the private address space. Public address space is normally under the control of a registration authority in charge of assigning these addresses to companies and/or individuals that require them.

PVC (Permanent Virtual Circuit)—In switching technologies, a statically defined pathway set up to provide a data pathway across a MAN/WAN internetwork.

Q.931—An ISDN call setup protocol that deals with the ISDN network layer between the terminal and switch.

queuing—The process of prioritizing traffic output on a Serial interface.

R Interface (Remote Interface)—In ISDN, the interface between the TE2 and TA.

RAM (Random Access Memory)—Volatile memory space in a router in which the running configuration is stored. Without power applied, the contents of RAM will be lost.

RARP (Reverse Address Resolution Protocol)—A process that dynamically provides addressing information to end clients that know only their MAC address. This process is similar to BootP and/or DHCP.

redistribution—*See* Route Redistribution.

redundancy—The process of providing fail-safe connectivity for hardware and/or software.

reliability—A measurement of dependability of a link on a scale of 1 to 255, with 255 being highly dependable.

repeater—A physical-layer device that only regenerates a bit stream. No intelligence is associated with a repeater.

RIF (Routing Information Field)—In token ring implementations, a field that consists of route control and route descriptor fields that provide pathway information for SRB hosts.

ring group—In source-route bridging, the definition of logical ring that exists inside the bridge to act as a destination ring for a multiport SRB.

RIP (Routing Information Protocol)—A standardized distance-vector dynamic routing protocol. RIP uses a number of hops to a destination network as a metric to measure the attractiveness of a route.

root bridge—A bridge in the internetwork that has been configured with the lowest bridge priority value, to make it the highest-priority bridge. All other bridges in the internetwork base path-determination decisions on the cost related to forwarding traffic to the root bridge.

rotary group—In DDR, a number of physical interfaces that have been associated and are under the control of one or more logical dialer interfaces.

route—Information in a router regarding reachability of a particular destination network.

route filter—A configuration, employing access lists, used to control the networks being advertised out of or into a router.

route redistribution—The sharing of routing information between two separate routing protocols. Redistributed routes are propagated throughout the network as routes derived by the protocol receiving the shared information.

route summarization—The process of condensing the number of routes in a routing table by configuring a single entry to represent multiple destination networks.

Routed Protocol—Any of the layer 3 protocols that can be implemented on a routed interface. Examples of routed protocols are IP, IPX, AppleTalk, DECnet, and VINES.

Routing Protocol—Any protocol that builds and maintains network reachability information in a routing table.

routing table—A listing of destination networks, metrics necessary to reach those networks, a next hop address, and an outbound interface through which to depart the router to reach that destination network.

runt—Any frame transmitted that is smaller than the minimum transmittable unit.

S Interface (Subscriber Interface)—In ISDN, the connection between the customer equipment (BRI interface or TA) and an NT1.

sample—In T1 technologies, a measurement of the height of an analog wave at 125-microsecond intervals, represented by an 8-bit codeword.

SAP (Service Advertising Protocol)—A Novell NetWare protocol used in providing service reachability for NetWare clients. All devices in a NetWare network that are capable of offering particular services issue SAP updates regarding those services.

SAP Filter—A configuration, using access lists, that allows the blocking of SAPs to prevent unnecessary traffic from traversing network segments.

scalable internetworks—Networks connected together by interconnectivity devices that are reliable, secure, accessible, and adaptable to the evolving needs of the network.

SDLC (Synchronous Data Link Control)—An IBM proprietary Serial encapsulation that is capable of transporting only a single protocol. SDLC is usually associated with mainframe connectivity.

serial interface—Any interface designed to access WAN services. Typical Serial interfaces include V.35, EIA/TIA 232, and EIA/TIA 449, etc.

session layer—The layer of the OSI Model that deals with interhost communications. This layer is considered to be one of the higher application layers.

SF (Superframe)—In T1 technology, an entity that consists of 12 T1 frames.

single point of failure—Any point in the network that exists without redundancy. If this point fails, much, or all, of the network suffers an outage as well.

SLIP (Serial Line Internet Protocol)—A technology developed to allow Serial connectivity of IP devices.

SMDS (Switched Multimegabit Data Service)—A cell-switching technology that utilizes a connectionless server function to forward data between edge devices.

SMTP (Simple Mail Transfer Protocol)—In TCP/IP implementations, a protocol that deals specifically with the propagation of electronic mail.

SNA (System Network Architecture)—A non-routable IBM protocol usually associated with mainframe connectivity.

snapshot client—A DDR-capable device that runs a distance-vector routing protocol that has frozen its routing table for a specified duration known as a quiet period. Once the quiet period has expired, the client dials the server router and exchanges routing updates.

snapshot routing—A DDR feature that allows distance-vector routing tables to be frozen for long periods of time known as quiet periods. When the quiet period expires, a client router dials a server router to initiate a period of active routing update exchange.

snapshot server—The router that receives the snapshot call to initiate routing update exchange.

SNMP (Simple Network Management Protocol)—In TCP/IP implementations, a protocol that deals specifically with the monitoring, configuration, and management of various internetwork devices.

Source Protocol Address—The layer 3 address of the originating host.

source-route translational bridge—A bridge that is capable of forwarding traffic between Ethernet and token ring clients by converting the frame type from one to the other and back again.

source-route transparent bridge—A Token Ring implementation of bridging between hosts that utilize a RIF and those that do not. The source-route transparent bridge adds or removes the RIF according to the end station's needs.

Spanning Tree Protocol—A bridging protocol employed by bridges to elect a root bridge and calculate the lowest-cost pathway to that root bridge. Should two bridge interfaces be connected to the same networks, the bridge with the lowest-cost path to the root bridge services that network. The other bridge interface is placed into a blocking mode and does not forward traffic.

SPID (Service Profile Identifier)—A number that identifies the service to which you have subscribed. This value is assigned by the ISDN service provider and is usually a 10-digit telephone number with some extra digits. The SPID can consist of 1 through 20 digits.

spoofing—The process of representing false information to show connectivity when there is none. In DDR with IPX, spoofing of watchdogs and SPX Keepalives is done to simulate client/server connectivity.

SPX (Sequenced Packet eXchange)—The connection-oriented protocol within the Novell IPX protocol suite.

SPX Keepalive—A message exchanged between client and server to verify that the client is still active.

SRB (Source-Route Bridge)—A Token Ring bridge with which frames are forwarded from ring to ring.

standard access-list—An access-list of limited functionality, generally used to permit or deny access to/from hosts and networks.

static route—A route that an administrator places in the routing table to override or augment the dynamic routing process.

stub area—In OSPF, an area that is allowed only a single point of access. Stub areas know only of the routes within the local area and summary routes to other areas.

subnet—A logical layer 3 network.

subnet mask—In IP, the information that specifies the distinction between the network and host portions.

SVC (Switched Virtual Circuit)—A connection that is dynamically set up and torn down based on service requests. An SVC can provide connectivity and fault tolerance within a switched internetwork.

switch—An internetworking device that makes forwarding decisions based on a layer 2 address.

switch type—In ISDN, the model of switch to which the CPE is connected.

T Interface (Trunk Interface)—In ISDN, this is usually coexistent with the S interface between the NT1 and the customer equipment.

T1—The physical coding characteristics of a 24-timeslot time division multiplexed circuit, such as Superframe or extended Superframe.

T1 Frame—One sample from each of 24 T1 timeslots placed end to end, with one additional bit added for framing.

TA (Terminal Adapter)—An adapter used in connecting non-native interfaces to ISDN facilities.

TACACS (Terminal Access Control Access Control Server)—An application used to provide remote authentication services for network access.

TCP (Transmission Control Protocol)—A transport-layer connection-oriented protocol that exists to provide reliable services for the IP protocol suite.

TE1 (Terminal Equipment 1)—A native ISDN-capable router interface.

TE2 (Terminal Equipment 2)—A non-native ISDN interface that must be attached to a TA for ISDN connectivity.

Telnet—An IP application that provides connection-oriented virtual terminal access to other IP hosts and/or servers.

TFTP (Trivial File Transfer Protocol)—A connectionless file-sharing protocol that requires no authentication for uploading and/or downloading of files.

timeslot—The space available for a single piece information from a particular channel in time division multiplexing.

Token Ring—A topology that employs a carrier sense multi-access/collision avoidance methodology known as token passing. End stations can transmit data only when they possess the token.

topology table—A listing of known destination networks and the number of pathways known to reach those individual destinations.

totally stubby area—In OSPF, an area that contains only a single exit point, routes for the local area, and a default route out of the area. No external routes are known at a totally stubby area.

traffic prioritization—The process of configuring the router to treat differing traffic types as more or less important in consideration for output priority.

transparent bridge—A bridging solution that only breaks up a collision domain. The end stations are unaware of the existence of the bridge.

transport layer—The layer of the OSI Model that deals with flow control and optional reliability of data transfer.

triggered update—A routing update spawned as a result of a topology change. These updates are not sent out regularly. They go out on an as-needed basis only.

tunnel—A logical configuration of the encapsulation of one layer 3 protocol inside the payload of another layer 3 protocol. Tunnel configuration requires the configuration of the source, destination, and encapsulation mode of the tunnel as well as encapsulated protocol attributes on the logical tunnel interface.

tunnel destination—The termination point of a logical tunnel.

tunnel interface—A logical interface to which encapsulated protocol attributes are assigned. The tunnel's source, destination, and mode are defined here as well.

tunnel mode—The encapsulation method used for a tunnel configuration. The default is **gre-ip**.

tunnel source—The origination point of a logical tunnel.

U Interface (User Interface)—In ISDN, the connection between the NT1 and the demarc.

UDP (User Datagram Protocol)—A transport-layer connectionless protocol used in providing transport services for the IP protocol suite.

UTP (Unshielded Twisted-Pair)—A type of physical media that employs eight wires that twist around each other to encourage constructive interference that in effect boosts the electrical signals being relayed across each wire.

virtual link—In OSPF, a link that must be configured when a non-Area 0 must be connected directly to another non-Area 0. The virtual link transits the non-Area 0 that is connected to Area 0 to create a logical connection of the new area to Area 0.

virtual ring—The configuration of a logical ring for implementations of multiport SRBs. The virtual ring must be specified as the destination ring in the SRB configuration of each interface.

VLSM (Variable Length Subnet Mask)—A subnet mask that does not remain constant throughout the internetwork for a given classful network.

VTY (Virtual Terminal)—A logical port to provide a means of accessing a router through the use of a Telnet session.

WAN (Wide Area Network)—Any of the various network technologies employed to cover wide geographical expanses.

watchdog—In Novell NetWare networks, the entity that monitors client/server connections for activity. Watchdogs clear inactive connections.

WFQ (Weighted Fair Queuing)—A Cisco queuing strategy employed to give low-volume traffic the priority for output consideration. Also called Last-Bit-In-First-Out (LBIFO).

wildcard mask—A four-octet mask used in the configuration of access lists to specify addresses for permission and/or denial. Also used in defining OSPF area membership.

X.25—A WAN technology used in many parts of the world. X.25 is generally a very low-bandwidth Serial technology.

Index

CORIOLIS HELP CENTER

Here at The Coriolis Group, we strive to provide the finest customer service in the technical education industry. We're committed to helping you reach your certification goals by assisting you in the following areas.

Talk to the Authors

We'd like to hear from you! Please refer to the "How to Use This Book" section in the "Introduction" of every Exam Cram guide for our authors' individual email addresses.

Web Page Information

The Certification Insider Press Web page provides a host of valuable information that's only a click away. For information in the following areas, please visit us at:

www.coriolis.com/cip/default.cfm

- Titles and other products
- Book content updates
- Roadmap to Certification Success guide
- New Adaptive Testing changes
- New Exam Cram Live! seminars
- New Certified Crammer Society details
- Sample chapters and tables of contents
- Manuscript solicitation
- Special programs and events

Contact Us by Email

Important addresses you may use to reach us at The Coriolis Group.

eci@coriolis.com

To subscribe to our FREE, bi-monthly online newsletter, *Exam Cram Insider*. Keep up to date with the certification scene. Included in each *Insider* are certification articles, program updates, new exam information, hints and tips, sample chapters, and more.

techsupport@coriolis.com

For technical questions and problems with CD-ROMs. Products broken, battered, or blown-up? Just need some installation advice? Contact us here.

ccs@coriolis.com

To obtain membership information for the *Certified Crammer Society*, an exclusive club for the certified professional. Get in on members-only discounts, special information, expert advice, contests, cool prizes, and free stuff for the certified professional. Membership is FREE. Contact us and get enrolled today!

cipq@coriolis.com

For book content questions and feedback about our titles, drop us a line. This is the good, the bad, and the questions address. Our customers are the best judges of our products. Let us know what you like, what we could do better, or what question you may have about any content. Testimonials are always welcome here, and if you send us a story about how an Exam Cram guide has helped you ace a test, we'll give you an official Certification Insider Press T-shirt.

custserv@coriolis.com

For solutions to problems concerning an order for any of our products. Our staff will promptly and courteously address the problem. Taking the exams is difficult enough. We want to make acquiring our study guides as easy as possible.

Book Orders & Shipping Information

orders@coriolis.com

To place an order by email or to check on the status of an order already placed.

coriolis.com/bookstore/default.cfm

To place an order through our online bookstore.

1.800.410.0192

To place an order by phone or to check on an order already placed.